Edited by
Michel Izard and
Pierre Smith

Between Belief and Transgression

Structuralist Essays
in Religion, History,
and Myth

Translated by John Leavitt
With an Introduction by James A. Boon

The University of Chicago Press
Chicago and London

Michel Izard is maître de recherche at the Laboratoire d'Anthropologie Sociale, and Pierre Smith is chargé de recherche at the Laboratoire d'Ethnologie et de Sociologie Comparativ, both part of France's Centre National de Recherche Scientifique.

Library of Congress Cataloging in Publication Data

Fonction symbolique. English
    Between belief and transgression.

    Translation of: La Fonction symbolique.
    Includes index.
    1. Structural anthropology—Addresses, essays, lectures. 2. Rites and ceremonies—Addresses, essays, lectures. 3. Symbolism—Addresses, essays, lectures. 4. Religion—Addresses, essays, lectures.
I. Izard, Michel. II. Smith, Pierre. III. Title.
GN362.F6613 306'.4   81-16377
ISBN 0-226-38861-1   AACR2

Originally published as *La fonction symbolique*
©Editions Gallimard, 1979

The University of Chicago Press, Chicago 60637
The University of Chicago Press, Ltd., London

Contents

James A. Boon

Introduction to the English Edition

In his recently translated *Dionysos Slain*, Marcel Detienne returns pursuits such as comparative mythology, classical studies, the history of religions, and structuralist and symbolic anthropology to their original impulses:

> To discover the complete horizon of a society's symbolic values, it is also necessary to map out its transgressions, interrogate its deviants, discern phenomena of reflection and refusal, and circumscribe the silent mouths that unlock upon underlying knowledge and the implicit (p. ix).

In its myth, ritual, and esoteric practices and texts, every society engages in a dialectics between rule and infraction, a dialectics that is stretched, whether ceremonially or discursively, toward what Detienne calls "the big taboos": incest, parricide, and cannibalism (p. 65).

Studies *of* transgressions are themselves transgressions in the institutional routines of academia. Anthropology and comparative religion, mythology, or literature—as well as efforts in political theory, sociology, or general human sciences that draw inspiration from these disciplines—flirt with forbiddens, dally in deviance, and scrutinize the socially scandalous in their explorations of the licentiousness of human meaning. A culture's "vices," insists Clifford Geertz in *The Interpretation of Cultures*, are "as stylized as its virtues" (p. 131). And some of the stylized, strangely legitimate vices of Western academic culture are those very disciplines assembled in the excellent volume in hand. You have, dear reader, a trickster by the tail.

v

Michel Izard and Pierre Smith offered the collection in France as an extension of Lévi-Strauss's insights into myth, ritual, and religion. A major thrust of Lévi-Strauss's corpus has been to consolidate three issues: (1) transformations between structures, (2) transpositions of one sensory code into another, and (3) translations across languages. In his *Mythologiques* tetralogy, myth is ultimately posed paradoxically: situated between languages rather than in particular langues. Yet myths provide an intellectual choreography, so to speak, of concrete-logics selected unconsciously by each population from an entire set of possibilities never known directly (but indirectly glimpsed through cross-cultural analysis of mythic *cum* contextual variations). Lévi-Strauss's literally operatic outlook on meaning ends not by reducing culture to nature but by reconciling the two as mutual information systems, manifest in the recombinative codings comprising everything from musical scales and mythic-logics to topology and genetic processes. At a moment recalling the retrospective gestures of *Tristes Tropiques*, he fleetingly salutes a previous reconciliation in Goethe, who ushered both nature and culture—texts, colors, weather, drama, biography—into an anti-Newtonian realm of organic models. The culminating strains of Lévi-Strauss's resounding "Finale" to *L'Homme nu* join these themes to a sweeping sense of tribal semantic universes and the musiclike logic of cultural variations. Music is to sound (*sons*) as myth is to meaning (*sens*). Both display a variational postponement, misperceived as "history," of a returning, indifferent void: *rien*.

In part a response to Lévi-Strauss's exhilarating, controversial arguments, *Between Belief and Transgression* addresses issues of religious belief, ritual practice, narrative performance, comparative institutions, and problems in the history of ideas and disciplines. Its traditional topics have a near-magical ring: big taboos, divine kingship, mortuary rites, solar myths, sacrificial victims, couvade, and all varieties of sacred wanderings. Here, as in many recent works on ritual signs, symbols, and structures by anthropologists and other scholars as well—Kenneth Burke, René Girard, etc.—the pages are stalked by shades of Bachofen, Müller, of course Frazer, and comparable ancestors. Was the nineteenth century, divested of its ingrained evolutionism, onto something? The volume thus returns an ever-spiraling structuralism to problems familiar to American and British readers in the anthropology of religion, more accustomed than a French audience to an accent on event and performance, native exegesis, and conflicts between cultural values and social norms. Such issues can be traced to classics by Van Gennep, Ruth Benedict, Gregory Bateson, and others, and to the array of predecessors, contemporaries, and successors represented in W. Lessa and E. Vogt's durable *Reader In Comparative Religion: An Anthropological Approach*.

British efforts to accommodate structuralism have been clouded by polemics between interpreters of Lévi-Strauss and the subject of their interpretations. One thinks especially of Edmund Leach, Rodney Needham, and Mary Douglas, who have tilted as much at as toward Lévi-Strauss.[1] In this volume, accommodation—with issues of action, belief, and contexts of performance—is again offered, this time in part by the next generation, and this time largely from France. Of course, French the twist remains, most obviously in the emphasis on polar categories that underlay the work of Durkheim's *L'Année sociologique* group on primitive classification, magic, and sacrifice. Above all, French is the methodological edge that characterizes every essay: sharp delineations between anthropological issues and either philological or historicist issues; distinctions between structure/affect, description/comparison, rules that originate versus rules that perpetuate, native models/dialectical models, and so forth. These articles follow Lévi-Strauss in challenging the philological or phenomenological priorities in other schools of interpretation; and many reject any comfortable functionalist sense of space-time isolates. To appreciate the profound impact of Lévi-Strauss's brand of critique in French philology and comparative studies, readers might again refer to Detienne's *Dionysos Slain*, whose opening polemic confronts the whole history of scholarly assumptions about classical Greek myths and political institutions and proclaims the special, exemplary quality of Greek culture to be problematic. Such doubled critique of method and of the history of ideas recalls Lévi-Strauss's *Totemism* and *The Savage Mind*. The fact that a similar complexity runs through his entire corpus makes the extraordinary popularity of his works—still in 1981 Lévi-Strauss was rated the most influential living author of any kind in France—all the more remarkable.

The perpetuation of methodological self-consciousness has obvious risks. Insiders and outsiders alike are right to feel exasperated with Left Bank disputation that adds a *pre-*, a *post-*, or a *redivivus* to every –ism, each suspiciously *proto* or worst of all an unawares *neo-*. Such routinization of methodological edge has the drawbacks of all routinization. Yet on the positive side this development aids escape from methodological naiveté, inevitably status-quo. And its rewards come when analytic sophistication is matched to an appropriate font of data.[2] Lévi-Strauss's structuralism has helped explode any confidence in, indeed any sense of, the empiricist's historical or ethnographic "crunch"; ethnographic information is as selected as any other kind. Structuralism joins other interpretive methods in heightening self-conscious and reflexive understandings (see, for example, P. Rabinow and W. Sullivan's *Interpretive Social Science: A*

1. I find the tenor of disputes in and around structuralism best conveyed by Buchler and Selby (1968), Leach (1967), Macksey and Donato (1972), and articles and introductions by R. Needham too numerous to cite. The side one takes is another matter. I treat such issues in *Other Tribes, Other Scribes* (in press). For some fresh readings from France of Lévi-Strauss, see C. Clément and R. Bellour (1979).

2. For recent, excellent overviews of issues and –isms in literary theory and related *sciences humaines*, see Harari (1979), with its wide-ranging bibliographies, and Culler (1981), whose spare essays touch all topics. Both works are fine guides to impossibly rich critical sources.

Reader). Every methodological common sense is, as Geertz reminds us regarding each society's common sense, a "cultural system." There is meaning in the method as well as in the meaning.

Whatever the fate of structuralism in the future of scholarly specializations—and it has been from the start an odder -ism than many—a lasting legacy is the enriched sense of methodological alternatives it fosters. I need only mention recent influential works that are simultaneously investigations of distinct cultural materials and treatises in method. On the pro-structuralist side, for example, Louis Dumont's *Homo Hierarchicus* and *From Mandeville to Marx* and Marshall Sahlins's *Stone Age Economics* and *Culture and Practical Reason*. On the anti-structuralist side we find among many others Victor Turner's extensive works, including *Revelation and Divination in Ndembu Ritual* and *Dramas, Fields, and Metaphors*; and Clifford Geertz's *Interpretation of Cultures* and *Negara: The Theatre State in Nineteenth Century Bali*. And on the ambivalently structuralist side (certainly the right attitude!) we have Paul Friedrich's *The Meaning of Aphrodite* and the works of Wendy Doniger O'Flaherty, including *Asceticism and Eroticism in the Mythology of Siva* and *Women, Androgynes and Other Mythical Beasts.*

With O'Flaherty we see another impact of Lévi-Strauss, in particular his rejection of sullen, exclusivistic scholarship. O'Flahèrty adapts Lévi-Strauss's sense of tribal mythic variants and their outlandish contents to investigations of Hindu myths, navigated along paths of "multiforms." She assimilates all the skills and seriousness of purpose known to Sanskrit philology but little of its conventional sobriety. O'Flaherty's always-elated works at times hearken back to Heinrich Zimmer's call, in *The King and the Corpse*, for responsibly dilettantish approaches to myth. And she can conclude a pluralist methodological introduction, accentuating both Freudian and structuralist components, to her study of Hindu myths of incest, bisexuality, bull-rape, and hosts of related topics with an insistent, courageous, and uncompromising: "These myths *are* funny" (1980). Of course, as Trickster (via Paul Radin) has taught us, where gods themselves are playful, indeed devious—that is to say, where gods laugh back—"funny" is deep.

The essays in *Between Belief and Transgression* share many qualities with the studies just mentioned. A brief introduction can only point toward several strengths of the volume. J. Pouillon's delicate pages on the verb "to believe" suggest that to profess belief is to establish a distance, more than an adherence, between the professor and the professed. Pouillon sets in motion all those paradoxical gray areas among belief, disbelief, and "unbelief." His formulations of the relation of doubt and conceivable "otherness" to creeds and tenets pertain equally to the practice and the interpretation of religion: *"C'est l'-incroyant qui croit que le croyant croit..."* (It is the unbeliever who believes that the believer believes...—"if," the irreverent American helplessly adds, "a woodchuck could chuck wood...."). Pouillon's deft touch in such matters may be contrasted with R. Needham's more skeptical, indeed philosophically cynical, efforts in *Belief, Language, and Experience.*

N. Belmont approaches categories of superstition and popular religion, and the European motives of and for their investigation, in light of the lack of an equivalent for the Latin *religio* in succeeding traditions. She demonstrates how the church undermined its own strength by stressing interiorization of beliefs that it radically distinguished from popular ones; her discussion of *credo* echoes Pouillon's concerns. While much more could be said about Sir James Frazer and about relations between Protestant/Catholic distinctions and later criteria of "popular religion," the article makes important connections between these issues and E. Benveniste's crucial work on the vocabulary of Indo-European institutions. Similar themes appear in Herrenschmidt's bold contrast between Brahmanical "effective sacrifice" and Old Testament "symbolic sacrifice." His typology cuts across what A. M. Hocart deemed rituals of "life" versus ethical ceremonies of "the good" (or what Max Weber and followers on through Robert Bellah have called traditional religions of the book) among other examples of ritual/renunciation distinctions. As in the works of L. Dumont, G. Dumézil, S. Tambiah, and others, these pieces relate structuralist formulations to the comparative religion anthropologists associate with Durkheim and Weber and, on the more textual side, M. Eliade.

Detienne's "Rethinking Mythology" argues against the view that myths are consistently identifiable across cultures. While he perhaps takes Lévi-Strauss too literally here, the resulting piece savors the development of studies in classical mythology as a "scandal" providing a basis of incessant dialectical commentary for cultures harboring them. Charachidzé's analysis of Prometheus-type legends in the classics and in the Caucasus is the most conventionally structuralist of all the articles. It hinges on an inversion: eagles facilitating regeneration in a "key" of fire on the one hand, of water on the other. It is this kind of twist that often disturbs critics inclined to functionalist views of codes as mere replication. Articles by Adler, Izard, Cartry, and Menget will interest area specialists and general students of divine kingship, couvade, spatial dualities, etc. The concentration on African materials in particular builds to a strength of the entire collection.

Each of the four remaining articles highlights different aspects of complex, symbolic transformations. Bidou's study of Tatuyo incest and death is right in Lévi-Strauss's domain. Yet his analysis of myth, rules of exogamy, and funerary codes accentuates narrative techniques and recent social change—both important extensions of the framework of *Mythologiques.* Smith's fine piece on African ritual also builds on Lévi-Strauss's distinction between myth and rite. Although he consolidates types of analyses developed by the Manchester school, he preserves the right to relativize any presumably determinant level of ritual, echoing Lévi-Strauss's rejoinders to V. Turner in *L'Homme nu.* Smith's three-way comparison of Bedik, Rwanda, and royal *Ncwala* rite of the Swazi is interesting both as ethnology and as a review of the history of ethnological ideas. He presents symbols of authority in various registers; and he relates the distinction between interpretation and analysis on the one hand and belief on the other to issues of participation versus distance in ritual that characteristically distinguish parent from child. (Other issues in culture and personality are revisited in Sperber's appendix.) Smith draws many general implications of the book together in a controlled comparison of ritual in practice.

Sahlins's article attempts a comparison of a very different sort. His pursuit of Captain Cook into the ritual and cultic imagery of Hawaii carries anthropological analysis into the domain of iconography, an area and methodology once claimed for us by Lévi-Strauss in a salute to E. Panofsky (cf. Boon 1972, p. 130). How the West has been construed (and has construed itself) in the act of contacting and interpreting "the other" has long been a marginal concern of anthropologists. With studies like Sahlins's—and Bernadette Bucher's fascinating *La Sauvage aux seins pendants* (translated as *Icon and Conquest*), on the meaning of the pervasive iconography of New World populations popularized by De Bry's *Grands Voyages*—the meaning and history of ethnological ideas promises to become central.[3]

I have reserved final comment for Héritier's stimulating review of "the big transgression." She develops possible sociological bases for regulations against so-called incest. One provocative suggestion is that logics behind varying incest taboos pertain to restrictions on two identicals (say father and son, or brother and brother) making contact with the same "other"—hence rules against sharing a mistress as well as a wife-mother. Some of Héritier's suggestions will doubtless require revision—e.g., explaining restrictions against homosexuality and masturbation by the same sort of identity/difference formula that distinguishes parallel from cross-relatives. Yet the article successfully unsettles our pat assumptions. It reviews Lévi-Strauss's notions of communication-signs with precision and moves smoothly from total social systems to menstrual taboos, shaded Mikados, and related topics that tie incest values to diverse domains.

Like David Schneider's *American Kinship*, the articles in *Belief and Transgression* dealing with social taboos, and with convictions (by investigators as well as "natives") that they both exist and explain something, point toward the "culture of kinship." Cultural practices that scholars have long considered to be lodged in nature turn out to operate more in ways we associate with religion: a Weberian position developed for anthropology most thoroughly by C. Geertz. Certainly incest is the touchstone transgression; and belief in its

---

3. Some lively views of the history of ethnological ideas are emerging from outside anthropology proper, for example, T. W. Herbert's outstanding *Marquesan Encounters* (1980) and, more problematically, E. Said's *Orientalism* (1980). Inspired by the opening chapters of Dumont's *Homo Hierarchicus*, I reviewed the history of holistic ideas of Bali in Boon (1977, Part I). Two recent books that taken together provide an unusual blend of symbolic and historical perspectives in ethnography and ethnology are M. Z. Rosaldo (1980) and R. Rosaldo (1980), both on the Ilongot of the Philippines.

general taboo is one of the earmarks of Western scholarship, and perhaps of Western ideology. Symbolic implications of the history of theories of kinship, marriage, and their antitheses formed a rich fabric of digression in Lévi-Strauss's *Elementary Structures of Kinship* (providing a point of departure for Héritier and others); consider, for example, his insistence on the "symbolic meaning" of mistaken explanations of exogamy:

> It will be recalled that McLennan believed that exogamy had its origin in tribes practicing female infanticide, and which were consequently obliged to seek wives for their sons from outside. Similarly, Spencer suggested that exogamy began among warrior tribes who carried off women from neighboring groups. Lubbock proposed a primitive opposition between two forms of marriage, viz., an endogamous marriage in which the women were regarded as the communal property of the men of the group, and an exogamous marriage, which reckoned captured women as the private property of their captor, thus giving rise to modern individual marriage. The concrete detail may be disputed, but the fundamental idea is sound, viz., that exogamy has a value less negative than positive, that *it asserts the social existence of other people*, and that it prohibits endogamous marraige only in order to introduce, and to prescribe, marriage with a group other than the biological family, certainly not because a biological danger is attached to consanguineous marriage, but because exogamous marriage results in a social benefit (p. 480; emphasis added).

In terms of sexual gratification, incest taboos establish surplus *cum* scarcity at the heart of "the group." From the vantage of any particular group, incest taboos employ the realm of sexuality to deny the self-sufficiency of "ourselves." Only positive exogamous rules in the realm of marriage categorically assert "others" in and of asserting "ourselves." Incest taboos alone cannot constitute society; they must be joined to positive marriage rules or to other symbolic means in "complex systems." For Lévi-Strauss *incest taboos are anti-isolationist without quite being prosocial*—a complexity in his views of incest versus exogamy many commentators overlook.[4] And the reasons for the cultural (indeed, religious) emphasis on transgressions such as incest would appear to be to convert them into symbolic supports for society, to add something positive to a prohibition.

Such digressions into the history of ideas of kinship and marriage in *Elementary Structures* prepared the way for *Totemism* as well. We recall Lévi-Strauss's demonstration that belief in the totemism of others (by outsiders) is as interesting and as fitting a topic for anthropological reflection as are the bits and pieces of tribal activity that were long artificially isolated and reified into this substantive category. In such studies ethnographic representations of actual practices, various native views, and the complex history of their detection and

---

4. A recent and profound misreading of Lévi-Strauss on this vital point is Fox (1980, pp. 10–11). For a serious and provocative return to the place of incest in Freud's *Totem and Taboo*, see R. Paul (1976). It is important not to isolate incest as a universal, distinctly uncanny taboo; cf. my attempt to approach Balinese incest themes as a cultural text relating values from several domains, in Boon (1982).

explanation cannot be divorced. Interpreting each requires confronting all. I need only add what strikes me as the fullest implication of Pierre Smith's and Michel Izard's own trickster-book: as with totemism, so with incest; and so with all manner and shape of terrible taboos and divine transgressions at the heart of the anthropology of religion.

References

Boon, James A. 1972. *From Symbolism to Structuralism: Lévi-Strauss in a Literary Tradition*. New York: Harper and Row.

___. 1977. *The Anthropological Romance of Bali, 1597–1972: Dynamic Perspectives in Marriage and Caste, Politics and Religion*. Cambridge and New York: Cambridge University Press.

___. 1982. "Incest Recaptured: Some Contraries of Karma in Balinese Symbology." In C. Keyes and V. Daniel, eds. *Karma: Its Meaning in Practice in the Popular Traditions of South and Southeast Asia*. Berkeley: University of California Press.

___. (In press). *Other Tribes, Other Scribes: Symbolic Anthropology in the Comparative Study of Cultures, Histories, Religions, and Texts*. Cambridge and New York: Cambridge University Press.

Bucher, Bernadette. 1981. *Icon and Conquest*. Chicago: University of Chicago Press.

Buchler, Ira R., and Henry A. Selby. 1968. *Kinship and Social Organization*. New York: Macmillan.

Clément, Cathérine, and Raymond Bellour, eds. 1979. *Claude Lévi-Strauss*. Paris: Gallimard.

Culler, Jonathan. 1981. *The Pursuit of Signs: Semiotics, Literature, Post-Structuralism*. Ithaca: Cornell University Press.

Detienne, Marcel. 1979. *Dionysos Slain*. Baltimore: The Johns Hopkins Press.

Dumont, Louis. 1981. *Homo Hierarchicus*. 2d ed. Chicago: University of Chicago Press.

___. 1977. *From Mandeville to Marx*. Chicago: University of Chicago Press.

Fox, Robin. 1980. *The Red Lamp of Incest*. New York: Dutton.

Friedrich, Paul. 1978. *The Meaning of Aphrodite*. Chicago: University of Chicago Press.

Geertz, Clifford. 1972. *The Interpretation of Cultures*. New York: Basic Books.

___. 1980. *Negara: The Theater-State in Nineteenth Century Bali*. Princeton: Princeton University Press.

Harari, Josué. 1979. *Textual Strategies: Perspectives in Post-Structuralist Criticism*. Ithaca: Cornell University Press.

Herbert, T. Walter. 1980. *Marquesan Encounters*. Cambridge: Harvard University Press.

Hocart, A. M. 1970. *Kings and Councillors*. Chicago: University of Chicago Press.

Leach, Edmund. 1967. *The Structural Study of Myth and Totemism*. London: Tavistock.

Lessa, William, and Evon Z. Vogt. 1979. *Reader in Comparative Religion: An Anthropological Approach*. 4th ed. New York: Harper and Row.

Lévi-Strauss, Claude. 1963. *Totemism*. Boston: Beacon Press.

___. 1966. *The Savage Mind*. Chicago: University of Chicago Press.

___. 1969. *The Elementary Structures of Kinship*. R. Needham, ed. Boston: Beacon Press.

___. 1964-71. *Mythologiques* (Four volumes: *Le Cru et le cuit; Du Miel aux cendres; L'Origine des manières de table; L'Homme nu*.) Paris: Plon.

___. 1974. *Tristes Tropiques*. John and Doreen Weightman, trans. New York: Pocketbooks.

Macksey, Richard, and Eugenio Donato. 1972. *The Structuralist Controversy*. Baltimore: The Johns Hopkins Press.

Needham, Rodney. 1973. *Belief, Language, and Experience*. Chicago: University of Chicago Press.

O'Flaherty, Wendy Doniger. 1973. *Asceticism and Eroticism in the Mythology of Siva*. Oxford and New York: Oxford University Press.

___. 1980. *Women, Androgynes, and Other Mythical Beasts*. Chicago: University of Chicago Press.

Paul, Robert A. 1976. "Did the Primal Crime Take Place?" *Ethos* 4, no. 9.

Rabinow, Paul, and W. Sullivan. 1979. *Interpretive Social Science: A Reader*. Berkeley: University of California Press.

Radin, Paul. 1972. *The Trickster*. Introduction by Stanley Diamond. New York: Schocken Books.

Rosaldo, Michelle Z. 1980. *Knowledge and Passion: Ilongot Notions of Self and Social Life*. Cambridge and New York: Cambridge University Press.

Rosaldo, Renato. 1981. *Ilongot Headhunting: 1883-1974*. Stanford: Stanford University Press.

Said, Edward. 1978. *Orientalism*. New York: Pantheon.

Schneider, David M. 1980. *American Kinship: A Cultural Account*. 2d ed. Chicago: University of Chicago Press.

Turner, Victor. 1975. *Dramas, Fields, and Metaphors*. Ithaca: Cornell University Press.

___. 1975. *Revelation and Divination in Ndembu Ritual*. Ithaca: Cornell University Press.

Zimmer, Heinrich. 1971. *The King and the Corpse*. Princeton: Princeton University Press.

Michel Izard and
Pierre Smith

Preface to the French Edition

There are few domains of anthropology which the work of Claude Lévi-Strauss has not contributed to renewing in a decisive way. There is probably none whose landscape has been more profoundly reshaped than that of the anthropology of religion, to the extent that this very appelation no longer seems to correspond to a homogeneous subject matter, the object in question henceforth appearing as fragmented, while at the same time dissolving into a wider perspective.

The texts brought together here propose to bear witness to this new situation. For beyond the diversity of the cultures studied and the themes approached, even beyond the heterogeneity of positions and methods, the anthropologists listed in the table of contents of this book share the sense of being engaged in carrying out a vast research program conclusively traced and authoritatively illustrated over the last thirty years by Claude Lévi-Strauss; it is this, first of all, that justifies the homage that we mean to render him with this publication.

In 1955, at the beginning of an article that has remained famous, Lévi-Strauss observed: "Despite some recent attempts to renew them, it seems that during the past twenty years anthropology has increasingly turned from studies in the field of religion."[1] In 1967 a British anthropologist belonging to a very different school of thought—John Middleton—could still remark, in his introduction to a collection of texts on religious anthropology: "Since then (the 1920s) the study of the religions of non-literate peoples has, with some monumental exceptions, met with a curious lack of interest by ethnographers."[2]

1. "La structure des mythes," in *Anthropologie structurale* (Paris, 1958), p. 227.
2. John Middleton, ed., *Gods and Rituals: Readings in Religious Beliefs and Practices* (New York, 1967), p. ix.

xv

While we risk appearing somewhat schematic, we can, in order to situate the state of researches in the anthropology of religion, note that three sets of theoretical assumptions[3] which dominated the development of the area have now been lifted.

The first sends us back to the works of the great founders like Tylor, Frazer, or Durkheim, who brought their main effort to bear on the nature of the religious. If we must grant them "the merit of having understood that the problems of the anthropology of religion fall into the province of an intellectualistic psychology,"[4] we must also recognize that their more specific postulates rapidly led to an impasse. In one sense, the work of Lévi-Strauss, above all such works as *Totemism, The Savage Mind*, or the four volumes of *Mythologiques*, can be understood as an immense effort to reorient the fundamental intuition of the authors invoked above, by bringing to light a set of operational rules, or, if one prefers, a logic of universal scope which could also be used to account for the specific details of what appear to be the most diverse and mutually irreducible cultural formations. In brief, the anthropologist accounts in his own language for modes of thought external to his own culture only to uncover, at the source of the other thought and of his own, a single matrix, whose productions are multiple yet determined; and he makes the nature of this determination the object of his interrogation.

The second set of assumptions is one of those that grows out of functionalism, which long occupied an impregnable position at the heart of anthropological theory. For functionalism—and this is one of the reasons for the long-standing lack of interest that we mentioned above—myths, rites, and beliefs were hardly worth considering except as projections of the social, whether they were considered reflections, expressions, formations of affective resonances, screens, or even emotional safety valves. From this perspective, and others which agree with it on this point, the ultimate coherence of facts of the religious or more generally the symbolic order can be isolated only on the basis of another instance, for which is reserved, a priori, a monopoly of relevance. Yet however one conceives the relations between the religious and social, and without thinking of denying these relations the privileged attention they deserve, we must certainly admit that cultural symbolism always monstrously, as it were, overflows the external determinations to which people seek to reduce it. Inversely, the work of Lévi-Strauss—which in this respect extends that of Marcel Mauss—has restored full freedom of action to anthropological investigation by tearing it free of its doctrinal moorings and exposing it once again to the fresh wind of new hypotheses, by inviting anthropology to grant the same credit to all social and cultural facts, including the most tenuous or the most strange, and, finally, by reuniting domains that have long been separated. The exercise of this liberty

3. Translator's Note: The French word here is *hypothèque*, which means a mortgage or a lien, and implies the way general outlooks in the area have been preconstrained by assumed theoretical goals.

4. *Anthropologie structurale*, p. 227.

does, however, entail respect for certain requirements. Let us cite two of these. One is that while the anthropologist can and should take on the study of myths, law, politics, in themselves and for themselves, he must also try to conduct his analytic procedure all the way to its end: "For every form of human thought and activity, one cannot ask questions of origin or of nature before having identified and analyzed the phenomena and discovered to what extent the relations that unite them suffice to explain them. It is impossible to discuss an object, to reconstitute the history that has produced it, without first of all knowing *what it is*; in other words, without having exhausted the inventory of its internal determinations."[5] But, and here another requirement is introduced, such a procedure makes sense only if one maintains the perspective that motivated it in the first place. If one seeks to grasp "for each one of these codes its mode of organization and its specific function," it is in order to have the means "to understand the nature of the relations that exist among them,"[6] this aim being given here as a long-term research goal.

The third set of assumptions leads us to consider more marginal currents of anthropology than those we have been discussing. The renewal we have been speaking of has, certainly, constituted a powerful incitement to approach field-work with new curiosity, and has contributed to revealing previously misrecognized characteristics of the objects studied. The religions and other symbolic systems that we are familiar with in civilizations that have long been using writing tend to present themselves, through their texts, as solidly built constructions which impose themselves on human minds from the outside. There is nothing like this in the societies that anthropologists usually study: we find ourselves more often faced with scattered myths, heterogeneous rites, lacunary discourses, practices related to each other by threads that we cannot grasp. In this situation the ethnographer may be sorely tempted to reach a system by himself supplying missing parts to fit the model he imagines, by soliciting local rationalizations, or by turning to a superficial comparativism. While it is true that nothing in such contributions is completely worthless, in the end they only provide supplementary documents to add to the file. For the specificity of the anthropological approach, in relation, notably, to that of the history of religions, requires that the specific traits of the objects studied be revealed on a logical and not merely historical or hermeneutic level—"upstream," not "downstream," from the data; the analysis should lead from explicit discourses and lived practices toward the conditions—largely unconscious—of their expression and their use. It is these conditions that Lévi-Strauss, whose thought has often been misunderstood and sometimes completely distorted on this point,[7] has identified under the name *structures*.

5. "Le champ de l'anthropologie," in *Anthropologie structurale deux* (Paris, 1973), p. 14.

6. Ibid.

7. On this point, see the vigorous reaction in the "Finale" to *L'Homme nu* (Paris, 1971), pp. 559 ff.

Whatever the degree of adhesion—and it can vary a great deal—of the different authors in this collection to the more specific formulations, the stronger hypotheses, or the particular demonstrations that Lévi-Strauss has proposed, we feel that these three very general points draw them all in the same direction, a direction indicated by the title we have chosen for this book.[8] As far as we know, the notion of "symbolic function" (where "function" implies "organ," this being in the end simply that part of the brain, the source of language and representations, which has developed only in man) is introduced by Lévi-Strauss only in two articles from 1949[9] and, more than twenty years later, in the "Finale" to L'Homme nu.[10] This discreet fidelity is easily explained if we notice that, as matrix of structures, unconscious determination, fabric of meaning, instance that "is necessarily interposed between the thought world and the lived world," the symbolic function is not in itself the immediate object of our discipline; it represents rather, if one accepts the positions sketched above, anthropology's necessary implicit reference, the invisible background on which the anthropological process must inscribe the formal results of the discoveries and intuitions that may justify our curiosity about what goes on in other places.

One of these intuitions, widely shared today, is that the symbolic function remains blind to what might be thought to be the specificity of the religious. If, trusting to etymology, religion has sometimes been defined as what "binds" [relie] men to each other, or "brings them together," the symbolic function fully answers this definition, but it operates on all levels of mental, social, and cultural life, without distinction and not only in a reserved sphere. So religions come to appear only as assemblages of variable composition, diversely defined, or not defined at all, by different cultures, whose constituent elements (myths, rites, glosses, moral codes, priestly groups, conceptions concerning individual or collective destiny, etc.) are very unequally developed in different cases. In addition, every one of these elements has, one might say, its own clinamen, which always tends to draw it out of the domain of the religious properly speaking. Thus, the Mythologiques do not treat myths in which religious resonances are evident any differently from others, the most numerous, which seem to be without such resonances, to reach results for which this difference is not relevant. Thus the mythical and the religious only intersect, they are not superposed. We also know, even while keeping to the strictly religious domain, that attempts made to establish systematic homologies between mythology and ritual quickly reach their limits. Rituals can both do without myths and contradict, overflow, or escape them. More generally, the study of the components of the person, or representations tied to biological and social destiny, conceptions concerning the nature and origin of power, and so on, can, without changing very much, either have or not have a "religious" coloring—which sometimes springs from the observer's eye alone—so that the religious appears to be of the

8. TN: The French edition of this book was entitled La fonction symbolique.
9. Reprinted in Anthropologie structurale, chap. 1, p. 28, and 10, pp. 224-25.
10. Cf. L'Homme nu, pp. 587-88, 609, 611.

order of the contingent and the local, whereas the symbolic, on the contrary, bears the mark of the necessary and universal.

The essays that make up this volume, while growing out of the same general inspiration, do not for this reason constitute a closed set; the order in which the texts are arranged is meant only to offer the reader one guiding thread among others. Still, the place of Dan Sperber's study[11] was determined by its axiomatic character: it affords access to the other texts in that it poses a preliminary question, which refers back to old but still pertinent discussions. To the question, "Is symbolic thought prerational?" Sperber replies clearly; for him the rational precedes the symbolic, and if we may justly speak of a "symbolic apparatus"[*disparitif*], this can only be an apparatus that is subject to the rational order. Following this text, Jean Pouillon and Nicole Belmont ask about the modalities of belief, but in different aspects, the exemplary avatars of belief being faith, the foundation of religion with universalist pretensions, on the one hand, and superstitions, the refuge of representations specific to popular religions, on the other, the distinct meaning of these two notions becoming confused as soon as the cultural context ceases to oppose them.

With myths we reach the most autonomous aspect of symbolic production, and the most thoroughly explored. Marcel Detienne, a specialist in ancient Greece, nevertheless opens his chapter, too, by inviting us to share in an enlightened doubt. For while researches on mythology concern civilizations with writing as much as they do those without writing, the transition from oral to written does not take place without raising questions about the ambiguity of a notion which, from its origins, is based more clearly on philosophical attitudes than on the objects studied. Georges Charachidzé confronts the oral and the written in another way by comparing the Hesiodic myth of Prometheus with tales that are still being transmitted by the populations of the Caucasus, and by showing that the most significant differences in the treatment of the common themes appear above all as the result of a change of "key," in the musical sense. Patrice Bidou then presents an extended and evocative commentary on the different parts of a myth that he collected in Amazonia and through which appear some of the fundamental questions that haunt all cultures.

The study of the internal determinations of that other great group of symbolic productions that constitutes rituals has scarcely been outlined. Through diverse considerations on the identity of rites, on their insertion into different autonomous systems, and on the way they are organized around characteristic acts, it is sacrifice which today is once again capturing the attention of anthropologists. Around the crucial theme of the effectiveness of sacrifice and its possible drift into symbolic sacrifice, Olivier Herrenschmidt compares the positions of Brahmanism, Judaism, and Christianity, which go from an ideology of effectiveness (Brahmanism) to a dialectic of the effective and the symbolic

11. TN: The order of articles in the present edition has been altered from that of the French edition, to which this preface refers.

(Judaism) and from there to the ambiguity of Christianity. The sacrifice is the "religious" act par excellence, but there are also "social" rites, whether we are speaking of "rites of passage" which effect the individual's insertion into society, or rites of power, which have their own symbolics. In the context of the Moundang kingdom (Chad), starting from an analysis of rituals of kingship, Alfred Adler points out the ambivalence of the person of the sovereign; the king bears witness to the cosmic order while at the same time he is a singular and mortal figure and thus subject to this order in an exemplary way.

All through the data on belief, myths, and rites, we continuously encounter essential preoccupations animating cultures—to account for man's relationship to nature, to society, and finally to his individual destiny. Man wanders between necessity and freedom, between norm and transgression, between transparency and mystery, without the question of the religious necessarily arising when the obviousness of the presence of the symbolic imposes itself. By the angle of a logic of the identical and the different at work in the symbolic order, Françoise Héritier reexamines the problem of the incest prohibition, introducing us both to the study of human destiny and the foundations of society and to that of categories of thought. Patrick Menget remains in the line of this dual inspiration, for it is, again, a dialectic of the same and the other that illuminates the relations—here studied in a South American Indian context—between the couvade and the incest prohibition. Through these two opposed but complementary institutions, what is in question is above all reproduction, biological reproduction in one case, social reproduction in the other. But these two modes of human reproduction cannot be separated and, together, have certain affinities with reproduction in nature. Nature/culture, wild nature/domesticated nature, bush or forest space/village space: if anthropology is attentive to these oppositions to the highest degree, it is because man lives in space, or rather in two spaces: that which he inhabits and in which he works, and that which, on the contrary, escapes the human transformation of nature without for this reason being a mere neutral referent. Michel Cartry starts from the opposition between "village" and "brush" to mark the necessary role this double territoriality plays among the Gourmantché (Upper Volta) in the process of individuation, which he deals with through the concept, introduced here for the first time, of "body-space." If space is present at birth, it is also present at death, and with it the "earth," ground of the living and body filled with the dead. Starting from the example of the kingdom of Yatênga (Upper Volta), Michel Izard shows how norm and transgression are inscribed in space and have meaning in relation to the ideology of the earth.

Exploring the domain of man in society, we have been forgetting the gods; dealing with the symbolic, we have lost sight of the lived world of man in history. Marshall Sahlins invites us to a double return, in telling us how a man, through being sacrificed, became a god, and in submitting to us, in guise of a conclusion, the enigma of this "apotheosis."

Jean Pouillon

1   Remarks on the Verb "To Believe"

The French verb *croire* ["to believe"]¹ is paradoxical in that it expresses doubt as well as assurance. To believe [*croire*] is to state a conviction; it is also to add a nuance to that conviction: "I believe" [*je crois*] often signifies "I'm not sure." This ambiguity involves the subjective side of belief [*croyance*]. As regards its object, the situation is no less equivocal, since the complement of the verb can be produced in two ways: direct or indirect. What is more, the indirect construction itself has two forms: *croire à* ... ["to believe in," "to think of"] is not the same thing as *croire en* ... ["to believe in," in the sense of being willing to rely on], which both differ from *croire* + direct object or *croire que* ... ["to believe that ..."]. Finally, the meaning of the verb and the construction of the complement can vary depending on the nature of the object: man, god, fact, value, statement. ...

     This suggests two questions (at least): is it possible to order this diversity of usages? If so, is this order universal or does it characterize only a certain type of culture, and in this case what is the basis for the word's unity? In other words: how is it that multiple meanings do not require diverse expressions?² But since

1. TN: The author's distinctions among different meanings of the verbs *croire, croire en, croire à*, etc., bear on the semantics of the word, not directly on its morphology. For this reason I have not followed the inflections of the French verb in my bracketed clarifications, but have usually put the infinitive form, whatever the tense, person, etc. of the verb in the text. For example, when the French text says *il croit* I have put "he believes" [*croire*], to make clear the opposition with, say, *il croit en*, which I translate "he believes in."

2. Diverse expressions do exist, however: credit [*créance*], confidence, trust [*confiance*], faith [*foi*]. ... But while one might turn to these for the sake of precision, they are not required by usage.

this is apparently the case, is a translation of the verb in all its senses possible in other languages, using a single term?

Croire à ... is to state that something exists; *croire en* ... is to have confidence; *croire que* ... is for something to be represented in a certain way. Although the difference between the two indirect constructions may appear slight, it is undeniable, as the following example shows: a person believes in [*croire en*, "trusts in"] God, while one believes in [*croire à*] the Devil, that is, one recognizes that he exists without, by definition, putting one's faith in him: one cannot *croire en* the Devil. *Croyance en* ["belief in, trust in"] God does imply *croyance à* ["belief in"] his existence, but implication is not identity. On the other hand, this implication seems so obvious that it often goes unformulated: a believer believes in [*croire en*, "trusts in"] God, he feels no need to say that he believes in [*croire à*] God's reality; he believes in [*croire à*] it, one would say, implicitly. But is this certain? In fact, the believer not only need not say that he believes in [*croire à*] the existence of God, but he need not even believe in [*croire à*] it; precisely because in his eyes there can be no doubt about it: the existence of God is not believed in [*crue*], but perceived. On the contrary, to make God's existence an object of belief, to state this belief, is to open up the possibility of doubt—which begins to clarify the ambiguity with which we started. So one could say that it is the unbeliever who believes that the believer believes in [*croire à*] the existence of God. One could call this a play upon words; but these words do lend themselves to it, and it is precisely this possibility that must be explored, if not elucidated, in trying to organize the field of their usages. Besides, what I have just said will appear much simpler if we leave the religious domain. If I have confidence in a friend, if I believe in [*croire en*, "have faith in"] him, will I say that I believe in [*croire à*] his existence? Certainly not; that existence is, simply, undeniable. It is only if it were not unquestionable that I would have to believe in [*croire à*] it, and believe in it explicitly. Again, it will probably be said that this is playing on words, this time on the word "existence," for man's existence, by definition, is not on the same level as that of the deity. By definition, yes, but by cultural definition: the distinction between a cultural world and a natural world, or between a "this world" and a "beyond," is widespread, but it is not universal. It is this distinction between two modes of existence that leads to a distinction between two ways of apprehending what exists: perception and knowledge on one side, belief [*croyance*] on the other. From this kind of perspective, the existence of supernatural beings can only be an object of belief, and this is why wherever this distinction is made the phenomon of belief as the affirmation of existence takes on this ambiguous aspect, between the certain and the questionable.

This is not the only reason. Let us now consider the relations between *croire à* ... ["to believe in (a fact)] and *croire que* ... ["to believe that ..."]. To believe in [*croire à*] the existence of X—"god, table, or washbasin"—can be expressed in a direct construction: to believe that [*croire que*] X exists. But this is a statement of a peculiar type—the existence of a god or of a hundred thalers is not an attribute—and is different from the statement that endows X with certain characteristics which permit X to be represented to oneself. The representation, the content of belief, is accompanied by an affirmation of existence but is separable from this affirmation; the affirmation can be bracketed—the Husserlian *epoché*—and this is what makes possible studies of beliefs as such: one need not believe in [*croire à*] what one believes in order to analyze it. The "I believe" [*je crois*] which precedes so many statements of the most diverse kinds, is the mark of a distancing and not of an adhesion.

These two movements, which a single verb is able to express, appear radically opposed, or else completely unrelated. Belief as representation, as statement, pertains to what is also called ideology; there is no isolated belief, every representation is part of a global system which is more or less clearly, more or less consciously articulated, a system which may be religious but may also be philosophical, political. . . . Belief as faith [*confiance*] is the conviction that he to whom one has given something will reciprocate in the form of support or protection; it calls forth a relationship of exchange, of which the relationship between the believer and his god is only a particular case, even if a frequently privileged one. One puts one's faith [*confiance*] to the same end, whether in an individual, in a party, in an institution. It is significant in this regard that Benveniste, in his *Indo-European Language and Society* (1969; English edition, London, 1973), discusses belief [*la croyance*] not in the section on "religion" but in that on "economic obligations." For he sees the original meaning of belief in this credit which has been accorded and should be returned. Must we then see belief-as-representation as a derivative meaning? Or else as a meaning that has been added on, and which would turn the verb "to believe" into a conglomerate without unity?

This derivation is certainly a possible one: to believe in [*croire en*] someone, to give him credit, is, among other things, to believe [*croire*] what he says, and in this way one goes from the trust to the statement that it allows one to take as established fact. This is especially evident when the belief appears in the form of religious faith: trust in [*croyance en*] a god is usually the basis of what we call a *credo*, a group of statements which become the direct object of belief. The same is true in many other domains. For political examples, there is an overabundance of choices. But it is also possible (more often than is usually . . . believed!) to accept a proposition that is said to be scientific just as one accepts a dogma or even the possibly fantastic assertion of a man who is judged worthy of trust; I believe it not because I am able to prove it, but because I have faith in those who say they have proven it, for example, in Einstein when, following him, I write $E=mc^2$. But we would miss the essential part of belief-as-representation if we reduced it to this sole case in which it is based on the argument of authority. The specific trait of a representation is to appear obvious, to be self-evident, and the fact that it is always possible to bracket the judgment or the feeling of obviousness changes nothing: the obvious is replaced by the arbitrary, but both simply mean that this form of belief is based on nothing but itself or the cultural system within which it finds its meaning.

So it seems impossible to overcome the polysemy of the word. Its religious usage does allow us to unify the verb's three constructions, but it does not eliminate the other usages; over and above this, it only unites the three constructions in religions of a certain type. This observation leads us to question its anthropological usage, now well established and apparently unproblematic.[3] What anthropologist would deny that he seeks to uncover the beliefs of those whom he studies, to compare them with our own beliefs or those of other peoples, as if this object of study and its designation presented no a priori problem, as if it were obvious that every human being "believes" [croire] — this being one of our beliefs—in the same way, if not, of course, in the same things? The danger in this situation is not simply the well-known if not always foreseen one of inappropriately applying a category that may have meaning only in our own culture; it has to do with the fact that this category may not be a single, unified one at all, even for us, or at the least that it is a shattered category, whose fragmentation is, precisely, a singular cultural phenomenon. What is more, anthropological usage reduplicates the paradox I emphasized above when I said that it is the unbeliever who believes that the believer believes. If for example I say that the Dangaleat[4] believe in [croire à] the existence of margaï, this is because I do not believe in their existence and, not believing in it, I think that they can only be believing in [croire à] it in the same way that I imagine I could, if I did. But how can one tell whether they believe [croire] and in what way? What question can one ask them, using what word of their language, in what context? Or, inversely, how is it possible to translate into French the word or words they use to talk about what is to our eyes an object of belief?

In J. Fédry's Dictionnaire dangaleat,[5] we find the verb àbidé "to perform the rites faithfully." It comes from the local Arabic abada, "to adore God," adoration being understood as a ritualized activity. It is a matter of worship [du culte], of faith in action, and not of the representation of a being whose existence must also be affirmed. This verb is used with a direct-object complement: this being, God for converts to Christianity or Islam, or the margaï for others. The best way to translate it is thus "to serve," in the biblical sense of the term: to worship [rendre un culte à]. No abday maragi, "I serve the margaï." Another verb, àmniyé, signifies "to bestow one's trust on," "to rest on," "to believe in"

---

3. Rodney Needham has done this (Belief, Language, and Experience), in a perspective different from my own. The two do overlap, however: the themes are necessarily the same, but they are put together in different ways.

4. The Dangaleat are one of the groups called Hadjeraï, who live in the central region of the Republic of Chad, Department of Guera. They worship [rendent un culte à] what one could summarily call local spirits: the margaï.

5. Thèse du troisième cycle, mimeographed (1971). I thank the author for having added to the information included in his thesis with a personal communication.

[*croire en*]. It is constructed with an indirect-object complement, introduced by the preposition *ku*: *no amnay ku marigo*, "I have faith in the *margaï*," "I give my faith to the *margaï*"; this is the verb that Christians use to say "I believe in [*croire en*] God," *no amnay ku bungir*. In contrast to the foregoing, this verb is not used exclusively in religious contexts: one can evidently, as in French, put one's faith in another person. The first sense given by the dictionary, besides this, is "to be used to, familiar with...," and one will say, for example: *no amniyiy-g pisò*, "I am used to horses." This too is a word of Arabic origin whose Semitic root has given us the"amen" of Christian liturgy which, as Fédry points out, marks adhesion to a person more than to a conceptual "truth." As this author notes, "one may wonder about the fact that both of these verbs come from Arabic, whose linguistic influence is very strong in Dangaleat, as in other Hadjeraï languages. But this should not make us doubt that what the Dangaleat have taken in has become an integral part of themselves." I will add in turn that from the language of a religion with a *credo* (an affirmation of existence and a set of statements and representations) the Dangaleat have taken what fits their own way of "believing" [*croire*]: the terms that designate a specific behavior and mental attitude—worshipping [*rendre un culte*] and trusting in the addressee of the worship—and not terms that are based on definite representations or propositions.

One may thus translate our "believe in" [*croire en*] into Dangaleat, and the fact that the Hadjeraï took the word from Arabic suggests that for them it expresses the essential aspect of belief (and of religious faith in general, says Fédry, who belongs to the Society of Jesus and should know whereof he speaks): faith [*la confiance*]. But in this case, how can we translate "to believe [that]" [*croire que*]? To find out, to know, to know about something, is *ibiné*; *pakkine* serves to render: think, suppose, figure out, foresee. These two verbs are pure Dangaleat. The first will be used to mark certainty and so translates "to believe" [*croire*] in cases where the French verb is more or less equivalent with "to know," when for instance Don Juan says to Sganarelle, who is questioning him about belief, "I believe that two and two make four." The second verb covers the doubtful usages of our verb, all those in which the speaker takes a certain distance with regard to what he is talking about.

In sum, we can translate all aspects of the verb "to believe"... except the verb itself. What we have been able to translate has been the French equivalent of "to believe" in each of its particular usages, but in Dangaleat there is no single term that serves as the basis of their unification. In other words, we can translate everything except the ambiguity. We must therefore return to the reasons for this ambiguity. Ambiguity is not simply polysemy, the fact that a verb sometimes has one meaning and sometimes another, each of them unequivocal; it is, rather, that all of these meanings, even the contradictory ones, are intrinsically liked; that, above all, there is always doubt at the heart of the conviction, and that the affirmation itself indicates that it could always be suspended. But why condense this paradoxical liaison into a single word instead of sorting out its elements, as the Hadjeraï do? The answer, "I believe," lies in the comparison between a religion like Christianity and a religion like that of the Dangaleat.

It is not so much the believer, I would say, who affirms his belief as such, it is rather the unbeliever who reduces to mere believing what, for the believer, is more like knowing. Nevertheless, the Christian cannot avoid expressing his faith not only as trust in God [*confiance en*], but also as belief in [*croyance à*] his existence and belief that [*croyance que*] God possesses such and such attributes, that the world was created, and so forth. He states this as a belief, even though he knows it—but also because he knows that by this very fact it is contestable and contested. Above all he knows that there are other beliefs, on the one hand because his religion has a history and was constituted against the "false" gods, on the other because this history is not over yet and there are still idols to be eliminated; and there can be *other* beliefs only because his own belief is one among others. Next, he knows—it is even an essential point in his *credo*—that the object of his belief is in a "reality" of a different order than the realities of the world of creation, which are the object of a permanently revisable scientific knowledge, or of calculations, of predictions that can be proven wrong; and he also knows that this possibility of revision lies in the demonstrable or verifiable character of the knowledge or the hypothesis, a character whose legitimacy he challenges in the case of his belief, but which, inversely, challenges the legitimacy of his belief. Thus he must simultaneously assume both his affirmation and the challenge to it, a challenge that belief is, nonetheless, supposed to make impossible on its own level. In other words, the contradiction is inside his faith, and that is what it is "to believe."[6]

This situation is the result of the distinction made between two worlds: the Kingdom of God and this world. In our culture such a distinction seems so characteristic of religion, to those who reject it as much as to its adherents, that religion in general and so-called "primitive" religions in particular are usually defined by a belief in supernatural powers and by their worship. There is even a tendency to think that the extent and importance of the supernatural world are much greater for "primitives" than for "moderns," that super-nature is not only the domain of gods and spirits but also, for example, the domain in which the power of the magician and the sorcerer operates. I certainly do not mean to deny that at any latitudes one can find people who believe in [*croire à*] the supernatural, but one equally finds people for whom such an affirmation is completely meaningless—without them being, for all that, areligious—far from it. For here we have a major misunderstanding: because we have constructed the concept of natural law, we are ready to admit the supernatural (whether as

---

6. It would be easy to show that today many "political believers" find themselves in an analogous situation. But they are not always as aware of it as Saint Augustine was when, according to Tertullian, he said: *credo quia absurdum*.

illusion or as other reality hardly matters) as a place to put whatever contravenes, or seems to contravene, natural law; but this is our own notion, whether we judge it well grounded or not, and not that of the people to whom we abusively attribute it. As Evans-Pritchard remarks, "many peoples are convinced that deaths are caused by witchcraft. To speak of witchcraft being for these peoples a supernatural agency hardly reflects their own view of the matter, since from their point of view nothing could be more natural."[7] For his part, Claude Lévi-Strauss has stressed the realist, materialist character of magic, its monistic, not dualistic, conception of the world.[8]

The *margaï*, these spirits who have such an important place in the individual and social lives of the Hadjeraï, are invisible, nonhuman powers; they act unpredictably, and are the cause of whatever disturbs the natural course of things. But they are no less a part of the same world as human beings. The latter believe in [*croire à*] the existence of the *margaï* like they believe in their own existence, in that of animals, things, atmospheric phenomena. . . . Or rather they do not believe in [*croire à*] it: this existence is simply a fact of experience:[9] there is no more need to believe in [*croire à*] the *margaï* than to believe that if you throw a stone it will fall. One fears and/or trusts in them, one gets to know them, one gets used to them, one performs the special sacrifices that please each *margaï*, and one is careful to make no mistakes, for fear of getting sick or being affected in some unpleasant way. If we can speak of a Dangaleat religion—another untranslatable expression—it is not in the sense in which the faithful share a single elaborated body of beliefs about supernatural beings, but rather in the etymological sense, according to Benveniste, of the Latin *religio*:[10] that of a meticulous concern for the proper carrying out of the cult, without, however, being able to define the necessary correctives in advance; at every occasion, one takes aim within uncertainty. One can only estimate what each *margaï* desires. The four verbs mentioned above define these behaviors equivocally and without contradictions: one serves the *margaï*, one trusts in them (that is, in the mutually fruitful nature of the exchange inaugurated by the sacrifice), one knows from experience that they exist, and one tries to guess their intentions. All this does presuppose a particular representation of the world, but one which excludes the possibility of its explanation in the form of "belief," of an assertion that in spite of itself is doubtful, relativized. The Dangaleat certainly know that others think differently, and it happens that many of them convert to Islam

7. *Theories of Primitive Religion* (Oxford, 1965), pp. 109–10.
8. Lévi-Strauss, *The Savage Mind*, English translation (Chicago, 1966), pp. 221–22.
9. In the same way, among the Nuer the expression *Kwoth a thin* ("God is present") "does not mean 'there is a God.' That would be for the Nuer a pointless remark. God's existence is taken for granted by everybody. Consequently, when we say, as we can do, that all Nuer have faith in God, the word 'faith' must be understood in the Old Testament sense of trust (the Nuer *Ngath*). . . . There is in any case, I think, no word in the Nuer language which could stand for 'I believe'." Evans-Pritchard, *Nuer Religion* (Oxford, 1956), p. 9.
10. Benveniste, *Indo-European Language and Society*.

or to Christianity. But this situation cannot surprise them: one does not believe in [*croire à*] the *margaï*; one experiences them, and this experience is first of all a local one; such spirits do not necessarily exist everywhere. While the encounter with otherness relativizes Christian belief in an otherworldly absolute, it confirms the Dangaleat experience of the world, which is relative from the beginning and so cannot be disturbed by diversity. This is why religions of the Dangaleat type are without the proselytizing inherent in religions founded on beliefs whose vulnerability impels their formidable dynamism.[11]

If the Dangaleat have no need of the verb "to believe" this is not solely because of their monism, as opposed to Christian dualism. Equally in play is another opposition, one between the historicism of the Christian religion and the empiricism of Dangaleat religion. This empiricism assures everyone of the presence of the *margaï*, and has no need of an intercessor. Every man performs his own sacrifices and will have recourse to the diviner only to know what animal, of what sex and what color, he should kill and on what day. A religion like Christianity or Islam is based, on contrary, on a revelation, testimony, a transmission whose fidelity is guaranteed by a church or specialized experts. This revelation is, precisely, that another world exists; the revelation is a unique historical event, its content is constituted by the words of its protagonist, God incarnate or prophet. So everything rests on a faith, which is simultaneously a trust and a specific *credo*. All the meanings of the verb "to believe" should then come together, but this necessity is nothing more or less than a cultural necessity. It is only in this perspective, in my opinion, that we can speak of "religious belief," and it is only when it is understood that this notion does not have universal value that we can appreciate how difficult the problem of a general definition of religion really is; but this may also be the point from which we can try to resolve the problem.

11. I do not mean to say that some beliefs are vulnerable and others are not. Any belief, in the fact of its communication, makes itself, and knows itself to be, vulnerable.

Nicole Belmont

2 Superstition and Popular Religion in Western Societies

> *The anthropomorphism of nature (of which religion*
> *consists) and the physiomorphism of man (by which*
> *we have defined magic) constitute two components*
> *which are always given, and vary only in proportion.*
>
> Claude Lévi-Strauss, *The Savage Mind*

The notion of superstition is fundamental both for the study of popular religion in Western societies and for the history of folklore as a discipline. For it was under the name of superstition that folkloric facts were taken down and collected, before the birth of folklore, by theologians and dignitaries of the Church and by the authorities of so-called learned culture. But they performed this task for centuries with a negative outlook: the goal was to condemn these facts and to try to make them disappear.[1]

It would probably be a misuse of language to speak of popular religion when referring to the superstitious beliefs and practices denounced by the Church, for they do not form a religion in the strict sense of the term, lacking as they do a body of doctrines and dogma and systematic organization into mythical and liturgical systems.

May we assume that this system exists nonetheless, but has remained submerged? The task, then, would be to bring the system to light. The inverse

1. N. Belmont, "L'Académie Celtique et George Sand. Les débuts des recherches folkloriques en France." *Romantisme, Revue de la Société des études romantiques* 9 (1975): 29–38.

9

hypothesis would be that so-called superstitious beliefs and practices had no need of their own religious system since the Christian religion could fulfill - this function for them. One does in fact frequently observe a syncretic situation in which it is difficult to distinguish the Christian religion and this popular religion, at least as far as their collective psychic mechanisms are concerned. The most important of these mechanisms is belief, and it is not by chance that the term "superstition," later felt to be pejorative, was sometimes replaced with "popular belief." One must therefore consider, besides the notions of religion and superstition, that of belief, and ask oneself exactly what each of these terms covers. In this regard I can cite a sentence from Freud's *Totem and Taboo*: "'Superstition'—like 'anxiety,' 'dreams' and 'demons'—is one of those provisional psychological concepts which have crumbled under the impact of psychoanalytic research. Once we have penetrated behind these constructions, which serve as screens between facts and knowledge, we begin to realize that the mental life and culture of primitives have not hitherto had all the recognition they deserve."[2] Not only superstition but also religion and magic are provisional constructs functioning as screens between the facts and scientific knowledge. With the help of anthropological reflection, I will attempt, in however limited a way, to reach the meaning and function covered by these terms.

To clarify their meaning I will turn to etymology and call upon Emile Benveniste's remarkable work, *Indo-European Language and Society*.[3] The Latin *superstitio*, says Benveniste, is an abstract term corresponding to *superstes*, "surviving," so that *superstitio* would signify "survival" and indicate a "remainder" of an old belief which appears superfluous at the time the term is used. "Super" signifies not only "above" but also "beyond": *superstare* is to stand beyond, to subsist beyond. Someone who has passed through danger, a test, a difficult period, who has survived it, is *superstes*. Another meaning grows out of this one: Someone who has subsisted beyond an event becomes its witness.[4]

Etymologically at least, the term "superstition" has nothing pejorative about it. It designates a survival, and it is worth noting in this regard that during the nineteenth century, when a substitute was sought for "superstition," it was "survival" that was adopted, a term which P. Saintyves in a 1932 article correctly attributed to the English anthropological school, which "both put the historico-scientific notion of survival at the disposal of scholars and cleared the air of theological preoccupation."[5] The theologians also used "superstition" in this sense, since they saw superstitions as vestiges of paganism. It was in

2. S. Freud, *Totem and Taboo*, 1913 (Standard Edition [London, 1953], 13: 92). [TN: The English translation has been modified to fit the French.]
    3. First published in Paris, 1969 (English edition, London, 1973). [TN: I have modified the English translation in spots to make it more literal.]
    4. *Indo-European Language and Society*, pp. 523–28.
    5. P. Saintyves, "Les origines de la methode comparative et la naissance du folklore. Des superstitions aux survivances." *Revue de l'histoire des religions* 105 (1932): 70.

order to express the same thing that the English anthropological school, in the person of Tylor, proposed the term "survivals," which he defined as "fragments of a dead lower culture embedded in a living higher one."[6]

The first attempt at a collection of folklore in France, that of the Académie Celtique at the beginning of the nineteenth century, in its efforts to purge the materials of traditional life of the disreputable name of superstition, had proposed another term, that of *monument*, to designate not only archaeological remains but also customs, beliefs, and local dialects.[7] Here too the etymology of the term contributed to what the members of the Académie Celtique wanted to express: in Latin a *monumentum* is anything that recalls someone or something, anything that perpetuates a memory; and it was only subsequently frozen into the more restricted meaning of a commemorative architectural monument. But in its beginnings the monument is the material trace of what is past, of what no longer exists. One sees, then, how much weight the notion of superstition-survival carries in the history of folklore.

The etymology of the word "religion" was also studied by Emile Benveniste, who remarks first of all that there is no common Indo-European term for this notion.[8] This absence is explained, in his opinion, by the fact that the very nature of this notion does not lend itself to a single and lasting expression. For while it is true that religion is an institution, in ancient civilizations this institution is not set apart from other institutions: "everything is imbued with religion, everything is a sign of divine forces." The need for a special term to designate it only makes itself felt when religion is set apart out and it becomes possible to know what belongs to religion and what is outside it. This is the case in Rome, quite late in the history of Indo-European civilizations, and that is why the Latin term *religio* has remained the sole and constant word, without equivalent or replacement, in all Western languages.

Its etymology was already a subject of controversy in Roman times. Two origins were proposed: one from the verb *legere* "to gather, collect," and one from *ligare*, "to tie." For Cicero *religiosi* are those who gather together all that has to do with worshiping the gods, whereas for Lactantius—a Christian author of the second half of the third century and beginning of the fourth—religion is a "bond" of piety which "binds" us to the divinity.

Emile Benveniste decides in favor of the first of these alternatives. In the classical period, he says, *religio* meant "scruples"; *religio est* meant "to have scruples"; it is meticulous care for the rites, a "hesitation, a misgiving which holds back, a scruple which prevents, and not a sentiment that impels to action or incites to ritual practice." Here we are closer to the meaning given by Cicero, who connects the word with *legere*, and this is born out by the fact that it is far more difficult philologically to connect it with *ligare*, "to tie."

6. E. B. Taylor, *Primitive Culture*, 2d ed. (London, 1873), 1: 72.
7. Belmont, "L'académie Celtique," p. 31.
8. Benveniste, *Indo-European Language and Society*, pp. 516–23.

Religere is "to recollect, to pull back to make a new choice, to reconsider a previous approach." For Emile Benveniste this is a good definition of the religious "scruple": to take up again a choice already made, to revise the decision which results from it—this is the proper sense of *religio*. "It indicates a subjective attitude, not an objective property of certain things. . . . Roman *religio* was at the beginning essentially subjective." The etymology proposed by Christian writers is interesting precisely in that it bears witness to a totally different conception of religion, which has become the expression of a bond of piety, of the dependence of the believer on God, of an *obligation* in the true sense of the word. For, as Lactantius says, God has bound man to him and attached him with bonds of piety.

The opposition between *religio* and *superstitio* is relatively late in Rome. It is to some extent a distinction between normal and exaggerated forms of belief or worship.

I will now turn to a source of material belonging to the culture that I have been mainly concerned with, that of traditional, preindustrial French society. I am referring to the *Traité des superstitions* of the Abbé Jean-Baptiste Thiers, to which F. Lebrun has devoted an excellent article.[9]

The definition Thiers gives of superstition occupies the whole of Book One of his first volume, *Le Traité des superstitions selon l'Ecriture sainte*, that is, around one hundred pages. The author bases himself on numerous texts drawn from the fathers of the church, from very early authorities such as Saint Augustine, Saint Eligius, and Origen up to the decisions of the councils, and also calls upon the major figures of Christian history up to the seventeenth century; in addition he makes use of examples which he could only have drawn from personal observation.

A first point should be stressed: for Thiers, as for the ecclesiastical authorities, superstition falls into the domain of religion—false religion certainly, but religion nonetheless. For Lactantius religion belongs to true worship, superstition to false worship. Saint Thomas Aquinas declares that superstition is a vice opposed by excess to religion, since it bestows divine honors on something that should not, or in a way that it should not, receive them. Superstition is excessive and extraordinary religion. One can be superstitious even in the worship of God, for example, when one gives him something that he has not asked for, and in a way other than that which he has commanded. There exist therefore two possible cases of superstition: either bestowing on some creature other than God the worship that is due to God alone, or else bestowing upon God a worship that he has not asked for or in a way that is not appropriate. What is interesting in this

9. F. Lebrun, "Le 'Traité des superstitions' de J. -B. Thiers, contribution à l'ethnographie de la France du XVIIe siécle," *Annales de Bretagne et des Pays de l'Ouest* 83, no. 3 (1976): 443–65. Thiers first published the *Traité des superstitions selon l'Ecriture sainte* (Paris, 1679), then in 1703–04 the *Traité des superstitions qui regardent les sacrements*. In later editions the two works are put together under the title of the second (Paris, 1741, and Avignon, 1777).

first approach is that the opposition between religion and superstition already sprang from the same conception at the time it was first noticed in Rome: superstition was taken to be an exaggerated, abnormal form of religion.

In the case of bestowing on a creature other than God the worship that he alone should receive, it is clear that this creature can be none other than the devil; thus one could even say that all superstition is founded on a tacit or explicit pact with the devil, or devils. Men, of course, ought to hate the devil, who is their mortal enemy and the enemy of God.

It follows that superstition is an enormous sin and forms part of what were called "reserved cases," which only a bishop had the right to absolve. Thiers declares that the seriousness of this sin "has not prevented superstitions from planting deep roots in the minds of people, where even today they cause strange disorders." In the preface to the edition of 1679 he expresses himself still more strongly on the wide extent of this evil: "[Superstitions] find credence in the minds of the great; they are current among middling people; they are in vogue among the simple people; every kingdom, every province, every parish has its own; many are guilty of superstition who do not believe in it; he is guilty of it who does not think so; they enter even into the most holy practices of the Church, and sometimes, which is wholly deplorable, they are publicly authorized by the ignorance of certain ecclesiastics who should be using all their strength to stop them from taking root in the field of the Church, where the enemy sows them among the good seed during the night."[10]

This text is remarkable in several respects and bears witness to the profound knowledge, not merely literary but concrete knowledge, that Theirs had of the problem. He sees that superstition is characteristic of all classes of society: the great, middling (petty and big bourgeoisie), and simple people; that besides this social extension it has a geographical one: every kingdom, every province, every parish has its own superstitions. He thus recognizes the local particularism of the data. He is also aware that one can be superstitious without thinking about it, involuntarily; and finally he knows that superstitions are present within the Church itself, either as a deliberate practice—and in the course of the book he has occasion to denounce the practices of monasteries which draw substantial profits from them (the belt of Saint Margaret, lent out by the monks of Saint Germain-des-Prés to women in childbirth for the price of one obol)—or because of the ignorance of the clergy, particularly in rural areas.[11]

If then it is possible to give oneself over to superstition without meaning to and without knowing it, then it is essential to determine with precision the rules by which it can be recognized. The first rule is that something is "superstitious

---

10. Preface to the 1679 edition. F. Lebrun also stresses the interest of this passage.

11. J. Delumeau, in his book *Le Catholicisme entre Luther et Voltaire* (Paris: P.U.F., 1971), shows the intellectual and moral insufficiencies of the pastoral forces of the sixteenth and seventeenth centuries, and of the efforts undertaken by the Counter Reformation to retrain the clergy, especially the rural clergy.

and illicit when it is accompanied by certain circumstances which are known to have no natural virtue for producing the effects hoped for from them," for example, the pronunciation of certain words whose meaning one does not know. This is a rule that Thiers takes from Saint Thomas, and it is worth citing in its entirety: "In things that are done to produce particular effects, we must consider whether they seem able to produce these effects naturally. For if they are able to produce them they will not be illicit, since it is permitted to use natural causes to make them produce the effects of which they are capable. But if they do not seem able to produce these effects naturally, it follows that they are not being used to produce them as causes but only as signs. And in this way they are connected with the pacts that are made with demons."

This text is remarkable in that Saint Thomas very reasonably places superstitions in the symbolic order: superstitious practices do not act as physical causes destined to produce effects, but as signs.

There is a second rule for recognizing something as superstitious: "It is superstitious and illicit insofar as the effects that one expects from it cannot reasonably be attributed either to God or to nature." For we could object to the first rule that supernatural effects with God as their cause must be superstitious by definition. This is not, of course, the case. But it is superstitious to imagine that when there are thirteen people at table one of those present will die within the year. Thiers remarks that he has observed this superstition even among "people who consider themselves above the ordinary." In this situation one of the thirteen is made to leave, or else a servant is added to the table "to break the number." Neither God nor nature has given this number a fatal or unlucky quality.

This belief was sometimes rationalized by an invocation of the Last Supper, which included thirteen at table, including one victim and one traitor. But in this case God would have to have institutionalized the belief through the mediation of his Church. And since this was not the case, we have the third rule: "Something is superstitious when the effects that it produces cannot be attributed to nature, and it has not been instituted either by God or immediately by the Church to produce them." The ceremonies performed by the Church, both by custom and in the administration of the sacraments, or in other circumstances, are not superstitious, even though they do not naturally produce the effects for which they are established. For the Church has received from God the power to establish ceremonies whose effects come only from God: "the Church, being led by the Holy Ghost, can never be sullied by any stain of superstition." "Thus, provided that the faithful keep themselves within the limits which the Church prescribes for them regarding Ceremonies, and add nothing of their own, nothing false, nothing new, nothing foreign, they need not fear falling into superstition from practicing the Ceremonies of the Church."[12]

This text is of interest on two accounts: it attempts on the one hand to stave off the objection that the beliefs and ceremonies of the Church could be super-

12. Thiers, *Traité des superstitions*, p. 89.

stitious since they do not *naturally* produce the effects which they are expected to produce, and so act as *signs* and not as natural causes; on the other hand we find here again the distinction that was drawn in the beginning between religion and superstition in Rome: superstition adds on, as it were, in relation to religion. It is an exaggerated form and, in the terminology of the church, unwarranted worship, a superfluous cult.

According to the fourth rule something is superstitious when it is performed by virtue of a tacit or deliberate pact with demons. There exist three possible cases of an explicit pact and eight cases of a tacit pact. Their detailed description, interesting in that Thiers illustrates them with examples, does not, however, add anything new to his definition of superstition. He next introduces the notion of "vain observance." Vain observances are defined as such for two reasons. On the one hand they do not always obtain the effects that they promise; and on the other hand, if one does sometimes obtain these effects, "those who practice [a vain observance] receive more trouble than profit, all the more so because for what is at most a temporal advantage they seriously compromise their consciences and miserably lose their souls."

The rules for recognizing a vain observance are the same as those for recognizing superstition. In fact Thiers seems to use this term to designate superstitious *practices*, while that of superstition covers the mental mechanism, the belief, and the practice.

If we try to summarize Thiers' prolix definition of superstition, we quickly see how equivocal it is. For superstition involves mechanisms that are supposed to act not as natural causes but symbolically, as signs, according to Thomas Aquinas. Yet Christian worship also involves symbolic mechanisms: its effects cannot be attributed to nature. To this Thiers replies that they emanate from God or from the institution of the Church. The ceremonies the Church performs are not superstitious since God has granted the Church the power to institute them, so that the effects of these ceremonies come from God. But the mechanism remains the same in both cases, and it is, as has been said, a symbolic mechanism. Thus the criterion is not really operational, even though there is no ambiguity in the eyes of Abbé Thiers: that which does not proceed from God through the intermediary of the institutions of the Church proceeds from the devil, but in fact does so by the very same symbolic mechanism. The most important point for us is that superstition is in the same category as religion; it is a religion, but a religion to which something has been added which does not proceed from God; it is a superfluous cult, an unwarranted worship.

If we turn now to the works of anthropologists, we may not find very much on superstition as such; but we do note that very early on, anthropologists studied magic as a fundamental concept of social and religious anthropology. The essential work in this regard is Marcel Mauss' *General Theory of Magic.*[13]

13. First published in the *Année sociologique* (1902-3), in collaboration with Henri Hubert (English edition, London, 1972).

Mauss notes the extreme importance of conditions of time, place, materials, and instruments in magical rites. These conditions are always numerous, imperative. If anything in a ritual is changed, it loses all effectiveness. This condition holds both for the actions of rituals and for the incantations and formulas used— what Mauss calls oral rites. From this formalism flow two consequences: the constraining character of magical rites, which impose themselves in an imperative way; behind this constraining formalism the content is much more mobile, more fluid, so that we find both a large number of magical practices having the same goal and similar practices with different goals.

This constraining character of magical practices is identical with that found both in superstitious beliefs and superstitious practices. This is easily seen for the practices, which involve formulas that must be followed to the letter. And the same is true for superstitious belief: let us recall the example Thiers cites of the superstition concerning the number thirteen, particularly eloquent in that it is still alive in our own times. To the extent that one believes in it, it is a real constraint that forces one to avoid getting into this situation.

In an article entitled "Obsessive Actions and Religious Practices,"[14] Sigmund Freud notes the similarity between the obsessives acts of neurotics, which seem to be imposed on them by force, as if by an external constraint, and religious practices. For neurotics any activities whatever can be made ceremonial if they are elaborated with small additions or given a rhythmic character by the use of pauses and repetitions.

But Freud also notes important differences between neurotic ceremonials and religious practices: (1) Individual ceremonial acts present a far greater diversity than do religious rites, which are much more stereotypical in nature. (2) The former have a private, even secret, character, while religious ritual is public and communal. But the difference does not hold so far as magical and superstitious practices are concerned, for these, too, are often performed in secret and in solitude. Marcel Mauss pointed out this private, secret, mysterious, nonpublic character of magical rites. (3) Finally, the "mini-rituals" of religious ceremonial are considered symbolic and charged with meaning (all the elements of the ritual of the Mass, for instance), while those of neurotic ceremonial seem foolish and senseless. "An obsessional neurosis presents a travesty, half comic and half tragic, of a private religion."

Major differences are evident here; but we could add a third term to this group, placed halfway between religious ceremonial and obsessional ritual, namely, magical and superstitious practices. For these possess both the diversity of individual ritual and the stereotypical character of religious ritual. Their character is less private than obsessional ceremonial, yet less public than religious ritual, and this is not only because these practices were condemned by the

14. The article dates from 1907. It is translated in Freud, Standard Edition, 9: 115-27.
15. Tylor, *Primitive Culture*, 1: 94.
16. Freud, "Obsessive Actions," p. 120.

Church: by nature they are both social and communal in origin since they are transmitted by tradition and are usually individual in practice. And, finally, they seem to be completely inept, nonsensical. Nineteenth century writers even thought that the absurdity of these practices could be used as a key to recognizing them. So Tylor declares: "It seems scarcely too much to assert, once and for all, that meaningless customs must be survivals, that they had a practical, or at least ceremonial, intention when and where they first arose, but are now fallen into absurdity from having been carried on into a new state of society, where their original sense has been discarded."[15] Superstitions do in fact often give the impression of being arbitrary and irrational. But one also sometimes notices an evident symbolism in them, usually metaphorical in nature.

Halfway between private ceremonies and large-scale religious rituals, magical and superstitious practices therefore share in the nature of both, being less fragmented than the former, less systematic than the latter. We could add to the senseless character presented by individual ceremonials the peculiarity of superstitions that Thiers emphasized, their "vanity": these are vain observances; they do not seem to be good for anything.

In reality, Freud restores to individual ceremonies the meaning and function that they seem to lack completely. For if they seem without meaning, it is for the simple reason that what is involved here is an unconscious meaning. "Obsessive actions are perfectly significant in every detail . . . they serve important interests of the personality and . . . give expression to experiences that are still operative and to thoughts that are cathected with affect. They do this in two ways, either by direct or by symbolic representation; and they are consequently to be interpreted either historically or symbolically."[16]

It is striking to rediscover in this text the same two modes of explanation that are applied to popular beliefs and customs: explanation by history, in which case they are considered *survivals*, and by symbolism, in which case the goal is to decipher their real, hidden meaning. These two modes of explanation are not mutually exclusive, as long as we keep in mind the fact that a historical explanation via an investigation of origins and evolution does not imply that the popular belief or custom has no contemporary function; on the contrary, if it persists it is because it has kept its full emotional charge.[17]

In another work[18] Freud opposes "conscious ignorance" and "unconscious knowledge" in the context of individual superstition: "*Because* the superstitious person knows nothing of the motivation of his own chance actions, and *because*

---

17. TN: Here the author uses the French term *investissement*, which in most contexts is translated into English as "investment." In a psychoanalytic context such as this one, however, *investissement* is used to translate Freud's German term *Besetzung*, meaning "the fact that a certain amount of psychical energy is attached to an idea or to a group of ideas, to a part of the body, to an object, etc." (J. Laplanche and J. -B. Pontalis, *The Language of Psychoanalysis*, 1967 [London 1973], p. 62). The idea of a psychic charge is here given the standard English translation "cathexis."

18. *The Psychopathology of Everyday Life*, 1901 (Standard Edition, 6: 258).

the fact of this motivation presses him for a place in his field of recognition, he is forced to allocate it, by displacement, to the external world." This mechanism of projection of an unconscious knowledge into the external world applies as well to collective superstitions, with the exception that here we are dealing with a store of beliefs and practices codified by tradition, which the individual has only to draw from, in place of a direct confrontation with chance and events. The constraining character of magical beliefs and practices, which has already been noted, would then be explained by this mechanism of projection: their constraining power would come both from the tradition which imposes a norm and, equally, from the unconscious.

Mauss's fundamental contribution to the theory of magic was to insist, in spite of appearances, on its social character. That of Frazer is quite different. As for Tylor, in Frazer's eyes magic falls into the category of science, but of a false, mistaken science. "Men mistook the order of their ideas for the order of nature, and hence imagined that the control which they have, or seem to have, over their thoughts, permitted them to exercise a corresponding control over things."[19] This theory is obviously open to criticism: why, for instance, should primitives and preindustrial European populations, who possessed a very refined and profound practical knowledge of nature, have suddenly let this knowledge lapse at certain moments and instead used magico-religious practices without effective action on their environment? It may be suggested that they used magical knowledge and technical knowledge to attain different ends—in the first case, ends that are unattainable by technical means (making the rain fall, for example), in the second case realizable ends (agriculture, hunting, and so on). But this is not the case, for agrarian rituals exist alongside agrarian techniques. People must therefore have been perfectly capable of telling technical effectiveness from magical effectiveness.

Frazer's contribution to the theory of magic concerns, rather, the problem of its mechanism. He distinguishes, as is well known, two kinds of magic, imitative or homeopathic magic (Thiers denounces a practice consisting of soaking a broom in water to bring about rainfall) and contagious magic (when, for example, one is careful to avoid the weapon with which one has been previously wounded). In one case there is similarity, in the other contiguity. These two principles are fundamental for ideational mechanisms, as Roman Jakobson has shown in the case of language.[20]

Every linguistic sign involves two modes of arrangement: combination with other signs, which are thus mutually contiguous; and selection within the code, which presupposes various degrees of similarity. We also know that in rhetoric

19. J. G. Frazer, *The Golden Bough. Part I, The Magic Art*. (London, 1911), 1: 420. Cf. Wittgenstein's critique of Frazer: J. Bouveresse, "Remarques sur le Rameau d'Or de Frazer," *Actes de la recherche en sciences sociales*, no. 16 (September 1977).
20. R. Jakobson, "Two Aspects of Language and Two Types of Aphasic Disturbances," in R. Jakobson and M. Halle, *Fundamentals of Language* (The Hague: Mouton, 1956).

these two principles are given the respective names of metonymy and metaphor. These are essential components of all symbolic processes. It is not surprising that they should be rediscovered in the system of magic and superstition. Homeopathic magic, which Frazer also calls sympathetic magic, is based on similarity or identity; it is like a metaphor in action. Contagious magic is based on the principle of contiguity: it is an acted metonym. At first glance superstitious practices seem metaphoric more often than metonymic. They seem to involve the mechanism of sympathetic, homepathic magic far more often than that of contagious magic. But to say this is perhaps to forget a large number of popular practices associated with the festivals of the Christian calendar but linked to that calendar in no other apparent way. Think, for example, of the crêpes or fritters made on Candlemas Day, the day of the Purification of the Virgin, on February 2.[21] The only link between the purely Christian ceremony and this popular practice seems to be one of contiguity—contiguity in time—to the exclusion of any link of sympathy or similarity. This is not the case with the other popular practice of the Purification, the blessing of candles which are then kept in the household all year long to ward off disasters, especially fire and storm. It is thus possible that a certain number of "superstitious" practices associated with the festivals of the Christian calendar have only a simple link of contiguity with the latter, and acquire their magical effectiveness solely by virtue of this link of contiguity. Less evident, therefore, than the link of similarity, it is nonetheless just as essential and effective as association by homeopathy or similarity, even though the latter is far more manifest, obvious, and immediately perceptible. These "metonymic" beliefs and practices seem, in addition, to have been much less easily tolerated by the Church than the others.[22]

It will be useful to restate the main points introduced up to now.

We noted first of all that the two notions of religion and superstition have been thought of as opposed categories throughout history. Anthropology considers them both as manifestations of the religious faculty, and so equivalent from this point of view, but nevertheless presenting differences: one is organized into a dogmatic and liturgical system, the other is seen in more scattered forms. This situation is specific to Christianized European societies. And, according to our hypothesis, superstitions in these cultures have no need to be organized into a system since they have been able to fit into the framework of the Christian religion. In "primitive" societies, it is magic that is opposed to a more organized and public cult, whatever its form may be. It seems therefore that this opposi-

---

21. J. -B. Thiers, *Traité des superstitions*, stigmatizes this practice: "Making what are called *Crêpes* or fritters, with eggs, water, and flour, during the Mass of the Purification; in such a way they should be done at the end of the Mass, so as to have money all year long" (I: 376).

22. Thiers gives an example that shows this dual symbolic effectiveness: "Attaching a nail from a crucifix to the arm of an epileptic, to cure him." On the one hand the nail is in a metonymical relationship with a sacred object, the crucifix; on the other hand, popular belief is certain that it *nails down evil*: its symbolic effectiveness is thus metaphorical.

tion is not merely postulated by the historian or the anthropologist: it also grows out of the facts themselves. But this too may only be one more construction serving as a screen, as Freud says, between the facts and knowledge.

Our glance at etymology showed that religion is in origin a subjective notion and indicates, as it were, a second movement: it is to have second thoughts about a choice that has already been made, to go back over an earlier course of action. Etymologically, superstition is not opposed to religion, since it is, strictly speaking, a survival, with no pejorative sense attached to this notion: a witness who has outlived a former state of things, a monument recalling that former state. Later in the history of ancient Rome the meaning shifts, and superstition comes to be opposed to religion as the exaggerated, pathological form to the normal form.

Anthropology, in particular the works of Marcel Mauss, has shown us that magical and superstitious beliefs and practices impose themselves with a coercive force that is felt to be external in two respects: on the one hand, these things are passed down by tradition, on the other hand they must be precisely observed. This same constraint is felt by the superstitious individual: it is chance, the play of events, that provokes the significant coincidence. Already J. -B. Thiers spoke of the superstition of coincidences. And the neurotic feels an obligation that he cannot escape, as powerful as if it came from outside himself, to perform compulsive acts which are equivalent to magical rituals in the constraints that they exercise. Freud speaks of "projection" with regard to superstition: that which arises from the unconscious but is censored by consciousness is projected into the outside world, either in the form of individual superstition or as a set of beliefs and practices codified by tradition.

From this point on, it becomes clear that the superstition/religion opposition is, in its deeper sense, an opposition between internalization and externalization: religion is a movement of return upon oneself (going back over a previous course of action, a choice already made, recollection), while superstition involves the projection of an unconscious knowledge out into random events or into a body of beliefs and practices passed down by tradition. Both processes grow out of the religious; they are simultaneously inseparable and antagonistic. No religion can be pure internalization, any more than it can be pure practice imposed from outside. It would be interesting to do a history of religions based on these two principles. It is likely that such a history would show an evolution from greater externalization to greater internalization: think, for instance, of the Protestant Reformation within Christianity. But there probably exists a limiting point in this movement of internalization: the point where religion becomes purely individual, loses all social character, which must therefore be the point where religion dissolves.

It is not my purpose here to produce this history of religions. What interests me is, rather, the fact that this opposition between religion and superstition, between internalization and externalization, has usually been felt to be a difficult, if not an impossible, contradiction to overcome. This is particularly true in the society that I have been studying, traditional, preindustrial society, which contained cultural discontinuities. An elite vainly sought to impose a greater internalization of religion by strict control of the process of externalization, by imposing an orthodox liturgy and system of worship on a multitude that it considered uncultivated. But this multitude needed beliefs and practices better suited to manifest their own deepest needs and tendencies, and so needed their own mechanisms of projection, which they invented themselves in order to express collectively and socially an unconscious knowledge that was far more heavily censored in learned culture.

The quest for the dividing line between "learned" religion and popular religion is thus a vain one. If such a line exists, it is constantly shifting, and so is impossible to grasp definitively. It is hard enough to grasp *hic et nunc*. In reality the dividing line is not on this level. It lies on a far deeper level, and combines two movements in opposite directions, one going toward the inside, one toward the outside, whose mechanisms and manifestations lean sometimes to the side of religion and sometimes to that of superstition. For neither of these expressions is ever really pure: in varying proportions there is always a mixture of the religious and the superstitious. But in practice that we are able to observe historically, this opposition and mixture have been experienced as an unbearable contradiction. We could say—with a paradox that is perhaps only so on the surface—that in the end the Church was fighting the wrong battle, the wrong enemy, since what it called "superstitious practices" were in fact a more active factor of social integration than was the opposed movement of internalization favored by the Church itself. For this movement of internalization can do more to dissolve religion than the necessarily collective movement of projection that is its opposite.

It remains for us to examine the notion of belief, which is also essential in this problem. As we did for religion and superstition, we will look first at etymology, which allows us, as it were, to get an idea of the archaeology of the notion.

Unlike for the word "religion," there seems to have been an Indo-European term for "belief." Emile Benveniste finds it in the Vedic texts: it is the word śraddhā, which signifies not belief in a thing, but a man's personal belief vis-à-vis a god, particularly the god Indra.[23] It is an act of faith manifested towards a god, but with a certainty of remuneration: this devotion is made in order to secure the benefits of what has been pledged. In the *Rg Veda*, it is an act of trust in a god, implying a return service in the form of divine favors bestowed upon the devotee. The Indo-European root *kred* reappears, in secular form, in the Latin *credo*, which first of all means "to entrust something with the certainty of recovering it." In this regard belief [*croyance*] and credit [*créance*]

23. Benveniste, *Indo-European Language and Society*, pp. 138–44.

are two equivalent notions, one of which concerns the religious domain, the other the juridical domain. For what, in fact, is a creditor? It is someone who holds a right by virtue of which he may require something of someone else, in particular a sum of money. Juridically this right is represented by the pledge, which can be a mortgage, a security deposit, or anything else.

Originally, belief thus means to hand over to another person something that belongs to you without consideration of risk, with the certainty of receiving back what has been entrusted. The mechanism is the same for specifically religious faith and for trust in a man, whether the commitment is by words, promises, or money.

In relation to religion and superstition, and to the two opposed movements that they contain, belief is thus paradoxically placed on the side of superstition, since it is a movement toward the outside, originally toward the divinity. Popular feeling is perhaps in agreement with this paradox. In a recent study on the chapels of a village in the diocese of Cambrai, the author reports the conviction of some informants that some priests nowadays are not "believers." It is possible to be a fervent and practicing Catholic without being a believer.[24] For belief is this movement toward the outside, toward a divinity, in this case the Christian God, or one of the saints, or the Virgin, to whom one entrusts something—an offering of money, a candle, or simply words, that is, prayer—with the certainty of receiving back a restitution in the form of a boon. It is thus apparent that "superstition" is more than a mere projection of unconscious tendencies toward the outside; it is necessarily accompanied by an act of faith, the certainty of a return. Superstition and belief are thus inseparable from one another. We can better understand why a third term has replaced both superstition and survival: the expression "popular belief" is superior to the extent that it rids the notion of any pejorative character as well as all reference to an ideological a priori which would send its meaning back into a departed past.

With these few propositions a third path suggests itself, which would provide a way out of the unsatisfactory choice presented by M. Vovelle in a recent article: "An 'other religion' or the *disjecta membra* of a system that may once have been coherent, but is now reduced to a few ill-sorted memories."[25] If we assume that "popular religion," the "other religion"—whatever we call it—has used Christianity as a system and a framework available for its own purposes, then we can locate their relationships on a level other than that of opposition, conflict, or reciprocal ignorance, since these relationships must be of a dialectical order. We thus resolve the hopeless problem of which one came first, and the string of assumptions that goes along with it: pagan survivals, fragments, "original" or "natural" religion, prerationality. It is probable, in fact, that Christiani-

24. F. Noiret, *Anor et ses chapelles, diocèse de Cambrai,* Diplôme de l'Ecole des Hautes Etudes en Sciences Sociales (Paris, 1976).

25. M. Vovelle, "La religion populaire: problèmes et méthodes," *Le Monde alpin et rhodanien,* nos. 1–4 (1977): 7–32.

zation and folklorization have always evolved in tandem, maintaining relations of tolerance, if not even of complicity, up until the fifteenth century, as J. Delumeau believes, and then of antagonism from the time of the Counter Reformation. At this time the internally divided movement of religiosity, perceived as antagonistic, crystallized a social and cultural opposition. If we are still wondering about origins, we can suggest, with Van Gennep, that folklore is the result of an autonomous invention from the time of the High Middle Ages, or, more specifically, from the time of a Christianization that was sufficient to provide a framework for a set of popular beliefs and practices but was incomplete from a symbolic point of view and was insufficient to express needs, desires, and tendencies that cannot find expression in articulate language.

Olivier Herrenschmidt

3

Sacrifice
Symbolic or Effective?

In a recent essay, the first stage of a reflection on what may prove to be a new view of sacrifice, I concentrated on the essential role played by the sacrifier as the bearer of desire in the sacrifice (Herrenschmidt 1978).[1] I felt, at the same time, that the victim's presence in the sacrifice had to be understood in terms of the necessity of exchange and the circulation of goods, and that the victim (or, more generally, the offering) should be thought of as the sacrifier's giving up of something that belongs to him—in the most extreme case, giving himself up through suicide, the sacrifice par excellence—to a receiver who must be present: the deity. Thus the destruction, the elimination, of the victim seemed to constitute what P. Mus has called "a formula of effective transposition," the only way to transfer a belonging from the realm of the visible to that of the invisible.

The sacrifier's desire constitutes the first axis of sacrifice, that of the individual. But there is also a second axis, that of the universal order, which is just as immediately involved here. It is these two axes that allow Madelaine Biardeau to speak of the sacrifice as a Janus figure (1976, p. 23). I believe that it is by con-

1. TN: French social science distinguishes between the *sacrifiant*, someone who has a sacrifice performed for his own benefit, and the *sacrificateur*, the person who actually performs the sacrifice. This follows the difference between the two voices of the Sanskrit verb "to sacrifice": *yajate*, in the middle voice, means "he sacrifices for his own sake," while *yajati*, in the active voice, means "he performs a sacrifice" (presumably for someone else's sake). The distinction is fundamental in the Brahmanic tradition (cf. Herrenschmidt 1978). I have followed the usage introduced by W. D. Hall in his translation of H. Hubert and M. Mauss, *Sacrifice: Its Nature and Function* (Chicago, 1964), translating *sacrifiant* as "sacrifier" and *sacrificateur* as "sacrificer."

24

sidering both of these axes, without neglecting one for the other, that we can come closest to the reality of sacrifice: that unique process, time, and place in which desire and order, the individual and the universal, are conjoined. For if we know anything about sacrifice, it is this: every time the sacrifier sets in operation the sacrificial process, it is the satisfaction of his desire and the order of the world that are brought into play.

The essential thing here is the specific effectiveness of sacrifice itself. There is no need to go into a demonstration: it is quite evident, and is sometimes explicitly stated. For the first part of this paper my guide will again be Brahmanic speculation, probably the most thoroughly developed that we know of in this domain: it has made explicit things which have undoubtedly remained implicit in many other cultures that have given a major role to sacrifice, while sometimes trying to empty it of its meaning—or of its power. I will be looking at the way in which Brahmanism accounts for the effectiveness and the effects of sacrifice, focusing on the following three points:

- —the way in which the order of the world can be linked explicitly to the sacrifice;
- —the way in which this intimate connection allows us to account for the effectiveness of the sacrifice;
- —how, particularly as the original sacrifice, it is not only the place where the individual and the universal join together, but also is the union of the one and the many, the totality and its determinations.

The fundamental notion of an order (or a law) of the universe is present from Vedic times. Four terms, remarkably analyzed by Abel Bergaigne over a century ago, designate this order: *dhāman, dharman, ṛta,* and *vrata*. These words "express originally not a moral idea, but the particular material conditions of the existence and of the stability of the world" (1883, 3:215), namely: foundation, support, and above all *adaptation* (in the sense of "mutual adaptation of the different portions of the world" [ibid.]), which is specifically designated by the term *ṛta*. According to Hymn I: 105 of the *Ṛg Veda*, cited by Bergaigne (3:269), *ṛta* is at the same time "the law of sacrifice, law which priests are eager to know"; "the law of celestial phenomena"; and "a moral idea" (we should note the immediate connection between morality and the natural order). Consequently it is not surprising that "the law of sacrifice and the law of celestial phenomena correspond to each other." And Bergaigne sums up his analysis as follows (3:270):

The regularity of celestial phenomena, that of the sacrifice assimilated to these phenomena and regarded as acting upon them, finally transported to heaven where they are in turn assimilated to the sacrifice; and, lastly, man's observance of the duties that are his to fulfill, not only towards the gods, but towards his own fellows; these three orders of facts in which the idea of law appears in three different aspects, nevertheless appear to us to be connected and to a certain point confounded in the eyes of the Vedic Aryans in their usage of the words *dhāman, dharman, vrata*, and *ṛta*, denoting in turn the laws of nature, the laws of worship, and moral laws.

The ritual thus acts upon "celestial phenomena" because it is in conformity with them, ruled by the same laws, homologous. The divinities are mediators, and sacrifice nourishes them (an extremely ancient idea), increasing their strength (Bergaigne 2:235): when they are well nourished, the gods work in the proper way and can fulfill their function in their place in the universe.

This whole process is powerfully summarized by Pierre Masson-Oursel:

> Far more than the worship of divine beings, the keystone of the doctrinal system is a theory of sacrifice (*yajña*). The religious operation (*karman*), the ritual act or word, directly controls things and events; it procures the desired objects, for the sacrificer or the person on whose behalf the act is done, by means of its own effectiveness—as long as the appropriate rite is known exactly and carried out with precision. . . . Nature obeys (the sacrifice) because the order of things coincides with the strict laws of the rite. The sacrifice is truer than reality; reality is an external evidence of this primarily cultural order. The world is, literally, a sacrifice (1948: pp. 81–82).

We are thus dealing with a ritualistic system, in the strong sense of the term, that is, with a formalism: the rite is effective if it is carried out correctly, since, in its very carrying out, the order of the world is reproduced and maintained. The right order of sacrifice is, and assures, the right order of the world.

So the world is, "literally, a sacrifice." And, Masson-Oursel continues, "the sacrifice, for example, of which the cosmic giant Puruṣa (= Prajāpati) is both author and object" (ibid., p. 82). The cosmos is an enormous man, but man is also a small-scale universe. Besides this, "the sacrifice is man, for it is man who offers it" (*Satapathabrāhmaṇa*, cited by Lévi 1966, p. 77). Hence the constant homologies and identities between the three orders: universal, sacrificial, human. The parts of the original *puruṣa* make up the whole universe, the stages (or parts) of the sacrifice make up the parts of the human body.

The sacrifice is thus a totalizing process: it is the whole as well as each of its parts. Differences disappear in it, and what remains distinct in the universe *so that* the sacrifice may be accomplished becomes one *in* its accomplishment. The character of Prajāpati says all this: he *is* the sacrifice as a whole; and he is its origin ("he gave forth the sacrifice"); he is its sacrifier and the first to enjoy its fruits (the first to go up to heaven); and he is its first victim. His myth tells us what we will keep finding again and again elsewhere: the fundamental identity of all or some of the "characters" involved in the sacrificial process: sacrifier, officiant, victim, divinity (and, as we shall see, we find the same doctrine in the Epistle to the Hebrews).

But the myth also tells us how the sacrifice is productive, "creative," that is, differentiating. Out of the sacrifice emerge the determinations without which a human world could not be lived. Prajāpati is aided by Speech (*Vāc*), who stands in the same relation to him as the ritual formula (*mantra*) does to the rite. But in the beginning Speech is undifferentiated, and the god Indra makes her distinct, specific, qualified. With this act Speech becomes effective and a part of this world: one quarter of Speech goes to man, another quarter to beasts, another to the birds, and the last to the insects (Lévi 1966, p. 35). Similarly, "Prajāpati gave forth the beings; they were without distinction, without consciousness, and ate each other; Prajāpati was unhappy about this; he saw the rite...and so organized the world: the cows were cows, the horses horses; the men men, the animals animals" (ibid, p. 25; cf. pp. 29–30). The order of this world is above all differentiation. There are no beings unless they are differentiated. The sacrifice creates (and maintains) the order of the world in creating (and maintaining) differentiations.

Having reached this point, I must leave the Brahmans and clearly formulate a number of propositions which I believe are of general validity and comparative value, and specify the questions that now face us.

It is evident that three facts are closely connected: there is no singular desire satisfied except by sacrifice, and this can only happen *because* sacrifice acts on the order of the world, *since* the laws of the former are identical to those of the latter. Beyond this, we now understand the priest's role to be relatively secondary—that of a necessary technician—as is that of the gods: this system provides little room for their will or free choice to operate.

As far as the sacrifier's desire is concerned I need say little. Everyone knows perfectly well that one never sacrifices for nothing and, what's more, someone who sacrifices always knows why. This is evident for any "religion" considered, including religions of "salvation."

Everyone knows, too, that the sacrifice possesses its own specific efficacy. But the problem, as I will be repeating more than once, is that our culture would like this not to be the case, since it has decided (it would be helpful to know exactly when) that this kind of efficacy is magical; with this value judgment our culture makes an understanding of the sacrifice, and with it of "religion," impossible.

What does raise a question is the fact that not all societies have, explicitly or implicitly, organized the whole of their representations around (or even starting from) a dominant notion of cosmic law, as this can be understood, for example, in the terms *dharma, tao*, or *kosmos*. We do not, in other words, always or everywhere find the idea of a systematically organized universe, in which every element—gods, creatures, things—has its proper place and its relations with others defined and fixed by an order or a law dependent only on itself. But in this kind of context what is to be made of the phenomena that we can still identify as sacrifice, and of the efficacy that it is supposed to have?

To answer this, one must turn to the religions of the Book which, at the opposite extreme from the Brahmanic universe, recognize no order in nature except insofar as it can be seen as the free and voluntary project of a divinity.

The respective positions of order and the divine are thus exactly inverted, thereby altering the place of man in the system—this place, however, remains an eminent one.

For one can suggest that in opposing Brahmanic thought and that found in the Old Testament one can define two mutually illuminating global systems of representations; that there is very likely no other course possible for human thought, which seeks to install meaning and order (i.e., a meaningful order) in the totality of the thinkable, visible and invisible, through a religious discourse; and that man always gives himself the privileged place in these systems, while at the same time masking the truth from himself: the truth that he is the sole producer of meaning in the universe, which would be quite meaningless if, precisely, man did not hold such a discourse. This, indeed, is what is meant by religious alienation.

I will, therefore, schematically oppose these two systems of representations, which, purely for the sake of the example, I will label Brahmanic and testamentary:

The Brahmanic system puts the divinities in the position of mediators between man and the world order, to which both man and the divinities are subject. The eminent place man occupies is due to his unique power to control and maintain the order of the universe through sacrifice.

The testamentary system teaches that there is no world order—no "natural law"—except insofar as a god has willed it, and that it is maintained, to man's benefit, only because this god wishes it so, a wish contingent upon man's obedience to the god's law: man can know what tomorrow will bring only because there is a contract agreed to by both parties. This contract is called the Covenant.

This means, consequently, that the first of these systems is organized around the sacrifice, the second around the Covenant.[2]

Sacrifice nevertheless remains present in both the Old and New Testaments, from the one offered by Cain and Abel to the sacrifice of Christ. What is remarkable is that in these texts the sacrificial fact is not homogeneous, and—from the time of ancient Judaism—possesses two very different characters and takes place at two different sites: the effective sacrifice, offered in the Temple at Jerusalem after the Restoration (which recalls the Brahmanic model) is opposed to a symbolic sacrifice (a term that remains to be explained), which accompanies the conclusion or the renewal of the covenant. In the latter case the sacrifice is a purely formal act, marking or sealing a sworn word or a commitment; in the

2. I warmly thank Luis Mallart for all our conversations about the ideas that are to follow, and for having directed me to Denzinger's *Enchiridion*. But this makes it all the more necessary to state that the opinions expressed here are mine alone. Except where otherwise noted, biblical citations follow the E. Dhorme translation for the Old Testament and the Jerusalem Bible for the New. [TN: I have tried to respect the author's choice of biblical translations: thus passages from the Pléiade Bible (Dhorme and Grosjean) are rendered directly from the French. Since the Jerusalem Bible exists in both languages, I have generally followed the English version, while feeling free to alter this in cases where it differs from the French. All such modifications have been noted.]

former it acts of itself, provided that it be correctly performed and adapted to its end (whence the classification of sacrifices in Leviticus).

The covenant, then, requires a sacrificial act (indeed, in Hebrew "to make a covenant" is literally "to cut a covenant").

Three major covenants are presented in the Old Testament: the covenants with Noah, with Abram, and with Moses. Each of these begin with a *sacrifice* (of a different sort each time); then Yahweh speaks, makes *promises*, decrees his *commandment*(s) to mankind, to whom, finally, he leaves a *sign* of his covenant. I should note in passing that all the texts describing sacrifices are old ones, from the E or J sources, while those that associate signs with the covenant come from the P redaction. The same priestly lawgivers are also responsible for the revelation to Moses in the cloud, which takes place between the sacrifice and the concluding of the covenant, and transmits the prescriptions concerning worship in the Temple—this being, precisely, the daily site of effective sacrifice (Exod. 25: 2–31: 11).

The most remarkable of the sacrifices we are considering here is the one involving Abram (Gen. 15: 9–17). Following Yahweh's order, Abram chooses the victims and cuts each of them down the middle. Then, in deep sleep, he hears Yahweh's promises, and, awakening, sees a smoking furnace and a flaming torch pass between the halves of the victims. The covenant is sealed. I will leave to the specialists the interpretation of this rite, which already interested Frazer (1918, 1: 392 ff), noting only that A. and R. Neher (1974, p. 61) compare it to the division of the Roman *tessera* (*hospitalis*) that is, the Greek *symbolon*. We are, indeed, dealing with a symbol, a material witness left for the future—of individuals and of their descendants—in order to recall a past *word*, a mutual commitment; it is the permanent material pledge of the ever-present validity of this word and this place. But it cannot bring about or realize anything in itself; it is in this sense that I consider the covenant sacrifice to be symbolic rather than effective.

The three covenants follow rigorously one from the other, each one more restrictive than the last. The first (Gen. 8: 20–22, source J; and 9: 1–17, source P) is made with Noah, his sons, and all the living things that are with them; the promise is of an order in nature (I will return to this) and the sign is a natural one: the rainbow. The covenant with Abram (who then becomes Abraham, Gen. 15: 1–18, source E; 17: 1–23, source P) involves only his descendants, and the sign is cultural: circumcision. The covenant with Moses, finally (Exod. 19 through 24: 8, E and J; and 24: 9 to 31: 18, P), is addressed only to the children of Israel (i.e. of Jacob), and, still more specifically to the "Aaronic priesthood" (H. Cazelles 1973, p. 234). It is still, however, fundamentally important for mankind: through this covenant, and through it alone, humanity enters into the age of the Law—a text of the Council of Trent calls all sacrifices before that of Moses on Sinai, from Abel on, "sacrifices in the period of nature" (H. Denzinger 1957, par. 939).

The human (social) order is thus distinct from the natural order, since the latter was fixed at the time of Noah. There is, then, in this testamentary system no necessary and immediate link between the two orders; and even less, of course, any relationship of homology between the universe, society, and mankind. We will find no variations here on the themes of micro- and macrocosms, for this system does not even have an equivalent for the term "cosmos."

With Noah we find out what the universal order is, why it exists, and what its limits are. Yahweh, having smelled the "appeasing fragrance" of the sacrifice (Max Weber has made it quite clear why Yahweh could not be nourished by it [1952, p. 135]), said "in his heart"[3] (which means that man does not even have to be informed): "No more will I curse the earth because of man ... and no more will I strike down every living thing as I have done: all the days that the earth will last, seedtime and harvest, cold and heat, summer and winter, day and night shall not cease" (Gen. 8: 21-22): by establishing differences, Yahweh orders nature. In deciding that things will be this way—and for man's sake—Yahweh guarantees that creatures will not live in disorder, uncertainty, and chaos; it will be a differentiated and stable, and therefore livable, world. The rainbow reassures the believer, for "God's gracious will is made visible to give mankind, terrified by the chaotic elements, the renewed assurance that God will support this aeon, and to guarantee the duration of his ordinances," says Gerhard von Rad (1961, p. 130); I will continue to quote this passage, for in each of its well-chosen words it reveals what the order ot nature can mean to a Christian:

> How does one explain the stability of nature and its orders, the continued blessing of mankind in spite of increasing human violence and barbarism? Answer: Here a divine will of healing forbearance is at work; indeed, faith even knows of a solemn guarantee of the cosmic orders which were disturbed by the temporary invasion of chaos. ... The *natural* orders, fixed by God's word, mysteriously guarantee a world in which in his own time God's *historical* saving activity will begin (ibid.).

It is tempting to represent the Brahmanic (I) and testamentary (II) systems by means of a simple schema of three terms: cosmic order (or law), divinities, mankind:

I: order $>$ divinities $>$ mankind
II: divinity $>$ order $>$ mankind

In I, the three terms are fundamentally related by an *act*: the *sacrifice*. But the place occupied by the sacrifice will reverse the order of the terms: as the only bearer of a desire that only sacrifice can satisfy, man becomes the master of the universe (which he maintains through the repetition of the rite) and of the

---

3. This remark points up the fact that Source J says almost nothing about covenants (H. Cazelles 1973, p. 242) and that it was the priestly lawgivers (P) who solidly built the history of the covenants, from Noah to Moses: for them (Gen. 9:8-9), Elohim really *spoke* to Noah and his sons: "I establish my covenant...."

divinities (whom he feeds through the rite); the knowledge of this essential homology guarantees that *in conforming* man can be in line with the truth (*satyam*) and ensures his survival and that of the world. And to conform is above all to act, that is, to sacrifice (correctly).

In II, it is a *word* [*parole*] which constitutes the fundamental relationship among the terms. There is no order except through the divine word, which guarantees it only for the sake of man, who occupies the summit of the hierarchy of created beings. Man has no control over this order, nor over divinity. He exists, in the end, only in the negativity of obedience to a Law which is guaranteed for the future, but not for all eternity. His only choice is whether to submit to this Law, or to disobey, transgress, and sin. Even his (positive) desire for salvation seems to distance him behind his fear and shame for trespasses still to be forgiven. And, curiously, it is at this point that effective sacrifice—which is not supposed to have any place in this system—reappears and, in the end, holds its own.

One of the fundamental issues throughout the history of the religions of the Book seems to have been the constant confrontation between prophets and priests over the value and efficacy of ritual. It would make things simpler to believe that Yahweh is not fed by the sacrifice, that it simply appeases his anger, that it reaches not his stomach but his nose—and he can threaten: "I will reduce your cities to waste and I will destroy your sanctuaries, I will no longer smell your appeasing fragrance" (Lev. 26: 31). Nevertheless, long after the time of Amos and Hosea, Mohammed must still remind his followers that Allah said: "I ask no provision of men, neither do I ask that they should feed me; for God is the All-provider" (Koran 58: 57, cited by M. Gaudefroy-Demombynes 1957, p. 562);[4] and that "Their flesh shall not reach God, nor their blood, but your piety shall reach him" (Koran 22: 38, ibid., p. 561).

This contradiction remains active throughout the history of Judaism. For even at the period of the restored Temple, the priestly lawgivers maintain both the symbolic sacrifice of ancient times and sources, the accompaniment of the covenant, as well as a daily practice of effective sacrifice, codified in Leviticus.[5]

These priests sketch out a "theory" of sacrifice (although, as Adolphe Lods has pointed out, they never arrive at a coherent doctrine [1937, pp. 294, 296]) and add two new forms to the ancient sacrifices (which consisted of burnt and

4. The reference given by M. Gaudefroy-Demombynes is in error. It should in fact refer to Surat 51, 57–58. I was unable to make this correction before the publication of the French text and I am grateful to Djafar Moïnfar for the correct reference.
5. The contradiction goes even deeper than this. Here we find it within the priesthood and the priests' functions; but it reappears between the synagogue, which arose during the Exile, and the Temple. While the ritualism of the priests is incontestably victorious after the Restoration, still the Romans' destruction of the Temple in A.D. 70 did not mean the end of Judaism, for the synagogues survived, carrying on a form of worship without sacrifice, "something unique in the ancient world" (R. Bultmann 1956, p. 60; cf. C. Guignebert 1969, pp. 93–94), and without priests; this worship essentially consisted of oral repetition and commentary on a now written Law.

"peaceful" offerings, such as *minha*, vegetable offerings): the "sacrifice for sin" and the "expiatory sacrifice," which are extremely similar to each other. If the old forms are not explicitly endowed with effectiveness—for they continue to appease Yahweh with their fragrance (Lev. 1: 17, 2: 9, 3: 16)—this is not the case for the new ones.

For to carry out a sacrifice now means to erase sin, to be forgiven, following a mechanism identical to that of Brahmanism—with the provision that we are still dealing with a universe of sin rather than a universe of desire. The Brahmans said, "Let him who desires such and such do such and such a sacrifice (and he will get it)"; the Levites say, "Let him who has committed such and such a sin do such and such a sacrifice, and he will be forgiven." Chapters 4 and 5 of Leviticus are based entirely on this scheme.

The prophets of this period share this point of view. God had said to Hosea, "I desire piety and not sacrifice, the knowledge of God instead of burnt offerings" (6: 6). But Malachi warns, "Cursed be the rogue who has males in his flocks, but vows and sacrifices a blemished animal to Adonai" (1: 14). And, says Malachi, if God is to be appeased it is in these terms: "Bring the full tithes to the storehouse so that there may be food in My house, and then put me to this test, says Yahweh of the hosts, and see if I do not open the floodgates of heaven for you and pour out blessings in abundance, if I do not forbid the locust to destroy the fruit of your soil, nor allow the vine in your fields to be barren" (3: 10-11). Along with the priests of the Temple, Malachi is definitely the prophet of effective sacrifice: give what is asked, in the way it is asked for, and Yahweh will give in return. The lawgivers, however, do not even bother with this conditional link (which shows perhaps that Malachi, "in spite of everything," is still a prophet); for in Leviticus it is clear that the result of the sacrifice is immediate and necessary: Yahweh no longer has any say in the matter.

I would like to draw attention to one point here, concerning later Judaism. We have seen that it knew and practiced effective sacrifice. But, unlike Brahmanism, it does not relate this to the order of the universe, which, of course, remains Yahweh's creation. Nevertheless (is this a significant correlation?) ideas about creation begin to change from the time of the Exile, in what are called the Wisdom Books.

This can first be seen in texts from just after the Exile, dated by commentators to the fifth century B.C., in chapter 8, verses 22-31, of the Book of Proverbs, whose entire prologue (chap. 1 through 9) was redacted, according to E. Dhorme, "at a time when Hebraic literature was undergoing a renaissance parallel to that of the Jewish community under the Achaemenid Persians"; and, on the other hand, in the Book of Job (38: 4-11), a work of the same century and therefore contemporaneous with the height of the Restoration, around the time of Esdras and Nehemiah.

For Job, Yahweh "fixed the measures," "stretched the line" (architect's expressions which recur in Zachariah 1: 16), "laid the foundations" of the earth.

Proverbs says that Wisdom, characterized by a rare Hebrew word signifying "artist, craftsman" (8: 30), was there with Yahweh at the moment of creation.

These notions recur later in a very different context: in the Book of Wisdom (of Solomon), written in Greek in the Hellenistic milieu of Alexandria before the time of Philo, in the middle of the first century. Here Wisdom is the *tekhnitis* (7: 21; 8: 6; 14: 2) of the universe, like Yahweh himself (13: 1), who revealed to Solomon (the designated author) the *sustasis kosmou* ("constitution of the world"—E. Dhorme; "structure of the world"—Jerusalem Bible). A. Lefèvre and M. Delcort observe that this Greek technical vocabulary "translates ideas that had long been admitted in the religious thought of the Israelites" (in H. Cazelles 1973, p. 723).

I will finally note, following Max Weber, a shift in the meaning of the word *hoq* which in Leviticus and Numbers is given the sense of "immutable ordinances," and for Jeremiah and Job will designate "natural law" (1952, p. 442, n. 35).

What is important here is to see that immediately after the Exile, under Achaemenid influence, there appears the notion of a "craftsmanly" creation and, under Greek influence, the notion of a cosmos. *Tekhnitis* and *kosmos*, so foreign to Old Testament thought, are to be found shortly before the time of Philo in the Wisdom of Solomon. Rudolph Bultmann has very clearly stated how, in Philo, "the original idea of creation has been surrendered with the adoption of the Greek notion of the cosmos. . . . The Creator has become the Greek *tekhnitis* (master workman). His work in the world is open to objective scientific observation, and its structure is rationally intelligible" (1956, p. 96).

New ideas thus penetrate the Judaic universe from the time of the Restoration. The representation of the universe as a systematically organized whole, which may have its own law (its "natural law") arises in correlation with the affirmation of a ritualism and a formalism, the monopoly of a definitively constituted priestly class, the only class to master and perform a sacrifice that is effective in itself.

Two of the elements of the Brahmanic system are thus evident in post-Exilic Judaism. But what must be noted is that in this society, these representations remain unconnected: they contradict too profoundly the idea of *creation*—and, therefore, the idea of transcendence. In so far as a "natural law" appears, it certainly does not rule God in the way it may rule nature or mankind—and we have seen that the law of nature is totally distinct, even as to its time of formulation, from the law of mankind. Yahweh remains the origin and the guarantor of this law, which is to say that he cannot be subject to it, any more than he can be within the cosmos. Sacrifice acts upon the ultimate reality, which is not the universe but the divinity. But because divinity is transcendent, there can be no valid explanation of the action of sacrifice upon him. And so this system cannot go beyond the simple affirmation of the effectiveness of sacrifice itself: it cannot be rationalized, it cannot be made into a "theory."

The two representations thus remain disassociated: on one side we have the effectiveness of sacrifice; on the other, the Law, the cosmos. But the latter, which cannot be superior to God, become associated with a new figure, that of Wisdom (*hokmah*) who, it is clearly stated, was also created, but "before eternity, from the beginning" (Ecclus. 24: 9; cf. Proverbs 8: 23). In the end, Wisdom makes her appearance not to make nature autonomous and so encompassing, but, on the contrary, to underline (like all the other divine hypostases) the radicalization of divine transcendence, by becoming an intermediary between God and his creation (cf. Guignebert 1969, p. 111).

It is in this context that Christianity appears. It will be important for Christianity, more than for any current or period of Judaism, to make sacrifice symbolic rather than effective. Nevertheless, the contradiction will remain unsurmounted with regard to the Last Supper and the sacrifice on the Cross.

The most interesting text in this connection is the Epistle to the Hebrews.

It is generally (although not universally) agreed that this epistle was written by Apollos, of Italy, to Christians of Jewish, probably Palestinian origin, after 62-63, and certainly before the destruction of the Temple by the Romans in 70 A.D. Apollos, as far as we can tell from the Acts of the Apostles (18: 24-28) came from a Hellenized Jewish environment in Alexandria, but he was also "a scholar well-versed in the scriptures" who "vigorously refuted the Jews" (translation of J. Grosjean). A main subject in this epistle is faith, which he defines in chapter 11, verse 1; but before reaching this point, he attempts to demonstrate by comparison that the rite constituted by the death of Christ is infinitely superior to all the rites of the Jews, whether these be Moses' sacrifice of the first covenant (9: 18-22) or the regularly repeated rites which the Levites and the High Priest continue to perform in the Temple. His argument, developed in chapters 3 through 10, is based on a primary opposition between the old and new covenants, and three other oppositions, expressed with varying force, between human and divine, earth and heaven, flesh and spirit. A single certainty underlies the whole demonstration: blood purifies all.

In fact, according to the Law almost everything has to be purified with blood; and if there is no shedding of blood, there is no remission. Thus it is necessary both that the copies of heavenly things be purified in this way, and that heavenly things themselves also be, but by a higher sort of sacrifice than those of this world (9: 22-23, Jerusalem Bible translation, modified to follow the French).

It is, precisely, different rites and their effectiveness that are going to be compared. The comparison bears on three elements: the sacrificer, the sanctuary, and the victim. It also refers directly, though not explicitly, to the rules of worship revealed to Moses on Sinai (Exod. 25: 8-29: 42).

The first thing said is that Jesus is a high priest (3: 1). As such he is opposed to the High Priest of the Temple and to the whole group of Levites (more specifically, the descendants of Aaron), as well as to Moses. He is likened, on the other hand, to Melchizedek, who is taken as a herald of Christ's coming. Melchizedek, king of (Jeru-)salem, was a priest of "God Most High"; he blessed Abraham, who had given him "a tenth of all" (Gen. 14: 18-20). He is "priest for ever" (Ps. 110: 4), especially since he has no genealogy (the Old Testament does not "situate" him). Melchizedek, who was a figure quite outside the ranks of the hereditary priesthood, was nevertheless the first to bless Abraham and received a tenth of all his goods. Melchizedek can clearly be compared and opposed to the priests of the Temple, descendants of Levi (and, in the case of the High Priests, of Aaron), who are born of men and receive a tenth of the goods of the descendants of Abraham. Jesus, on the other hand, born from God, is priest for all eternity—and not through heredity, for he "belonged to a different tribe, the members of which have never done service at the altar; everyone knows he came from Judah, a tribe which Moses did not even mention when dealing with priests" (7: 13-14; cf. Matt. 1: 2-3 and Luke 3: 33-34). The fact of not having inherited the priesthood confers a priesthood which is eternal and superior.

In addition, the priests are human and therefore weak, and so must sacrifice not only for the sins of the people but also for their own (5: 3): at the same time that they are sacrificers, *they are also necessarily sacrifiers*. It is worth noting that here, too, man's role is to sin and sacrifice.

The human, sinful priests who descend from Aaron are feeble sacrificers compared to Jesus, being mere mortals: "There used to be a great number of those other priests, because death put an end to each one of them; but this one, because he remains forever, can never lose his priesthood" (7: 23-24).

In addition to this, there is a change in the nature of the sanctuary in which the two kinds of priests officiate. Jesus is "the minister of the sanctuary and of the true Tent of Meeting which the Lord, and not any man, set up" (8: 2). In this respect, too—and no longer only as the Son of the house is to the servant of the house (3: 5-6)—Jesus is superior even to Moses: for when Moses built the Tabernacle he was only following the plan revealed to him on the mountain (8: 5), while Jesus has passed through "the greater, the more perfect tent, which is better than the one made by men's hands because it is not of this created order" (9: 11). Unlike the priests, therefore, it is enough for him to have entered the Tabernacle once and for all time (9: 12). For the priests—and this is the second time that the text insists on the repetition of the sacrifice as proof of its inadequacy—must, as their condition requires, "constantly" reenter the first tent for worship, if they are ordinary priests, or, in the case of the High Priest, enter the second tent once a year for a blood sacrifice (9: 6-7).

The tent of Moses, the Temple of Jerusalem, thus represents an inadequate sanctuary, of inferior quality: "All the priests stand at their duties every day, offering over and over again the same sacrifices which are quite incapable of taking sins away. He, on the other hand, has offered one single sacrifice for sins" (10: 11-12).

In the end, of course, it is the quality of the victim that will make all the difference. For there is certainly some efficacy in spilling the blood of animals, and consequently "the blood of goats and bulls and the ashes of a heifer are sprinkled on those who have incurred defilement and they restore the holiness of their outward lives; how much more effectively the blood of Christ, who offered himself as the perfect sacrifice to God through the eternal Spirit, can purify our inner self from dead actions so that we do our service to the living God" (9: 13-14). For Jesus entered the sanctuary "taking with him not the blood of goats and bull calves, but his own blood" (9: 12).

One sacrifice is thus being compared to another. Or, rather, to many others, for there is a necessary repetition marking the limits of efficacy. The Jerusalem Bible translates this in the strongest sense: "The Law is quite incapable of bringing the worshippers to perfection, with the same sacrifices repeatedly offered year after year" (10: 1).

In the first Covenant, each component of the sacrifice was related to the others in the following way:

sacrifier / sacrificer-priest / victim / god

In the new covenant we have:

sacrifier / priest-victim-god

(We can even speak of an absolute identity of all the components, since Christ is, above all, both man and god.)

In this way, especially from the sacrifier's point of view, the whole sacrificial process is carried to a higher level of effectiveness. This is summarized in 9: 24-26:

> It is not as though Christ had entered a man-made sanctuary which was only modelled on the real one; but it was heaven itself. . . . And he does not have to offer himself again and again, like the high priest going into the sanctuary year after year with the blood that is not his own, or else he would have had to suffer over and over again since the world began. Instead of that, he has made his appearance once and for all, now at the end of the last age, to do away with sin by sacrificing himself.

And the Jerusalem Bible appreciates what is at stake here in terms of the rite and its effectiveness: "The sacrifice of Christ is unique: being offered 'at the end of time,' i.e., at the end of human history, there is no need for it to be repeated, since it wipes out sin, not with non-human ('alien') blood, but with Christ's own blood, cf. 9: 12-14, so its effect is unconditional" (9: 26, n.k [modified to follow the French version]. And, in the note to 7: 27, it speaks even more strongly of "the absolute and definitive efficacy of the sacrifice of Christ" [French version].

We see, then, that Christ's sacrifice is to be read and understood in direct comparison with the sacrifice in the Temple and, consequently, that what is being compared here is the respective efficacy of two rites. It must have been evident to converted Palestinian Jews that what was involved here was no image or metaphor but something quite real.

Let us turn now to the act that constitutes the Last Supper.

It has been noted for many years that there are variations in the different accounts. Luke (22: 19-20) and Paul (1 Cor. 11: 23-25) speak of a "new covenant" signified by the Last Supper, which Christ asks his disciples to perform "in memory of him." Matthew (26: 26-28) and Mark (14: 22-24) speak only of a covenant, and do not mention the institution of a rite. John does not report the Last Supper, but goes on at length about an event that took place the year before, a little before Passover, when Jesus multiplied the loaves and fishes (chap. 6). Here again we find a comparison to Moses, the point being that the manna, the heavenly bread (Exod. 16: 4), was not truly such: it is Jesus who is "the living bread that has come down from heaven" (John 6: 51). The Jews protest: "How can he give us his flesh to eat?" (6: 52). Jesus makes this clear: "Anyone who does eat my flesh and drink my blood has eternal life and I shall raise him up on the last day, for my flesh is real food and my blood is real drink" (6: 54-55).

So opinions differ from the beginning: if the Last Supper heralds an act to come—the sacrifice of Christ—then we may read it both as the founding of a commemorative, symbolic rite and as an effective act—like the sacrifice it announces—in which blood, really consumed (or shed) has full powers of redemption. And if opinions differ, it is because the Last Supper refers to two distinct events that, as we have seen, are kept quite separate in the Epistle to the Hebrews.

The model for the Last Supper is the covenant sacrifice performed by Moses on Sinai, in which the victim's blood seals the covenant (Exod. 24: 8), and in which we therefore find the following relations:

sacrifier-priest / victim / god

But what the Last Supper announces is the real sacrifice of Christ; and from this point of view the relations are:

sacrifier / priest-victim-god

If my reading of the Epistle to the Hebrews is correct, this sacrifice is effective in the same way as the sacrifice in the Temple, but to an even greater degree; it continues, therefore, to be based on the reality of the effectiveness of the victim's blood, something we are reminded of in John's report of the words of Jesus, above.

So the Last Supper is both a symbolic act which seals a covenant (like the earlier sacrifices, especially the Mosaic) and, at the same time, an anticipation (and so still symbolic) of a sacrificial act endowed with its own efficacy, which by itself ensures the remission of sins and definitive salvation. And so, like the act it anticipates, the Last Supper too is an effective act. It thus involves two quite different kinds of sacrifice. The Christian tradition, however, will keep trying to confuse them, that is, to reduce the effective to the symbolic. Thus the Jerusalem Bible, in complete contradiction with its unavoidable interpretation of the Epistle to the Hebrews, gives the following note to Matthew 26: 28:

> As at Sinai, the blood of victims sealed the covenant of Yahweh with his people, so on the cross the blood of Jesus the perfect victim, is about to seal the "new" covenant, cf. Luke 22: 20, between God and man—the covenant foretold by the prophets.

We should note that unless the expression "perfect victim" is to be understood by its usage in the Epistle to the Hebrews, then it cannot be understood at all.

For Catholicism, the sacrifice becomes the mere "seal" of the covenant; it is no longer considered to have its own efficacy and, in the end, we must no longer take literally either the words of Jesus as reported by John (who did not hear them himself), or the commentaries of Apollos (who was not a witness). These are only parables (although we know how dangerous it is to take parables at their word) or, if worse comes to worst, metaphors, such as our culture delights in. The letter can capture interest and edify only when it hides or is hidden; only the poor in spirit would think of taking it literally.

But it turns out not to be so easy to eradicate belief in the effectiveness of the rite. Beaten down, it keeps reappearing. Perhaps (only perhaps) it was only with Calvinism, as Max Weber thought, that this process reached its end-point; perhaps this "great historical process in the development of religion, the elimination of magic from the world (*die Entzauberung der Welt*, the disenchantment of the world) which had begun with the old Hebrew prophets and which, in conjunction with Hellenistic scientific thought, had repudiated all magical means to salvation as superstition and sin, came here (i.e. in Calvinism) to its logical conclusion" (1958, p. 105). The whole problem is here: for our culture, the effective rite can only be magical.

Despite all this, in the very midst of "religious" ritual the Catholic church continues, in the face of and against everyone else—against itself, these days—to preserve rites that are defined above all by their specific efficacy: the sacraments (including, of course, the Eucharist).

We will simply recall what the Council of Trent had to say about this.

The sacraments are necessary for salvation, for which faith alone does not suffice (Denzinger 1957, par. 847), and they do not exist simply to "nourish" the latter (par. 848); they contain and confer the grace which they signify (par. 849; here we are very close to the definition of the sacrament given by Peter Lombard, bishop of Paris, in the eleventh century: "signum est gratiae Dei et invisibilis gratiae forma ut ipsius imaginem gerat et causa existat"). If anyone says the opposite, let him be anathema, such as him who says that: "per ipsa novae Legis sacramenta ex opere operato non conferri gratiam" (par. 851: "that by the said sacraments of the New Law, grace is not conferred from the work which has been worked").

The sacrifice is thus effective in itself and by itself; which is to say that it is formally effective, regardless of the faith of the sacrifier or the officiant (who, in performing the rite, is asked only to have the intention to do what the church does: par. 854). Still more false, declared Pius X in 1907, is the modern doctrine that "sacramenta nuda sunt symbola seu signa, quamvis non vi carentia" (par. 2089: "... although not lacking efficacy").

Let us turn, finally, to the Mass—a sacrifice in which a sacrament is administered.

The Mass refers above all to the sacrifice of Christ, a sacrifice which it cannot, for the reasons we have just seen, merely commemorate or symbolize. Nor can it be a sacrifice in addition to that of Christ, for the latter was effective in a definitive and absolute sense. The Mass therefore derives its efficacy from the fact that it reactualizes Christ's sacrifice, in the strongest sense of the term. In doing so, it abolishes time.

I will conclude, then, by looking at the nature of religious time. The linear time of monotheistic religion, so often taken as history, is a false lead. It is true that here "time begins with the creation, and ends with the creation, which is unique" (H. Rousseau 1968, p. 86); that this time, in principle, is not rhythmic but points in one direction, which is to say that it is oriented. It is the time for the carrying out of the divine project. But for man this time has stopped. "Becoming," as François Châtelet has said, is nothing more than "the accomplishment of what was foreseen" (1962, p. 19); it is a "negation of history." "In the end," says Châtelet, "the—a priori—reference to transcendence, which is ahistoric by definition, always, in one way or another, annuls historicity" (ibid., p. 20). The loop is closed, in spite of everything, in the calendrical ritual of the church, patterned and cyclic and always, at its apogee, referring back to this founding and final act in which time is suspended. And the believer, like every sacrifier, waits, held in the long anticipation between the moment of the real performance of the sacrifice and the moment—whose coming, he is told, depends on his belief in the efficacy of the rite—of the obtaining of fruits, of the satisfaction of desire.

Brahmanism is based entirely on effective sacrifice. Judaism maintains two parallel representations of sacrifice, one effective and one symbolic. What for it was only a small contradiction becomes confusion and ambiguity for Christianity: effective sacrifice cannot be denied (it is the foundation of the religion), but the church will continually attempt to reduce it to the symbolic. In doing so, it will be aware that it is losing something essential: precisely what defines it as a *religion*. Faced with the Reformation, Catholicism will maintain its positions in the teeth of all opposition (the Council of Trent). So it will remain a religion, but one that appears more and more as a form of magic to a Reformation which is itself turning into a morality. For when a religion ceases to believe in the efficacy of its rites, it can turn into anything at all; at the worst, we have Joseph de Maistre's view of Protestantism: "It does not submit to anything, it does not believe in anything; and if it pretends to believe in a book, it is a book that does not bother anybody" (1957, p. 122); and this heresy, as much a civil as a religious one, "unleashes general arrogance against authority, and puts discussion in the place of obedience" (ibid., p. 120).

But Judaism, too, is hardly monolithic. Its history shows, in contradiction to the narrow-minded evolutionism still rife in the anthropology of religion, that effective sacrifice appears only at a late period. The long history of Judaism begins with a confederation of tribes with no place for a priestly class, the essential religious functions being divination, oracles, and dreams. It is only with sedentarization, agriculture, urbanization, and the appearance of royalty that we find a priestly class laying exclusive claim to a religious function which came essentially to consist in the performance of sacrifice. Even this was imposed only gradually (but it was in force before the reforms of Josiah in 622 B.C.). In the meantime the prophets arose, and struggled on two fronts: they eliminated all the old specialists in *signa* (to use a Dumézilian term), who used techniques of interpretation, and themselves relied only on Yahweh's word, which they received clearly and transmitted as such to the people; and, secondly, they rose up against the increasing belief in the efficacy of the rites, a belief that was being affirmed by the priests. It took the Exile to silence the great prophets and grant victory to the priests. But around the synagogues, first with the scribes and then the rabbis, there survived a Judaism freed of effective sacrifice but still cast in a ritual form.

As to the history of Hinduism, we know that Brahmanism has had its day, and religion is no longer organized around the sacrifice. Since the fifth century B.C., in any case, sectarian and devotional movements have proposed new paths to salvation and have protested against the Brahman's monopoly of the effective rite. The divinities are affirmed—salvation must come through them and their power—but now salvation is the unveiling of the devotee's oneness with his chosen divinity.

The three examples offered here thus demonstrate that there is no necessary historical evolution of belief from an effective sacrifice to a symbolic one. If the history of Judaism suggests correlations between religious forms and other instances (economic, political...) of the kind vigorously investigated by Max Weber, no such conclusion can be drawn for Hinduism, or even for Christianity. In the end, the crucial point appears to be precisely the relation that societies establish between order and the divine in relation to man, who is both inferior and privileged, and the power they grant him over the one and the other. Again, it seems evident that relations between certain instances could be pointed out: people cannot think whatever they want, at any time. But it still seems premature to make any claims beyond this.

I hope at least to have shown that "sacrifice" covers a number of very different realities, and that these should not be confused. Through them we can grasp the basic attitudes that societies take in relation to the world, as well as their different modes of intellectual appropriation of nature: the discourses in which and through which the ordering of the thinkable takes place, and without which no praxis is possible. And one might, for example, begin to question, and so put an end to, this universality of the Law of the Father, which is nothing but God's Law, which is itself, precisely, nothing but one historical form of representation of the Law or of Order, but one understood by us, always, as commandments.

References

Bergaigne, Abel. *La Religion védique d'après les hymnes dú Rig-Véda*. 3 vols. Paris: PUF, 1963. (First edition, 1877-83.)

Biardeau, Madeleine, and Malamoud, Charles. *Le Sacrifice dans l'Inde ancienne*. Bibliothèque de l'Ecole des Hautes Etudes, Sciences religieuses, vol. 79 (Paris: PUF, 1976).

Bultmann, Rudolph. *Primitive Christianity in Its Contemporary Setting*. New York: Meridian, 1956. (First German edition, 1949.)

Cazelles, H. *Introduction à la Bible*. vol. 2, *Introduction critique à l'Ancien Testament*. Paris: Desclée, 1973.

Châtelet, François. *La Naissance de l'histoire*. Paris: Minuit, 1962.

Denzinger, Heinrich. *The Sources of Catholic Dogma*. St. Louis: Herder, 1957. (Translation of the *Enchiridion Symbolorum*, Editio 30, 1955.)

Frazer, J. G. *Folklore in the Old Testament*. London: Macmillan, 1918.

Gaudefroy-Demombynes, Maurice. *Mahomet*. L'évolution de l'humanité, no. 36. Paris: Albin Michel, 1957.

Guignebert, Charles. *Le Monde juif vers le temps de Jésus*. L'évolution de l' humanité, no. 18. Paris: Albin Michel, 1969. (First edition, 1935.)

Herrenschmidt, Olivier. "A qui profite le crime? Cherchez le sacrificant." *L' Homme* 18 (1978): 7-18.

Lévi, Sylvain. *La Doctrine du sacrifice dans les brahmanas*. Bibliothèque de .' Ecole des Hautes Etudes, Sciences religieuses, vol. 73. Paris: PUF, 1966. (First edition, 1898.)

Lods, Adolphe. *The Prophets and the Rise of Judaism*. New York: Dutton, 1937. (First French edition, 1935.)

Maistre, Joseph de. *Du Pape, et extraits d'autres oeuvres*. Libertés, no. 12. Paris: Pauvert, 1957.

Masson-Oursel, Pierre. *La Philosophie en Orient*. Supplementary volume to E. Brehier, *Histoire de la philosophie*. Paris: PUF, 1948.

Neher, A. and R. *Histoire biblique du peuple d'Israël*. Paris: Adrien-Maisonneuve, 1974.

Von Rad, Gerhard. *Genesis, a Commentary*. London: SCM Press, 1961. (First German edition, 1949.)

Rousseau, Hervé. *Les Religions*. Que Sais-je? no. 9. Paris: PUF, 1968.

Weber, Max. *The Protestant Ethic and the Spirit of Capitalism.* New York: Scribner's, 1958. (First German edition, 1904-05.)

___. *Ancient Judaism.* New York: Free Press, 1952. (First German edition, 1917-19.)

Translations of the Bible

La Sainte Bible, traduite en français sous la direction de l'Ecole biblique de Jérusalem. Paris: Editions du Cerf, 1961.

The Jerusalem Bible. New York: Doubleday, 1966.

La Bible. Bibliothèque de la Pléiade. Paris: NRF.

    L'Ancien Testament, vol. 1, 1956; vol. 2, 1959. Edited by Edouard Dhorme.

    Le Nouveau Testament, 1971. Edited by Jean Grosjean and Michel Léturmy.

Marcel Detienne

4 Rethinking Mythology

Who thinks of protesting when, at the beginning of his enterprise, Lévi-Strauss recalls that a myth is perceived as a myth by any reader throughout the world? Yet at the same time Dumézil confesses that he has spent his whole life trying to understand the difference between the myth and the folktale, to no avail. Nothing is easier than recognizing a myth intuitively, and yet no theoretical definition has been able to carry the field from the time that mythology was first conceived of as a science, as scientific knowledge about myths.

In our linguistic usage, mythology is a semantic locus where two discourses intersect, the second of which, belonging to the realm of interpretation, speaks of the first. A double semantic register informs the figure of mythology. On the one hand mythology is a set of discursive statements and narrative practices: the tales and stories that, in the eighteenth and nineteenth centuries, everyone was supposed to know. On the other hand mythology designates a discourse about myths, a knowledge that claims to speak of myths in general, their nature or their essence. How is it that mythology-as-story has come to be inhabited or possessed by a desire to know? How has it come to be invested with a will to know the reason for its own discourse? Fifteen years after the high tide of structural analysis, it still seems necessary to interrogate the ambiguous status of what we have come to call "mythology." Through what practices has this double knowledge come to define its own territory? Through what partitions did it take shape? How has it been instituted, yesterday and in the more distant past? And who is it that speaks for mythology-as-knowledge? Who enunciates it? To whom is it addressed?

In a genealogical history that goes from the Greeks to Lévi-Strauss (and from Lévi-Strauss back to the Greeks, with whom his dialogue has never ceased), the configuration of mythology has involved two essential steps: in the nineteenth century, with the establishment of a new knowledge which explicitly claimed to be the science of mythology; and, at the other end, in the perspective that gave the new science its name, professing the model of its own development, when, between Xenophanes and Thucydides, a first figure of mythology was drawn, whose soul was a novel notion of *mythos*. Two reasons, at least, justify this order of presentation: the analysis of myths, today as in the past, is deployed entirely in the space laid out by the mythological science that sprang into existence around 1850; while, on the other hand, privileged and fundamental relations tie this nineteenth century science to a certain idea of Greece.

Between 1850 and 1890, academic Europe became filled with chairs of comparative mythology, history of religions, and mythological science. From Oxford to Berlin and from London to Paris, the new discipline states its project in terms that are rigorously identical, from Max Müller to Paul Decharme and from E. B. Tylor to Adelbert Kühn and Andrew Lang. In his Oxford lectures, Max Müller summarizes the motives which now necessitate a scientific discourse on myths: it is a matter of explaining the stupid, savage, and absurd element in mythology. It is suddenly realized that mythology—and the only familiar mythology comes from Greece—is full of indecent incidents, contains absurd propositions, and speaks an insane language. It is generally accepted at this period that the poets of Greece had an instinctive aversion to all that was excessive or monstrous; yet these same Greeks, writes Max Müller, "relate of their gods what would make the most savage of the Red Indians creep and shudder. Among the most backward tribes of Africa and America it is difficult to find anything more hideous or revolting."[1] What is it that horrifies Max Müller's Red Indian? It is the infamous adventures of the adulterous, murderous, cruel, and cannibalistic gods: Ouranos castrated by his son, Kronos devouring his newborn children, Dionysus carved up and skewered. A whole vocabulary is used to convey the scandal; it starts with "shocking" and "embarrassing," goes on to "extravagant" and "ridiculous," then plunges from "absurd" to "infamous," "savage," "hideous," "revolting." The new mythology is established in a state of scandal.

Why is it that the fables of antiquity, the "ancient fictions" of the eighteenth century, suddenly cease to be disseminated by the decorative figures of cultivated society, in salons and drawing rooms, and from being a condition of intelligibility for the whole cultured world[2] the long-familiar mythology of the

---

1. F. Max Müller, *Lectures on the Science of Language*, 2d ser. (London 1864), p. 385. [TN: The French translation of Müller's lectures includes a phrase not in the original English text. I have used the English text here and have added the phrase in question. Cf. Max Müller, *Nouvelles leçons sur la science du langage* (Paris 1868), 2: 113–15.]
2. J. Starobinski, "Le mythe au XVIIIe siècle," *Critique* (1977): 977.

Greco-Roman world should come to be perceived as an insane and absurd language in which the society of Homer and Plato—supposed to have reached the very apogee of civilization—seems to be speaking a discourse that is more savage than that of the peoples of nature? Several reasons probably converged to produce this result. But two seem to have been decisive. There is first of all the invention of a new linguistic horizon with the discovery of the Vedas, the Gathas, and comparative grammar; a science of language is constituted around word inflections and an autonomous system of sonorities. At the same time the idea develops that language arises out of the people and the nation, and that mythology can only be its lost or forgotten voice. The second reason is that the Greek and the Iroquois no longer meet, as in the days of Fontenelle and Lafitau, under the sign of the fable and of shared ignorance. After romanticism and the philosophy of Hegel, which saw in the Greek world the natal soil of "cultivated European man," Greek man no longer has any right to foolishness or mistakes. The scandal erupts when it is first suspected that the Greek, bearer and witness of reason, speaks in his mythology in a way typical of "a mind struck temporarily insane." The new mythology presents itself as a campaign for public safety.

To account for the existence of these irrational and scandalous elements, two competing strategies run through the productions of the science of myths between 1850 and 1890. The school of comparative mythology, grouped around Max Müller, and contemporary with the progress of comparative grammar, was based on the science of language, and believed that the explanation had to be found in the system of language and its history. The anthropological school, on the other hand, with Tylor and Lang, undertook the project of a comparative history of the human mind, through its different stages of thought. It is sufficient to recall that the first orientation, a linguistic and comparative one, reconstructed a stratigraphy of human speech in which man, at the dawn of his history, had the faculty of producing words which directly expressed part of the substance of the objects perceived by the senses. Confronting the world, the human being emits sounds which materialize as roots and engender phonetic types from which the body of language is constituted. But this language of origins is charged with a disturbing power, a kind of excess of meaning. As soon as the force of the first great words escapes the speakers' control, mankind becomes the dupe of the words he pronounces, prey to the illusions of a language within which proliferates the strange and disconcerting discourse of myths. For Max Müller, mythology is the unconscious product of a language of which man is never the producer, only the victim. Myth is a clinical matter, whereas language has a formal science: mythology is a disease whose extent and ravages can be precisely measured by comparative grammar. All that is left to the artisans of comparative mythology is to discover, behind the screen of "mythological" names and personifications, the forms of the spectacle of nature that so affected the first human beings: some sided with the sun; others declared for darkness and the storm.

But the medicine the linguistic technicians administered was too brutal. While it dissipated the fog of words and the mists of phrases, the whole of mythology evaporated and disappeared along with them. And the rival enterprise of Tylor and Lang was free to object that Max Müller's theory was unable to justify the stupid, absurd, and savage details whose presence, it was generally agreed, laid bare the scandal and cried out for an indictment.

The anthropological school mobilized comparison in its turn, but this time on the level of civilizations, from the primitive to the most evolved, and without granting language any privilege other than of being an original product of mankind. Speech arose in a human community still in the state of savagery; and all languages, in their beginnings, are ruled by the same "intellectual art," as Tylor says, the same "nursery philosophy."[3] Mythology is everywhere, it saturates grammar, spreads into syntax, invades language through metaphor. In its organic structure and its first developmental steps, myth belongs to the primordial stage of the human mind, but its growth is limited to the childhood of mankind—a childhood, our childhood, which still lies before our eyes. Myth is no longer to be found in diachrony, in the archaeology of language, but everywhere that savage peoples are to be found: Iroquois, Bushmen, Australians, who still today tell the same savage stories, which no one would dream of explaining as the peculiar result of a few badly understood phrases. The human mind mythologizes under certain conditions: the proof of this is given by the savage hordes who even today speak the language of myth. The absurd contents of the Greek fables, the shocking and embarrassing stories of Homer's contemporaries—if they are put side by side with the mythology of peoples of nature—can be explained with certainty: they are survivals of a coarse and primitive state, survivals that have sometimes been taken for history, sometimes rejected as absurd lies.

But we must go farther than this, beyond the description of these competing strategies, and investigate the developments that shaped what both strategies call "the object of scientific mythology": insane propositions, savage sentences, absurd discourses. All through the exposition of the motives behind the new science there is an admission of its attraction to the very thing that repels it. For what makes it shudder with horror is the sole object of its activity, to the extent that the interpretation developed by this discourse on the shape of a new and necessary science seems to give itself the primary task of discussing and displaying a scandal whose effects very clearly delimit the field of the new mythology-as-knowledge.

The whole discourse proceeds by repeated and successive movements of partition. For authorities over the science of myths, religion imposes a first, fundamental partition. In the general system of Christianity, which includes all of the founders of the history of religions—Catholics, Protestants or agnostics—knowing God (or knowing about God) constitutes both the proof and the guarantee of the rationality of the human race. Because of this the gods of the Greeks and the

---

3. E. B. Tylor, *Primitive Culture*, 2d ed. (London 1873), 1: 237.

Aryans can only be seen as an immediate product of human intelligence. As Paul Decharme wrote in his *Mythologie de la Grèce antique*, in 1884, "when the Greeks are not speaking in their mythological tongue, their conception of divinity does not differ in essentials from our own."[4] In other words, mythology is what is left of the religious tradition of the Greeks after scholars in the second half of the nineteenth century, all sharing the same implicit knowledge, have removed from the tradition all elements that are compatible with their own dominant representation of the divine. Everything held to be immoral or indecent thus immediately falls into the domain of mythology. Other, less summary, partitions are superimposed on this first one. Lang, for instance, distinguishes two different groups among the myths of civilized people, among whom the Greeks are included by divine right: rational myths, in which the gods are presented as beautiful and wise beings; the others, labeled irrational, that are marked by savagery and senselessness. There is no need to explain the first group, since they are part of Religion. A true mytho-logic begins with the others.[5] Thus, exclusionary procedures multiply in the discourse of the science of myths, borne on a vocabulary of scandal that indicts all figures of otherness. Mythology is on the side of the primitive, the inferior races, the peoples of nature, the language of origins, childhood, savagery, madness—always the *other*, as the excluded figure. At the same time, with each of these partitions mythology shifts, changes form and content: it becomes the incredible which religion lays before itself; the irrational that reason grants itself; the savage as the inverse of the civilized; it is what is absent, what is over and done with; it is ancient madness.

To go any further requires a vote of confidence: for might not mythology be a figure entirely created, in its double register, out of a sense of scandal? This is a question that the science of mythology itself invites us to ask. For when comparativists and anthropologists explain their projects between 1850 and 1890, they refer constantly to a privileged model: that of the Greeks of the sixth century before our era, delicate and refined people whose religious feelings, already shocked and embarrassed by mythical tales, lie at the source of the first intrepretations. Along with Max Müller, Lang evokes the pious and thoughtful men who for so many years "tried to account to themselves for their possession of beliefs closely connected with religion which yet seemed ruinous to religion and morality."[6] In pointing to a philosopher like Xenophanes of Colophon as their precursor, the initiators of the science of myths send us back to the Greek world which also, in fact, gives us the word *myth*, the thing that was already

4. P. Decharme, *Mythologie de la Grèce antique*, 2d. ed. (Paris 1884), p. viii.

5. A. Lang, "Mythology," *Encyclopedia Britannica*, 9th ed. [TN: The author uses the word *mythologique*, a pun on "mythological" and "mytho-logic" coined by Lévi-Strauss for his four-volume study of Amerindian myths, better known in this country under the titles of each volume: *The Raw and the Cooked*, etc. The title for the whole multivolume work, *Mythologiques*, has been changed in English translation to *Introduction to a Science of Mythology*; an interesting switch, considering the argument of this essay. I have rendered *mythologique*, used as a substantive, as "mytho-logic."]

6. *Myth, Ritual and Religion* (London 1887), 1: 10.

called *mythology*, and even the sense of scandal that seems so closely tied to the apprehension of a first mytho-logic. To investigate the beginnings of inter-pretation, at least in ancient Greece, we must first distinguish interpretation from exegesis.[7] The latter, we can say, is the incessant commentary that a culture makes on its symbolism, its gestures, its practices, on all that constitutes it as a system in action. Exegesis proliferates from inside; it is a speech that nourishes the tradition of which it is a part, whereas interpretation emerges the moment there is an outside perspective, when some in a society begin to question, to criticize the tradition, to distance themselves with regard to the histories of the tribe. There are two ways to begin looking as an other at what has been received and accepted by all. One of these, a minimal one, begins with the prose writings of those whom the fifth century will call *logographs*, and who have already for a century been disposing traditional tales and histories, from genealogies to the great historical sagas, in the new space of the written sign. But at the same time as this discreet and silent distancing, produced by the operation of writing alone was going on, another approach was being manifested in maximal form with the new forms of knowledge connected with the appearance of writing: the first philosophy, with Xenophanes of Colophon, or the historical thinking conceptualized by Thucydides; knowledges [*savoirs*] that radically questioned a tradition which they denounced as unacceptable or no longer credible, as immediately or even ultimately meaningless.

It is in this work of interpretation that a novel notion of *mythos* is con-structed, and that the figure of *mythology*, in the Greek sense of *mythologia*, is sketched out with its distinctive features. A series of landmarks in a historical field extending from the sixth century to the beginning of the fourth allows us to follow the way in which the territory assigned to *mythos* came to be organ-ized. Around 530, Xenophanes, in the name of the first philosophy, brutally condemns all of the stories about the Titans, Giants, Centaurs, including "Homer and Hesiod." These are so many scandalous adventures which attribute to the gods or superhuman figures all that is injurious and hateful in the world of men: thievery, adultery, treachery. Rejecting all stories of this genre, Xenophanes expels them by assigning them a dual status: (1) these are forgeries, *plasmata*, pure fictions; (2) these are barbarous stories, the stories of *others*.[8] But the word *mythos*—which from the time of the epics is part of the vocabulary of language and the word—has not yet been mobilized to designate the discourse of others, at which philosophy, barely born but already scandalized, points the finger and so noisily cries out. It is, however, around the same period that the new sense of *mythos* appears, as witnessed in a poem of Anacreon of Samos: between 524 and 522, the party of Samian rebels, fighting the tyranny of Polycrates, is known by the name of *mythietai*: these are, as the ancient gram-

---

7. Cf. Dan Sperber, *Rethinking Symbolism* (Cambridge 1974).
8. Fr. I, 19–24: Diels Fr. 14 to 16; cf. the analyses of J. Svenbro, "La parole et le marbre. Aux origines de la poétique grecque" (Thesis, Lund 1976), pp. 75–108.

marians explain, rebels, troublemakers; more precisely, probably, people who hold seditious opinions.[9] An adverse figure for the eunomy claimed by Polycrates, *myth* connotes revolution, *stasis*. And this semantic development, which we know about from Anacreon's blow-by-blow account, becomes increasingly specific in the course of the fifth century, in the vocabulary of Pindar and Herodotus, for whom the word *myth*, employed rather discreetly, ends up designating only the discourse of others, in that it is illusory, unbelievable, and stupid. In works like Herodotus's *Histories* and the poems of Pindar, which seem to devote such a large part to what we are tempted to call "myths," the occurrences of *mythos* could be counted on the fingers of one hand: two occurrences in the nine books of Herodotus, three in the Pindaric corpus.[10] When Pindar sings the eulogy of a victor at the Games he is pronouncing a *logos*; myth appears with the rise of the speech of illusion, *parphasis*. *Mythos* is born along with rumor. It grows up along with deceitful stories, misleading words, which seduce and do violence to the Truth. Made like one of Daedalus's statues, *mythos* can be recognized by its apparel of glistening lies: an appearance that perverts what is trustworthy and shamefully betrays the manifestation of being. But these are always the tales of others, those who usurped for Ulysses the glory earned by Ajax, who keep on repeating the scandalous version of Tantalus's feast, in which the gods are supposed to have greedily devoured the flayed flesh of Pelops.

Herodotus makes the same partition; his own stories are never anything but *logoi*. And when he invokes particularly holy traditions, Herodotus speaks only of sacred *logoi, hiroi*. The famous "sacred discourses" which our usage interprets as "myths" all the more easily since these traditions are often connected with ritual gestures and actions—these are never called *mythoi*. On the contrary, it is a myth for Herodotus when certain people want to explain the flooding of the Nile by alleging the existence of an enormous River Ocean flowing around the earth, for this is a pure fiction which excludes all forms of argumentation and leaves no room for empirical observations. It is also *myth* when the Greeks claim that Busiris, king of the Egyptians, wanted to sacrifice Hercules: foolishness and absurdity, for how could the most pious of men, the Egyptians, even conceive of such a grave impiety? It is unbelievable, and what is more, unlikely.

To speak of *myth* is a way of crying scandal, of pointing the finger. *Mythos* is a very convenient word-gesture which suffices to denounce silliness, fiction, or absurdity, and, in so doing, to confute them. But *myth* is still only a signpost to a distant, barely indicated site. In order for it to designate a more or less autonomous discourse or form of knowledge we must wait until the very end of the fifth century, when both the tales of the ancient poets and all that the logographs had written in the meantime fall into the domain of *mythos*. One of the places where this break takes place is in the historical activity of

9. Anacreon, Gentili (1958) Fr. 21. Cf. S. Mazzarino, *Il pensiero storico classico* (Bari 1966), I: 155 ff.
10. Herodotus II, 23; II, 45. Pindar, *Nemeans* 8, 32 ff.; *Olympics*, I, 27–59.

Thucydides: when he defines the domain of historical knowledge he outlines its conceptual territory by excluding the fabulous, the *mythodes*, which in turn, in addition to its own boundaries, receives a domain which takes in a different manner of recounting and remembering.

The logographs recounted the histories of the tribe in writing; Herodotus sought to give the city a new way of remembering; Thucydides now intends to construct a model of political action, a futurologist's knowledge in which the historian thinks of himself as the ideal political leader. His purpose is not to tell what happened but to attain the truth of an effective discourse, a discourse built of such well-fitted reasoning that it constitutes the best means of acting in the space of the city, today and in the future. Still, a history up to the present, like the *Peloponnesian Wars*, must confront the problems of memory and oral tradition, and this is done in what has come to be called the *Archaeology*, in a critique of stories that are passed down from mouth to mouth.[11] The memory is fallible, it interprets, chooses, reconstructs; and the more troubled the times the more fragile it is, the more the marvelous proliferates and anything at all can be believed. In Thucydides' eyes all that circulates orally, *akoai*, is fundamentally false because of the lack of critical spirit in the people who tell or recall events of long ago or yesterday, even in their own country, the place where they should be able to get information to verify and correct the story. The traditional memory is found guilty of gullibility, of accepting ready-made ideas, of passing on unchecked information which swells the tide of the *fabulous*. Poets and logographs are put in the dock by a suit brought against the mouth and the ear, because the rumors, the received ideas that are already part of the incredible do not become any more credible when poets make them into tales and lend these events beauties which enlarge them, or when, parallel to this, logographs seek to combine prefabricated ideas more for the ear's pleasure than for the establishment of the truth.

With Thucydides the breach is opened: on one side, a spoken tradition that still includes public recitations and proclamations up to the end of the fifth century; on the other, writing, sure of itself, rejecting pleasure and the marvelous, and wanting to address itself only to a silent and separate reader. The author of the *Peloponnesian Wars* is convinced that everything woven between the mouth and the ear drifts ineluctably towards the fabulous, towards what blocks the effectiveness of a discourse whose abstract writing should reinforce its action in the political order. He intends, therefore, to proceed by means of a confinement of the oral tradition of ancient times, in prose as well as verse, bringing together in a single enclosure both what philosophy had been calling the forgeries and fictions of the ancients and the whole tradition that had been put into writing from Hecataeus to Hellanicos and Hippias of Elis.

Parallel to Thucydides and at the same period, the totalizing knowledge of Platonic philosophy was proceeding, with still greater rigor, to the confinement

11. Thucydides, *Peloponnesian Wars*, I, 20–22.

of what Plato and his contemporaries bring together under the names of *mythology* and *archaeology*.[12] The radical critique with which the *Republic*, through its attack on the poets and fabricators of *logoi*, challenges the entire tradition, takes particular aim at the mimetic nature of mythology, or forms of expression with formulaic, rhythmic, musical aspects; these are aspects which answer the needs of memorization and aural communication, but which are, for the philosopher, the irrefutable sign of their belonging to the polymorphous and motley world of all that panders to the lower part of the soul, that solitary realm where passions and desires run wild. Not only is the discourse of mythology scandalous—and the *Republic* draws up the catalogue of obscene, savage, and absurd stories—it is also dangerous, because of the illusionary effects of mouth-to-ear communication whenever it is not surveyed or controlled. However—and this is a major point of difference with Thucydides—while it is easy in the ideal city to outlaw ancient memories by driving out the poets and censoring traditional stories, the Platonic project makes it necessary to fashion, to invent another, new mythology,[13] a useful beautiful lie which would make everyone freely do what is right. Still barely bereft of her old memories, the new city is already seeking to rediscover the secret unity of tradition. For a society, even if it is conceived and governed by philosophers, still needs that which alone can give it cohesion: a shared and implicit knowledge through which—as the *Laws* insist—a community seems to have a single opinion all through its existence, in its songs, its tales, and its histories.[14]

At the opening of the fourth century, under the convergent action of two types of knowledge—the philosophical and the historical—what had been furtively designated as *myth* gave way, disappeared, to melt into a new landscape, henceforth baptized *mythology*, in which the scriptural activity of already professional mythographers would be deployed.

At the end of this detour in the direction of a history of the sixth to the fourth centuries, we can say that the founders of the science of myths had good reasons for recognizing in Xenophanes and the scholars of ancient Greece the initiators of a partition which they themselves, nineteenth century men of science, were content to reaffirm. Plato and Thucydides are indeed the forerunners of the sense of scandal that mobilized Müller and Lang from the moment it became evident that mythology contained a language characteristic of a temporarily insane mind. But this clairvoyance has its inverse, for none of the artisans of the new science became aware of the strangeness of the figure called mythology, a figure that had sprung from ancient movements of partition, and which since then had never ceased to produce the most diverse questions.

Rethinking mythology means, certainly, to deconstruct the conceptual form of an apparently immediate and legitimate knowledge by registering the specific

12. Plato, *Greater Hippias*, 285d–286a; Thucydides, VII, 69.
13. The *Republic* is a "mythology" (501e), as are the *Laws* (752a).
14. *Laws*, 663–64.

procedures put to use from Xenophanes to Max Müller and from Thucydides to Tylor. But from this point on it also means taking into account some things that we have learned about mythology since then.

1. Mythology is written. There is no mythology, in the Greek sense, except in mythographic form, in writing, through the writing that traces its boundaries, that outlines its figure. And it is through an illusion, that, since the nineteenth century, mythology has come to be the speech, the song, and the voice of origins.

2. Being a cultural product of the Greek world, mythology develops from the moment of its formation along with *interpretation*, which constructs it and takes it as the object of a discourse whose alternatives can be summarized very briefly:[15] mythology either has a meaning or it does not have one. If it does have one—and here it is philosophy that leads the field—the meaning must be sought in one of three ways: in mythology itself—this is the tautegoric approach of Creuzer, of Schelling, and also of Lévi-Strauss; outside of mythology—the allegorical road, with a hidden meaning beneath the immediate meaning, an approach which the Pythagoreans, the Stoics, and others considered unacceptable; or finally, *through* mythology—this is the path of symbolism, of the quest for an ineffable which cannot be produced by rational discourse. Here we have the neo-Platonics, and, nearer to ourselves, Kerényi and Ricoeur.

3. A heterogeneous figure drawn by procedures of exclusion and movements of partition, mythology designates neither a specific literary genre nor a particular type of narration.

It is only after a profound misunderstanding that it has become possible, today or yesterday, to found an enterprise of vast scope on the assumption that a myth is perceived as a myth by any reader in the world. A misunderstanding for which the reader, and through him writing, written culture, are largely responsible.

15. Cf. G. Van Riet, "Mythe et vérité," *Revue philosophique de Louvain* 58 (1960): 15–87.

Georges Charachidzé

5 The Eagle in the Key of Water

Thought in action, thought dramatized, mythology—the making and telling of myths or their by-products—can only be understood if grasped in its activity. The interest of mythographers—we are those who recopy—bears or should bear on this singular activity engaged in by the creators and repairers of myths. But very often, either due to the nature of the material itself or because of an inclination due to the literary character of our disciplines and our training, we are constrained or tempted to deal with the finished product and it alone, the fine tale that is both our delight and our torment.

Such analyses should, of course, be undertaken, wherever our curiosity leads and whatever the paths chosen. But by themselves they seriously risk resulting in autopsy reports: the object handled in this way hides from investigation the living links that implant it among men and through which it is bound to other myths. In many cases the mythic narrative is only available to us stripped of its festal apparel, the sound and movement that accompany its production. All that we get is what we end up calling a "text."

There is only one way to conserve or restore to it a little bit of life: this is by bringing to light and resuscitating the dynamic relations that unite it to other objects of the same nature, either its variants or myths foreign to its purview but without which it would not be what it is.

More concretely, one of the essential services the mythographer performs consists of bringing to light the conceptual pathways and literary techniques which fabricators or repairers of myths use in operating upon a base of pre-existing material. It is one of these processes that will be illustrated here. I propose the name "conservation by inversion" for it: within a single society, or passing from one society to another, a mythical, legendary, or epic narrative transforms itself while maintaining its identity through a reversal of all or part of its values.

I believe I have shown, or at least demonstrated the probability, that the Greek myth of Prometheus and the Caucasian, particularly Georgian, tale of Amirani should be considered variants of each other.[1] When one looks at both cases, it becomes difficult if not impossible to treat them separately, without, however, being in a position to explain the origin of this solidarity: the two mythical sets appear to be mutually interdependent, whatever their historical relationship may have been.

The homology goes quite far if we focus on the major articulations of the myths, particularly on the sources of the (certainly unequal) renown of these two great figures: their revolt against God, their punishment. The parallel is not limited to the developmental schema of the narrative, the number of steps, their order and content: it extends as well to the variations that Greek and Caucasian mythologists have developed out of the initial theme.

MP (= Myth of Prometheus). According to Hesiod, because "Prometheus ...dared to match his wits against almighty Zeus"[2] he is chained to a stake or a column: Zeus "bound (him) in cruel chains unbreakable, chained round a column."[3]

According to Aeschylus, Zeus has Prometheus fastened to the rock itself with metal clasps forged by Hephaistos, the blacksmith god.[4] In a second phase of the punishment, Zeus sets off an explosion on a cosmic scale: he "shatters" (Aeschylus, 1016) the mountain, covering the captive with a heap of rocks in the shape of a dome or a skullcap (*petraia d'angkale*, 1019). Finally, after "a long period of days" (1020), the prisoner, still in chains, is brought back to the earth's surface, on a peak of the Caucasus,[5] to be tortured by an eagle which Aeschylus calls "the winged hound of Zeus" (1022).

LA (= Legends of Amirani). Born of the Melusinian love between a hunter and the goddess Dali, patroness of horned game, Amirani does not attain the grandiose proportions of the Greek Titan: the contemporary Caucasian epic unfolds in a more humble setting than that of the ancient theogony.[6] But the

---

1. This demonstration is presented in an unpublished text, "Prométhée ou le Caucase," forthcoming from Librairie Hermann.
2. Hesiod, *Theogony*, 535.
3. Ibid., 521–22.
4. Aeschylus, *Prometheus Bound*, 1–87.
5. Aeschylus does not mention the place where the last phase of the punishment takes place. But he did specify this in the—alas, now lost—second play of the trilogy, as is witnessed in the texts of Apollonius of Rhodes (*Argonautica*, II, 1246–49), who knew the lost tragedy, and of Cicero (*Tusculanae*, II, 23, v. 28), who cites several verses from it in Latin translation.
6. The legends of Amirani in Georgia, Abrskil in Abkhazia, have been collected over the last hundred years. The mythological workshop is not yet out of business: at the present

Caucasian hero's pride is certainly equal to that of the Greek god: the defiant speeches of *Prometheus Bound* would not seem out of place in the mouth of Amirani.

1. And, in fact, it all starts with a defiant challenge to God, whose answer comes quickly. He chains the rebel—or has him chained by supernatural blacksmiths—either to an iron or a wooden stake, or even to the rock itself.

2. Then God buries the prisoner underground: he moves and shatters whole mountain ranges (Kazbeg or Elburz) which cover Amirani with a rocky shell in the form of a "skullcap" or "helmet":

"There arose a terrible storm, with thunder and lightning; the mountains shattered and closed off the path leading to Amirani."[8]

"The mountain covered him over like a helmet."[9]

Amirani shares his underground captivity with a "winged dog" born of a pair of eagles, which gnaws on the prisoner's chain for a year; at the very instant it is about to give way, all the blacksmiths in the country strike their anvils, and the links regain all of their former thickness.[10]

3. Every year Amirani, still chained to his stake, is brought back up to the outside world on the highest peak of one of the great glaciers of the Caucasus. With the aid of a helpful human (a lost hunter or shepherd), he tries to free himself—in vain. Because of the lying or excessive speech of a woman (the wife of the human savior), he sees his rocky prison close up again for another year.[11]

This is why, if he escapes from his bonds one day, he will exterminate the broods of women and blacksmiths, responsible for his being kept in captivity.[12]

Spatial localization. In both MP and LA, the triplicity of phases of punishment conforms to the same principle of progression and the same distribution among levels of the world: first on the earth, in an undetermined place;[13] then underground; finally on a peak in the Caucasus.

Temporal pattern. MP and LA both follow, if not the same periodicity, at least the same proportions. The subterranean captivity follows swiftly upon the enchainment on the surface of the earth: it happens immediately in the Caucasus, in Greece it leaves just enough time to perform *Prometheus Bound*. The new

time, new versions are still being produced in the high valleys of the Caucasus. The texts cited here as LA refer to my own numbering of the Georgian originals. Whenever possible, I refer the reader to the Russian translation of Chikovani (cited as Ch.): M. Chikovani, *Narodnyj gruzinskij epos o prikovannom Amirani* (Moscow, 1966).

7. LA 1, Ch. I; LA 19, Ch. X and passim.
8. LA 24, Ch. XXV, p. 303.
9. LA 19, Ch. X, p. 267.
10. LA 1, Ch. I, p. 217, and in most of the variants.
11. In the majority of the variants, with a cycle of one, three, or seven years.
12. LA 20, Ch. XIII, p. 275.
13. According to Aeschylus, Prometheus is at first in "Scythian country, in a desert devoid of human beings" (vv. 1–2), which is a way of saying "very far away," somewhere between the Danube and the Urals.

phase lasts "a long period of days" according to Aeschylus; one, two, or seven years, according to the Georgian legends.[14] The final punishment, according to MP, is eternal: "Hope for no ending to this pain," threatens Hermes (Aeschylus, 1026). The qualitative and abstract eternity of the Greek myth finds a measurable, patterned, and humanly observable equivalent in the limitless period which the Georgian story expresses in the rhythmical form of cyclic punishment. In the last count—if counting is possible where eternity is concerned—Amirani's final punishment, like that of Prometheus, should have no end.

These points of contact between MP and LA have to do above all with structure and content and involve the story's progression and proportions. But the parallel goes beyond this: it also concerns the forms and figures of the action, the modalities of its dramatization. Here are some examples, among others.

The Apparatus of Punishment

According to MP, this can take three different forms, the first of which gives rise to two variants.

MP, variant A1. According to most Greek paintings of the scene, Prometheus is chained to a stake of modest dimensions, on a human scale.[15]

MP, variant A2. If we follow Hesiod (*Theogony*, 522), the Titan is attached to a "column" (*dia kiōn*). This item has been exploited in vase paintings, which represent the "column" as a sort of pillar connecting sky and earth. A whole Hellenic tradition, which may be anterior to Hesiod, sees in the *kiōn* a pillar holding up the sky.[16]

MP, variant B. Aeschylus, describing the chaining of Prometheus in detail, fastens him directly to the rock: "Put this clasp on his arm; then strike the hammer with all your might and rivet him to the rock" (55–56 and, for the whole, 51–81).

MP, variant C. There exists a "vegetal representation" of the punishment, a symbolic substitute that is also probably a ritual equivalent for the usual apparatus of punishment. According to a tradition already known to Aeschylus,[17] Zeus granted the prisoner his freedom on the condition that in compensation for the removal of his metal chains he agree to wear a crown of osier.[18] Athenaeus, who reports this substitution and is surprised by it, assimilates it to a ritual attested at Samos which consisted of tying up a wooden statue within an osier grove.[19]

---

14. Usually one year, beginning either in the spring or at the New Year.
15. O. Gruppe, *Griechische Mythologie und Religiongeschichte*, I–II (Munich, 1906), pp. 382 and 1226.
16. L. Séchan, *Le mythe de Promethée* (Paris 1951), p. 36.
17. Ibid., pp. 45–46 and 75.
18. J. -P. Vernant, "Métis et mythes de souveraineté," in M. Detienne and J. -P. Vernant, *Métis ou les pièges de l'intelligence* (Paris, 1974).
19. Athenaeus, XV, 672a-e, 674d-e.

Caucasian mythologists exploited the same possibilities and produce the same kinds of variations on the theme of the apparatus of punishment.

LA, tradition A1. In most of the variants, Amirani is chained to a stake of iron or wood:

"God punished him. He tied him up with a great iron chain and attached him to a great iron stake."[20]

LA, tradition A2. Several tellers of the tale turn this support into an enormous column, a sort of world pillar, "whose roots are long enough to encircle the whole earth, and whose top reaches to heaven."[21]

LA, tradition B. According to other, less numerous, variants, Amirani is chained directly to the rock:

"Then God commanded that he must be chained to that rock itself."[22]

LA, tradition C. The tale of Amirani also has a vegetal interpretation which conforms to the Greek conception. Here too, as in Greece, the vegetal equivalent of the apparatus of punishment does not appear as a concretely applied technique. It functions on the edges of the story, on the imaginary and symbolic level among the Abkhasians, on the ritual level among the Svans and the mountain Georgians. In the Abkhasian myth, vine-shoots in place of chains, thorn bushes instead of a stake, and rhizomes of fern for the underground fastening of the apparatus, come together to announce confusedly to the hero the tragic fate to which he is doomed.[23] The Svan and Georgian mountain-dwellers assign a very precise ritual function to bramble branches, which are symbolically supposed to ensure the rechaining of Amirani when the latter has, so to speak, exhausted the three techniques corresponding to the successive phases of punishment. Parallel to this, in another ritual the symbolic rechaining of the hero is performed by tying up a wooden chair with cotton threads.[24]

In the Caucasus as in Greece, the vegetal bonds act only as ritual substitutes, appearing *after* the punishment and equivalent to a second, renewed chaining, this time a symbolic one.

The Burial

In both MP and LA, the burial takes the form of a meteorological and geological cataclysm: crashing thunder, a sky on fire, and the shock of mountains "shattering." In both stories the result of the catastrophe is the same: the prisoner is buried under "a curved stone" according to MP, under a heap of rocks in the shape of a helmet according to LA.

These precise and organized similarities do not exhaust the parallelism, which I have so far limited to the narrative itself. They also concern the ideological

20. LA 2, Ch. II, p. 350, and passim.
21. LA 1, Ch. I, p. 217.
22. LA 1, Ch. XII, p. 271.
23. LA 14, Ch. XXVII, p. 309; LA 23, Ch. XXVIII, p. 310.
24. M. Chartolani, *Kartveli xalxis mat'erialuri k'ult'uris ist'oriidan* (Tbilisi, 1964), pp. 157–59.

extensions of the two mythic ensembles: a negative relationship of the hero with women and marriage, an ambiguous position with regard to blacksmiths, the congruence of the hero's "reign" with a golden age free of labor or production, etc.

Such points of contact, which are not isolated and localized but form a system, make all the more glaring the gaps and distortions found in passing from the Greek myth to the Caucasian legend: for the latter lacks the very element responsible for the fame of Prometheus, namely, his torture by the eagle intermediary and the theft of fire.

It is true that the winged dog who intervenes on Amirani's behalf between the second and the last phase of his punishment could easily fill the role of a substitute or avatar of the Promethean bird of prey. Especially if we take Aeschylus's image literally: *ptēnos kuōn*, the "winged dog"; this is not a stylistic figure, a stereotype: according to the *Thesaurus*, it appears only twice in all of Greek literature, in *Prometheus Bound* and in *Agamemnon*.[25] The winged dog of Amirani is also a creature in the service of God, a doer of high deeds; and he is also, despite his peculiar anatomy, an eagle through and through, but a poorly made eagle.[26] We should note that Prometheus's eagle is also a kind of monster, born of Tychon and Echidna;[27] in the words of Apollonius of Rhodes, "his nature was not that of a bird of the air" (*Argonautica*, II, 1254).

But the winged dog of the Caucasus performs his function in an opposite way from that of the Greek eagle: he comes to the prisoner's aid instead of adding to his punishment. This reversal of values still remains an enigma at the present time.

As for the fire in the tale of Amirani, one may say that it shines by its absence. For it appears less absent than negated, systematically refused. All of the versions show a kind of desperate desire to avoid it or, if it still appears, to suppress it: materially, by putting it out, or symbolically, by negating it. Amirani and his two human companions live far from even the most rudimentary hearth—they do not even have a campfire. In spite of their numerous hunting expeditions and the permanence of their savage life (they have no home), it never happens that they light even the smallest fire to cook their game. Only once does Amirani make the slightest movement in the direction of fire: he attacks the house of a demon at the request of his adopted brothers, whose nostalgia for a more comfortable, more human existence had been awakened by the sight of flames shining on the demon's hearth. But it is in vain. Not content with slaughtering the people of the house, Amirani destroys everything...and puts out the fire.[28]

25. H. Estienne, *Thesaurus graecae linguae* (1572), *sub voce*.
26. B. Nizharadze, *Ist'oriul-etnograpiuli c'erilebi* (Tbilisi, 1962), 1: 146.
27. See F. Vian's notes to his edition of *Argonautica* (Paris 1974), 1: 236, n. 3.
28. LA 1, Ch. I, pp. 210–11.

In addition to this, Amirani's behavior while in chains, in the final phase of his punishment, is equivalent in several ways to a symbolic abolition of fire. For instance, he persuades a peasant to go and unhook his own hearth chain and bring it to him: such an action means the destruction of the hearth and in reality would be punished by immediate death.[29]

Finally, the rituals which even today accompany the replacing of the hero's bonds (when his rocky prison closes for another year) clearly illustrate this negative relation: the extinction or reinforced protection of domestic fires coincides with his attempted escape, the failure of which in turn permits their relighting or continuation.[30]

Here we are in the presence of a new homology, but an inverted one, between MP and LA. Prometheus is being *honored* at the lampaedromia of the Prometheia, during which fires are renewed;[31] Amirani, too, is involved in rituals with the same goal, but the success of these rituals requires his continued captivity and are really performed *against him*.

This insistence on rejecting fire, pointing out the vanity of its use, or opposing it to Amirani, appears too regularly not to be considered a response to a deliberate intention on the part of the Georgian mythologists. *Negated fire* thus fulfills a real function within the tale of Amirani. This important fact completely changes the relationship between the two mythical ensembles, at least within the mode of fire. Its presence in MP and its negation in LA cease to appear as mutually exclusive traits and are revealed, on the contrary, to be united by a relationship of inversion.

But this "involuting" operation—whose reproduction leads back to the initial state, whether we start from MP or LA—would remain a quite arbitrary step, ascribable to a sort of sophism on the part of the mythographer, if we could not be sure that the negation of fire is seen as compensated by a positive correlate in the Caucasian tale. To confirm its validity we must find a narrative episode, a belief or a symbolic action which inverts the Greek myth in positive relief [*en plein*], as it were, rather than in *intaglio* [*en creux*].

Such a document appears in one of those miraculous versions which sometimes come along to delight the mythographer: the teller had accumulated, as if for his own pleasure, themes that are rare or obscure elsewhere, which the other variants treat only by allusion or mention without understanding. The texts belonging to this version were collected only recently—between 1936 and 1953—but in spite of this late date they are noteworthy for the archaic and traditional character of their style, as well as for their profound links with

29. M. Chartolani, *Kartveli*, pp. 135–44 and 153.
30. Ibid., pp. 160–63.
31. N. Wecklein, "Der Fackelweltlauf," *Hermes* 7 (1873).

Georgian cosmology.[32] The last variant, in particular, makes abundant use of sacred formulas and contains numerous passages in verse sung during the ritual dance which accompanies the production of myths: these are, in fact, veritable liturgical texts, performed as part of the celebration of the cult.[33]

The positive counterpart of *fire refused* appears in the form of a *reconquest* of *subterranean water*. It occurs during a crucial event in the history of the world, for it fixes for eternity one of the essential norms which assures the functioning of the cosmos.

Amirani confronts an enormous black serpent or dragon, the one who devours the sinking sun every night in the depths of the underground world. At the urging of the sun, the hero is swallowed by the dragon, who immediately seeks refuge in his natural domain, the underside of the earth (or in the Black Sea). Amirani emerges from the belly of the beast by cutting through its side, then seals the fissure with a wooden board—not with a sheet of metal, as had been agreed on by the dragon. Thanks to this trick, the sun that is swallowed every night can now emerge at dawn by burning through the wooden prosthesis which Amirani put in place: in this way the periodicity of day and night is ensured until the end of time. The hero, however, once out of the dragon's belly, is still trapped in the underground realm. Searching for some means of transport to the outside world, he meets an old woman busily making bread dough. But instead of mixing the flour with water, she urinates to moisten it. Explanation: "Our country is under the domination of a dragon who won't let anyone get water." Amirani goes to the body of water guarded by the dragon, kills him, and brings water back to the old woman.

This adventure shows him a way to reach the world aboveground: the dragon killed by Amirani used to devour the young of a giant eagle who is quite capable of making the journey. The eagle, grateful to the hero, agrees to carry him and sets him down on the surface of the earth.[34]

This adventure of Amirani is a fairly exact inversion of Prometheus's theft of fire.

LA 30. A mythical, nonearthly humanity is deprived of the free use of water by a hopochthonian supernatural being—a giant dragon or serpent. According to Georgian cosmology, as we will see below, the dragon who forbids access to the body of water is none other than the master of underground water. Amirani grants men access to and use of the water they had been deprived of. Following this good deed he is saved by a hypochthonian eagle.

MP. A still-mythical humanity ("It was when gods and mortal men had a dispute...," *Theogony*, 535) is deprived of fire, which originates celestially, by the master of the fire himself: Zeus, the supreme god. Prometheus restores

---

32. LA 30 and 31; Ch. IV, XXIV.
33. This trait has been pointed out by Georgian ethnologists; cf. Ch., commentary on XXIV. For the sacred character of the dance movement in question, see G. Charachidzé, *Système religieux de la Géorgie païenne* (Paris, 1968), p. 712.
34. LA 30; Ch. IV, pp. 240–41.

to men the celestial fire which Zeus had kept from them. Following this act, which is a crime from the point of view of the gods, he is tortured by a celestial eagle.

LA	A hypochthonian	} eagle {	saves	} the hero
MP	A celestial		tortures	
LA	{ in gratitude for a good deed	}	related to the reconquest	
MP	{ in punishment for a crime			
LA	{ of underground water	}	which had been kept from a	
MP	{ of celestial fire			
LA	mythic humanity by a {	hypochthonian	} supernatural	
MP		uranian		
LA	being who is master {		of the water below.	
MP			of the fire above.	

The Greek myth and the Caucasian tale conserve their essential traits, which are inverted in passing from one to the other. What factor could have provoked this reversal of values and turned the mythic universe upside down, with recourse to such extremely opposed natural elements as celestial fire and subterranean water?

The necessity for such a reversal was imposed on the mythologists because of the place assigned to the eagle in the popular ornithologies of the Greeks and the Georgians, respectively.

For the former, the eagle is tied symbolically and almost congenitally to celestial fire. He is a *purphoros*, a "fire-bearer."[35] The eagle alone has the power to look straight into the sun, and goes so far as to kill any of his offspring who cannot stand this test. His relation to the sun is in fact ontological in nature, as is expressed in the belief in the periodical renewal required by the eagle's peculiar physiology. Weighed down by the years, he is no longer able to rise into the air and would be doomed to crawl along miserably if he did not have recourse to a sort of "sun treatment." Tearing himself in one final effort from the increasing grip of the earth, he ascends all the way to the empyrean heaven, close enough to the sun for it to burn his plumage. Thus revivified, he regains for a time his vigor and the mastery of celestial spaces.[36]

The mythical ornithology of the Georgians, inverting that of the Greeks, populates its sky with birds of prey who are closely, even physiologically,

35. Aristophanes, *The Birds*, 1248; cited in M. Detienne, *Les Jardins d'Adonis* (Paris, 1972), p. 60.

36. M. Detienne, *Les Jardins*, p. 61; J. Hubaux and M. Leroy, *Le mythe du Phénix dans la littérature grecque et latine* (Paris, 1939), pp. 72-76.

linked to the *water below* in a positive or negative way. The giant vulture is the opposite of the Greek eagle: while the latter is *regenerated through contact with celestial fire,* the former *degenerates through the absorption of terrestrial water.* The bird in question is the *Aegipius monachus L.,* or *svavi* in Georgian (sometimes confused with the gypaetae, *k'ravi–c'amia*). The *Materials on Fauna* report the following belief concerning this bird:

"The shepherds say that vultures will sometimes steal a lamb, and there is nothing impossible about this. This is why shepherds—at least according to themselves—sprinkle salt on a carcass that is going to be eaten by the vultures. As a result the vultures drink so much water that they can no longer take off, and the shepherds can beat them to death with sticks."[37] Now the Georgian eagle is opposed both to its Greek homologue in terms of fire and to the great vulture because of its positive relationship with terrestrial water. Here is how (the text is from the end of the seventeenth century): "Eagles (*arc'ivi*). On this subject they say: in his five-hundredth year he becomes young again by dropping from the highest heavens and is reborn through his fall into the midst of the waters." The same author again underlines the eagle's affinity for terrestrial water by assimilating him to the white-tailed sea eagle,[38] one of the largest birds of Europe. "The sea eagle (*psovi*). Nowadays the peasants call this bird an 'eagle' (*arc'ivi*)."[39]

Now this bird of prey, *Haliaetus albicilla,* is doubly connected with water. First by its environment and habits: living near oceans, rivers, and lakes, it spends its time fishing (whence its name of "fishing eagle," *haliaete*), which provides its staple food. Secondly, by its name, which definitely contains the root for "water or fish"; *psov–i,* as a matter of fact, is not Georgian, and results from a borrowing from northwestern Caucasia, either from Circassian *psy,* "water," or Oubykh *psa,* "fish" (this last term, too, deriving from the root *ps–,* "water").

Other beliefs allow us to verify this natural relationship between the eagle and terrestrial water. There is this one, among many others: the Svans divide wild animals into four classes, each of which is under the supervision of a "master" or "mistress" of game. Thus the goddess Dali, the mother of Amirani, reigns over "horned game of the mountains"; the Angel of the Forest reigns over carnivores (except for the wolf); Dzgrag is the master of wolves; the spirit Apsat (Aefsati among the Ossetians) rules both trout and high-flying birds, especially the eagle.[40]

Thus there can be no doubt about the eagle's affinities for water. But what is involved in most Georgian beliefs is terrestrial rather than subterranean water, while at the same time it is the latter which plays the essential role in the mythic

37. *Masalebi sakartvelos paunisatvis* (Tbilisi, 1966), 1: 106.
38. TN: This is *pycargue* in French, as opposed to *aigle.*
39. Saba Orbeliani, *Sit'q'vis K'ona,* ed. Iordanishvili (Tbilisi, 1949), col. 31; ibid., col. 694.
40. Charachidzé, *Système religieux,* p. 483.

episode inverting the theft of celestial fire. In fact, the *Natursystem* as conceived by the Georgians assimilates the hydrosphere to the mass of water located under the earth, the hydrosphere representing only the outcroppings of this mass on the earth's surface.

Fire and water, concretely and symbolically, are subsumed in a precise and constraining classification, itself integrated within a tripartite division of the world, whose effects are felt in all domains, from the most grandiose to the most humble.

The universe consists of three superimposed spaces, three *sk'neli*, from top to bottom:

I.   *Ze-sk'neli*, "the space on high," or the celestial world.

II. *Gare-sk'neli*, "the space above," or the earthly world.

III. *Kve-sk'neli*, "the space below," or the underground world.

The gods are on the top level; in the middle, humanity and wild nature; underneath are demons and monsters.[41]

Whatever their mode of being (gods, demons, natural elements), only two categories of entities have an ontological status: those above the sky and those below the earth. Between these two extremes, the space which is in proximity to human beings can only be a place of passage, of mediation, or meeting; the creatures that populate it and the elements which animate it are merely emanations of the celestial world or the underground world. This is true even for mankind:

In the beginning the gods inhabited the surface of the earth (space II), sharing it with the demons, against whom they waged permanent war in order to keep them at a reasonable distance. One day the gods left definitively for the sky, leaving men (*viri*, the males) in their place. Alone against the demons, men proved incapable of resisting them. At this point the gods intervened, hunting down the race of demons without respite and forcing them to seek refuge underground, where they have remained ever since. The vanquished, for their part, left women on the earth. And the situation as it exists in our time is the result of this double process.[42]

As a result of this, the men and women who populate the surface of the earth emanate respectively from the gods on high and the demons down below; they are their substitutes in the world in between. The existence of the human race and its perpetuation through marriage are due to the conjunction of the celestial and the subterranean.

The same is true for fire, which is divided into two opposing substances: the fire on high, at the celestial level, manifests itself to human beings in the form of lightning; the fire below, on the subterranean level, becomes perceptible on the occasion of outcroppings such as volcanic phenomena.

41. Orbeliani, *Sit'q'vis K'ona*, col. 615.
42. Cf. references in Charachidzé, *Systemè religieux*, pp. 280–81, 343.

Terrestrial fire is thus, like humanity, conditioned by its double origin, divine and demonic, it too surviving only thanks to the hearth, which holds a position and function identical to the position and function of marriage.[43]

The system of waters is parallel to that of fire, and I suggest that this structural similarity may have favored the inverse relationship between the Greek and Georgian mythic ensembles. There exist two masses of water, one celestial, on level I, including a store of snow, the other underground on level III. As for the water that gives life to humans, animals, and plants, it wells up onto level II without really belonging to it, being simply the result of an outcropping of the subterranean body of water. The water on the earth's surface either descends from the sky in the form of rain and snow or comes up from underground. This rising of the waters is controlled by a hypochthonian dragon (the one confronted by Amirani) who sometimes provokes inundations which the Georgians call "little floods" (the flood here being thought of as coming from beneath the earth).[44]

Earthly animals are divided up ontologically according to the same principle: thus the wolf is a being of celestial origin, who nourishes and protects the sun; the same is true of the snake who, despite the fact that he crawls along the ground, is thought of as a solar being (in Georgia he serves as the mount of the sun; among the Circassians he is the mount of the lightning).[45]

There is a remarkable parallelism, but with an inverse dynamic, between the comings and goings of the eagle and those of the sun. Like the bird, the sun makes his cycle between the water on high and the water below; night is the result of his plunge into the watery mass of the underworld. That night continues until morning is because the sun is swallowed by the dragon, who is master of the subterranean water and from whom the sun escapes by burning through the dragon's side.

The eagle's cycle is accomplished in the same way, but his aquatic affinities are oriented in a different way: the ascent of the sun takes place *in spite of* the subterranean waters, that of the eagle *because of* them, since his plunge into aquatic hypochthonian space regenerates him and permits him to fly once again.

The cosmological constraints by virtue of which entities, living beings, and natural elements are connected through dividing, repelling, or attracting each other, have their effects on all human activities, and especially on mythology. For millennia this dynamic has been influencing and redirecting the mechanisms by means of which myths evolve and are transformed through differentiation or opposition. Its incessant and profound action explains the fact that a single mythical schema can be maintained in its essentials while at the same time being partially inverted.

Let us suppose, to simplify things, that the ancient mythologists of the Colchid or Svanetia, inspired by the Greek model, took it upon themselves to

---

43. Ibid., p. 87, n. 32.
44. N. Shamandze, *Mcire c'arghvnis legendebi*, Macne, 2 (Tbilisi, 1971), pp. 61–70.
45. B. Nizharadze, *Ist'oriol-etnograpiuli*, p. 146.

deal with the theme of fire regained. The adaptation, however supple and free it might be, must maintain a minimal group of original elements, those whose connection with the original myth is too significant to be broken or even loosened. Such is the case with the eagle, whom we know to have a powerful relationship with Prometheus's act, its consequences, and its object—fire. But the Georgians could not conceive and represent the eagle without connecting him with subterranean water, on which he depends for his very being: the presence and maintenance of the eagle in the story automatically produced a transposition "into the key of water," as Claude Lévi-Strauss says. Whence the process of inversion whose principal comments have been analyzed here.

It may seem unwise or irresponsible to base such large-scale conclusions, involving whole mythologies, on a single confrontation between a Greek story several thousand years old and a brief episode from a contemporary tale which, to boot, is only attested in a small number of variants. One would wish to find at least one document that would confirm that the theft of fire was read "in the key of water" on the shores of the Black Sea. Such evidence does indeed exist, but it must be sought some two thousand years earlier. We find it in the scholia to the *Argonautica* of Apollonius of Rhodes, canto II, verses 1246–59.

The Argonauts arrive within sight of the peaks of the Caucasus, where, says the poet, Prometheus is chained, with the eagle feeding on his liver. The scholiast reports a number of local traditions as the source of the myth. These in particular:

Variant 1. The river whose flooding destroyed the best lands of the country of Prometheus was named the Eagle (*Aiētos*); as for the liver, many see it as a symbol for the fertility of the earth. When Herakles changed the course of the river through irrigation works, it appeared to the local inhabitants that the eagle had been destroyed and that Prometheus had been freed from his fetters.

The second variant is even more interesting.

Variant 2. According to Herodorus of Herakleia, Prometheus was a king of Scythia. He lacked sufficient resources to assure the subsistence of his subjects, for a river named the Eagle (*Aiētos*) destroyed the harvest with its floods. The Scythians put their king in chains. Herakles succeeded in reconnecting the river with the sea. For this reason the belief that Herakles had killed the eagle and freed Prometheus from his bonds spread among the people.[46]

Considered in itself, this *interpretatio scythica* seems to be a gratuitous game based on an attitude of heavy-handed euhemerism: a sort of medieval allegory as imagined by an erudite Voltairean, thoroughly in the style of what has been called "Ionian rationalism." But in the face of the principles of Caucasian cosmology and their application in the tale of Amirani, the scholiasts' explanation seems, on the contrary, to be based on a vigorous native tradition, which is still producing its effects in our own time. We note the presence of a number of "Amiranian" traits: the assimilation of the hero with a king, attested in several Georgian legends; his reign being concomitant with the impossibility or the

46. C. Wendel, *Scholia in Apollonium Rhodium vetera* (Berlin, 1935).

vanity of agricultural pursuits; his bondage by his own people, which we find in some Circassian variants.

But for us the main interest of this ancient version remains that of a witness authenticating beyond any possible doubt the process of inversion of a myth of fire into a myth of water.

Here the mechanisms of transposition have worked differently than in the Georgian story; far from bringing about the reversal of all values, they affect only celestial fire—which becomes terrestrial water—and the natural affinities of the eagle, now identified with the aquatic element.

Important modifications, involving the processes of shifting [glissement] and transposition, different from the phenomenon of inversion but amplifying it, differentiate the "Scythian" version from both MP and LA. These transformations will not be studied here. I will limit myself to indicating those which involve the actual mechanism of inversion.

One of these bears on the initial situation, on the very anomaly that the events it sets off are meant to remedy. According to MP, there is a lack of celestial fire (of subterranean water in LA), which is transformed in the tradition reported by the scholiast into an excess of terrestrial water. In both of these cases, the action consists of granting men mastery over a natural element, by regaining it in the Greek and Georgian fables, by taming it in the Scythian transposition.

The latter, indeed, totally identifies the eagle with terrestrial water; the eagle and the flooding river are now one; being and denomination confused together, the eagle *is* the water of this world. This has a triple consequence: the eagle keeps its negative sign (which is inverted in LA30); on the other hand, the water becomes harmful, whereas it is beneficial, even vital, in LA30; finally, the hero's position remains unchanged: he is in the camp opposed to that of the eagle, who on the contrary becomes Amirani's ally in the Georgian tale.

These problems, and others—notably Herakles' intervention against the eagle, shared by Greek mythology and the Scythian version—deserve an in-depth study, which will be undertaken elsewhere. But this is not my purpose here: my purpose has simply been to show that the reading "in the key of water" does not constitute an isolated fact, a result of the fantasy of a Georgian narrator using "folk-tale motifs," but that it is part of an ancient tradition and belongs specifically to the Caucasus.

This being the case, we must return to the Georgian story to point out a difficulty which appears to challenge not the phenomenon of inversion itself but its vigor and extent. For this mechanism appears not to apply to the respective affinities of Prometheus and Amirani towards fire and water.

We know that the hero of the Greek myth is connected with fire: he is defined as a *purphoros*, a "fire-bearer" (this is the title of a lost tragedy of Aeschylus, the last of the trilogy), and it was under this title that he was honored in ancient rites of the renewal of fire. We would then expect from a "reading in the key of water," such as is attested in the Caucasus, that it would also bear on this point and make the Georgian hero, if not a *hydrophoros*, at least a person linked in one way or another with the aquatic element. Certainly, as we have seen, Amirani appears on many occasions as resolutely "anti-fire," the exact inverse of Prometheus. But this definition by default lacks a positive counterpart: nothing in the whole of the Georgian tale suggests a relationship between Amirani and the water below. Nevertheless, the process of inversion has operated here, too, but its effects on the tale are discoverable only indirectly.

We must first take note of a restriction: if Amirani was put in relation to water, this could only be with the water *on high*. The rigorous and precise cosmology which locates every being at its own level of the world could hardly tolerate a creature of celestial origin being confounded with the mass of subterranean water. Now Amirani indisputably belongs to the spaces above, at least by birth and heredity (the latter being a social rather than a biological affair in the Caucasus). For his mother, the goddess Dali, is a celestial entity, even if her functions as protectress of game require earthly visitations and hideaways. Besides this, his sociological father—his "godfather," according to the indigenous term, from whom he takes his name, his genetic patrimony, and his destiny—is none other than the supreme god himself. Endowed with this double celestial guarantee, which wholly determines him in his being and his doing, Amirani can have affinities only with the water above, the hydrosphere remaining, as it were, forbidden to him. If the mechanism of the inversion of fire into water has operated here, it could not have been with the subterranean water as in the rest of the myth, but only with celestial water.

The hero's relationship with celestial water is attested triply if we refer ourselves to the Caucasian corpus in its entirety, with the arsenal of beliefs and rites from which it draws some of its substance.

1. He is born of a goddess who performs a double service. Besides her quality as patroness of deer, Dali has the function of providing or afflicting men with snow and rain. This is in fact why she is most commonly invoked, to provoke or prevent, depending on the circumstances, one of these natural phenomena.

We are dealing here with a true theologeme:[47] the rites involving hunting and its celestial guarantees have a meteorological end. In particular, the arrival of bad weather, with rain or snow, is tied to the relationship between hunters and the

---

47. TN: "Theologeme" and, later, "meteorologeme" are constructions with the suffix -eme, which indicates the smallest meaningful unit of a system of signification. What is implied by the use of these terms is the existence of coherent systems of symbols underlying discourse about the gods on the one hand, the weather on the other. The use of -eme indicates that the incidents in question are elements of these larger systems. The usage is derived from linguistics, in which "phoneme" is used for the smallest meaningful unit in a language's phonological system, "morpheme" is used for the smallest meaningful morphological unit, etc. Lévi-Strauss popularized this use outside of linguistics with his invention of the "mytheme" in "The Structural Study of Myth" (1955; reprinted in his collection, *Structural Anthropology*, which has gone through several English editions).

masters of game. This belief is attested throughout the Caucasus. According to the Mingrelians, the appearance of the *mesepi*, the patrons of wild animals, means a change in the weather. The coming of a male *mesepi* brings good weather, that of a female *mesepi* brings rain or snow.[48] In *Rac'a*, the divinity who protects game appears in the form of a black cloud, soon turning into rain, to hunters who have violated a taboo.[49]

There are many religious hymns and mythological narratives that tell of the intervention of the goddess Dali in the form of rain or snow, following an unvarying scenario: a hunter violates a taboo (by killing too much game or forbidden game), the goddess provokes a deluge of rain or snow:[50] "A hunter surprised a piebald sheep which he captured with the help of his dog. But Dali was in the forest. She snowed and buried the village."

A hunter's professional fault incites Dali to manifest herself to the guilty party: and the apparition of a mistress of game cannot occur without the accompaniment of rain or snow. The texts puts this as strongly as possible: "Dali snowed [*dalim itova*]."

Amirani's mother is thus not only connected with the precipitation of snow or rain, she *is* the snow, she *is* the rain.

On the other hand, a large number of variants show the hero himself acting as rainmaker. An important group of Svan versions, in fact, see his punishment as the consequence of a hunting *hybris*, for which he shares responsibility with his companion in captivity, the winged dog Q'ursha.[51] The same kind of causality intervenes in the traditions of eastern Georgia, notably among the Xevsur: Amirani or his biological father (himself a famous hunter) tracks a "marked," i.e., a sacred, deer, thus provoking the appearance of the goddess Dali, which, as we know, automatically means rain or snow.[52]

The hero of the Georgian tale is thus invested, independently of his own will, with the function of meteorological agent, whose behavior sets in motion the mass of celestial water.

Finally, like his mother, Amirani is directly assimilated with the rain in the popular imagination. The verse passages of the tale, which follow an archaic meter, and which represent the last fragments of a great mythological epic, provide a definition of the hero which differentiates him from his human half-brothers. The latter are described as being, respectively, like "an ornamented bride" and "a fortress of crystal."

"Amirani is like a great black cloud ready to burst into rain."[53]

48. A. Dirr, "Bezestvo oxoty i oxotniçyj jazyk u kavkazskix gorcev," S.M.O.M.P.K., X, IV, 4, p. 8.
49. A. Robakidze, *K'olekt'iuri nadirobis gadmonastebi raç'asi* (Tbilisi, 1941), pp. 191-92.
50. E. Virsaladze, *Kartuli samonadiro ep'osi* (Tbilisi, 1964), pp. 70-73; texts on pp. 217-20.
51. B. Nizharadze, *Ist'oriul-etnograpiuli*, p. 159.
52. LA 32, Ch. XVIII, and passim.
53. LA 1, Ch. I, p. 206.

2. This aptitude for making it rain and for raining himself which Amirani bears is confirmed indirectly by the misadventure of his hunting homologue, the "hunter hung upside down," whose sad and beautiful tale has been told in a very rich set of hymns and myths down to the present day. Georgian ethnologists, notably E. Virsaladze,[54] correctly see in this character a double of Amirani. In a still unpublished study ("Prométhée ou le Caucase"), I have taken up and extended the demonstration.

The narrative—generally in the form of a hymn which is both sung and danced—serves as the etiological myth for a ritual which is still practiced nowadays. The story is basically as follows:

Accompanied by his winged dog Q'ursha—the same one who shares Amirani's captivity—a professional hunter tracks or kills a deer at the top of a mountain. The goddess Dali then appears and punishes him, either because he has taken forbidden game or because he has betrayed her with a mortal woman, his own wife. The two themes are most often mixed together, following exigencies specific to the doctrine of hunting in force in the Caucasus.

The excessive hunter—or the hunter who is unfaithful to his Melusinian love—finds himself suspended on the side of a rock by the sole of one of his moccasins, his head hanging down. He soon starts to suffer from hunger. Then the dog offers himself as a sacrifice; his weeping master kills him, skins him, and cooks him on a fire made from his bow and arrows, but cannot bring himself to eat him.

His family and the whole village find out what has happened, and throw ropes down from above and set up ladders from below. All in vain: the mountain keeps growing to defeat their efforts. Finally the hunter hurls himself into the void and dies, followed by his dog Q'ursha, resuscitated for the occasion.

Let us remark in passing that what we are witnessing is really an inverted hunt: the mechanism consists of attributing to beings, accessories, and behaviors purposes contrary to the ones they have in normal practice. To summarize: having become nonweapons, the bow and arrows serve to roast an antigame which will serve as nonfood for a hunter who is hanging upside down by the sole of his moccasin, which is normally meant to tread upon the earth.

This process of inversion deserves our interest for two reasons. First of all because it puts the hunter—like his homologue Amirani—in the position of antifire: he lights an inverted fire to cook nonfood which he will not eat. On the other hand, processes of reversal are often used to make it rain, to reverse time. This is the case both in the Caucasus and elsewhere; see for example the role attributed to the mirror in Kabyle practices, and those in which this utensil intervenes as an "agent for the reversal" of time.[55]

54. In the remarkable study that she has devoted to "The Georgian Hunting Epic," and in which the essential texts are brought together: *Kartuli samonadiro ep'osi* (Tbilisi, 1964); texts on pp. 189-223.

55. P. Bourdieu, *Esquisse d'une théorie de la pratique* (Geneva and Paris, 1972), p. 69, n. 84.

And in fact the ritual for which the myth constitutes both the etiological warrant and the musical accompaniment has the sole purpose of calling and provoking the rain. It is sufficient even to sing the hunter's hymn backwards to obtain the same result.[56]

The hunter-homologue of Amirani is thus also a rainmaker, and so connected with celestial water.

I will not resist the pleasure of noting in passing a curious parallelism between this meteorologeme from the shores of the Black Sea and one that exists on the West Coast of the United States, among the Makah Indians: a gull-hunter finds himself immobilized on top of a rock that grows by itself. His family organizes rescue efforts that prove to be in vain, using ropes (from above) and arrows (from below). Suffering from thirst, he sings the "invocation which is still used to make it rain." Finally he leaps into the void and is killed.[57]

3. We know that the Georgians, having to conform to a demanding cosmology, found themselves intellectually unable to connect the demigod Amirani with terrestrial water, and for that reason the inversion operated not upon the myth's spatial coordinates but only on the substance of a necessarily celestial natural element. The reversal is limited to transforming celestial fire into celestial water. But their Ossetian neighbors, the last descendants of the Scythians and the Alans, are not bound by the same constraints. And they have represented the aquatic affinities of their hero Amyran quite differently. This evidence is valuable, for while it is clear that the Ossetian epic of Amyran, their most popular epic after that of the Narts, was based on Georgian themes, it is equally certain that the work of borrowing and adaptation took place on the basis of an archaic state of the Georgian tale, to which we no longer have direct access today. Thus the comparison of the two versions offers us a way of clarifying and enriching the possibilities latent in the myth, only some of which are actualized in the legends that have been collected in Georgia in our time. The latter, for instance, attribute the enchaining of our hero to blacksmith demons, the hypochthonian Kadzhi, while his Ossetian homologue is chained up by the celestial spirit of the forge, Kurdalägon. This variation on a single theme—extremely instructive in relation to Prometheus, fastened to his rock by Hephaistos—was not exploited or was lost by the Georgian tradition.

The Ossetian epic closely associates Amyran with terrestrial water. Nephew or grandson of God, he is confided at birth to the spirit of the waters, Don Bettyr, who serves as his adoptive father and raises him at the bottom of the Black Sea until adolescence. The young Amyran sometimes shows himself to fishermen, emerging from the waves, perched on a bull or cow of the sea.[58] Later he leaves his marine universe and on earth undertakes the exploits that will lead to his

56. E. Virsaladze, *Kartuli*, pp. 190–91.
57. C. Lévi-Strauss, *L'Homme nu* (Paris, 1971), pp. 137–38.
58. Chikovani, *Narodnyj*, pp. 190–91.

punishment. But his early life, his upbringing, his childhood, make him an aquatic being, completely bound to terrestrial water.

Thus bolstered by a set of independent but convergent facts, the affinity of Amirani for atmospheric water (the hydrosphere in the Ossetian parallel) contrasts with the affinity of Prometheus for celestial fire. This not unexpected, but unsolicited, reversal provides the mechanism of inversion with the cog that appeared to be missing.

If the preceding analyses have convinced the reader, and if he admits that the reconquest of celestial fire by Prometheus and of terrestrial water by Amirani are indeed in a relationship of reciprocal inversion, he will naturally raise the question: in which direction did the transformation take place? There is no clear answer to this legitimate query.

At first glance it seems simpler to take the Georgian tale as a transposition of the Greek myth: a number of considerations support this. First, the dating of historical relations between the two peoples: the establishment of uninterrupted contacts between the Greek world and the Colchid was established after Hesiod had fixed the story of the rebellious Titan for prosperity. Next, the preponderant role of fire in the Greek myth, in which it invades everything, while water plays only a secondary role in the legends of Amirani. Finally, the coexistence on the shores of the Black Sea of a double tradition, attested by the authors of antiquity; one, which we have analyzed, is based on a "reading in the key of water;" the other, however, maintains the preeminence of fire. Philostratus, in the second century of our era, reports a belief current among the peoples of the western Caucasus, to the effect that Prometheus, chained to one of their mountains, had been tortured by an eagle and then rescued by Herakles. This is why, since then, the natives destroy the eyries of eagles by burning them with flaming arrows.[59] From this one could conclude that the transposition "in the key of water" took place in the ancient Colchid on the basis of a fire myth imported by the Greeks.

But the very existence of these documents could be interpreted otherwise: a whole Hellenic tradition attests that the myth of Prometheus, or at least a number of its versions, were current among the inhabitants of the Colchid, and that they were taken to be autochthonous. Particularly noteworthy are the accounts of Strabo, Flavius Arrian, and that of Philostratus, cited above.[60] For these authors, and for others still, there is no question about the Caucasian roots of the myth. We should note in addition that the practice reported by Philostratus of destroying eagles with flaming arrows in itself situates the eagle in the position of antifire: we understand how the Caucasian eagle, identified

<hr>

59. The Greek (and Latin) texts have been brought together conveniently and translated in V. V. Latyshchev, *Scythica et Caucasica* (St. Petersburg, 1890), 1: 635.

60. Ibid., pp. 162 and 223, respectively.

with water, might be destroyed by fire. But such a technique could not be used on the Greek eagle, who, on the contrary, is regenerated in the igneous element.

Faced with these problems, irresolvable within the limits of an article, one must cease trying to open up the pathways of history. I shall, then, limit myself to a modest but well-established conclusion: the same mythic ensemble, involving the reconquest of a natural element essential to the survival of humanity, was read "in the key of fire" among the Greeks, "in the key of water" among the Caucasians.

Marshall Sahlins

6

The Apotheosis of Captain Cook

> *When one god vanquishes another, he perpetuates the memory of his victory by the inauguration of a cult.*
>
> Hubert and Mauss, *Sacrifice*

European scholars have sometimes found it difficult to credit the idea that the people of Hawaii took Captain Cook for their own god Lono when he visited the Islands in 1778 and 1779. True, the Hawaiians did kill Cook on February 14, 1779—although why this should strike Christians as casting doubt upon his divinity is hard to say. In any case, within forty-eight hours of his death they asked when he was coming back. On the night of February 15, two priests of the temple in which Cook had been ritually received as Lono—one was the so-called tabuman, who had "constantly attended Captain Cook with a wand on shore, marching before him and making all the natives bow to him as he passed" —defied death at the hands of their own chief and the English by coming off to the *Resolution* while the hostilities following Cook's martyrdom were still in

This is a somewhat expanded version of the Kroeber Anthropological Society Annual Lecture delivered on May 7, 1977, and appearing in the *Papers of the Kroeber Anthropological Society*, nos. 53–54 (Spring and Fall, 1978) (used with permission of the publisher). Aside from standard sources in Hawaiian ethnography, as are cited in the text, the descriptions here rely on manuscript collections, mainly in Hawaii; a more complete exposition and documentation of Hawaiin kinship and polity will appear in a later work.

In citations from older accounts and journals, I have usually modernized spellings, especially of Hawaiian names.

course. According to Lieutenant King, one of the priests, "after his fears subsided and he had shed abundance of tears at the loss of the Erono [Lono], told us that he had brought us a part of him. He had a bundle under his arm" (Beaglehole 1967, p. 560). The bundle contained about ten pounds of Cook's hind parts. This share of the body had been given the head priest by the ruling chief, Kalaniopu'u–apparently for ritual disposal in the sea, as was normally done with the corruptible parts of a high chief's remains. (Nevertheless, the two priests took the opportunity to inveigh against the paramount; nor was it the first time he had allowed them the posterior end of the many wonderful things the English left on Hawaii.) For Lieutenant King the horror of the occasion was rendered bizarre by the "singular question" the priests asked of him, namely, when would Lono return, a question King afterwards heard from other Hawaiians, along with fears about what Cook would do to them then. It is something like Lévi-Strauss's observation on similar incidents in Latin American history, where the Indians killed the Spaniards in order to see if they really were gods, even as the Spaniards were slaughtering Indians because they took them to be less than men–thus posing the question of who did more credit to the human race (Lévi-Strauss 1974, pp. 75-76).[1]

In the published account of the *Voyage*, King adds that the idea the Hawaiians entertained of Cook's return "agrees with the general tenour of their conduct toward him, which showed that they considered him as a being of superior nature" (Cook 1784, 3:39). A later and more skeptical historiography would turn on the equivocation in this phrase, "a being of superior nature." Motivated I believe by a concern to show that Hawaiians are as realistic and rational as anyone else, and could not mistake a man for a god, some scholars have supposed that the homage accorded to Cook, such as the prostration tabu, indicates only that he was conceived as a being of superior *social* nature, like their own titled chiefs. The elaborate deference was merely the kind of hospitality Polynesians afford any visitor of high status. But quite apart from the empirical evidence that must be brought to bear, what this secular interpretation neglects is, first, that the distinction between a tabu chief and a god is not true to Hawaiian thought and, second, that Cook was as immortal in the European view as he was in the Hawaiian.

1. Trevenan (Beaglehole 1967, p. 561n) and Samwell (Beaglehole 1967, p. 1217) also report Hawaiian assertions that Cook would return in a short time. Only Bligh among contemporary observers denied the Hawaiians believed this, characterizing the idea as absurd in marginal notes to the part of the *Voyage* published by King–whom Bligh detested (Gould 1928, p. 383).

Apropos of Lévi-Strauss's remarks, there were remarkable parallels between the Hawaiian reception of Cook and the Aztecs' welcome of Cortes, the god Quetzalcoatl returned. These parallels will be developed in another paper.

For recent views on Cook's divinity, see the Introduction to Beaglehole (1967), especially p. cxliv. Note that the skepticism of the great Maori anthropologist, Sir Peter Buck, regarding the pre-mortem deification of Cook is rather the opposite of the opinions of the nineteenth-century Hawaiian historians, such as Kamakau. These scholars allowed that Cook was originally taken for Lono but that his death proved him otherwise.

The Hawaiian view runs parallel to classic concepts of divine kingship (Hocart 1927; 1936). Chiefs entitled to prostration were "gods, fire, heat and raging blazes" (Kamakau 1961, p. 4); they were called "divine, *akua*" (Malo 1951, p. 54). Gods, fire and heat were interrelated—but not simply because people who violated the chief's tabus would be consumed in sacrifice. Like the personified Polynesian notion of brilliance or light from whom they descended (*Wakea*), these high chiefs represented the heavenly generative powers of form and visibility; like the sun, they caused all things to be seen but could not themselves be gazed upon without injury. It is consistent that one Hawaiian account attributes Cook's murder to a lowborn person of the backcountry who could not recognize the Captain (Martin 1817, 2:67). Such commoners were *makawela*, people of "burnt eyes"—just as the eyes of the transgressor of the chief's tabu, placed in a bowl of kava, were swallowed in sacrificial rites by a ceremonial impersonator of the chief (Malo 1951; Valeri 1976). Prostrating himself, the commoner escaped such a fate, but he arose only to see the earthly traces of the chief's passage. When the great King Kamehameha received the Russian explorer Kotzebue in 1816, he had to explain why he appeared in such simple dress: "The uniforms which King George wears," he said, "shine very much. But they can be of no service to me, because Kamehameha outshines everything" (Kotzebue 1821, 2:193). Later kings and chiefs, less sure of their celestial position, would practically monopolize foreign trade to import for their own use the brightest silks of China and textiles of New England. Exasperated Honolulu traders sent back letters to Boston pleading for "articles of a showy kind" (Marshall Letters: Jones 9/3/1823). "Don't send any more blue," wrote one, "they will not sell" (Marshall Letters: Crocker 16/8/1823). For the Hawaiian market, the capitalist mode of production was being organized by the Polynesian conception of *mana*. What was happening in Hawaii may be judged from the observation of an early Christian convert, compelled to disabuse the traders' missionary countrymen by explaining that the people were flocking to the churches not to hear the Word but to see the chiefs (Stewart and Richards 1825, p. 250). Therein lies a tale of why the Hawaiian to this day has an aloha shirt on his back.

In sum, such were chiefs who were gods, *akua*. Cook likewise had been greeted by prostration from his first moment ashore to the day of his death, and by the god-name Lono ("Orono," "Erono," etc.) throughout his second visit. This did not mean that the divinity of traditional Hawaiian chiefs was thereby eclipsed. With unconcealed delight, the American merchant Charles Hammatt relates in his diary that on a certain day in June, 1823, when the head missionary Hiram Bingham went to remonstrate with the royally drunk King Liholiho, "and told him God was not pleased with such conduct," Liholiho replied, "I am God myself. What the hell! Get out of my house; go to your own house. God damn!" (Hammatt, 1/6/1823). Clearly, to suppose that Cook was to the Hawaiians only a chief and not a god is merely to impose a late and inappropriate set of native European categories.

Besides, the secular interpretation neglects a basic agreement between eighteenth century European and Hawaiian thought on the divinity in the relation of hierarchy. If Hawaiians did not believe that Cook was truly dead, finished, once they had killed him, neither could many of Cook's own crew. James Trevenan, midshipman of the *Resolution*, recalled the sentiment in a marginal note penned on his own copy of the published *Voyage*. In phrases that faithfully echo the Hawaiian reaction, he wrote: "The fact that I (as well as many others) had been so used to look up to him [Captain Cook] as our good genius, our safe conductor, and as *a kind of superior being*, that I could not suffer myself, I did not dare, to think he could fall by the hands of Indians, over whose minds and bodies, also, he had been accustomed to rule with uncontrolled sway" (Trevenan, MS, emphasis mine). Durkheim might have been pleased with this one well-chosen (if draconic) experiment in support of his thesis that spiritual power is a transfiguration of societal constraint.

Yet more, the intercultural agreement on Cook's transfiguration organized historical practice as much as religious theory. In the seven days following Cook's death, the English entered into protracted negotiations, punctuated by hostilities, with a view towards recovery of the body. At one point the English seamen cut off the heads of two Hawaiians and waved them before the assembled savages in order to make them understand the Christian imperatives of revenge and proper burial. People were dying that Cook might live, for among Hawaiians and English alike this struggle over the corpse was motivated by the conviction that only its proper disposition could guarantee the perpetuation of Cook's spirit. True that on the English side it was a matter of whether the remains would rise at Judgment; whereas, for Hawaiians it was more a question of whether they would sit in judgment. All along, the ritual dignities that Cook had enjoyed were designed to encompass his power and appropriate his protection to the Hawaiian chiefs. Now compromised by his murder at the hands of a rival—for such is the fate of all ruling chiefs however they may actually die— this protection would have to be secured through the ceremonial appropriation of his bones. In the strongest form, Hawaiian doctrine required that the long bones and skull, arranged in proper relative position, be set in a sacred effigy casket made of basketwork or sennit (*kai'ai*) and deposited in an appropriate temple. Ritual defleshment had rendered the dead chief a "true god" (*akua maoli*), while for his would-be successor, the acquisition of these deified bones, whether by violence or inheritance, was an essential condition of chiefly legitimacy; it was the acquisition of a proper godly ancestry (Malo 1951; Stokes 1930; Valeri 1976). Hence the proverb, applied to a great paramount of the past, but as we have seen also applicable to Cook, "Keawe returns, his remains bound in the sennit container" (Pukui and Elbert 1965, p. 100).[2]

2. The concept of a victory over one's predecessor is a common motif in installation rites of divine kings (Hocart 1927). On the *ka'ai* or sennit caskets, see also Hiroa 1957, pp. 573–77. As late as 1829, the caskets of previous rulers figured symbolically in attempts of the Hawaiian king (then Kamehameha III) to restore a traditional authority—this notably includes the *ka'ai* of Lonoikamakahiki, an instantiation of Lono, as was Cook (I'i 1959, p. 155).

The historical accounts of the Hawaiian treatment of Cook's corpse seem ambiguous on the point of whether Cook was also offered in temple sacrifice by the chief—which normally is followed by an ignominious disposition of the corpse—as well as ceremoniously defleshed.[3] This ambiguity is not altogether critical since it would be in a few years conceptually resolved by the place Cook assumed in the political cult, and in any case the death of a high chief is always testimony to the sacrificial powers of his successor. There is no doubt that the paramount Chief Kalaniopu'u, along with the head priest, went into ritual seclusion after Cook's death, which is the customary behavior of the successor to royal power during this liminal period of twofold corruption: of the corpse and, through temporary suspension of the tabus, of the social organism as well (Cook 1784, 3:66; Law, MS). But a second ambiguity is more intriguing and enduring. From here on out, both the English and the Hawaiians would claim to possess Cook's bones. The historical journals relate that on February 20 and 21, 1779, the Hawaiians ceremoniously surrendered to the English virtually a complete set of remains, said to be Cook's. These consisted mostly of defleshed and partially burnt bones, but the hands, which had been preserved, were indisputably the Captain's. The bones were appropriately confined to the deep, full fathom five at least. Yet in the first decade of the nineteenth century, contemporary accounts tell, they reappear, bound in a sennit container and carried by the priests of Lono in the annual rites of fertility, tax collection, and chieftainship called the Makahiki.[4]

By the same date at least four different engravings depicting the assumption of Captain Cook into heaven had been published in European books (Murray-Oliver 1975, p. 199). One, by Loutherbourg, was called "The Apotheosis of Cook" (fig. 6.1). Another, appearing as frontispiece to Bankes's *Modern System of Universal Geography*, bears the legend: "*Neptune* raising *Captn Cook* up to Immortality; a *Genius* introducing him with a wreath of Oak, and *Fame* introducing him to History. In the Front Ground are the *Four Quarters* of the *World* presenting to *Brittania* their various Stores" (fig. 6.2). The front ground thus

3. For representative Hawaiian statements on the treatment of Cook's body, see: Lahainaluna Students 1839, p. 66; Dibble 1909, p. 27; Kamakau 1961, p. 103; Westerwelt 1923, p. 112; Ellis 1828, p. 117; Tyerman and Bennet 1831, 1: 376. The book by the Lahainaluna Students (1938), assembled by the missionary Dibble and translated by Tinker (1839), contains information gathered from old Hawaiians in the Lahaina area in the 1830s; much of this is repeated in Dibble's own history (1909; first published in 1843) and in later Hawaiian accounts.

4. For detailed accounts of Cook's death and the incidents that followed, see Beaglehole 1967.

Lieutenant King had also noted that subsequent to the defleshment and before the return of the remains to the English, various parts of the body as well as the skull and long bones had been distributed to several chiefs (Cook 1784, 3:78). It is, of course, possible that many of the bones received on the *Resolution* were not Cook's, since four marines were also killed and carried off in the action at Kealakekua. Nineteenth-century historians, Hawaiian and European, often compromise the discrepancies by indicating that the Hawaiians gave some of Cook's bones back and kept some for worship. Ellis (1828, p. 120) is specifically the most consistent with the Cook journalists, since he writes that the ribs and breastbone only were carried in procession by the Lono priests, and these were not mentioned among the remains returned in 1779.

Figure 6.1 "The Apotheosis of Captain Cook," by Jacques de Loutherbourg

Figure 6.2 Frontispiece to *Bankes's Modern System of Universal Geography*

gives a clue to the tenets of the faith in which Cook held such exalted position: it was Imperialism.

This being the doctrine, it was inevitable that the Anglo-Saxon cult of Cook should outlast the Hawaiian. By 1819, the Makahiki Festival had been suspended, the ancient tabus abolished, the temples and images of Hawaiian worship largely destroyed. All this happened in the famous "overthrow of the tabus," the event reckoned in one Hawaiian source as "the time they tabued the temples." American missionaries arrived in 1820 and began to spread through the Islands. In July, 1825, Lord Byron, cousin to the poet and commander of H.M.S. Blonde, visited the Bay of Kealakekua where Cook had fallen. There, in a rite of four days, beginning with a reverential collection of pieces of the true rock where the deed was done, Byron's party administered the coup de grace to the Hawaiian cult. By 1837, incidentally, this rock had been reduced to less than a quarter of its original size by various Europeans repeating the Byronic ceremonies, including some Spaniards who not only collected relics of the rock but, as an entire ship's company, "knelt upon it, and offered up prayers for the hero's soul" (Taylor 1929, p. 77). By 1846, the rock had entirely disappeared. (See also Taylor 1929, pp. 42-43, for the oration delivered at "this sacred and hallowed spot" at the sesquicentennial celebration of Cook's visit.) Progressing a few miles south, Byron's company, by permission of the reigning chiefs in Honolulu, then penetrated the sacred "house of Keawe" where the bundled remains of Hawaiian kings were still enshrined (Stokes 1930). To the dismay of the guardian priest, they stripped the temple of its images and artifacts on the pretext of taking these "curiousities" for display in Britain. Although the priest resisted any indignities to the royal bones, Byron writes, he "assisted us with civility, although with reluctance, to spoil the *morai* [temple] of its previous contents [*viz.*, the wooden temple images], and the *Blonde* soon received on board almost all that remained of the ancient deities of the Islands" (Byron 1826, p. 202). Byron, it should be noted, had come to the Islands to return the remains of the Hawaiian king Liholiho, who died of measles in London in 1824. For his part, Liholiho, visiting Westminster Abbey shortly before his death, could on no account whatsoever be induced to enter the Chapel of Henry VII, since upon hearing that the ancient kings of *England* were buried there, he declared it was much too sacred for him. Although Byron reports this himself (Byron 1826, pp. 62, 199-202), he showed not even a decent sense of irony, let alone a reciprocal reverence for the Chapel of Keawe—a building "so sacred," wrote the artist of the *Blonde*, "that no white man before our arrival had ever by his presence profaned its threshold" (Dampier 1971, p. 67).

Returning after the pillage to Kealakekua, Byron completed the English reformation by erecting "a cross sacred to the memory of Captain Cook on the spot where his body was burnt." This "humble monument" had as its vertical piece a pillar of oak, ten feet high, into which a copper plate was inserted, bearing the following inscription:

Sacred
to the memory of
Capt. James Cook, R.N.
who discovered these Islands
in the year of our Lord 1778.
This humble monument is erected
by his countrymen,
in the year of our Lord, 1825.

The spot was promptly tabued by the local Hawaiian chief; later, to the same effect, it was deeded to the British government. And, although the Hawaiians had by 1825 largely ceased to believe in the divinity of Cook, or at least to ceremonially practice it, it was not (nor will it be) the last time the tribes of Angles and Saxons would piously erect a monument to him at this place (cf. Taylor 1929).[5]

I do not mean to suggest that the Hawaiian concept of Cook's divinity was a simple assimilation of European beliefs. We have to deal rather with a parallel encoding, of the kind that Laura and Paul Bohannan have described (in the African context) as "a working misunderstanding." It is a sort of symbolic serendipity, or at least a congruent attribution from two different cultural orders of a special meaningful value to the same event, so as to give it a privileged and determining place in history. The process does, then, raise a fundamental point concerning the role of structure in history, about which I digress for a moment.

At issue is the widespread and profound idea that history unfolds as a physical process, as an expansion in the modality of cultural order of the real-material resources and forces in play. Being thus constituted by prevailing material constraints, culture would appear as the self-mediation of nature, the natural world reproduced as social form through the effects of utilitarian interest and empirical rationality. Yet what anthropologists often observe in just such phenomena as "acculturation" is an unaccountable disproportion between the "objective causes" and the "cultural effects" when these are considered simply in terms of physical magnitudes and mechanical relationships. When the first missionaries debarked in Hawaii, they found the traditional religion had already been abolished because, the ex-high priest confided to them, there was but one great god in heaven.[6] In the same vein, neither could Cook's divinity have been

---

5. For other versions of Byron's pillage of the Hale o Keawe and related activities at Honaunau and Kealakekua, see Dampier 1971 and Bloxam 1925. In contrast to Byron's language, Dampier describes the priest of the temple as moved to "indignation at this sacrilegious rape.... He was obliged, however, to submit." Dampier had to interrupt his sketch of the inside of the temple-house (thus doubling the historical losses) as a consequence of the sudden manifestation of "rapacious inclinations" on the part of the English; he thereupon, "and regardless of the divine punishment attending such shameless sacrilege, took ample share in the depopulation of this ancient sanctuary" (Dampier 1971, p. 67).

6. This vignette appears in the recollections of James Hunnewell (Hunnewell Collection, Box 58), citing a conversation with the high priest Hewahewa (respecting the abolition of

the logical *sequitur* to the force he exerted, since in his relations with Hawaiians he took great care to keep violence at a minimum—not to mention that it was *they* who killed *him*. In all such instances, the disparity between the "real pressures" and the historical outcomes has to be made up from the cultural structures at issue, from the significance they had to bestow on persons, objects, and events. Pragmatic influence and functional efficacy are themselves symbolically constituted. True that if Cook had managed to get back into the ship's boat, everything would have been different. In this sense the event is irreducible. But that particular tide in the affairs of men at Kealakekua Bay cannot demonstrate any sort of ecological determinism or great-man theory of history apart from the way it was culturally appropriated. Henceforth, Cook in distinction to all other men and the British as opposed to all other nations were destined for a critical role in Hawaiian history—long after the English imperial presence had in fact been superseded by the American. For by virtue of Cook's sacrifice, the *mana* of the Hawaiian kingship was itself British.

To this day, the Union Jack flies in the upper left-hand corner of the state flag of Hawaii. King Kamehameha used to have the English colors waving in front of his house and from his canoe before he ever ceded the Island of Hawaii to Vancouver in 1794. By that year, each of the three principal chiefs of Hawaii had named one of their sons "King George." Indeed, the reason why Kamehameha's son Liholiho went to England (and to his untimely death) in 1824 was to secure King George's protection "against the encroachments of his chiefs" (Raquet to Adams, 8/3/1824, AH: Hist. and Misc.). In opposition to Liholiho, whose revenues and authority they were subverting by novel claims of hereditary right, these chiefs had become the party of the Americans. Especially they entered into a convenient religious and political alliance with the New England missionaries. Whereas Liholiho was never to join the American church—nor for that matter did any of his royal successors, although Kamehameha IV (Alexander Liholiho) was baptized in the Church of England—his rival chiefs showed themselves increasingly susceptible to Puritan tabus. Liholiho accordingly fell back on a received and opposing doctrine of sacred power, choosing to reactivate the protective *mana* of the English as it had been secured from his father's "good friend" and "brother," King George, through the manes of Cook and the machinations of Vancouver.[7]

the tabus in 1819) on board the *Thaddeus* before the pioneer missionaries had landed. The belief in Jehovah—"Akahi wale no Akua nui i loko o ka lani," as Hunnewell has it—was not necessarily general among Hawaiians. Nor was it a simple conclusion regarding European power so much as a selective appropriation of that power by certain chiefs—an issue that will be treated at length in a forthcoming work.

7. Although Kamehameha's cession of Hawaii was not accepted by the British Crown, Kamehameha and, after him, Liholiho conceived themselves and their territories as subordinate to "King George" (cf. Mathison 1825, pp. 366–67). Kamehameha continued to refer to the English king as his "brother" at least until 1811 (Franchère 1969, p. 63; Bell 1929, 1(6):83). On Liholiho's struggles with his chiefs, the general situation is described in Kuykendall 1968 and Bradley 1968; excellent political and economic detail is found in papers of New England traders of the period, such as John C. Jones (Marshall Letters), J. Hunnewell, C. Bullard, and C. Hammatt.

We begin to see why Byron could exercise such high-handed authority in Hawaii, despite the fact that the English had been out of the running in the Pacific sandalwood and fur trade for decades. The enduring and effective British presence in Hawaiian international relations remained that of Captain James Cook. By going back to the accounts of English captains in the years immediately after Cook's death—when these captains were still considered by Hawaiians to be his sons—we get some idea how his instrumental value was structurally developed. When Meares came into Kealakekua in 1787,

> The numbers of them which surrounded the ship, with a view to obtain permission to go to *Britanee*, to the friends of their beloved Cook, are incredible. . . . Presents were poured in upon us from the chiefs, who were prevented by the multitude from approaching the vessel, and the clamorous cry of *Britanee*, *Britanee*, was for a long time vociferated from every part, and without ceasing (Meares 1790, p. 9; cf. p. 388).

James Colnett, at Hawaii as master of the *Argonaut* in 1791, records in his journal that since Cook's death the Hawaiians had suffered "a great deal of sickness which never before this affected them, which they alleged to having killed him." (Note that in this respect, the Hawaiians' perception of Cook's persisting influence—or is it influenza?—was not empirically unsound.) Colnett continues:

> They made strict enquiry of me, if ever he would come back again, and when I saw him last. I told them [that] having been constantly in their part of the world, I could not tell, but this I knew, the Spaniards were coming to take their country from them, and make them slaves. They enquired if C[aptain] Cook had sent them, and how long he would be angry with them, and what they should do to get C[aptain] Cook to entreat his ares [*ali'i*, "chiefs"] to send and assist them against the Spanish. Since I was [in Hawaii] in the *Prince of Wales* [1788], two volcanoes have opened on the sea side of the Isle, which burned night and day with great fury and tremendous explosion, which they say C[aptain] C[ook] has caused (Colnett MS).

Now Colnett's complicity in Hawaiian ideas about Cook's godliness was something more than "bad faith." It suggests how a given code of the conjecture may become the organizing frame of history: functionally encompassing the event and also ordering the further empirical course. Colnett exploits the Hawaiian link to Cook in order to develop the English opposition to the Spanish—who were likewise in the Islands at the time, in a ship recently captured from Colnett. The values thus bestowed on the English and Spanish in Hawaiian eyes thenceforth affect their commercial and other dealings with the two nations. The sacrifice of Cook becomes a meaningful condition of historical praxis. Of course, the finalities as well as the categories involved in this intergroup coding must be sought in the respective cultural orders. Broadly speaking, the Europeans entered into political contact with Hawaiians as a means to economic ends; whereas, for Hawaiians, the trade with Europeans was an economic means to political ends.

But within each side of the intercultural equation, internal competition then developed through a motivated engagement of corresponding oppositions on the other side. We have already seen an example in the way the differentiation between Hawaiian chiefs and people was made to turn on a European distinction between "fancy goods" and "plain goods" in the matter of imported cloth. The opposition of indigenous categories is symbolically linked to parallel contrasts within the European vis-à-vis, thus mapping the course of history on coordinates of meaningful difference. In the same way, the opposition between the protective Cook and malignant influences, exploited by Colnett and others in the eighteenth century, was built into a structure of political relations that, by Liholiho's time, assumed the familiar form of a Saussurean proportion. Ritual heir to Cook, the young Hawaiian king stood to the chiefs threatening his rule as the British were to the Americans.[8] In their own struggles, king and chiefs respectively valorized the conflicting interests of English and Americans—and of course vice versa. The dialectic of valuation thus constitutes the relations and changes of the so-called "acculturation." Surely, I have condensed the process, but perhaps not too much to raise doubts about the common conviction that a structural understanding is antithetical to a historical sense.

In arguing against the secular historiography of Cook I may also be guilty of a quixotic exaggeration. The idea that Cook was not really considered a god is actually the minority scholarly opinion. On the other hand, the standard explanation of his deification, common to European and Hawaiian historians alike, may also be exaggerated. The standard explanation is that Cook was taken for Lono because his arrival coincided in time and objective details with the annual rites of this god, the Makahiki. The masts of his ship looked like the image of Lono carried in procession around the island during the Makahiki—in the same clockwise direction, moreover, that Cook took around Hawaii. Kealakekua, "The Road of the God," was supposed to be the home place of Lono, or else of several later chiefly incarnations of whom Cook was also identified; the temple at Kealakekua (Hikiau) where Cook was adored was a temple of Lono; its priesthood was of that cult; and so forth. While we can retain the idea that Cook, arriving appropriately with the rising of the Pleiades during his second visit, was associated with Lono among all other gods, and that the priests in question among all other Hawaiians believed in and promoted his divinity, beyond that the standard opinion needs to be revised. This temple (Hikiau) at Kealakekua was devoted to the war god Ku, not Lono; it was a temple of human sacrifice, specifically forbidden in the peaceful rites of Lono. When Cook came on his second visit, the Hawaiian ruling chief, Kalaniopu'u, was fighting a war on Maui, though the received descriptions of the Makahiki

8. On another level, the continued opposition between Kamehameha's domain and the quasi-independent chiefdom of Kauai (acknowledging the superiority of the former but itself never conquered) was linked to the opposition of England and American during the War of 1812 (Anon, *Atahualpa*). Afterwards, the Kauai paramount chief formed an alliance with the Russians, in contrast to Kamehameha and his English (Pierce 1965).

assert that war is interdicted throughout this period. It would take another paper to detail all the empirical objections to the standard theory. Apart from the contradictions to it my subsequent discussion will imply, suffice it to say here that we have no evidence of a protracted four-month Makahiki cycle until Vancouver's voyages of 1793 and 1794, during the reign of Kamehameha on Hawaii. Cook was not considered a god because of empirical resemblances between the events of his voyage and details of the Makahiki rites; rather, these rites were latterly elaborated, primarily by Kamehameha, *as an iconic representation of Cook's voyage.* The Makahiki as we have come to know it is testimony to Cook's sacrifice as a source of legitimacy of that chieftainship, and at the same time of the transformation of that chieftainship into statehood under a sign of peace, Lono, thereby eclipsing the cult of tribal violence whose focus had been the god Ku.[9]

Nor was Cook the only European captain to become the object of veneration. Nathaniel Portlock, also British, landed in Hawaii several times as commander of a fur-trading vessel. Of his first visit it is necessary to mark only that he came in May and June, 1786 (rather than in the Makahiki period of November-February), that his crew fished up a large shark which was given to the Hawaiians, and that he made a present of an armchair from his cabin to the priest-chief of Kauai named Opunui. On his next visit to Kauai, in February, 1787, Opunui escorted him to a certain "house" in Waimea Valley:

> I found this house to be very large, commodious and clean, with a new mat on the floor; on the left side of the door was a wooden image of a tolerably large size, *seated in a chair which nearly resembled one of our armed chairs.* There was a glass-plat all around the image and a small railing made of wood; beside the chair were several to-e's [iron adzes] and other small articles. My friend informed me that this house had been built with the to-e I had given him on my calling at Oneehow [Niihau], and that the other articles were presents that I had made him at different periods, and that *the image was in commemoration of my having been amongst them.* Few people were admitted into this house. Amongst other articles in it were several drums; one in particular was very large, the head of which was made out of the skin of

9. Dorothy B. Barrère first suggested to me that the Makahiki ceremonies were developed as a representation of Cook's voyage; it is her genial idea. This does not mean there was no such ceremony before. Firstfruits and renewal ceremonies coinciding with the phases of the Pleiades cycle are common in Polynesia and Micronesia, often under terms cognate to "Makahiki"—normally the name of the Pleiades (cf. Makemson 1941). Various elements of the Hawaiian Makahiki rites as described by Malo (1951) and Kelou Kamakau (Fornander 1916-19, 6(1): 34-35) are analogous to harvest rites on other Polynesian islands; other elements of the Hawaiian ceremonies have clearly been integrated from the local human sacrifice and *akua* fishing rites (the latter corresponding nearly to the date of Cook's death). Hence the position taken here is not that a Makahiki ceremony was previously lacking but that it was subject to considerable manipulation and development by Kalaniopu'u and Kamehameha. As we shall see, the appropriation of Cook's death within the Makahiki eventually resumed and replaced the traditional sacrificial rituals sponsored by Hawaiian ruling chiefs.

the large shark I have already mentioned; and I was told *these drums were dedicated to their gods* (Portlock 1789, pp. 192-93; emphasis mine).

By what distinction, then, did Cook become a uniquely powerful god? To answer correctly we have to recognize that he was not in the first instance unique. Divinity inhered in the relation the Hawaiians conceived to all these strangers with "white skin and bright, flashing eyes" come for a far off place. Nothing foreign was merely human to them. Cook's godliness was a specialization of the generalized relationship the Hawaiians more or less widely entertained to all the Europeans, not excluding the ships themselves and the objects carried on them. And whereas the divine status of the general body of Europeans would be eroded in the pragmatic oppositions of trade, and by an arithmetic of pollution that despoiled the white man's tabus by the secularity [*noa*] of the women with whom they had intercourse, the sacrifice of the body of the Great Commander insured that he lived on as representation of the initial relation of hierarchy.

The very first Hawaiians who came off to Cook's ship at Kauai on January 20, 1778, made a peculiar and pious oration before they dared climb aboard. The prayer was a way of freeing the ship from its tabus, or else of consecrating themselves that they might enter it, in the way they would before entering a temple—which, according to one Hawaiian recollection, they took it to be. Coming on deck, they stared at the things about them in indescribable amazement, until one of them, without the least trouble to conceal it, took up the sounding line and proceeded to carry it off. Halted by the sailors' incantations of bourgeois doctrines of private property, he was asked what he thought he was doing. "I am only going to put it in my boat," he said (Beaglehole 1967, p. 265). Clearly the cargo cult that Melanesians would later dream about, these Polynesians for one fleeting moment actually realized. "They thought they had a right to everything they could lay their hands upon," reads the published *Voyage*. But, "they soon laid aside a conduct which, we convinced them, they could not persevere in with impunity" (Cook 1784, vol. 2:205). Nonetheless the idea persevered and, according to Hawaiian tradition, the good news was spread from island to island: "They have doors in the sides of their bodies (i.e., pockets)... into these openings they thrust their hands and take out many valuable things— their bodies are full of treasure" (Dibble 1909, p. 23).

For Hawaiians, the outside place—as the outer parts of the known world, or as the sea is to the inhabited land—is traditionally the site of ultrahuman powers. This distance in space is also a remove in time; the far-off is the homeland of the gods and thus the origin of cultural things. At the furthest horizon the ends of the earth meet the limits of the sky; hence, "Kahiki," the distant foreign lands, are also above, "heavenly." That too is the status of ruling chiefs—*lani*, "heavenly"—since tradition tells they came from foreign parts to impose by divine powers (*mana*) the separations (*tabus*) that constitute the cultural order. Cannibals and sharks, they effected this order through violence: they "ate" the land, a metaphor at once of chiefly rule and of the appropriation of women from the native "sons of the land" (*kamaaina*). But as we have already seen, this human world of forms was likewise an act of chiefly impregnation: of generation by the celestial light that renders all things visible. I mention these arcane doctrines to help explain a passage in Lieutenant King's account where he says that, even apart from Cook, "they regarded us *generally*, as a race of people superior to themselves," saying often that the great *akua* (god) "dwelled in our country" and the paramount chief's god likewise "lived among us" (Cook 1784, 3:159, 160; emphasis mine).[10] On the Hawaiian side, the kind of cultural coding this entails can be found in the same chant of the great Oahu chief, Kauli'i, whose reputation (asserted by some) as conqueror of the Islands is motivated precisely by his exploits as voyager to foreign lands, to Kahiki:

> Kahiki,
> Where the langue is strange,
> To Kahiki belong the people who ascend
> To the backbone of heaven;
> And while above they tread,
> And look down below.
> There are none like us in Kahiki:
> Kahiki has but one kind of people, the *haole*
>   "foreigner," "white man."
> They are like unto gods;
> I am like a man.
> A man, indeed,
> Wandering about,
> And the only one who got there.
>   (Fornander 1916-19, 4(2):374.)

Now Kauli'i lived several generations before Cook, and it is possible that this reference to the *haole*—a term applied in historic times to the white man exclusively—is a post facto insertion in the traditional chant. But to then dismiss the text for its anachronism would be, paradoxically, to miss its historical sense. Exactly by its retrodiction (or retention) of the *haole* in the context of indigenous categories, the chant discloses the structural logic in the Hawaiian interpretation of the European experience. Should we also by the same his-

10. Certain Hawaiian categorical distinctions and relations alluded to in this paragraph are exemplified further along in the text. The mythical corpus (e.g., Fornander 1916-19) is a main source of the present analysis, along with commentary such as Beckwith's (1919; 1970; 1972) and Luomala's (1949). Also valuable in this connection are Mary Kawena Pukui's ethnographic observations (see Handy and Pukui 1972; Pukui, Haertig and Lee 1972). A text particularly germane to the coding of Cook and European power is Kamakau (1845). Above all, I should like to pay tribute to Valerio Valeri's excellent analysis of Hawaiian myth and polity (1976), which has been a source of much useful reflection and inspiration.

toricist scruples ignore the Hawaiian tradition, recorded in the nineteenth century, that the Europeans were at first taken to be cannibals? This is again like Lévi-Strauss's remarks on the mutual slaughter of the Indians and the conquistadores. Both the English and the Hawaiians were very anxious to determine if the others ate human flesh—although for different and opposed reasons: the English because they feared the natives were dangerous savages, the Hawaiians because they believed the foreigners were powerful gods. As it turns out, the Hawaiians were not cannibals in practice (that is, apart from the symbolism in rites of chieftainship), but they had good reason to conclude the white men were. Upon seeing Cook's crew devouring red watermelons (from California), they could only exclaim, "Gods, indeed! They eat the flesh of man" (Lanainaluna Students 1839, p. 64). My point, however, is that the divinity which eventually settled upon Cook was not an intellectual mistake, contingent on substantial if accidental analogies between the empirical behavior of the English and the mythical thought of the "natives." The substantialization of reference, this idea of meaning as the naming of objects of observation, is an error of our own thought. The Hawaiian response applies in the first place to the *relationship* of hierarchy, which for them was an established fact before the first white man from Kahiki ever stepped on their shores. The supernaturalism, then, was not so much an interpretation of the European experience as it was indistinguishable from the perception itself of that experience.

Analogy then followed from the principle of divinity, rather than vice versa, and it was widely applied to the whole of Cook's people as well as to the objects they brought and the actions they took. A pile of coconuts on deck and a heap of bullock hides evoked allusions to legendary sea monsters, presumed to have been slain en route by the powerful strangers. Kamakau records other recollections:

> Good-looking gods they were! They spoke rapidly. Red was the mouth of the god. When they saw the strangers letting out ropes the natives called them Ku-of-the-tree-fern (Kupulupulu) and Coverer-of-the-island (Mokuhali'i). These were gods of the canoe builders in the forest. When they say them painting the ship they said, "There are Ma'ikoha' [a man transformed into the first paper mulberry] and Ehu [Fair-haired] daubing their canoe, and Lanahu (Charcoal) daubing on the black!" When they saw the strangers smoking they said, "There are Lono-pele and his companions [of the volcano family of gods] breathing fire from their mouths! (Kamakau 1961, p. 99).

European fireworks provide another significant anachronism, since Hawaiian tradition alleges they were shot from the ships on the very first night (Kamakau 1961, p. 95), though the Cook sources do not mention them until the second coming, a year later. But the historical displacement of this astonishing mediation between earth and heaven—in the form moreover of the flying sorcery of the chief's god Ku—can be reconciled by the recorded reaction to fireworks displays put on by later visitors, such as Vancouver in 1793:

The first Skyrocket actually staggered them with surprise; as if with one voice a general sound was heard expressive of wonder and amazement. Balloons, Flower Pots, Roman Candles, Mines, and Water Rockets astonished them past conception; they could only express the inferiority of Owhyhee [Hawaii] and praise the prodigies of Brittania (Manby 1929: I(3):43). To Maiha-Maiha, [Kamehameha, King of Hawaii] would frequently cry in the midst of his surprise, "poor Owhyhee [Hawaii], you are no more" (Bell 1929, p. 82).

Fear and despair were not the only reactions to the sudden arrival of these beings "of superior nature." It is important that the gods—or what is here the same, chiefs come from Kahiki—were ambiguous in Hawaiian conceptions: usurpers, they were also protectors; by violence, they established order; blinding, they caused all things to be seen; by sacrifice, they gave life to the kingdom. In brief, the chief holds the power of death—but as ultimate sign of the control of life, including the power to bestow it. Hence the observation repeated over and again in the Cook documents: everywhere the English were greeted with inexpressible joy. I can only allude to the fantastic scene at Kealakekua in 1779, when the ships came to anchor surrounded by a flotilla of 1,000 canoes and thousands of other people swimming in the water and standing on the beaches—singing. Lieutenant Riou's log book entry laconically captures the emotion, "towed and sailed in, amidst an innumerable number of canoes, the people in which were singing and rejoicing all the way." The Hawaiian historian completes the tableau of the same event as viewed from the other side: "Their happiness knew no bounds; they leaped for joy: 'Now shall our bones live; our *aumakua* [ancestral god] has come back" (Kamakau 1961, p. 98).

The way the English then behaved at Kealakekua Bay was not calculated to disabuse the Hawaiians of this belief. Quite apart from Cook's own passive acceptance of the dignities of his installation as Lono at the chiefly temple of Hikiau and again at the adjacent "House of Lono," the English generally, if unwittingly, entered into the role the Hawaiians cast for them so as to give "concrete thought" opportunity after opportunity to draw the appropriate metaphoric conclusions. I mention only a few incidents born of this working misunderstanding. The astronomical observatory was pitched directly adjacent to Hikiau temple, where it was protected by the tabu sticks of the priests. Asked what they were doing there, the English replied they were looking at the sun—of all things; the Hawaiians promptly dubbed the astronomical instruments "by the name of the Etua [gods], and supposed they were our gods and that we worshipped them" (Samwell in Beaglehole 1967, p. 1186). The sacred houses of the temple itself were taken over as an infirmary and by sailmakers to repair the ships' canvas. Since all the while the priests were bringing offerings to the Europeans about the temple, given without the hint of a demand for repayment—and in the manner, form, and trembling appropriate to prestations to the gods—there was not even any objection when Lieutenant King asked to have the wooden fence of the shrine for firewood, not even when the sailors thereupon proceeded to carry off the wooden images for the same purpose. As the English understood this temple to be a burying ground, based on previous experiences in Polynesia, it did not surprise them either that the ruling chief, Kalaniopu'u, asked them to bring there the body of a seaman who had died aboard ship. The fact was that Hikiau was a temple of human sacrifice, and the skulls the English saw there were the testimony of the chief's power over those who transgressed his tabus and whose death transformed the central temple image into his "living god." So when Captain Cook and Lieutenant King read the Christian services over poor old William Watman, they had an attentive and "well-behaved" audience in the priests of the temple, who, after the English had finished, proceeded to recite their own prayers and throw offerings of pigs and bananas into the grave. Lieutenant King seems to have been touched and he suffered them to stop, but for the next three nights, "Kao [the high priest] and the rest of them surrounded the grave, killed hogs, sung a great deal, in which acts of piety and good will," as King deemed them, "they were left undisturbed" (Beaglehole 1967, p. 517).

One need not suppose that all Hawaiians shared the interpretations incident to the cult of the *haole* that was developing at Kealakekua Bay.[11] Indeed the people's very joy at the Europeans' coming evoked customary practices that could not help but pollute these gods—that eventually would secularize them, even as the martyred Cook was uniquely apotheosized. History reenacted that separation of earth and heaven, men and gods, which gives the famous "evolutionary" character to Polynesian myth. As the structure stood at Cook's arrival, the Europeans were to Hawaiians in general as their own chiefs, likewise godly beings from Kahiki, were to the common people. Still another anachronistic prophecy, said to have applied equally to the conquest of Oahu by Maui chiefs in 1785 and the arrival of Cook, encodes this epigramatically: "The land is the sea's" (Kamakau 1961, p. 134; Fornander 1916-19, 6:287n; Thrum 1921, pp. 203-4). The meaning can be gauged from a few lines of the Kumulipo origin chant:

> Those of the sea take to the land,
> Creep this way and that,
> The family of creepers multiply,
> The ancient line and the new line intermingle,
> The new line becomes the genealogy of chiefs
> (Beckwith 1970, p. 294).

11. King cites one apparently (though not necessarily) secular view that the Europeans had come from a place where food was short (Cook 1784, 3:26). He also notes that one man put a number of ethnographic questions to him about European customs and beliefs, including "Who was our god?"—questions attributed in the published *Voyage* to the priest Kanaina of Kealakekua (Cook 1784, 3:131), but in King's journal to the Kauai chief Ka'eo (Beaglehole 1967, p. 625).

The reference of the last lines is to the taking of women, hence of indigenous fertile powers, by the invading chiefs; as in Western Polynesia, the people of the land are wife-givers to the chiefs. This helps explain the so-called mass prostitution that made of every European voyage a successful observation of the transit of Venus. It is critical, however, that the sexual receptivity of Hawaiian women did not initially have the notorious character of "prostitution" that was destined to transform it into a mode of commoner trade. For the women were "but little influenced by interested motives in their intercourse with us, as they would almost use violence to force you into their embrace regardless whether we gave them anything or not" (Beaglehole 1967, p. 1085; Ellis 1782, 2:153). The Hawaiian sense is better judged by an incident attending Cook's departure for the last time, thirteen months after his first visit, when a number of men and women came off in canoes, and, under the direction of the women, the men came on the deck and deposited in its crevices the naval cords of newborn children. Behind this lay a whole panoply of custom of which we need only retain *wawahi*, "to break open." *Wawahi* was the offering of a commoner woman to a ruling chief (alternatively to a god) in the hope that the firstborn child would be sired by the chief. The practice in turn has to be referred to the customary redistribution of land at the accession of a paramount, who thus "acts as a conqueror," threatening to progressively displace and impoverish the people who once held stewardships in favor of the chief's immediate followers. The recognition of kinship with the chief, however, could forestall or reverse this decline in status; then, Hawaiians say, "the bones of our grandparents will live."

Now when the commoner women flocked aboard Cook's and later ships, they did not confine their intercourse to the sexual. Pressed by their sailor consorts to enjoy the civilizational benefits of what one explorer called "social living" (as opposed to natural), they also ate with European men, and of forbidden foods such as pork, thus violating key tabus of the Hawaiian religion. The whole process affords a nice illustration of the fact that the deployment of a received structure in a new context produces no simple or stereotypic reproduction, but rather assigns new functional values to old oppositions and thereby orders an unprecedented course of events. For in the event, the Europeans were polluted. The combination of their tabu status with the secularity (*noa*) of women generated contamination. So in an extraordinary contrast with the ritual liberties taken by Cook and his crew, when Vancouver came to Kealakekua the English were strictly enjoined, on the strong request of King Kamehameha, from entering the temples or otherwise interfering with Hawaiian observances (Vancouver 1801, 3:221-23). When Vancouver left, Kamehameha could not even escort him up the coast, as was his wont, because the king had to go into ritual seclusion, (in part) to purify himself of the consequences of "his having lived in such social intercourse with us, who had eaten and drank in the company of women" (Vancouver 1801, 3:275). By 1793, the English had lost their godliness. But the gods had not yet lost their Englishness. And if the functional values accruing to the exchange of goods and women had separated the Hawaiians from the divine power loose upon the land, there remained the sacrificed Cook to mediate between them.

Malinowski (to invoke another ancestral spirit) has left us with mythical ideas insufficient to account for the way Polynesians encompass the present by the past. In his famous notion of myth as "charter," Malinowski understood the legend to be the justification of existing relations, supposing the relations themselves were pragmatically fashioned out of the interests and practices of "real life." A utilitarian praxis is accorded the privileged analytic position, instrumentally shaping the past according to its own project—if not also formally constituting the past as a projection of itself. In the case of Hawaii, we have seen some of these anachronistic tricks the living play on the dead, but it deserves reemphasis that the retrodiction is a secondary formation on a much more fundamental movement from the past into the present. For a people who do not distinguish the genealogical bard from the political counselor, history must always repeat itself, since only the second time is it event. The first time it is myth.[12]

The structure of Polynesian mythical time is logically adapted to this paradigmatic function. The earliest mythical figures are divine personifications of basic cultural categories—as Papa and Wakea, Earth Mother and Sky Father or, more generally, surface and light—whose narrative interaction is an active form of the right relationships between these abstract concepts. As myth gives way to legend, divine forces are replaced by heroic chiefs, but the logical continuity between the two is guaranteed by their genealogical connection, since by Polynesian kinship-ideas the ancestor is a general class of which his descendants are particular instances. Nor does it merely follow that legendary chiefs are instantiations of cultural relationships; the present itself reproduces the same code—"life is ours; our ancestors have returned."

There is a story often repeated in early historical texts about various attempts to convince King Kamehameha of the relative superiority of the white man's gods. Usually (but not always) the European protagonist is identified as Vancouver. The American trader Townsend, for example, heard the following in 1798:

> Captain Vancouver was very anxious to Christianize these people, but that can never be done until they are more civilized. The King Amma-amma-kah [Kamehameha] told Capt. Vancouver that he would go with him on to the high mountain Mona Roah [Mauna Loa] and they would both jump off together, each calling on their separate gods of protection, and if Capt. Vancouver's god saved him, but himself was not saved by his god, then his people would believe as Capt. Vancouver did (Townsend 1888, p. 74).

12. I owe the following general ideas on the passage from the abstract categories to chiefly instantiations in Hawaiian myth to Mr. Gregory Schrempp, who is presently working comparatively on Hawaiian and Maori folklore.

The Russian explorer Golovnin added, in 1818:

> This experiment did not appeal to Vancouver, and he not only declined to
> perform it, he did not even mention it in his *Voyage*. Thus ended the dis-
> cussion on religion (Golovnin 1974, p. 49; cf. Cleveland n.d., p. 211).

Now this story is in fact a legendary allusion to a famous priest, Pa'ao, who
arrived from Kahiki (foreign lands) many generations past to overthrow the
indigenous ruler and install the line of outside chiefs in which Kamehameha
traced his own descent. As the myth goes,

> It was said that many gods asked Paao to accept and worship them as his
> deities. He had built his house on the edge of a precipice from which the
> koae (Bos'n bird) flew. Whenever any gods came to him Paao told them to
> fly from that precipice. The one returning alive should be his god and receive
> his worship. But when they leaped from the cliff they were dashed to pieces
> at its base. [To abbreviate: such was the fate of Lelekoae and Makuapali, but
> Maiuakaumana flew and became Pa'ao's god (Thrum 1923, pp. 46-47).]

It is mainly to their ancient predecessor Pa'ao that the American missionaries
owe the wary, if not cool, reception they were given by Hawaiian ruling chiefs
in 1820. Even the sacrificial idiom of disapproval later voiced by the Hawaiian
priest Hewahewa takes inspiration from the cult of Pa'ao: "Hevaheva said,"
according to the diary of the merchant Stephen Reynolds, "it was good to cut
Mr. Bingham's head off, for he was sending people to hell with their eyes shut;
but [at least] he sent them there with their eyes open" (Reynolds 4/9/1826).
As it did in fact prove true of the American missionaries, Pa'ao likewise had been
the religious harbinger of a novel and more powerful political order. Not only
did he impose a new ruling line, but also the entire theory of legitimacy through
violence that would make of every succeeding paramount a conqueror, including
the rites and temples of human sacrifice and the chief's dreadful god, "Ku-
snatcher-of-the-island" (Kukailimoku). The victim of Pa'ao's usurpation, one
Kapawa, had been the embodiment of a different idea: of rightful rulers installed
by birth rather than force, before the assembled and consenting multitude at the
inland temple of Kukaniloko on Oahu. Recall the prophecy "the land is the
sea's." Inland rather than seaward, thus associated with indigenous and natural
powers as opposed to foreign cultural sources, this ancient temple often appears
in mythical contrast with Pa'ao's as the symbol of a chieftainship that rules
through kinship with the people, hence by *aloha* rather than by sacrifice, and
by reciprocity instead of by appropriation.

Given the theory of a religiously effected usurpation, it is not surprising that
the first Christian missionaries were greeted with suspicion—the more so as they
were Americans, not English. Fear was not allayed when the missionaries dug a
large cellar for their house in Honolulu, intended, Hawaiians said, to hide American soldiers and their arms, who would emerge to take the kingdom. Rumor
after rumor of similar missionary plots against the chiefs fill traders' journals

of the 1820s, of which the following is at least faithful to the Hawaiian categorical opposition between food and excrement.

Natives put a story in circulation that the Mission houses were burnt at Mowee
[Maui] the Mission sent off. Pitt [Kalaimoku, the "Prime Minister"] gone to
Owhyhee [Hawaii] to send them forever from that Island, because the mission gave the young prince [Kauikeaouli, later Kamehameha III] and princess
[Nahienaena] shit to eat. It appeared they were at the mission house and were
offered bread and butter—the natives who were standing about the Prince not
being acquainted with butter raised the report as above (Reynolds, 25/4/
1824).[13]

Part of the problems the missionaries suffered from Pa'ao was in fact mediated
by Cook, since he and English power had forestalled the Americans as initial
beneficiaries of the paradigm of foreign usurpation. Lieutenant Peter Puget,
commander of *Chatham* in Vancouver's H.M.S. squadron, had a fascinating inter-
view on theological issues with the high priest of the temple at Kealakekua
where Cook had been venerated as Lono fourteen years earlier. The priest told
Puget the story of Pa'ao's voyage, ascribing to it the origin and form of the
existing religion. In the same context, he made two observations on Captain
Cook. He said that Cook had been killed because he carried away the fence
and images of the temple for firewood. Secondly,

Their gods he told us were numerous and good. One he distinguished as
superior to the rest, that always accompanied the King. It has the same
name as that given to Captain Cook, Orono. This Divinity always accompanied the King on his excursions. . . . The memory of Capt. Cook appears
on all occasions to be treated with the greatest veneration by all ranks of
people, and his name is still mentioned with a sort of enthusiastic respect
(Puget, MS).

Edward Bell, clerk of the *Chatham*, confirms that the central image of the
temple was a "preposterous figure" of Orono (Bell 1929-30, 1(6):78-79).
Herein lies one of many curious discrepancies between the Vancouver and Cook
reports, and between the two together and the standard scholarly explanations
of Cook's deification. In the Cook documents, the central god of this temple was
not Lono but Kunuiakea (King, in Beaglehole 1967, p. 621) or Kukaohialaka
(Samwell in Beaglehole 1967, p. 1159), who are respectively the generic and
sacrificial versions of the kingdom-snatching god of Hawaiian paramounts,
Kukailimoku. This is consistent with the status of the temple as a place of
human sacrifice (*luakini*), even as human sacrifice is inconsistent with the rites
of Lono. Moreover, apart from the suspicions of Zimmermann and the allega-

13. One of the Lahainaluna student compositions, "Mistaken Ideas Concerning the
Missionaries," dated April 9, 1842, contains a very similar account of this incident as well as
other anecdotes of the early Christian period. This valuable paper and a translation prepared
by Mary Kawena Pukui are in the Bishop Museum Library, Honolulu.

tions of the unreliable Ledyard, none of the Cook chroniclers indicate the Hawaiians took any exception to removing the fence and images; on the contrary, they voluntarily assisted the sailors in carrying them off; so that few historians since have accepted this explanation of Cook's martyrdom (Beaglehole 1967, p. cxlvi, n). I personally agree that this was not the actual reason Cook was killed. On the other hand, the high priest's assertions to Puget make a good deal of sense within the system of Hawaiian thought. Indeed they resolve all these and other mysteries of Cook's divinity in the following way.

By taking the temple paling and images, Cook was a transgressor of sacred tabus. As a transgressor, he was accordingly sacrificed by the king, Kalaniopu'u —which explains why later accounts have Cook both defleshed as a chief and offered as a sacrifice (see n. 3, above). As a sacrifice, Cook becomes substantially incorporated into the king's god, Ku—this by the well-known logic of identity between sacrifier, victim, and god explicated by Hubert and Mauss as well as by the explicit Hawaiian logic that the sacrificial victim, consumed by the deity, transfers life to the image and grows it to adulthood: it becomes a living or true god (*akua maoli*). Hence the reports by Samwell and Trevenan of the Cook expedition that Hawaiians not only asked when the dead Cook would return but asserted he would come back soon, in two months' time (Beaglehole 1967, p. 1217; Trevenan: MS). Two months would make it about mid-April, which is the customary period for placing and giving life to a new image of Ku by the traditional rites of sacrifice (Fornander 1916-19, 6:8-9). Also, by the same logic of sacrifice the god Lono/Ku is a spiritual double and protector of the king, which explains why, as the priest told Puget, he "always accompanied the King on his excursions."[14] On the other hand, as chiefly predecessor of the ruler, Cook's own bones ought to have been appropriated and preserved as the sign of royal legitimacy. And so they were—whatever the English might have confined to the deep on February 21, 1779. Manby of the Vancouver expedition relates that Cook's bones, as of 1793, were under a heap of stones close to a temple about a quarter of a mile from the spot where he was killed (Manby 1929, 1(3):39)—to which Puget (MS) adds the politically significant detail that they cohabited there with the remains of Kalaniopu'u, the Hawaiian ruler of Cook's time. As Kamehameha, the current king, had killed Kalaniopu'u's rightful heir and taken the Island by force, and as Kalaniopu'u for his part had sacrificed Cook, the possession of the bones of both fallen chiefs was the sign that Kamehameha had captured their *mana* and demonstrated his own. At the same time, as heir to a chieftainship that combines Cook with Kalaniopu'u, the foreign ancestry with the indigenous, as well as the god of peace (Lono) with the

14. The incorporation of Lono in Ku, as it were, does not mean that the two would not also be distinctly imaged and worshipped. As John Papa I'i describes the system at ca. 1810 in Honolulu, where Kamehameha and his heir Liholiho were staying, there were three godhouses: the Hale o Lono, or house of Lono; the Hali Hui, "the dwelling for miscellaneous gods"; and the Hale o Kaili, "for the god Kaili, or Kukailimoku" (I'i 1959, p. 58).

god of war (Ku), Kamehameha had worked a veritable revolution in Hawaiian polity and cult. Still, it was not the first such revolution: the priest told Puget the story of Pa'ao.

By 1809, we have evidence that Cook's bones are not just lying there; they are the subject of annual rites. Writing of the place of sepulcher (as he was told it was) in Kealakekua, the American seaman George Little observed that the Hawaiians in approaching it, "seemed to be awed into a profound reverence.... They also informed us that, once in a year, all the natives assemble here to perform a religious rite in memory of his lamentable death" (Little 1845, p. 132). Such notice of an actual worship is confirmed by several other European reports for this period—as, for example, the missionary Samuel Whitney, whose journal of 1820 records, "They say he was a god, and for a long time worshipped him as such" (Whitney MS; cf. Von Chamisso in Kotzebue 1821, 3: 239; Tyerman and Bennet 1831, 1:376; Beaglehole 1967, p. 561n re Dimsdell; Byron 1826, pp. 25-28, 123, 196; Dibble 1909, p. 27). But the specific and critical details come from the famous William Mariner and the Reverend William Ellis. Mariner had it on the authority of Kamehameha's harbor master (John Harbottle) in 1806 at Oahu, and independently later on from several Hawaiians resident in Tonga, that

> The people of the Sandwich Islands, although they actually did kill him [Cook], have paid, and still continue to pay him, higher honours than any other nation of the earth; they esteem him as having been sent by the gods to civilize them, and one to whom they owe the greatest blessings they enjoy. His bones (the greater part of which they have still in their possession!) they devoutly hold sacred; they are deposited in a house consecrated to a god, and are annually carried in procession to many other consecrated houses, before each of which they are laid on the ground, and the priest returns thanks to the gods for having sent them so great a man.... [Mr. Harbottle] informed Mr. Mariner that the natives of Owhyhee returned very few of the bones of Captain Cook, but chiefly substituted the bones of some other Englishman that was killed on that melancholy occasion; and those of Cook were carried annually in procession as above related (Martin 1817, 2:66-67).

Ellis in 1823 indicates that the bones in question were the ribs and sternum; these bones

> were considered sacred, as part of Rono, and deposited in a heiau (temple) dedicated to Rono.... There religious homage was paid to them, and from thence they were annually carried in procession to several other heiaus, or borne by priests round the island, to collect the offerings of the people, for the support of the worship of the god Rono. *The bones were preserved in a small basket of wicker-work,* completely covered over with red feathers... (Ellis 1828, p. 120; emphasis mine).

Hence, Cook returns, "his remains bound in the *ka'ai.*" But what is more, these notices of the procession of Cook's bones perfectly match the conventional ethnographic descriptions of the Makahiki festival, excepting only that the sacred bundle of Lono (i.e., Lonomakua, Cook) had been replaced in the last years before 1819 by a wooden crosspiece hung with tapa, owing inspiration in part to the indigenous representation of the god of sport, also a feature of the Mahahiki—and in part to the mast of a ship in full sail. It is apparently to this image that Mathison alludes, in an account gathered soon after the abolition of the Makahiki and other traditional ceremonies:

> It is generally well known, that after the death of Captain Cook the inhabitants repented them of the deed. . . . To perpetuate his memory, therefore, they resolved to deify him; and accordingly made an appropriate image, which for many years was actually carried in procession round the island of Owhyhee, under the appelation of *The Wandering God*. This image, during the procession, was immediately preceded by a person bearing in his hand a spear, to which was prefixed an instrument containing twenty lashes, each a yard in length, woven with the same sort of feathers that are used in the manufacture of cloaks and idols. He brandished it before the image, as it were to clear the way; and any person who had the misfortune to be touched by it, was summarily put to death as guilty of violating the tabu regulation (Mathison 1825, pp. 431-32).

With these new ritual elements in hand, we can rapidly bring the story to a close. Not that the denouement is unworthy of another chapter as long as this, however. The revolution Kamehameha had effected was nothing less than the conquest of the archipelago and the formation of the state. And the cult of Cook figured decisively in these events. The legitimation of Kamehameha's own power as English power, had set a policy of submission to the British Crown—recall that Kamehameha had ceded the Island of Hawaii to King George through Vancouver in 1794—and of honorable foreign trade that gave him the military means to vanquish the other islands, whose own chiefs had not had the good fortune of sacrificing Cook. Kamehameha would then play upon the ambiguities of the sacrifice to progressively replace the warlike dimension of the kingdom-snatching Ku by the peaceful aspect of Cook/Lono, initially incorporated in Ku as victim. During the first decade of the nineteenth century, the Makahiki Festival of Lono in fact completely superseded the sacrificial rites of Ku, which had been the traditional prelude to war. Already in 1794, Kamehameha began to limit human sacrifice; by 1817, it was a rare thing, evidently reserved to capital punishment in criminal cases. But while the customary rites of sacrifice were allowed to fall into disuse, Kamehameha replaced them with the Makahiki, even to some extent incorporated them in the newly elaborated Makahiki that he spread from island to island with the conquest. This circuit of the Lono priests carrying symbols of Cook and collecting tribute, for example, is the transformation of an analogous preliminary of the traditional Ku ceremonies into the central performance of the Makahiki (Malo 1951 and Kelou Kamakau in Fornander 1916-19, vol. 6). Again, the exchange of salience between

Cook and Ku is epitomized by the fact that whereas Kamehameha formally announced his choice of successor by allowing the young Lihiliho to offer the human sacrifices during customary Ku rituals in 1803, he formally installed Liholiho as heir in 1809, precisely at the Makahiki (I'i 1959, p. 37; Campbell 1967, p. 130). Thus the ultimate efficacy of the god, Captain James Cook: he could protect the royal power from the dangers of usurpation and sacrifice to which it had traditionally been vulnerable; and, above all, substitute a cult of internal peace—the hallmark of the state—for the indigenous polity of tribal violence.[15]

The final act of the drama at once confirmed Cook's supremacy and ritually undermined it. The abolition of all the tabus in 1819 was specifically directed against the old war god, "Ku-snatcher-of-the-island." At Kamehameha's death, Ku had been inherited by a cousin of King Liholiho (Kekuaokalani). But if this presaged a new struggle for power, the king and his chiefs sought to foreclose it by declaring there were no gods anyway, and that they now intended "to live as the white men do." With this, the divine Cook, like his own bones, would disappear from historical sight. Perhaps, then, the most fitting epitaph of the god was that set in doggerel by Anne Seward, in an "Elegy on Captain Cook" composed when the news of his death reached England:

> Ye, who ere-while for Cook's illustrious brow
> Pluck'd the green laurel, and the oaken bough,
> Hung the gay garlands on the trophied oars,
> And pour'd his fame along a thousand shores,
> Strike the slow death-bell!—weave the sacred verse,
> And stew the cypress o'er his honor'd hearse;
> In sad procession wander round the shrine,
> And weep him mortal, whom ye sung divine!

* * *

Requiescat in Pace.

References

Note: asterisk (*) indicates unpublished manuscript.

Anonymous. *Log of the Atahaulpa*, 1811-16. Microfilm, Massachusetts Historical Society.

Archives of Hawaii (AH). *Historical and Miscellaneous Files; US Consul Raquet, Rio, to Hon. John Quincy Adams, Sec'y of State, 8 March 1824.

Beaglehole, J. C., ed. 1967. *The Journals of Captain James Cook on His Voyages*

---

15. On the decline of human sacrifice from 1794 onwards, see, among others, Bell 1929-30, 2(1):90; Lisiansky 1968, p. 120; Shaler 1808, p. 167; Corney 1896, p. 102; Golovnin, MS. On the corresponding changes in ritual, note that the ceremonial calendar given by Kelou Kamakau—a participant in the rites he describes—completely reverses the war and peace periods alleged in standard ethnographic treatments (in Fornander 1916-19, 6:2-45).

of Discovery. III: *The Voyage of the* Resolution *and* Discovery, *1776-1780.* Cambridge: The University Press for the Hakluyt Society. (Contains also the journal of Samwell and excerpts from the journals of King, Clerke, etc.)

Beckwith, Martha Warren. 1919. "The Hawaiian Romance of Laieikawai," Thirty-third Annual Report, Bureau of American Ethnology, 1911-12: 285-666.

___. 1970. *Hawaiian Mythology.* Honolulu: University of Hawaii Press.

___. 1972. *The Kumulipo.* Honolulu: University of Hawaii Press.

Bell, Edward. 1929-30. "Log of the Chatham," *Honolulu Mercury* 1(4): 7-26; 1(5): 55-69; 1(6): 76-96; 2(1): 80-91; 2(2): 119-29.

Bloxam, Andrew. 1925. *Diary of Andrew Bloxam, Naturalist of the* Blonde *on Her Trip from England to the Hawaiian Islands, 1824-25.* Bernice P. Bishop Special Publication 10. Honolulu: Bishop Museum Press.

Bradley, Harold Whitman. 1968. *The American Frontier in Hawaii.* Gloucester: Peter Smith.

Bullard, Charles B. *Letterbook of Charles B. Bullard, supercargo for Bryant and Sturgis at the Hawaiian Islands and Canton, March 20, 1821-July 11, 1823. Typescript copy at Hawaiian Mission Children's Society Library.

Byron, Captain the Right Honorable Lord [George Anson]. *1826. Voyage of H.M.S.* Blonde *to the Sandwich Islands in the Years 1824-25.* London: John Murray.

Campbell, Archibald. 1967. *A Voyage Around the World, from 1806 to 1812...* Honolulu: University of Hawaii Press (facsimile of the third American edition of 1822).

Cleveland, Richard J. n.d. *In the Forecastle: or Twenty-five Years a Sailor.* New York: Manhattan Publishing Company.

Colnett, James. *The journal of James Colnett aboard the *Prince of Wales* and *Princess Royal* from October 16, 1786, to November 7, 1788; aboard the *Argonaut* March 29, 1791-April 18, 1791. Archives of Hawaii, Cook Collection (photostat of original in P.R.O., London).

Cook, Captain James. 1784. *A Voyage to the Pacific Ocean... in His Majesty's Ships the* Resolution *and* Discovery... *In the Years 1776, 1777, 1778, 1779, 1780.* 3 volumes. [Vol. 3 by Captain James King]. Dublin: Chamberlaine et al.

Corney, Peter. 1896. *Voyages in the Northern Pacific: Narrative of Several Trading Voyages from 1813 to 1818.* Honolulu: Thrum.

Dampier, Robert. 1971. *To the Sandwich Islands on H.M.S.* Blonde. Edited by Pauline King Joerger. Honolulu: University of Hawaii Press.

Dibble, Sheldon. 1909. *A History of the Sandwich Islands.* Honolulu: Thrum (reissue of the 1843 edition).

Ellis, William (Rev.). 1828. *Narrative of a Tour through Hawaii.* 4th ed. London: Fisher et al.

Ellis, William (Surgeon). 1782. *An Authentic Account of a Voyage Performed by Captain Cook and Captain Clarke... during the Years 1776, 1777, 1778, 1779, and 1780.* 2 vols. London: Robinson, Sewell, and Debrett.

Fornander, Abraham. 1916-19. *Fornander Collection of Hawaiian Antiquities and Folklore.* Translation revised by Thomas G. Thrum. Memoirs of the

Bernice P. Bishop Museum, vols. 4, 5, 6. Honolulu: Bishop Museum Press.

Franchère, Gabriel. 1969. *Journal of a Voyage on the North West Coast of North America during the Years 1811, 1812, 1813, and 1814.* Trans. by W. T. Lamb. Toronto: The Champlain Society.

Golovnin, Vassili. 1974. Chapters on Hawaii and the Marianas in *Voyage Around the World...1817, 1818, and 1819.* In. V. M. Golovnin, *Voyage...1819.* Trans. Ella Wiswell. Pacific Islands Program, University of Hawaii Working Papers, 1974.

Gould, Lieutenant-Commander Rupert T. 1928. "Bligh's Notes on Cook's Last Voyage," *The Mariner's Mirror* 14: 370-85.

Hammatt, Charles H. *Journal of Charles H. Hammatt [in the Sandwich Islands, May 6, 1823, to June 9, 1825]. Xerox copy in Hawaiian Mission Children's Society Library; original in Baker Library, Harvard.

Handy, E. S. Craighill, and Mary Kawena Pukui. 1972. *The Polynesian Family System in Ka-u, Hawai'i.* Rutland, Vermont: Charles E. Tuttle.

Hiroa, Te Rangi (Peter H. Buck). 1957. *Arts and Crafts of Hawaii.* Bernice P. Bishop Museum Special Publication 45. Honolulu: Bishop Museum Press.

Hocart, A. M. 1927. *Kingship.* London: Oxford University Press.

____. 1936. *Kings and Councillors.* Cairo: Printing Office, P. Barbey.

Hunnewell, James. *Hunnewell Collection [letters, journals, business papers, etc.]. Baker Library, Harvard.

I'i, John Papa. 1959. *Fragments of Hawaiian History.* Trans. Mary Kawena Pukui. Ed. Dorothy B. Barrère. Honolulu: Bishop Museum Press.

Kamakau, Samuel M. 1845. *"Some Very Ancient Things of Hawaii." Thrum Collection, Bernice P. Bishop Museum. Trans. from *Ka Elele Hawaii* (newspaper), February 10, 1845, by Thomas G. Thrum.

____. 1961. *Ruling Chiefs of Hawaii.* Honolulu: Kamehameha Schools Press.

Kotzebue, Otto von. 1821. *A Voyage of Discovery into the South Sea...in the Years 1815-1818.* 3 vols. London: Longman.

Kuykendall, Ralph. 1968. *The Hawaiian Kingdom.* Vol. 1, *1778-1854.* Honolulu: University of Hawaii Press.

Lahainaluna Students. 1838. *Ka Mooolelo Hawaii.* Lahainaluna: Press of the High School.

____. 1839. "Hawaiian History Written by scholars at the High School" (translation of the above by Rueben Tinker), *Hawaiian Spectator* 2: 58-77, 211-31, 334-40, 438-47. (This translation was concluded in the Honolulu newspaper, *The Polynesian* for August 1, 8, 15, and 22, 1840.)

____. 1842. *"Mistaken Ideas Concerning the Missionaries." Original composition in Bishop Museum Library. Trans. Mary Kawena Pukui.

Law, John. *Journal of John Law, Surgeon of the *Discovery*, later the *Resolution.* Cook Collection, Archives of Hawaii. Photostat of original in the British Museum (Additional MS 37327).

Lévi-Strauss, Claude. 1974. *Tristes Tropiques.* New York: Atheneum.

Lisiansky, Urey. 1968. *A Voyage around the World in the Years 1803, 4, 5, and 6...Ridgewood, N.J.: The Gregg Press (facsimile of the London edition of 1814).

Little, George. 1845. *Life on the Ocean; or, Twenty Years at Sea* ...3d ed. Boston: Waite, Peirce and Co.

Luomala, Katharine. 1949. *Maui-of-a-Thousand-Tricks: His Oceanic and European Biographers*. Bernice P. Bishop Museum Bulletin No. 198. Honolulu: Bishop Museum Press.

Makemson, Maud Worcestor. 1941. *The Morning Star Rises*. New Haven: Yale University Press.

Malo, David. 1951. *Hawaiian Antiquities*. Bernice P. Bishop Museum, Special Publication 2. 2d ed. Honolulu: Bishop Museum Press.

Manby Thomas. 1929. "Journal of Vancouver's Voyage to the Pacific Ocean (1791-1793)," *Honolulu Mercury*, 1(1): 11-25; 1(2): 33-45; 1(3): 39-55.

Marshall Letters. *Copies of Letters rec'd [by Josiah Marshall, Boston] from the Sandwich Islands and Canton, 1820-1832. Haughton Library, Harvard University.

Martin, John, ed. 1817. *An Account of the Natives of the Tonga Islands... Compiled and Arranged from the Extensive Communications of Mr. William Mariner*. 2 vols. London: Murray.

Mathison, Gilbert Farquhar. 1825. *Narrative of a Visit to Brazil, Chile, Peru and the Sandwich Islands during the Years 1821 and 1822* ...London: Chas. Knight.

Meares, John. 1790. *Voyages Made in the Years 1788 and 1789, from China to the Northwest Coast of America, to Which are Prefixed an Introductory Narrative of a Voyage Performed in 1786, from Bengal, in the Ship Nootka*. London: Logographic.

Murray-Oliver, Anthony. 1975. *Captain Cook's Hawaii: As Seen by His Artists*. Wellington: Millwood Press.

Pierce, Richard A. 1965. *Russia's Hawaiian Adventure, 1815-1817*. Berkeley: University of California Press.

Portlock, Nathaniel (Capt.). 1789. *A Voyage Around the World... in 1785, 1786, 1787, and 1788*. London: John Stockdale.

Puget, Peter. *Journals of Peter Puget, with Vancouver (1790-1795). Hawaiian Historical Society: photostat copy of journals in the possession of Judge F. W. Howay; apparently same as those in the British Museum (Add. MSS 17546, 17547, 17548).

Pukui, Mary Kawena, and Samuel H. Elbert. 1965. *Hawaiian-English Dictionary*. 3d ed. Honolulu: University of Hawaii Press.

Pukui, Mary Kawena, E. W. Haertig, and Catherine Lee. 1972. *Nana i ke Kumu (Look to the Source)*. Honolulu: Hui Hanai; Queen Liliuokalani Children's Center.

Reynolds, Stephen. *The Diary of Stephen Reynolds. Microfilm, Hawaiian Mission Children's Society Library (original in Peabody Museum, Salem).

Riou, Edward. *"A Log of the Proceedings of His Majesty's Sloop *Discovery*," Archives of Hawaii, Cook Collection (photostat of original in P.R.O., Adm. 51/4529/43).

Shaler, William. 1808. "Journal of a Voyage between China and the Northwestern Coast of America made in 1804," *American Register* 3: 137-75.

Stewart [Charles], and [William] Richards. 1825. "Journal of Messers. Stewart and Richards at Lahinah [sic]," *Missionary Herald* 21: 276-80.

Stokes, John F. G. 1930. "Burial of King Keawe," *Papers of the Hawaiian Historical Society* 17: 63-73.

Taylor, Albert Pierce. 1929. *Sesquicentennial Celebration of Captain Cook's Discovery of Hawaii (1778-1928).* Honolulu: Captain Cook Sesquicentennial Commission and the Archives of the Hawaii Commission.

Thrum, Thomas G. 1921. *Hawaiian Folk Tales.* Chicago: McClurg.

_____. 1923. *More Hawaiian Folk Tales.* Chicago: McClurg.

Townsend, Ebenezer, Jr. 1888. "The Diary of Ebenezer Townsend, Jr.," *Papers of the New Haven Colony Historical Society* 4: 1-115.

Trevenan, James. *Marginal notes to the 1784 edition of Cook's *Voyage*, vol. 3. Photocopy in Archives of Hawaii, Cook Collection; full transcription is in the Archives of British Columbia (Victoria).

Tyerman, Daniel, and George Bennet. 1831. *Journal of Voyages and Travels.* Vol. 1. London: Westley and Davis.

Valeri, Valerio. 1976. *"Le brulé et le cuit: Mythologie et organisation de la société hawaiienne ancienne." Thesis for the doctorate of the 3d cycle, E.P.H.E., Université René Descartes.

Vancouver, Captain George. 1801. *A Voyage of Discovery to the North Pacific Ocean... in the Years 1790, 1791, 1792, 1793, 1794 and 1795...*New ed. London: John Stockdale.

Westervelt, W. P. 1923. *Hawaiian Historical Legends.* New York: Revell.

Whitney, Samuel. *Journal of Samuel Whitney. Hawaiian Mission Children's Society Library.

Pierre Smith

7

Aspects of the Organization of Rites

In the "Finale" to *L'Homme nu*, Claude Lévi-Strauss suggests that we "study ritual in and for itself, in order to understand the ways in which it constitutes an object distinct from mythology, and to determine its specific characteristics" (p. 598), that is, to take on this great anthropological domain in a spirit similar to that which presided over his earlier research on myth, kinship, and so-called totemic classifications. He illustrates his proposal by presenting and analyzing the fact that, on the level of pronounced speech, performed acts, and manipulated objects, the "ritual makes a constant appeal to two processes, dividing up [*morcellement*] on the one hand, repetition on the other" (p. 601). In what follows, I will seek to demonstrate the importance of two other interdependent constants whose implications, it seems to me, must be understood to better situate the identity of ritual phenomena. For the latter, contrary to what some of the current types of interpretations would have us believe, cannot be reduced to a simply display of social mechanisms, a faithful reflection of myths, or even a confused forest of diversely associated symbols. Usually requiring the coordination of the acts and thoughts of a great many people, and sometimes even of an entire society, they do not arise by chance or solely as a function of external constraints specific to the domain from which they borrow and on which they are nourished. Like the various forms of art which are often integrated with or rooted in them, rituals are particularly elaborated cultural creations, and one can hope to clarify their incredible complexity and their captivating strangeness only by trying to find the principles of their own specific elaboration.

103

The two aspects that I will examine here are the following: rituals are generally organized, on the one hand, around central focalizing elements, and, on the other, within one of the distinct ritual systems which coexist in a single culture. So whatever the specific characteristics of the procedures used, the symbolism put into play, or the myths evoked, it is these focalizing elements and this integration into systems that makes rituals from around the world seem to draw upon a relatively limited repertoire and obey common schemas. A clarification of these aspects should, therefore, permit both a more solid comparison of rituals from different societies, a domain in which there has been almost no progress since Frazer's great exploits, and the isolation of a number of criteria helpful in choosing among the different possible or proposed interpretations of a given rite, an activity in which great confusion exists today. In the first part of this essay I will limit myself to brief remarks illustrated chiefly by examples drawn from African cultures which I have studied directly, and, in the second part, to a reconsideration of the interpretation of the *Ncwala* of the Swazi, one of the most complex and best described African rituals, and one whose interpretation has been extremely controversial.

The focalizing elements of the rite, if we take this term in the strong sense, are those acts around which the different sequences revolve and are organized. They are distinguished from the many other symbolic acts which surround them by the fact that, from the point of view of the participants or the believers, something really happens at this moment, a mysterious or mystical operation which cannot be reduced to the symbolism of the act performed. To take a limited example, let us say that putting flowers on the tomb of the Unknown Soldier can hardly be taken for anything but a symbolic action and remains "on this side" of ritual in the strict sense; on the other hand, the act of relighting the flame (if one does not deny all relevance to this act a priori) can already be considered a ritual operation. Similarly, in our culture, the dedication of a public building is a purely symbolic manifestation, whereas the christening of a ship takes on characteristics of a rite. On the other hand, the same act, for example the blessing of bread which is going to be eaten in common, can, depending on the context, be simply a gesture evoking piety or can constitute a central ritual operation of what we are accustomed to call the sacrifice of the Mass. While we admit these differences intuitively, we also can see that they do not depend on the absence or presence of reference to religious belief or worship. Rather, they are based, from a certain point of view, on the absence or presence of a simulation, an operation whose supposed efficacy is simulated. This point of view is difficult to place exactly: let us say that it is that of someone who takes rituals seriously without giving them too much credence, and who thus observes that the fact of giving a ship a name and breaking a bottle on its bow at the moment the ropes attaching it to the land are cut and it shakes and slides into the sea for the first time, produces a peculiar effect in him, as if this machine were also a gigantic person and this conferred aura would stay with it throughout its machine life. In the same way, the attitudes of the priest and the faithful at the moment of consecration, prepared for by the whole first part of the Mass, make one think that even if the bread and wine have not changed, something important has happened. Theoretically, the priest's actions and the words of consecration are sufficient to cause transubstantiation, but it is hard to imagine this happening in a living room, before a distracted audience, with a relaxed priest. In a certain way, the celebrant and the faithful at the Mass are tricking themselves. By their attitudes in an appropriate context, they are endeavoring to reflect a transformation that has not taken place in the consecrated substances.

This way of looking at things will probably not be acceptable to the fervent believer, unless, perhaps, it is applied to rituals in which he does not believe; but it is precisely at this point that the interest of the problem lies, in the fact that thought devoted to ritual activities lets itself be caught in this way in the trap laid for it, which in the end is its own trap. This paradoxical point of view, which can be maintained only by stripping the rites of their mythological and exegetical contexts, could be rejected as a pure rationalization alien to all true religious experience, if it were not, on the contrary, imposed on us by the major ritual systems, astonishingly recurrent around the world, of a great many so-called archaic societies. Throughout the world, in black Africa, Amazonia, Australia, Melanesia, and elsewhere, men on the one side, women and children on the other, clearly divide ritual roles between them: the former convince the latter that the gods, spirits, or ancestors are among them in a perceptible way. To do this, they put on masks or costumes, change their voices and their bearing, or play instruments which the others do not see, such as bullroarers, flutes, hand drums, and so on, and the women and children believe, or are supposed to believe, or at least are supposed to act as if they believed, often under pain of death, that these really are supernatural manifestations. The central theme in the collective initiation of young men is their passage from the second group into the first, and it involves the exposure of the simulation. But what is even more striking is that this passage takes nothing away from their beliefs; on the contrary, when they are given the mission of simulating the manifestations, they only become closer to the gods and come to consider this the most excellent way of worshiping them. And very often their mothers, who must have some idea of what is going on, reinforce this conviction by acting as if they believe their sons are going to be killed during the initiation and will come back reborn and different afterwards (cf., for example, Eliade 1959).

I have been able to observe these ritual performances, well-known to ethnologists, among the Bedik of eastern Senegal, a small Tenda-speaking people living in the confines of the Upper Gambia and Fouta-Djalon, and I took down these significant words from an initiator: "when we announce to the future initiates that the masks are going to cut off their heads, they should act as if they believe it. If one of them acts skeptical or put out, it is very serious and he must be severely punished. But if one of them believes too strongly and gets upset, tries to run away or loses control, it is even more serious. This is the sign that he will never be able to live among us as a man, and in the old days they preferred to kill him and be done with it." This statement bears out the paradoxical viewpoint suggested above: take the rite seriously, but not too seriously.

We encounter a comparable situation in possession, in which man, instead of hiding behind a mask of a god, makes the dazzling revelation that he is inhabited by the god. And when the true trance is produced and submerges the consciousness of the adept, this is taken as the very proof, sufficient to defeat any skeptic, of the presence of the god. Still, in many cultures an actual trance is not produced, and this changes nothing. This is the case, for instance, in Rwanda, where I had several opportunities to observe the *kubandwa* rites, in which the adepts merely—as they themselves recognize—consciously play the stereotyped roles of the divinized hero Ryangombe and his legendary companions; they do not consider themselves any less inhabited by the spirits of these beings for this reason, and so consider themselves perfectly free of responsibility, since, they assure us, it is the spirits who are acting through them. Here we are not far from a purely theatrical situation in which the actor disappears behind the character he is playing, takes himself and others in with his acting, and in which a certain type of complicit belief (one believes in it) is established which is more the specific effect of the performance than simple result of any independent belief in the reality of the character represented.

If we admit that the kernel of rituals lies less in the translation of a mythology, a vision of the world, or a symbolism than in their encounter with what I would call a certain type of "snare for thought" [*piège à pensée*], many of the questions traditionally posed by anthropologists and historians of religions will appear ill-conceived. We can cite, for example, the case of bullroarers, oblong plaques of wood, metal, or bone that are turned and spun at the end of a long string, and which produce a deep throbbing hum whose intensity varies with the speed at which the string is swung. Where it is found, which is throughout most of the world, this barely musical instrument is either a simple child's toy or else a central element of rites, particularly of initiations. In this second function—which excludes the first—it serves most often to make the spirits speak to the ears of women or other noninitiates, from whom its appearance, its use, or even its existence, are hidden. Struck by the astonishing similarities, noted all over the world, of the ritual uses and symbolic connotations attached to this instrument, A. C. Haddon wrote in 1898 that it was "perhaps the most ancient, widely spread, and sacred religious symbol in the world" (p. 258). In a recent article in the journal *Man*, a well-known American folklorist, Alan Dundes, takes the problem, as many others have done, and cites more than one hundred studies on the subject. The psychoanalytically inspired solution he proposes is the following: the bullroarer is not only a phallic symbol, as has often been stressed, but also has anal connotations evoked by the noise it makes, which is often associated with the sound of wind or thunder; it is a "flatulent phallus," which could be compared in the modern context, with the farting motorcycle; this double connotation is connected to the fact that in certain rites of initiation, the men are supposed to reconceive (phallic aspect) and give birth (anal aspect) to the initiates, without recourse to women; this is why the latter are forbidden to see the bullroarer and are kept away from initiations (Dundes 1976).

It would be easy to refute Dundes's model solely on the basis of his own examples; for while the bullroarer's phallic connotations seem quite common, its anal connotations are far less so, and they seem to mark other aspects of the initiation than does the bullroarer itself. In addition to this, the model is put together from assorted elements extracted from a number of cultures, which are not related among themselves, and the model does not seem to be attested as such anywhere. And even if it were attested in one place or another, it is difficult to see how this would explain the use of the bullroarer in all times and places. Even so, Dundes's explanation remains no sillier than the many others which would have the most widespread ritual procedures derive from an arbitrarily borrowed or reconstructed symbolism with universal pretensions, and which claim to reveal, for example, the ultimate or original *signification* of sacrifice, circumcision, or initiation.

To get back to the bullroarer, we must follow a procedure which is the reverse of Dundes's and recognize that it is, first of all, no more than a prehistoric gadget. It does not become holy, phallic, etc., until the moment when it is used ritually, not as a mere toy. On the other hand, the bullroarer is only one artifice, one aural mask, among many which men use to indicate the presence of supernatural beings while keeping women away. In Melanesia (on the island of Wogeo, for example), and in certain Amazonian societies (the Yurupari cult), it is flutes or trumpets which are used in ritual performances of this sort. Among the Bedik of Senegal, the subordinate bush spirits are represented by various types of masked men with distorted voices, while the three superior spirits manifest themselves only to the sound of drums, friction drums, and bullroarers, respectively. In brief, the problem is not that of the intrinsic signification of the bullroarer, but of its insertion (frequent but optional) into this type of rite. Once this is accepted we will be able to note certain specific traits of this gadget which make it particularly appropriate for playing this role and bearing certain symbolic connotations rather than others. Except for its extreme simplicity and its rudimentary character, which suggest that its existence goes back into the depths of time, the bullroarer is of no interest from a musical point of view; there is thus no great loss in forbidding its use outside of ritual mysteries. On the other hand, it is a wind instrument that does not depend on human breath; unlike instruments played with the mouth or the fingers, it can indepefinitely produce a continuous sound which does not betray its human origin to the ears of those who are not supposed to know about it (this may also be one of the reasons the organ is played in churches). Its humming is naturally appropriate for representing the voice of elemental forces like wind and thunder. It is also an instrument whose handling is dangerous for the audience and which, if it is let go or if the string breaks, turns into a dangerous projectile. This, associated with its exclusively masculine shape and use, probably explains the phallic and aggressive connotations which are frequently attached to it, and why it is used more often than other artifices of the same sort to frighten women and keep them away. Among the Bedik, for example, its use is accompanied by violent hurling of stones on the roofs of the huts in which the women are hiding and sometimes the bullroarer itself is hurled into the thatch of the roof. Thus the bullroarer becomes a "sacred" object only when it is made part of a preconceived ritual schema, but once it is part of such a schema it brings its own characteristics along with it, and it is on this common base that cultures elaborate various but deeply related glosses. And the same is the case for other "snares of thought," such as masking play, the play of sacrifice, the play of prayer, the play of trance, and so on, which constitute the kernel of rituals throughout the world.

If we now move from the content of ritual performances to the form that contains them, we reach a second essential aspect of the organization of rites, one which is equally determinant for their analysis. Every rite is linked to circumstances which determine how it is performed, and these circumstances themselves form series. The various rites associated with circumstances of the same series tend to form a system, that is, to respond to, oppose, complete, or repeat each other in a way that is certainly more evident, at any rate, than is the case with those connected to circumstances belonging to different series. On the other hand, it seems that no society limits its ritual activities to a single series of circumstances, and it follows that several ritual systems generally coexist within the same culture. As a first hypothesis, we can schematically distinguish and define four universal series of circumstances apt to determine the characteristics of ritual systems. For every rite is tied either to periodical or occasional circumstances; and these circumstances can, in either case, primarily affect either the life of the collectivity or that of individuals.

   Rites that are connected with a series of periodical circumstances form a system along an axis of the syntagmatic type; each rite in the series will necessarily be preceded and followed by another in a clearly determined order which will be repeated with each recurrence of the cycle. In relation to the collectivity, for example, in a great many societies the seasons determine a cycle of annual rites, although it is also possible to observe cycles of longer or shorter periodicity (the daily prayers of the Muslim community, for example). In relation to the individual, it is the major steps of the life cycle (birth, marriage, death) which generally constitute the base of ritual systems, but other periodicities may be grafted onto this (birthdays, for example). To become part of a periodical series, the circumstances and the rites attached to them must necessarily refer to the natural order, whether this be the astronomical calendar or what we could call the biological calendar. Thus the Catholic liturgy officially commemorates only the events of its own mythology; nevertheless, since this liturgy is arranged along the course of the year, Christmas cannot be prevented from also being a winter solstice festival, Easter a festival of the return of spring, St. John's Day a festival of the summer solstice; on the other hand, by referring essentially to the story of Christ, the liturgy also respects the order of the biological calendar, since from Advent (expectation of his birth) to All Saints' Day (the Last Judgment), it clearly follows the steps of his terrestrial, then eschatological, life, with Christmas also appearing as a children's festival, and All Saints' Day (Halloween) as a festival of the dead. Periodicity thus improves its own specific constraints on every ritual system which respects it; and we can say that the rites of the seasonal cycle and the rites of the life cycle, whatever the differences in their temporal bases, have this at least in common: both make a period of passing time, in itself irreversible, appear as an ordered series of eternal re-beginnings and repetitions.

Occasional rites, on the other hand, react to time's surprises, to circumstances which are foreseeable only from a statistical point of view. They form a system along an axis of the paradigmatic type, offering a number of types of ritual responses adapted to various situations, and among which the conjuncture alone, interpreted as need be through divination, will determine the choice. Thus a single rite can be repeated before others of the same series intervene in an order which remains unpredictable. On the other hand, the temporal surprises to which occasional rites may respond may, as is often but not always the case, be connected with the seasonal or life cycle. In relation to the life of the collectivity, for example, there may be rites responding to natural disasters (droughts, epidemics), but also rites responding to purely social disasters such as war. In the same way, on the individual side, occasional rites can be responses either to natural accidents (sickness, sterility), to purely social accidents (failures, conflict), or even to symbolic ones (bad dreams, the violation of a taboo). In a general way, periodic rites follow an order which must be respected; for this reason they have a tendency to celebrate the expected, or at least to seal the acceptance of the ineluctable (death, for example); occasional rites, on the other hand, are based on the idea of a disorder which must be dealt with, while at the same time good surprises (a victory, for example) also can be ritually celebrated.

While a ritual system considered as a whole constitutes a global response to a series of circumstances which determine its occurrence, different societies develop these systems to unequal degrees, and each one elaborates them in its own way. The general configuration thus obtained is a significant dimension of any culture. For example, the great rituals of the Ndembu of Zambia, for which Victor Turner has given us particularly rich descriptions and analyses (cf. Turner 1967 and 1968), are almost all based on a single system: they are rites of affliction, that is, occasional rites responding to the accidents of individual life (sterility, sickness, conflicts, tensions, various sorts of personal failures). Turner thus has an ideal situation for revealing all the affective implications of the symbolism at work in these rites. He is mistaken, however, in suggesting that this is the determinant raw material of rites in general. It is solely because Ndembu culture has chosen to develop and privilege above all else a ritual system based on the accidents of individual life that its symbolism works the way it does, and that the Ndembu have such a tendency to use ritual to make manifest and to treat their affective problems. In other cultures in which these problems also exist this type of system may not be found or may be poorly developed, and in this case it is another order of realities, such as the seasonal cycle, which will appear most strikingly in the rites and furnish a rich harvest of symbols of another type altogether. Not only does the symbolism at work in rituals not explain those rituals—it does not even explain itself, except in function of the systems within which it is elaborated.

While cultures develop their ritual systems unequally and in different ways, they also establish complex and diverse links among them. For example, they may group them together and assign them to a given period (puberty or marriage rites), then integrate the rites into an annual cycle involving society as a whole. In the same way, the accidental or predictable circumstances of the life of certain individuals, kings for example, can be treated ritually as events involving the collectivity to the highest degree. On the other hand, certain periodic circumstances, as we shall see below, can be treated in the mode of occasional accidents, and not as elements in a cycle. Events of the occasional type can in turn be occasions for the holding of periodic rituals (the commemoration of historical events). Finally, an event of the life cycle (the death of certain personages) can set off either a cycle of seasonal rites (the treatment of a skeleton can be extended over several years), or the holding of occasional rituals (the worship of family spirits in reaction to some misfortune). In a general way, a single type of ritual act, such as sacrifice, initiation, prayer, or the display of ritual masks, can be integrated, either centrally or accessorily, to various systems, differently interconnected among themselves, and in this way receive different colorings or orientations, pertinent for its analysis.

Let me illustrate some of these remarks with a rapid sketch and comparison of two ritual systems, one of which I observed among the Bedik of Senegal, the other in Rwanda. The Bedik have a fairly sparse but regularly utilized system of occasional individual rites, used particularly to combat witchcraft. They follow a highly developed cycle of annual rites, which completely dominates their social life and mobilizes the attention and energies of the entire group for an appreciable part of the time. They have no occasional rites involving the collectivity, although certain calamities sometimes appear to be evoked within the framework of the seasonal rites. Finally, as far as the life cycle is concerned, the practices associated with birth, marriage, and death really fall more into the realm of good manners and etiquette than into that of ritual properly speaking. Still, from birth on, the life cycle closely follows the seasonal cycle. The whole male population passes through nine age grades from childhood to old age, and each group thus constituted has its own role to play in the cycle of annual rites (cf. Smith 1971). The progression of the life cycle is thus put at the disposal of the seasonal rites, the various age groups being manifested as such only in the framework of these rites. The initiations that mark the passage from the first to the second age-grade and open up access to the secret of the masks, from which women are excluded, take place only every two to three years, during an annual festival which, while more complicated those years than others, undergoes no change in nature on this account. From a certain point of view, the initiations and the progression through the age grades constitute systems for providing actors for the cycle of annual rites, for organizing the whole male population for this purpose (girls and women also have various minutely regulated parts to play). The same thing could be said about the division of lineages into two moieties, the Keita and the Kamara; for these are manifested, and opposed, solely in the framework of the same ritual system. Every village is further divided into two wards, call High and Low, located on either side of the central plaza, which always contain Keita lineages and Kamara lineages juxtaposed in a definite order. Outside their topographical reality, these wards are not manifested as such on the social plane except on the occasion of seasonal rites and the preparations for them. The lineages themselves have no differentiated roles, privileges, or statuses except in the framework of these same rites, and it is solely during festivals that the different families of a single lineage leave the hamlets located near their fields and come together for a few days in the main village. Finally, the distinction that is made between these hamlets and the "real" village (which is sometimes less populated than the hamlets, outside the festival periods), rests entirely on ritual prerogatives: the "real" villages, which cannot be moved once they have been "bought" from the bush spirits with sacrifices, alone may serve as the setting for the seasonal rites and have their men's houses arranged to this effect. In brief, most of the social dimensions which intersect in this way and situate each individual within the group by a complex formula (sex, age grade, moiety, lineage, ward) can be effectively manifested only as mechanisms in the cycle of seasonal rites.

The Bedik talk a great deal about these rites, but only in order to know what should be done, before or after a particular sequence, by whom and in what way. They do not interpret the rites, and each festival is identified only by the ritual procedures it involves, without other references. The myths, rare and meager, merely justify certain ritual prerogatives on the following model: in the old days women held the drums and masks; then they did something wrong, and the drums and masks passed over to the men; in the old days, the Keita were of the bush and the Kamara of the village, then when they met they exchanged their respective spheres. The whole system is based on the opposition of the bush and a village thought of as a human clearing in the midst of an omnipresent bush inhabited by innumerable spirits, to which the souls of the ancestors are assimilated. Within the village, the men, because of their initiation into the secret of the masks which incarnate the spirits, are more marked by the bush, and the women by the village. The ritual year is divided into two unequal parts, the first including the rainy season (June-November) and the cool part of the dry season (December-February), the second covering the hot part of the dry season (February-May). The Keita, masters of the village and of agriculture, direct the rites of the first period, while those of the second period are entrusted to the Kamara moiety, responsible for bush activities such as hunting, initiations, and the display of masks, which take place during that time. The Kamara moiety is itself divided into lineages responsible for the mystery of the masks and lineages of blacksmiths who, during certain festivals, mediate between the bush and the village on the one hand, between men and women on the other. The age grades are divided between two men's houses, one marked by the bush, the other by the village. The first is associated with the grade of new initiates and the two grades reserved for men who have passed their prime; the second is associated with the five grades of adult men, from youth to maturity. The life cycle of men thus appears, after an initiation which is a "departure for the bush," as a movement of the bush towards the village, then, at the time of approaching death, of the village toward the bush once more. The hamlets, in which festivals may not take place, are thought of as belonging to the bush in opposition to the "real" village. The first part of the ritual year, marked by field labor and harvest, is an active and joyous period during which the village and its surrounding fields conquers the now generous bush, whereas the second part, marked by bush activities, is a dangerous and difficult time during which the bush lays siege to the village and reconquers the fields.

Within this framework, the various ritual procedures can be understood only by comparing those of one period of the year with those of the other. Thus, during the festivals of the first period men and women dance together, while the two great festivals of the second period are reserved respectively to men and to women. Large drums and transverse flutes are used only in the first period; little drums and vertical flutes, associated with the masks, are used only during the second period, each of these four types of instruments thus receiving a symbolic coloring connected to the central opposition; and the same is true for many other aspects of these rites (different genres of songs, each assigned, even outside the festivals, to a particular period of the year; alternating competitive and authoritarian relationships between age grades; variations in the topography of the rites, etc.). Thus the interpretation of the various ritual sequences is pertinent only within the framework of the system as a whole. For example, if we want to look at the fact that during the first festival of the second period the men who have been dancing alone suddenly stop to insult the women's genitals by beating the earth, we must first know that in the next festival the women will do the same thing in regard to the men, and second, that every other year it is gifts, not insults, that they exchange at these moments. When the sequences are taken as a whole, then, they invalidate many of the interpretations which we would have been tempted to give of the first sequence, and appear more as a vast dance movement, stretched over two years and four festivals, than as a significantly oriented expressive progression. If the sexes are opposed in this way during the second part of the ritual year, this above all because the opposition bush (where the men go)/village (where the women stay) is believed to be more virulent at this time, whereas in the first part of the year it is mediated by field labor, in which men and women collaborate.

The ritual system of the Bedik is a way of mobilizing the village to confront the bush in all of its aspects and impose upon it collective responses adapted to the different phases of the village's relations with the bush in the course of the year. This is especially marked in the fact that it is the ritual system that instigates the generalized custom of collective agricultural labor, each person in turn inviting others to come and work in his field. For some of the labor done in the field of the "village chief" [le responsable du village] is first and foremost part of the rituals themselves; in addition, the millet beer that supplies the festivals and is used for sacrifices is furnished either by the age grades or by the wards, depending on the seasons, and these groups can obtain these obligatory prestations only in return for collective labor performed in the fields of one person or another; finally, ordinary collective labor, which is not for the purpose of furnishing ritual prestations, is usually enlivened at the beginning of the rainy season by the presence of masks, brought out of the bush during the second part of the dry season, who sing and shake rattles to encourage the laborers, disappearing only at the time of the first harvest before the first great festival of this part of the year.

In Rwanda, the situation is entirely different. The rites of the life cycle are highly developed and interrelated in many ways (for all rites, for instance, sexual relations are imposed or forbidden to the kin of the individual concerned); they do not, however, involve an initiation or passage between ritual grades, and take place without reference to cults or to the intervention of identifiable supernatural forces; the fact of spitting a certain liquid into the face of a girl, even against her wishes and those of her family, even by surprise and outside of any ceremony, creates a marriage, and it will not be possible for the young woman to marry a second time in this way. The occasional rites involving the individual are essentially those of worship, either of familial ancestors or of divinized heroes (the kubandwa cited above), involving an individual initiation which can take place at any age, depending on the circumstances. These cults aim above all at reestablishing momentarily threatened vital values (fertility, luck, health, prosperity) by appeasing the spirits or obtaining their protection. The only rituals concerning the population as a whole—who in most cases take only a passive interest in them—are the royal rites, whose content was kept largely secret by the ritualists of the court. These rites have not been performed since 1931, and they were almost impossible to observe before that, but the ritualists preserved a long oral text which they could recite only to the king, and which described the various ritual processes to follow in various circumstances. A. Kagame was able to collect this text in 1945, and it was later edited and translated by other authors, with numerous notes and commentaries (Kagame 1947; d'Hertefelt and Coupez 1964). It is divided into seventeen "ways" or rituals. Five of them aim at reestablishing the sometimes disturbed natural course of production, namely, (1) driving away drought; (2) stopping excessive rains; (3) restoring the productivity of bees; (4) improving hunting; (5) driving away cattle diseases. These rituals share the characteristic of treating these natural problems in political terms: drought must be "defeated" and the rains, which have proper names, must be "awakened" (p. 25); "when the bees foment a rebellion," the king "puts down the rebellion of the bees," and warrior eulogies are recited (pp. 33–35); excessive rains and the "unproductivity" that results from them should also be "defeated," and for this the "banishers of monsters" curse enemy countries and drive off unproductivity, notably by executing a woman without breasts or past menopause, who comes from the Twa (pygmoids) "who do not pay tribute to the king" (pp. 27–31). Cattle plague is "defeated" and the country "freed" of it by a similar procedure (p. 47). In each of these cases the king, assisted by his ritualists, intervenes decisively. To defeat drought, for example, he makes a ritual drum (the symbol of power) which will awaken the rains. The simulated character of these ritual exploits appears even more clearly in the rite for improved hunting: it is solemnly announced to the people that the king is going hunting, bearing dangerous and precious weapons; he does not use them, lest they be carried off by a wounded animal (which would be inauspicious), and he sticks to easy game, lest he risk failing; at the time of his solemn return, the royal procession displays an elephant tusk and a lion or leopard skin which has been taken discreetly from the royal treasury (p. 41).

Five other ritual "ways" are war ceremonials, offensive or defensive; these are just as occasion-based as are the five I have already described. War with a foreign country is considered a "revolt" which the king must put down (p. 159), and the theme of fecundity is as present in the war rituals as in the political or war theme in the fertility rituals: the Rwandan warriors should be "lively" (p. 165) and the enemy country, its weapons and warriors, must be "made to waste away" (p. 167); the king is invited, depending on the circumstances, to suspend or resume sexual relations (pp. 185, 193); the testicles of dead enemy kings are attached to the Rwandan dynastic drum (p. 171); a bull (symbol of virility) of the enemy is captured and slaughtered (p. 179); the decoy drum which the enemy is deliberately allowed to capture is made of wood from a tree that has been completely uprooted, so that its roots cannot grow again (p. 187).

The seven other ritual "ways" can be divided into three groups, each one corresponding to a dangerous transition of the periodic type. The three rituals of the first group are involved in the transition from one reign to another, namely: "the way of indecency" bearing on the treatment of the royal corpse and mourning rites; "the way of competition," an optional rite performed by the queen mother to put down possible competition among pretenders to the throne; "the way of enthronement," involving especially the lifting of mourning, the obligatory resumption of fertilizing activities (copulation, sowing) and a ritual war against a small neighboring country, with the king and his mother pledging, in a single phrase, to "wipe out foreign countries, cattle plagues and diseases" (p. 267). We see that, as in the previous cases, it is a question of correcting a potentially dangerous situation, on the natural as well as the political plane. The same is true for two other rituals, associated with the transition from one cycle of four kings to the next, in which the same reign names will be reused in fixed order. The fourth king of a cycle is required by the first of these rituals to renew the sacred fire that burns perpetually in the court and symbolizes the dynasty. He may no longer leave the western half of the region, which is considered the heart of the country and is surrounded and divided in two by the bends of a river. The first king of the next cycle should, following the second ritual in which cows and pastoral symbolism play a large part, pass with the tanned and preserved remains of his fourth predecessor into the eastern half; this half, which corresponds to the primitive Rwanda and from which the conquering armies set out toward the west, is where these remains will be buried. The new king may no longer leave this half of the region until he dies; then his successor will perform the inverse transfer and, the dynasty thus having been recycled and reinvigorated to ensure a new start, he may from then on, like the third king of the cycle who follows him, leave the center of the country to make conquests in distant lands and increase his territory.

The two last "ways" constitute the only annual rites of Rwanda and come one after the other at the same period, which is also considered one of dangerous transition. The first is a sort of national mourning period which begins at the invisible (final and inauspicious) phase of the moon of *gicuraasi* (May), just at the end of the major rainy season. This period is considered dangerous for people's health both because of the diseases stirred up by changes in temperature and because food stores are lowest at this time. When the next moon appears life is reborn, under the impulsion of the king, by the resumption of all the happy and lifegiving activities which had been momentarily suspended. A few days later the second ritual takes place; its central theme is the arrival at court and the ritual manducation—initiated by the king, who is then followed by all of his people—of the first fruits of the new sorghum, the token of renewed vitality and abundance. As before, fertility symbols and political and warlike symbols are closely linked. These two isolated and juxtaposed annual rites do not, as I understand them, enter into the framework of a seasonal system but respond to one difficult transition among others with different periodicities. In addition, these various periodic rituals are conceived on the same model as the occasional rites with which they form a system. In all of these, the king and his ritualists intervene at the desired moment to correct a dangerous situation, on the natural as well as the political plane. This situation may actually be a difficult one or may simply be foreseen as dangerous. In this case, the first part of the ritual is used to dramatize the conjuncture (the mourning of *gicuraasi*, for example) and the second to entrust the king with the vigorous reestablishment of the normal, that is the happy, course of nature and the polity, which thus receive a new impulsion.

Seasonal among the Bedik, primarily occasional in Rwanda, rituals involving the collectivity respond in each case to radically different conceptions of the relationship between nature and society. For the Rwandans, society is identified as an extension of nature and benefits spontaneously from nature's generosity and life-forces. The king, conceived of both as the political agent of natural phenomena and the fertilizing agent of the social order, is the guarantee of this preestablished but sensitive harmony—sensitive to the extent that any anomaly in the natural order brings about sociopolitical disorder, and vice versa. The most desired goods, abundance of cows and children, incarnate this fusion between natural fecundity and political fecundity. The accidents that are most severely repressed are those that announce a natural disorder in the midst of society, like child-mothers and girls without periods or without breasts: the court must have these monstrous embarrassments banished or eliminated to avoid an epidemic of drought in Rwanda. Government by ritual is thus reduced to the court's occasional interventions to repress deviations and restore the flow of a life-giving current.

For the Bedik, on the contrary, the human village must not be abandoned to the bush. It must be torn out of the bush and constantly affront it. The whole population is permanently organized and mobilized for this, and all relations with the bush are planned to fit the channel of the ritual cycle. The latter aims less at restoring spontaneously positive contacts with nature than at establishing and constantly maintaining them. Difficult times are not anomalous, as in Rwanda, but a normal phase of a cycle which includes several phases, all of which, joyful or dangerous, are treated ritually. Highly egalitarian and solidary, Bedik society severely represses, sometimes by death, only those crimes that are associated with the secret of the masks, the ideological pivot around which turns the order which Bedik society has constructed to confront the harsh realities of the bush.

As we have seen, ritual systems can also be a way of administering, if not a society, at least the minds that make it up. In this regard we should perhaps note (with all the reserves due in this kind of comparison) that on the condition of replacing the above references to the natural order or the bush with references to economic laws (considered as spontaneously beneficent or maleficent), the formal opposition between the two systems that I have been comparing resembles in many respects one that is more familiar to us in the contemporary political world.

Several thousand kilometers to the south of Rwanda, at the other end of the Bantu world, is held the annual *Ncwala*, the royal ritual of the Swazi. The brilliant and detailed description that Hilda Kuper (1947, pp. 197-225) has given of these exceptionally long and complex ceremonies in itself constitutes a major accomplishment. This author has, in addition, analyzed certain aspects of the rite. She first turned her attention to what was also the subject of her book that was just cited: ranks and social statuses. Later, she gave us an interesting analysis of the symbolism of costumes and ornaments, put in relation with the animal species from which most of them are drawn (1973), as well as a study of the pertinence of the changes the ritual has undergone through various periods (1972). In a long article, T. O. Beidelman (1966) has, for his part, analyzed other aspects of the symbolism involved in the *Ncwala*, notably the cosmology and the symbolism associated with colors, the body image, and so on. Beyond these analyses of particular codes, all are agreed that what must be sought in the *Ncwala* is something other than a simple sum of its aspects. If, indeed, analysis tends to show that these aspects converge, it is toward, or around, something else: a function to fulfill, a message to convey, or at the least a central theme which should allow us to establish the identity of the rite in question.

Hilda Kuper begins by citing, without accepting, the interpretations of earlier authors: for one, the *Ncwala* is above all "a great propitiation"; for another, "it is a celebration in which ancient Swazi life is replayed in dramatic form"; for a third, it is "pre-eminently a First Fruits Ceremony." One can certainly see a great many things in the *Ncwala*, which mobilizes all the forces of the kingdom for almost a month, but the examination of the rites themselves in no way corroborates the first two interpretations. The first fruits, on the other hand, really are at the center of the ceremonies. Yet, as Kuper justly remarks, this is only "an essential rite in a complex series of rites." It remains to be explained what connects this theme to various other ones. For Kuper herself, "the *Incwala* is first and foremost a ceremony which ... aims at 'strengthening kingship', at 'showing kingship', 'to make stand the nation'." It also "dramatizes actual rank developed historically: it is a 'play of kingship'. In the ceremony the people see which clans and people are important" (1947, pp. 223, 225).

These conclusions, functionalist in nature, invite a number of objections. Most of the royal rites around the world, which are very different from each other in other respects, all dramatically display the king and the hierarchy that supports him. This explains nothing about the particularities of the *Ncwala*, especially since a well-orchestrated parade would amply suffice to fulfill this function. Why should there be in addition this extraordinarily complex series of extravagant rites, many of which take place out of the sight of the masses?

Why, also, should the Swazi insist, as Kuper underlines, on the fact that everyone must participate in the *Ncwala*, and not watch it as mere spectators? As for the notion of "strengthening the kingship" and "making stand the nation": many sequences do aim explicitly at fortifying the king and sustaining him, but this is to prepare him for still more important sequences in which he passes from the role of central object to that of principal actor, who does not merely use his power but uses it dramatically for various precise ends which cannot be reduced to the above-mentioned functions. Besides this, certain other ritual sequences—and this is the whole problem—seem on the contrary to have as their object and effect to underline and accentuate the weakening and isolation of the king. In brief, the various interpretations suggested seem doomed to oscillate between overly general explanations which let the specific identity of the *Ncwala* slip away, and explanations which are only partially pertinent and find themselves contradicted by other aspects of the ceremonies. The only generalization we have been able to retain up to now, because it is both relatively precise and pertinent for the ritual as a whole, is that the *Ncwala* is a dramatization and not a simple celebration, commemoration, or public rejoicing.

What, then, is the drama being performed? Max Gluckman, in a famous article (1952), has attempted to answer this question by interpreting certain peculiar aspects of the *Ncwala*, particularly the sacred chants which evoke hatred and rejection of the king, and the fact that at a certain moment the king must pass naked through his people while his wives and the queen mother weep and lament over his fate. Because of this, for Gluckman the *Ncwala* is to be classed among "rituals of rebellion." These sequences, in which fundamental tensions and conflicts are ritually expressed, especially the ambivalent attitudes of the people and the princes towards the sovereign, would represent a kind of social catharsis, an institutionalized opposition. They alternate with sequences in which cohesion and loyalty are reaffirmed and thus, in the end, lead to a reinforcement of loyalty.

T. O. Beidelman, in the article cited above, reproaches Gluckman for treating as privileged a very limited aspect of the ritual: rather than first seeking to understand "the vocabulary and grammar" of the symbolism specific to Swazi culture, Gluckman immediately proposes an interpretation in functionalist terms, that is, in terms of sociological and psychological effects which are neither consciously sought by the actors nor suggested by a detailed analysis of the ritual system. It is unquestionable that Gluckman does force the facts in interpreting the songs which evoke hatred and rejection of the king—and this is his main, if not his only, argument—as a cathartic expression of this hatred and rejection. At no time do the singers assume this position; they merely attribute it to others who are not clearly identified but whose supposed existence is put in relation with the difficult situation which the king is believed to be in during this part of the rite. As a Swazi cited by Kuper writes (1947, p. 207): "it is a national expression of sympathy for the king.... The songs show the hatred evoked by the king, but they also demonstrate the loyalty of his supporters. The people who sing the songs sing with pain and suffering, they hate his enemies and denounce them."

So Beidelman in turn proposes a new solution. For him, "the main theme of the *Incwala* is... the separation of the king from the various groups within his nation so that he is free and fit to assume the heavy supernatural powers of his office as king-priest of the nation" (p. 401). It is this separation which is the goal especially of the aforementioned songs and the king's nakedness. These sequences, "far from being periods when the king is symbolically weak..., mark his assumption of great power" (ibid.). In the same way, the complex symbolism of ritual sequences which seem to contradict each other all through the *Ncwala* aim only at conferring an ambivalent, ambiguous, quasi-monstrous personality on the king, so as to make him effective in the supernatural order.

While Beidelman's analyses provide useful clarifications of some particular points of the symbolism, his interpretation is far from convincing as a whole. He himself, indeed, simply says that at least it is better than Gluckman's, and therefore acceptable until a better model has been put forward (p. 401). One can object first of all that, contrary to Beidelman's presentation, which suggests that his global interpretation results from analyses of particular sequences, the latter in fact manifestly result from the former. The royal rites in general would make hardly any sense at all if the king were not treated and did not act separately from the other participants, at least at certain times. The rites whose object is to separate and construct the king, and not only to make use of his unique, already-given position, are the rites of enthronement, and it is hard to see why these should be annual. The most characteristic sequences of the *Ncwala* in this regard have the manifest purpose of reinvigorating, not reinstating, the king. In addition, the sequences which employ songs that evoke hatred for the king and in which he appears naked are, for Beidelman, those in which the king is the most separated; far from being symbolically weak in them, the king assumes his greatest power in these sequences. But it is hard to understand on the basis of this why these are also the sequences in which his people— Kuper's text insists on this repeatedly—identify with him the most intensely, weep, act as if they feel pity for him, suffer with him. These sequences, it is true, are generally followed by another sequence in which his power bursts forth; but the whole problem lies precisely in knowing whether the latter sequence is supposed to illustrate what precedes, as Beidelman thinks, or to contrast with it, as Gluckman thinks. Gluckman, I believe, is correct on the formal plane even while he is mistaken about the content of the contrast, the first sequence clearly not being a rite of rebellion in the sense that he intends. Finally, Beidelman supports only a part of his demonstration with a reasoned analysis of Swazi cultural symbolism; a whole other part, the most contestable one, is based on a reference to a depth psychology of the body in which the effectiveness and the signification of symbolic gestures are referred to as pre-

verbal and prerational affective states which escape both investigation and veri-
fication just as much as the latent sociological functions for which Gluckman
is criticized. Attacked by Beidelman in the same article (p. 402) for the priority
he gives to operations of the intellect, Claude Lévi-Strauss answers him at
length in the "Finale" to L'Homme nu (pp. 569 ff.). One could add that Beidelman, a disciple of Turner's, tends to interpret Swazi royal rites as if they were
Ndembu rites of individual affliction.

On the basis of the positions defined above, one cannot, certainly, exhaust
the analysis of so rich and diverse a symbolism as that of the Ncwala, but one
can, perhaps, at least help to establish the identity of this ritual so as to be able
to compare it globally with others and to put the analysis of particular sequences
into a general framework which would allow us to narrow the field of possible
interpretations of any particular aspect. In brief, what are the principles that
preside over the organization of a cultural phenomenon as complex as this?

For the Swazis, the Ncwala is clearly not just one more ritual among others.
It is the great national event of the year, but it is not integrated into a cycle,
annual or otherwise, which would precede and follow it with other periodic
ceremonies. The only other great royal ritual mentioned by Hilda Kuper is that
in which the king and his mother are given the task of making the rain fall; this
takes place in October, but only "if necessary" (1947, p. 53), that is, when
the first rains expected in September have not arrived and the natural order is
disturbed. As in Rwanda, the responsibility for this disturbance is generally given
to the political order, since the people get angry at the rulers and the rulers
blame the Europeans (pp. 171-72). There are also "irregular" agricultural rites
performed by the queen mother when the crops are poor (p. 242). In a general
way, says Kuper, "there is a ritual for every dangerous situation and ritual must
be performed when the situations arise" (p.166). These formal similarities with
the Rwandan system examined above are reinforced by similar descriptions.
As Beidelman correctly remarks, "Swazi see an order both in the sphere of
natural objects and events and in human society. In most respects it would seem
that a distinction between nature and society is not made by them; rather, the
two are manifestations of the same principles of order in the universe, interdependent and validating one another. Order in one affects order in the other,
and disorder in either jeopardizes the order of both" (p. 376).

The Ncwala is connected to the summer solstice (in December). For the
Swazi, every year the sun makes a great journey in the sky from south to north
and back again. When he reaches the southernmost point of his journey, the sun
is thought to have one "into his hut" and to rest there and get ready to reemerge
vigorously in a new yearlong trek. The Ncwala can neither end before nor begin
after the solstice, for it is said that "the king races the sun," that is, at the
moment the ceremonies end he and his people should have assimilated the new
vigor of the sun, whose departure toward the north marks the new year. The
Ncwala is also tied to the phases of the moon. It includes two parts, the Small

Ncwala and the Great *Ncwala*, separated by an intermediary period of fifteen days. The Small *Ncwala* lasts for two days and is held before the first crescent of the lunar month which includes the solstice, that is, when the preceding moon is supposed to "die," the nights are dark, and human beings are supposed to be weak. The Great *Ncwala* lasts for six days and begins at the full moon, which is associated with human health and vigor. The moon is considered the wife of the sun, walking behind him. The lunar month preceding that of the solstice, the month at the end of which the Small *Ncwala* takes place, when the sun gets back from his long voyage, is called "Little Chief." The lunar month which includes the solstice and the Great *Ncwala*, and which marks the new departure of the sun and the beginning of the new year, is called "Great Chief" (Kuper 1947, pp. 53, 201-2, 208). We see therefore that the sun, the moon, the year, and with them the king and his people, reach the end of the race before setting off again, and that the *Ncwala* itself conforms to these two-part rhythms.

To these cosmic correlations is, however, added another which justifies them, but which neither Kuper nor Beidelman draws upon in their interpretations. When she describes agricultural life, Kuper tells us that the period preceding the December solstice is that of the peak of hunger before the first crops ripen and may be eaten. It is the time when "the highest output of energy is required, [while] the food supply is at its lowest"; the lunar month during which the *Ncwala* takes place is also called "to swallow the pickings of the teeth." The month that follows is, on the contrary, called "Everyone is satisfied," for it is the time of abundance (pp. 36, 50-53). Gluckman notes this opposition, but does so only to refer it immediately back to his interpretative model: this season in which "socially disruptive forces [are] working" would also be propitious for internal struggles and the ritual of rebellion (1963, p. 132). But the content of this drama is far more grandiose than that to which he reduces it. It is first of all a dangerous transition, a disorder on the cosmic plane tied to the productivity of nature, which the king, guarantor of universal harmony, must confront—and the whole of Kuper's text shows that his people are with the king at this time to support and sympathize with him in "his heavy work" (p. 215). It is only if he does not emerge victorious from his ordeal that "disruptive forces" would rebound into the political and social order. Since this dangerous transition is a regular one, it does not call, as would an unpredictable drought, for reciprocal censure of the king and his people. We do, however, find its echo or prefiguration tied to the ritual dramatization of the crisis, in the songs alluding to the unidentified enemies of the king (and so of the Swazi in general).

Having thus situated the *Ncwala* in its general framework, one may now ask what central act it is organized around—what I above called the "snare for thought" or the simulation. Here one must look at the exploit of the king, or rather a series of exploits which respond to the various aspects of cosmic and natural transitions, accompany them, and are believed in the end to be based on a single necessity. Upon a concrete dramatic base, the height of famine, the

Swazi superimpose two different dramas, one in the cosmic order, the other in the sociopolitical order. This is not gratuitous. The new harvests close the drama only because this victory of nature is also the victory of the sun and moon, who determine the recurring cycle of years, seasons, months, and days, and the victory of men who have been able to produce, thanks to the beneficent order maintained by the king. Just as all of the productive forces of nature are eminently incarnated in the few products of the earth which are kept for the rite of consumption of the firstfruits and in the two gourds which symbolize the old year and the new year, so all the forces of the cosmos are incarnated in the voyage of the sun and the rebirth of the moon, and all the forces of society in what the Swazi call "the play of the king," with supporting parts for his close kin and his faithful warriors and ritualists.

The astonishing complexity of the *Ncwala* is probably the result of a slow historical development tied to the development and diversification of the Swazi nation, in which more and more diverse specialists and social groups had their role to play; it is also the result of the general principle stated by the Swazi that, when one must change a rite, "it is better to add than to discard" (Kuper 1947, p. 224). But all through the ceremonies, it is the same dramatic schema in double time that is prefigured, played in different ways, repeated at different levels, some of which are nested inside others. And the first beat, which marks the weakening of the cosmic forces, the exhaustion of nature, the end of the year, the distress of men, and the "passion" of the king, is thus as necessary to the basic structure of the rite as, for Christians, Good Friday is necessary for Easter Sunday. The various sequences that are negatively marked by the state of crisis are always followed by a new exploit of the king and the triumphal sequence that goes along with it.

This happens, first of all, on the scale of a single reign. When a king dies, his successor is generally a minor under the authority of a regent. Mourning has "darkened" and weakened the nation. The *Ncwala* is then reduced to a bare sketch in which neither the negative nor the positive beat is marked, the essential thing being the consumption of the firstfruits. The ritual then grows from year to year, paralleling the development of the young king. It is only when the king reaches maturity, is married to his ritual wives, and fully assumes his functions, that the *Ncwala* is played in its entirety and with its full intensity.

We find a similar opposition between the Small and the Great *Ncwala*. The former, which takes place during the inauspicious period of the new moon (the old dead moon for the Swazi), only prefigures the second, which takes place during the auspicious period of the following full moon. The Small *Ncwala* is dominated by an atmosphere of crisis, the Great *Ncwala* by one of triumph. Each, however, includes both phases. The first day of the Small *Ncwala* is dominated by songs evoking the difficult situation of the king, but a twilight the formation of dancers changes from a crescent to a circle (full moon), prefiguring what will happen fifteen days later. It is at this time that the king, aided by the ritualists, accomplishes his first feat, which consists of breaking the old year and preparing the advent of the new. Hidden in his hut, he spits toward the East and the West through two small holes in the hut walls—this gesture being associated with the fertilizing power of the king (Kuper 1947, pp. 80, 215)—while the principle ritualist cries, "He stabs it with his two horns, our bull!" The crowd outside applauds, then chants the final song, a triumphant eulogy.

The next day, at dawn, the same sequences are reproduced briefly, then the Small *Ncwala* ends with the weeding of the queen mother's fields by the warriors; but although they do the work, they are thought to do so without energy. For Gluckman, this is "at least an unconscious protest against work for the state" (p. 122). But Kuper's text clearly states that while it is their lack of energy that is stressed, they may still be perfectly happy to do the work (p. 206); their lassitude simply expresses the fact that the time of the Small *Ncwala* is one of general weakening connected with the expiration of the year; at the end of the Great *Ncwala*, the same work will be performed again for two days by the same warriors and, this time, without any negative connotation (p. 221).

The first sacred song of the Great *Ncwala* is a lullaby in which the warriors say they are rocking a baby (the king) who will grow up and become as big as the world. The first three days are devoted to a complex series of rites to prepare the king, who should be "reborn [and] revitalized" (p. 210). The vitality of bright green, resistant, tough, rapidly growing plants is made to contribute, as well as the vigor of bulls, the king being identified as the "bull of the people." Next he "bites" various magical substances several times and the crowd again applauds for these feats, which mark his development and are supposed to prevent evil during the course of the new year. The dancing warriors again move from a crescent into a circle. The fourth day is the "Great Day." It opens with songs of crisis, but this time one hears at the same time the above-mentioned lullaby of hope, which is sung by the youngest people present. It is at this time that the king passes naked among his weeping or pitying people. Shut up in his hut, he again spits a magic potion through holes to the East and West of the hut, while the ritualist cries, "He stabs it!" and the crowd cheers. It is at this time that he consumes the firstfruits; he is followed in doing this by his close kin and, in the succeeding days, by all his people. Just as when he spits it is announced that he "stabs," when he eats it is said that he "bites"; this, with the applause that follows, underlines the fact that these ritual actions are taken as heroic feats. At the end of the afternoon, the king is pushed into his sanctuary by the members of his clan, who intone a new, sad song in which they announce that they are going to leave the country and its people. Then the princes, who have remained outside, call him back: "Come, the sun is leaving you, come, king of kings, father. . . . !" It is now that, passing the point of the solstice along with the sun, the king emerges in the fantastic costume of a legendary monster and performs a wild dance. He hesitates to return to his people, and disappears back into his hut. The princes call him and he reappears. This happens several more times, in general tension and excitement. The last time, when the scene reaches its climax, he holds in his hand the gourd symbolizing the past year that was cut at the previous year's *Ncwala*, and throws it onto the black shield of one of his warriors, who is supposed to die in battle during the year.

Throughout this sequence, the king is clearly identified with the sun, who, after resting in his solstitial hut, springs forth with new vigor to recommence his annual voyage. His fantastic costume and his mad dance invert and justify his morning nakedness and his sad passage through his people. Like the sun resting in his hut at the end of his journey, the king in his own hut, to use the image suggested by a Swazi (Kuper 1972, p. 604 n. 1), refuels his engine. The heroic nature of his dazzling emergence and his toss of the gourd is accentuated by his dramatic appearances, departures, and returns, which reproduce at an accelerated rhythm, pushed on to a climax, the two-beat structure—each beat here separated by the king's retreat into his sanctuary—which, repeated with various connotations and at various tempos, makes up the scenario of the *Ncwala*.

We find this structure again, in a different mode, in the rites that mark the last two days of the *Ncwala*. After the peak of the "Great Day," the king and his people must observe a day of confinement and restrictions similar to those for the state of mourning; normal activities and behavior are suspended: it is forbidden to work, have sexual relations, to scratch one's head, to make merry, to sing, and so on. The death of the old year requires this one final transition from inauspicious to auspicious evocations, "to come again into lightness" (Kuper 1947, p. 220). On the last day, a great purifying pyre, lit by the king, will consume the gourd symbolizing the old year and with it all the ornaments and ritual objects, which will be remade for the next year. Finally the rain will fall and put the fire out. The people sing and dance around their king, but the sacred songs evoking crisis are now forbidden for another year. All activities are resumed in an atmosphere of joy, prosperity, and amorous license. All that remains to be done is for the faithful warriors to devote two days to agricultural labor, spontaneously energetic labor this time, in the royal fields, while throughout the country the heads of families give the signal for the consumption of the firstfruits.

The similarities between the *Ncwala* and the annual royal rites of Rwanda are striking. In both cases, the ritual takes place at the end of the heaviest rains (May in Rwanda, December among the Swazi), at what is considered the most critical period of the year, when food stores are at their lowest. In both cases we have a first set of ceremonies associated with the inauspicious connotations of the next moon. In both cases, too, the king's consumption of the firstfruits, followed in this by his people, is at the center of the second set. We have seen that in both cases, the central role of the king results from the responsibility he is supposed to assume in maintaining or reestablishing harmony in the natural and social orders, which are conceived of as closely interdependent, if not identical. There are also many similarities in detail, particularly in the ritual roles of the queen mother and of cattle. Let me give another example here. In Rwanda, the first sorghum is grown by ritualists in a particular region of the country; the text of the Rwandan ritual describes the voyage of these ritualists to bring this precious sorghum to the court: "They rob and beat people.... At the places where the *igitenga* basket spends the night, people make gifts of hospitality. If someone does not do this, his hut is destroyed. And even if they come upon tribute on its way to court, or provisions for the chiefs, they confiscate it without anyone complaining" (d'Hertefelt and Coupez 1964, p. 83). Among the Swazi, before the *Ncwala*, specialized ritualists go to seek "the waters of the world" drawn by the ocean and mountain rivers and brought back to the capital (to resupply the king and the nation) in a sacred vessel; Kuper's text (p. 200) describes their return as follows: "They behave with studied arrogance. They accost anyone who crosses their path... and demand a fine. They pillage the countryside and take any beer they find in the huts." Finally, in both cases the ritual exploits of the king are inscribed in cultural contexts in which the heroic feat is an essential social value linked to the definition of a man as a warrior and fertilizing agent, and in which it also constitutes the privileged source of poetic inspiration.

In brief, despite the enormous distance and the dozens of very different societies which separate them, one suspects that the Rwandan and Swazi cultures, and more generally those of the Bantu kingdoms of the regions of the great lakes on the one hand, and those of the extreme southeast of Africa on the other, both marked by the "cattle complex," have a relatively close historical relationship. In this case, the comparison of rituals is all the more revealing in that it permits us to uncover an abstract schema that has been maintained through the centuries, in spite of numerous differences both on the level of the symbolic content of particular procedures (privileged by Beidelman), and on that of the sociological pertinence of the whole (privileged by Kuper and Gluckman). In Rwanda, there is almost no hint of the deployment of hierarchies and roles characteristic of the *Ncwala*; most of the royal rites take place where they cannot be seen, or even without the people's knowledge. I found nothing that could be interpreted in terms of catharsis, either in the theme of the nakedness and isolation of the king, or in its sequel (the wild dance of the costumed king). The annual rites of Rwanda, too near the equator, were associated neither with the course of the sun nor with the idea of a new year. They were more hieratic, simple, and sober than the *Ncwala*. Their dramatic schema was relatively discrete and linear, simply moving from a symbolic national mourning to the ritual resumption of activities, followed by the consumption of the firstfruits, without the prefigurations, reversals, and dramatizations, on several levels inside each other, characteristic of the *Ncwala*. The theme of death and rebirth is common to both, but while the Rwandans code the first phase in terms of mourning, the Swazi code it in terms of a manifest crisis; in Rwanda, they stop farming and beating drums, while the Swazi farm in spite of themselves, without energy, and sing sad songs. The attitudes of mourning, then of the lifting of mourning, appear only at the very end of the *Ncwala*, as a final exorcism of the inauspicious evocations linked to the year that has just been buried; in Rwanda, too, they celebrate the lifting of the state of mourning, says the text, "to abolish (the lunar month of) *Gicuraasi*" and "to keep this moon from remaining in your enclosures!" (pp. 74-75).

In the preceding descriptions I have not considered many ritual procedures which surround the central schema, and which clearly have no object but to prepare for it by, for example, strengthening the king or sacred objects and materials. To understand these, one must draw on a thorough knowledge and a detailed analysis of the (Swazi and Rwandan) cultural symbolism of animal and vegetable species, gestures, colors, substances, and the like, and also on a thorough knowledge of the history, or other connotations, attached to places, clans, and so on. Kuper and Beidelman have attempted this in a partial way in their analyses of the *Ncwala*, but it seems quite evident to me that in this case all of these symbolic and sociological aspects come together simply to fortify and enrich the central schema; they are only the flesh on a skeleton which organizes the rite within a particular species, and around particular neurological nodes. Even the sacrifice of cattle, which is very common in the Rwandan royal rites and re-peated in the *Ncwala*, manifestly plays only a supportive role and is indispen-sable neither to the ritual nor to its interpretations, whereas in other types of rituals it may constitute the central fact. In brief, it is by considering rites first of all in their most stripped-down aspect, rather than by accumulating glosses, that we can best assign them an identity allowing us to guide and control subse-quent analyses.

Concrete ritual phenomena are situated at the intersection of two dimensions that are often forgotten by those who analyze them: on the one hand, the coherence of the attitudes specific to a ritual system taken as a whole; on the other, the ludic, aesthetic, and illusionistic aspect. These dimensions come together to produce certain parallel, mutually reinforcing effects: first, those which believers impute to the rites and, second, those which the rites produce in believers. The latter would hardly be different from the aesthetic effects pro-duced by various forms of art, which are often integrated with rites, or have their deepest historical roots in ritual—except that the belief that is called religious causes believers to take this second effect for the first.

Art itself, however, never quite breaks free of this ambiguity; when it suc-ceeds, it always maintains a simulation which is experienced as magic. The dif-ference between this and thé recourse to "snares for thought" is perhaps of the same order as that between the stage magician who simulates prodigies and more or less pretends to make us believe in them, and the prestidigitator who quite simply recognizes himself as such but skillfully ends up making us wonder about it. The preference for one or the other of them is surely a subjective thing. In the "Finale" to *L'Homme nu*, Claude Lévi-Strauss compares, among other things, myths to music (pp. 577-96), and then immediately afterwards to rituals (pp. 597-611), attempting in a certain way to make myths seem similar to music, which he delights in, and to make them seem unlike rituals, of which, curiously, he draws a rather repellent picture. He does, however, recognize a single illusionistic component in both music and ritual. By the dividing up and repetition which characterizes its procedures, ritual "feeds the illusion that it is possible to go in the opposite direction from myth, to remake the continuous out of the discontinuous"; this is, however, "a hopeless attempt, forever doomed to failure," a "bastardization of thought, resigned to the servitudes of life" (p. 603). Music, on the other hand, "provides the healthy illusion that contradictions can be overcome and difficulties resolved" (p. 590). The reason for the contrast—and his brilliant pages attempt to demonstrate this—lies in the fact that music (probably like other forms of art) succeeds in its illusionistic project, whereas rituals, attempting the impossible, fail. Still, the excellent analysis, here presented as an example, of Ravel's *Bolero* (which is also marked by dividing up and repetition), once it escapes from strictly technical language, is summarized and concluded in phrases that could just as well fit a ritual experience such as the *Ncwala*: "So . . . the superimposed planes of the real, the symbolic, and the imaginary follow, capture, and partially cover each other until the discovery of the correct tonality, even though this has remained in a state of Utopia through the whole of the work. And when the modulation finally makes the orders of the real and the imaginary join and coincide, the other oppositions are absorbed. . . . The apparent antinomy . . . gives way under the effect of a mediation whose proof has just been administered. . . . After a supreme tumult cut short, the score ends in the consecrating silences of a labor well fulfilled" (p. 596).

References

Beidelman, T. O. "Swazi Royal Ritual." *Africa* 36, no. 4 (1966): 373-405.
Dundes, Alan. "A Psychoanalytic Study of the Bullroarer." *Man* 11, no. 2 (1976): 220-38.
Eliade, Mircea. *Birth and Rebirth*. New York: Harper and Row, 1958.
Gluckman, Max. "Rituals of Religion in South-East Africa" (The Frazer Lecture, 1952). In *Order and Rebellion in Tribal Africa*, London: Cohen and West, 1963, pp. 110-36.
Haddon, A. C. *The Study of Man*. London: John Murray, 1898.
d'Hertefelt, M., and Coupez, A. *La royauté sacrée de l'ancien Rwanda*. Tervuren: Musée royal de l'Afrique centrale, 1964.
Kagame, A. "Le code ésotérique de la dynastie du Rwanda." *Zaïre* 1, no. 4 (1947): 363-86.

Kuper, Hilda. *An African Aristocracy. Rank among the Swazi*. London: Oxford University Press, 1947.

———. "A Royal Ritual in a Changing Political Context." *Cahiers d'Etudes Africaines* 12, no. 4 (1972): 593-615.

———. "Costume and Cosmology: The Animal Symbolism of the Ncwala." *Man* 8, no. 4 (1973): 613-30.

Lévi-Strauss, Claude. *L'Homme nu*. Mythologiques IV. Paris: Plon, 1971.

Smith, Pierre. "Les échelons d'âge dans l'organisation sociale et rituelle des Bedik." In D. Paulme, ed. *Classes et associations d'âge en Afrique de l'Ouest*. Paris: Plon, 1971, pp. 185-204.

Turner, V. W. *The Forest of Symbols. Aspects of Ndembu Ritual*. Ithaca: Cornell University Press, 1967.

———. *The Drums of Affliction: A Study of Religious Processes among the Ndembu of Zambia*. Oxford: Oxford University Press, 1968.

Patrice Bidou

8

On Incest and Death
A Myth of the Tatuyo Indians
of Northwest Amazonia

Since there were no women . . .

For one or two seconds the thread of discourse is held back, then the teller picks (himself) up again and adds:

. . . no women of an "other" group,

and he goes on:

Moon took out the end of his penis to satisfy himself against the trunk of a banana tree.

So in this first burst of speech, my sister who lives next to me under the great common roof of the maloca is not a woman: "Since there were no women . . ."; she is forgotten as a person with whom I can express my sexual desire. But things are not so simple—and the words, too, can falter—for my sister *is* a woman if I want to think so even for a second or two. The immediate enunciation, here that of the myth, expresses the rule, the custom (immediate to the extent that it is true that the rule or rules—culture—constitutes the nature of man), while speech picked up again expresses a reflection on the rule. What is being reflected on is this: *even though my sister is a woman, I still must not sleep with her and even less take her as a wife.* This is above all—one might say classically—a reflection on the social; but it is also, and at the same time, a reflection upon the individual who lives the rule (in whom the rule lives). For as soon as there is a rule, there is, somewhere in the individual, constraint, coercion. And no coercion

129

takes place without pain: it is thus a question of analyzing how (for what we are interested in is not only what the myth says, but how it says it) the myth points to and signifies the wounds created by work (the "work of culture") in the depths of individuals, in a given society, at a given moment.

The Tatuyo[1] speak of incest (of the prohibition of incest)—and of death—when they tell the following story, which relates the adventures of Moon and of his sister, Mênê-Riyo.

Since there were no women ... no women of an "other" group, Moon took out the end of his penis to satisfy himself against the trunk of a banana tree. Moon is a man, he is the son of Sun, he is "the one of the night."[2]

She is his sister.

She had finished peeling the manioc and went out to throw away the peels. There she saw him: "Ah, you're doing that all alone, you poor thing, I feel sorry for you! Come on and 'do it' with me, but only one little time," so she said, to her own brother.

She let him do it and they made love together.

She had told him, you can do it, but only once.... But he didn't want to stop and he came back to her that night. The next night he went with her again, the same thing the next night, every night he went with her.

She had enough of it: "Who comes every night to 'play' with me?" she wondered. She was pregnant. She prepared black dye, genipa. She poured it into a pot and put it down near the fire next to her. That night he showed up. While they were "doing it," she soaked her hands in the pot of genipa dye and smeared the face of Moon, "the one of the night."

(Look up there, you'll see, he still has his black spots.)

When he was finished, he went back to stretch out in his hammock. At daybreak he looked in a mirror: aiie! there it was, his face covered with black spots. In the pale light of dawn he went into the forest, he went to a "pegaro-so" tree, gashed it, and covered his face with rubber sap to get rid of the stains. Nothing worked, they remained indelible.

His sister was looking for him: "Where can he be? It was surely he, my younger brother, who was coming every night to 'do it' with me," she thought. She went off to look for him; she met him down there on the road in the forest, he was sitting with his eyes fixed on the mirror. He saw her come up behind him, she who was the cause of all his troubles. So he flipped the mirror, and in a flash she was hurled into the air, up into the sky,

Moon was very angry and so he did this to get rid of her and make her disappear.

1. The Tatuyo (*Pámwa mahã*), who call themselves the "Sons of the Celestial Anaconda," constitute a small tribe of around three hundred individuals belonging to the Tucano linguistic and cultural ensemble. The Tucano live on the upper reaches of the Pira Piraná (Vaupés, Colombia) (cf. P. Bidou 1974, 1976, 1977). For the semantic analysis of certain indigenous words we have benefited from Mme E. Gomez-Imbert's knowledge of Tatuyo linguistics; this text was read by Mme J. Duvernay, Mme S. Picon, M. C. Gros, and M. M. Perrin. I thank all of these individuals for their valuable help and advice.

2. The same word (*mwipî*) designates the sun and the moon (both being masculine figures); in opposition to the moon, who is called "the one of the night," the sun is called "the one of the day," or "the warming one."

This is sorcery; the words for blowing to get rid of women go like this . . .[3]
Moon couldn't manage to pull out his blackened hairs: he thought bad
things, he was ashamed. Then he called the *mwipîkakáa* ants, they ate him
completely, he died right there, there in the forest. Moon is the first one to
get sick and die. He died like that, by himself. Sun, his father, was angry:
"Where is my son, what has happened to him?" he said, and he went off to
look for him. By this time Moon had no flesh left; he was rotten, decomposed. Only his bones remained, scattered on the ground. Sun went off to
look for him to put him back together again, to remake his body; This is
why people later will blow to heal diseases. . . .

We will stop the teller here, but the tale goes on; this "myth" in fact constitutes only the opening sequence of a long story whose principal hero is named
"Bitter."[4] Bitter is the fruit of the incest between Moon and his sister (respectively son and daughter of the Sun), he is thus the Sun's grandson by direct
descent. After his birth, which is an extremely long and complex affair, Bitter
undertakes the making of a "piece of anaconda" drum to "call people to be
born." After this he will follow and protect them the whole length of their
journey back up the river, furnishing them with all the necessary elements—
"natural" as well as "cultural," for their life on earth. An orphan, bitter, unwell
(he had a withered leg), Bitter appears essentially as a mediating character:
between the sky and the earth on the one hand, between "People" (*mahâ*) (this
is what the Indians call themselves) and the whites, on the other. Synthesizing
these two points of view, young Indians who had "passed" through the missions
identified Bitter with Jesus [or vice versa], and his mother Mênê-Riyo with the
Virgin Mary. What irony! The former is the fruit of a carnal union, an incestous
one to boot, the latter of an immaculate conception. But when all is said and
done, couldn't the latter means of procreating be considered a kind of hyper-
incest?

The "Story of Bitter" is very popular among the Tucano populations of the
Vaupés (the linguistic and cultural ensemble to which the Tatuyo belong); it is
certainly the best-known story, to women and children as well as to men. Many
versions have been collected and we will not fail to call upon them whenever it
seems necessary to illustrate the analysis.[5]

3. "Shamanic" speech is closely tied to the discourse (the story) of the myth. In other
words, every time the myth recounts a certain order of things, and the teller is himself a
shaman (as is the case here), at the same time "shamanic" words, which allow an intervention in this order, are pronounced. In this myth, the dots represent the "shamanic" speech,
which we have omitted to keep the text a reasonable length.
4. To keep him from being eaten by the Four-Tooth Jaguars (who are the whites), his
grandfather (the Sun) smeared him with the juice of a bitter plant, whence his name "Bitter"
(*higê*). Bitter is also commonly known under the name Warimi, which seems to mean "the
one who went away." Bitter has many other names as well, based on the important times
and events of his life.
5. This study is based in the first place on a dozen versions I collected personally (always
directly in the indigenous language), mainly among the Tatuyo (of various clans), but also
among their northern neighbors, the Carapana. Outside of this I have drawn primarily on
three sources, all from Tucano populations: Alfonso Torres Laborde (1970), which includes

The Tatuyo speak of incest—in its direct or its metaphoric form—in many other contexts of their mythology. Thus, a man lives with his daughter—who is named "Breast"—and the two constitute a monstrous couple which devours people. Bitter goes to their maloca. He is almost killed several times, notably by Breast's deadly stream of urine, and finally succeeds in killing the latter by striking her in the genitals. He cooks her with very hot peppers. The father comes home and is delighted at the good "food" that his daughter has been able to find. He starts to eat, and it is at the precise moment when he is eating his daughter's breast that he realizes his mistake; he dies poisoned. In the inversion of this, another myth recounts how a father who lives in intrigue with his daughter constantly tries to kill a suitor of hers (Morning Star). Finally the daughter kills his father in order to eat him—she cuts off his head with her weeding tool—thinking that it is her suitor.

Still, the story of Moon and Mênê-Riyo is exemplary, for several reasons: It is about the first act of sexual relations per se, and this is incestous.

Incest here appears in a direct and explicit manner, it is one of the principal themes "treated" by the myth.

The protagonists are a brother and a sister; in Tatuyo society, my sister is certainly the most consumable member of my family, but she is also par excellence the one whom I must renounce in order to give her to an "other," so as to get his sister in exchange as my wife. We should note that in many contexts this brother/sister relationship turns into a father/daughter relationship; the latter can also be one I exchange to get a wife, either for myself or for my son. Thus, in the mythology of the Desana (another group of the Tucano ensemble), the primordial incest takes place between the Sun and his daughter.[6] We should note in addition that son/mother (or mother/son) incest seems to belong to a much more hidden discourse, and poses a certain number of problems which we can only indicate here. In other words, in taking—as the myth invites us to do—the brother/sister relationship as the paradigm of incest among the Tatuyo, we can in no way claim to exhaust this theme.

Finally, this tale is exemplary to the extent that the character of the incestous moon represents one of the most widespread mythic themes of the New World, and is, in fact, found from one end of the American continent to the other.

Whatever the versions, they all open on to two facts that are absolute preconditions of incest, namely: on the one hand, a (social) structure, the *family*;

a fairly complete version of the "Historia de Luna"; Martin Von Hildebrand (1975) in which several passages appear, embedded in the story of the Imarikakana (figures who are called Ayáwaroa by the Tatuyo), relating the incest between Moon and his sister. Last but not least, Steve and Christine Hugh-Jones were kind enough to share all of the (unpublished) versions they had collected among the Barsana, southern neighbors of the Tatuyo, for which they have my warmest thanks.

6. Reichel-Dolmatoff (1968): the sun commits incest with his daughter (pp. 24, 41). Reichel-Dolmatoff (1975, p. 127): "The sun and the moon (Tukano myth) were brothers, and the moon's daughter lived on earth. At night the moon came down and committed incest with her...."

on the other hand, a desire (a drive), *sexual desire* (Moon takes out his penis to masturbate against the trunk of a banana tree).

The whole affair proceeds from the encounter of these two liminal facts: the first resolutely social (cultural), the second profoundly natural. We know the results of this immemorial encounter: the drives must be regularized for society to exist. Nevertheless, this procedure has something in it which may surprise us; for what does mythic speech do in its very enterprise of reduction, but give voice to sexual desire as such, and increase it in doing so? In other words, far from making the listener *forget* sexual desire with all its disorderly force, the myth (a public discourse which is ceaselessly said and resaid, discussed, commented on, interpereted, even disputed) reminds one of it constantly, constantly rekindling in Indian thought and experience the maxim that we can give as follows: "Sex is one thing, its social expression should be something else."

So it appears crucial for us to stress from the beginning that, unlike our society in which no one really knows any more why he shouldn't sleep with his sister ("It just isn't done"),[7] the Tatuyo have been careful to explain the deep signification of this interdiction, the relation between this rule of incest prohibition and the survival of the group appearing too immediately to be left unclear.

From the beginning, then, there is the family: one is among one's own. (One is among one's own; but already, in the very constitution of the self, the hesitation of [mythic] speech clearly shows that the latter can only be constituted as one element in a larger system in which the "other" [or the "others"] is also included.)

There is Sun, the father, but at the beginning of the story he remains off-stage. There is his son Moon, and his daughter Mênê-Riyo. And, stresses the myth: "She is the sister," and "(he is) her own brother." This is fundamental, for without it nothing happens. It thus appears clearly that the incest prohibition cannot found the family (this is meaningless) but that on the contrary it reproduces the family, and in this sense it appears as the *co-naissance* of the family.[8]

But isn't there a strange vicious circle here? For it seems to be necessary to institute a rule, the prohibition of incest; but in order to do this it would seem necessary that a structure (the family) already be given, which, in itself, signifies that the whole society is also present and so, of course, the rule also. This would indeed be a vicious circle if we considered the myth as a narrative retracing the origin of the prohibition. But while everything appears to invite this—the linear structure of the discourse, the diachrony of the narrative, and finally and above all our own mental structuralism in relation to history and explanation—to proceed in this way would be a strategic error in the enterprise of understanding

---

7. In our society one of the reasons for this structural indetermination should probably be looked for in the extreme distance that lies between the individual and the social totality.

8. TN: Here the author is playing on two possible senses: *connaissance*, "knowledge," and *co-naissance*, "co-birth," "birth together."

mythic thought. From the beginning of the myth, the rule is there, totally present. It could not be more clearly stated from the first sentence on: there are women on one side and "other" women on the other. It is not a problem of origin but of structures, or of "knowing," as the Tatuyo say. *Mahî* is knowledge, and it is also power. *Ka mahã* (= the People) comes from the same root; it is literally "those who know," "those endowed with knowledge."

In other words, it is not so much a question of considering the sexual drive in the raw state and its social expression as two limits marking the distance to be covered, or that have been covered, by humanity in passing from nature to culture, but as two concomitant givens whose relations connect and disconnect within society and within individuals. In order to do this, the myth narrates: it narrates a story [*une histoire*] (and it is here, and here alone, that there is a real diachrony), the story of the actual transgression of the rule and what results (resulted) from this. If a rule, a taboo, has never been broken, then it is not known, "it stands there, as it were, in its sovereignty."[9] By recounting the actual transgression of the incest prohibition, the myth brings to light, in every domain and at every level, the whole set of complex mechanisms that are involved; running through the rule in this way, it defines the rule in extension, it lays out the synoptic table of its violations. And the shaman is above all the one who knows how to read this table.

So this day, since there weren't any women, Moon, full of sexual desire, used the trunk of a banana tree to satisfy himself. But it happened, as if by chance, that at that moment his sister came out of the maloca to throw out the peels of the manioc she had been peeling; and she saw her brother there. Nobody, of course, believes in chance, but it is important to play at it, for what is involved if not precisely "the substitution, in this domain as in all others, of organization for chance"?[10] "She had finished peeling the manioc..."—an insignificant detail? To think so would be to miss the nature of myths totally; this "detail," in fact, produces the conjunction between brother and sister. A spatial conjunction first of all; for it is at the foot of the banana trees which grow in a border around the open area surrounding the maloca that women come to throw away rinds and garbage in general. Next a sexual conjunction; for when she says to him: "you are all alone, you poor thing..." she expresses the reality that, for her too, he is the only man, or rather that there are no "other" men. We should point out, also, that the work of transformation of manioc—particularly its grating—is an activity with strong sexual connotations. Immediately after they are peeled, the manioc tubers are shredded: the woman sits on the ground with her legs spread, the grater rests between her thighs, one end is jammed against a beam of the

---

9. "The rule *qua* rule is detached; it stands there, as it were, in its sovereignity; although what gives it its importance are the facts of daily experience." (Ludwig Wittgenstein, *Bemerkungen über die Grundlagen der Mathematik*, cited by J. Bouveresse [1977, p. 43]).
10. Lévi-Strauss 1967, p. 32.

maloca, the other is supported on the lower part of her abdomen. The tubers are then seized by the handful and with a rapid back and forth movement they are shredded on the little stone teeth embedded in the wood.[11] But on this day Moon's sister, after peeling the manioc, when she was about to start grating it, saw her brother masturbating; she invited him, "Come do it with me ...," and according to another version, "I have what it takes to do that. Come try it a little." ("Luna culeaba con un palo. 'Para qué hace con el palo?' dijo la hermana. 'Yo tengo para hacer eso. Pruébelo una vez.' Era la propria hermana, mismo papa, mismo mama" [M. Von Hildebrand 1975, pp. 345-46] .)

There is a sort of substitution, both for her and for him: "and they made love together." At these words the teller of the tale, an adult clan elder, laughed. And in fact, to speak of having sexual relations with one's sister, or even to really have them—it happens—does not seem to have any serious consequences: it makes people laugh, and the men joke about this in the evening in the maloca while they smoke and take coca. We must, however, specify that this generally involves classificatory sisters who do not live under the same roof.

We can note in passing, at any rate, that in the indigenous theory of the prohibition of incest no "voice of the blood," no "repugnance due to over-familiarity," no "lack of stimulation" is invoked as a natural obstacle to a sexual relationship between a brother and a sister. Most of the versions stress: "He found it good," and "She liked it."

So sleeping with one's sister does not seem to have consequences. Yes, but on condition that, as in the myth, it just happens once or twice, in passing. But Moon didn't want to stop, and every night he came to "do it" or "play" (as the Tatuyo say) with his sister: he came at nightfall and, neither seen nor known, took off before the break of day. Thus the sexual relation between brother and sister, if it is to continue, or in order to continue, turns from being diurnal—open— to being nocturnal—hidden. In other words, from being visible and social, the sexual relationship becomes secret, it burrows into the private lives of individuals, while at the same time speech gives way to silence and to caresses.[12] We are at the heart of incest.

Thus, at the price of a plunge into the night, everything apparently (so to speak) goes well; "he found it good," "she liked it." Certainly, but only until the day she found herself pregnant: at this point everything falls apart, this

11. It was Professor G. Reichel-Dolmatoff who pointed out the sexual symbolism of the manioc grater (personal communication): this grater, which consists of an oblong, slightly concave wooden board, represents the *vagina dentata*. On its upper part a long protuberance indicates the clitoris, the little stones incrusted underneath are the teeth, and the edges are the labia.

12. On this subject, C. Lévi-Strauss notes: "Although night is a necessary precondition for sexual communication, by a compensating movement which is intended to restore the balance, night would seem to forbid linguistic communication between the partners." A few lines further down he adds, based, precisely, on a Tucano example: "Individuals of opposite sexes can exchange either words or caresses, but not both at the same time, since this would be considered an abuse of communication" (Lévi-Strauss 1967, p. 418, n. 19).

event is decisive, it constitutes the instance on which the rule of the incest prohibition is really founded. For a child is to be born, and so immediately poses that essential question which no society can avoid, since it is what founds society: to what group does (or will) this child who is about to greet the day belong? We must come out of the night whether we want to or not. (Another solution is possible—that the child not be born—this is infanticide, which is sometimes practiced in such cases.)

For the Tatuyo this question is particularly crucial, since the child's deepest nature, its social membership and identity, depend exclusively on the identity of the father. For in Tatuyo society everything is brought to bear, on the level of ideology in general as well as on the level of myths and rituals, to deny the role of woman (of the mother) in the reproductive process. The child who is born is uniquely and entirely the flesh of its father, flesh which is itself that of its father's father and, beyond the generations, the flesh of the celestial Anaconda, the ancestor of the Tatuyo. The mother, who comes from somewhere else,[13] is only a receptacle, a place of gestation, and finally a "deceptacle," when she gives up the child (the flesh, the sperm—*puná*—elaborated in her womb) to (her husband's) group. My family, *yi yána*, "my own ones" as the Tatuyo say, is constituted on the basis of this extremely strong principle of patrilineal descent, and it includes, vertically, father, sons, daughters; horizontally, brothers (older or younger) and sisters (older or younger).

But let us go on with our reading of the myth. Moon's sister, Mênê-Riyo, is pregnant. Let us observe her actions closely; we see her prepare a little trap. She prepares the black dye of the genipa (*wée*), puts it in a pot, puts the pot down near the fire next to her, within reach, and she waits. (Another version (that of Stephen Hugh-Jones), after exposing the details of Mênê-Riyo's preparation in extremely rich detail, finishes like this: "When she had done preparing paint, she lay in her hammock *thinking*" [my italics, P.B.].)

No hurry, but a great deal of cold blood; we would call this a premeditated crime.[14] In addition, the myth gives no attenuating circumstances, even though it appears indulgent, even complicit, toward Moon. It is clear that she is not concerned with finding out who this nocturnal lover is (besides, can we seriously believe that she doesn't know?)[15] What is fundamentally important is

13. The mother comes from somewhere else, she is not part of the "family," she is the flesh of another anaconda (the ancestor of the members of her group); she is not, cannot be, and never will be a Tatuyo. And reciprocally the sister (or the father's sister), while she is married out (the Tatuyo, like the Tucano generally, are patrilocal), will never lose her Tatuyo identity. Thus taken in the strict sense the rule of exogamy does not by itself forbid sexual relations between a son and a "mother."

14. We must, nevertheless, see who profits from the crime. For if on the one hand this nocturnal "caress" betrays Moon and leads to his death, on the other hand, what is Mênê-Riyo doing acting this way—what does the myth say?—if not affirming as an obvious truth the essentially paternal function in the process of constituting the expected child?

15. The version collected among the Ufaina leaves no doubt as to this subject: "Luna llego otra noche y ella Manariyawa (Moon's sister) le pintó la cara (*ella sabio pero por puta*)." The parentheses are in the text, but the emphasis is ours. (M. Von Hildebrand 1975, p. 346.)

that the identity of the father, and so, immediately, the identity of the child who is going to be born, be clearly—socially—defined, seen and recognized by all in the full light of day.

This is indeed the heart of the problem, and it seems crucial to emphasize, in approaching it, that in Indian experience as well as Indian thought *it is not possible to separate (for very long) sexual relations from the process of procreation*. When, instead of masturbating against a banana tree, Moon comes to copulate with his sister—"who has what it takes for that" says the myth—the substitution is only apparent. A radical change has taken place, for, for the first time, a man and a woman are involved, and their relationship cannot be considered as a thing in itself that will somehow find all its finality in sexual satisfaction. The whole logic of the myth and the very diachrony of the narrative establish, on the contrary, this fundamental aspect of things: in the end, every sexual relation becomes or is a relation of procreation. And every relation of procreation concerns society as a whole; it is society's reproduction that is at stake not only because of the birth of a new element but also and at the same time the reproduction of society as a constituted, organized totality. So what really comes into question with the problem of incest, and here it seems that the Tatuyo myth has a very general import, is not so much a codification of sex as such, but far more of sex as the process of procreation: the rule of the incest prohibition consists essentially of a *regulation of sexual reproduction*.

We would be tempted to specify "heterosexual" reproduction: but, while what is involved in homosexual relations has a great importance in the general context of interpersonal relations, it does not seem to involve the problem of incest directly, except, perhaps, on the level of a "dream": for the Tatuyo are haunted by nostalgia for a lost world in which men reproduced among themselves, a world, perhaps, in which they were immortal in the image of the primordial sun. This dream of "absolute endogamy" is expressed periodically during initiation rituals (whose essential parts are out of bounds for women), in which yurupari trumpets serve as a masculine version of women's menstrual periods, and in which young men, "borne" by men, are (re-)engendered by men.[16] The Tatuyo undoubtedly find here, (borrowing the words with which Lévi-Strauss closes the *Elementary Structures of Kinship*), "the joys, eternally denied to social man, of a world in which one might live among one's own."[17]

In other words, to come back to the myth—and to reality—just "doing it" once is not (yet) procreation and, if it involves a brother and a sister, it isn't

16. For the ensemble of the Tucano populations of northwestern Amazonia, yurupari trumpets (*pohé*) represent the key instruments of the passage between the "other world," the "world from before fleshly existence," and "this world here," "the place where people (*mahá*) live." Essentially masculine instruments, possessed and manipulated exclusively by men, they constitute a system of opposition with female periods. For a detailed study of yurupari ritual (the ritual of initiation), cf. Stephen Hugh-Jones (1974).

17. TN: To "live among one's own (people)" is a literal translation of Lévi-Strauss's phrase *vivre entre soi*, with which he closes the *Elementary Structures of Kinship*. The English version of this work translates its final phrase as to "keep to oneself" (Lévi-Strauss 1967, p. 497). An incursion of "Anglo-Saxon individualism"?

really incest, and we can laugh about it. But if this relationship continues, it quickly becomes a relationship of procreation and, in the case of a brother and a sister, an incestous relationship. In passing, we can note that the opposition between incest prohibition and exogamy, which may be valuable in other contexts, does not appear particularly pertinent in the Tatuyo context. For, as we have been stressing, there is a thin line between a sexual relationship without social implications and the conjugal bond; from the moment when a man and a woman begin to have regular sexual relations, *we* (i.e., the social group) begin to talk marriage. (We can also note that while a relationship of procreation is inconceivable outside the socially recognized marriage relation [a child who is conceived outside marraige does not usually survive: there is, in particular, the practice of infanticide] ; inversely, a sterile sexual relation means the annulment of a marriage.)

Besides this, the conjugal bond is deployed at every level: in particular, a man starts a plantation (*chagra*) for the woman who is becoming his wife, and while the woman works the soil the man will provide the products of fishing and hunting. The "complementarity" between the sexes on the level of "work" constitutes the basis of the economic reproduction of society.

Let us pick up the thread of the myth again. That night, when the visitor slid into her hammock, Mênê-Riyo, to "unmask" him, covered his face with black genipa dye with her hands (here again we see how the "caress" takes the place of speech at night). At the break of day, before the dawn, Moon went out of the maloca and looked at himself in a mirror (according to other versions he looked in the water): his face was covered with black stains. He thought bad things, he was ashamed. He tried to make the stains go away, but all his efforts were in vain, he decomposed right there, died.

Let us leave Mênê-Riyo for the moment to follow the fortunes of her brother Moon. For him, things happened according to the following scheme:

incest → *shame* → *death*

By the simple play of transitivity—and here again the entire context authorizes this procedure—we get:

incest → *death*

(= incest brings about or signifies death.)

But we will wait before pursuing this further and look at the shame whose intermediary position seems to be of fundamental importance.

It was, says the myth, "at daybreak" or "in the pale light of dawn" that Moon looked at himself in a mirror and saw his face covered with stains. This is important, for we have seen that the myth has developed a whole game based on the opposition of day and night and the passage from one to the other. We see immediately that shame, like the dawn, occupies a mediating position between the two full states of night and day.

But everything starts, at the emergence from the night, with a game of mirrors. The mirror—the theme of the mirror in the sense of a reflecting surface—occupies a central position in Tatuyo thought; the mirror *reveals*. It appears in this role in many mythological contexts.

Jaguars, for instance, use the mirror in a myth to see the distant places where they can find dried meat. In a sequence of the "Story of Bitter," the jaguar chief looks in his mirror and so becomes aware of the presence of Mênê-Riyo, who is spying on him, hidden on a shelf high in the maloca. In another sequence, the troupial bird searches for his mistress Mênê-Riyo; the latter cannot be found (Moon having sent her to the sky to punish her) until the day when the bird leans over a pot to drink, and there sees her image reflected in the water's surface; he flies up to join her in the sky. For the shaman the little stone mirrors which he possesses are an aid to seeing, they are his power of perception. In all these cases (and the examples could be multipled) the mirror—reflection—makes visible what is not normally or directly so; it allows one to perceive what is hidden, whether the persons or things in question are found at a great distance (in space, but also in thought), behind, above, etc. In the present context, the mirror reveals to Moon what was hidden in himself; there, spread out over his face, the black stains of genipa send back the image of his internal rottenness (for the black dye of genipa in fact represents decay and death):[18] in the mirror is reflected his shame. But the play of visual reflection is itself only a metaphor; for when Moon looks at the mirror he is thinking, and he is thinking bad things. "To think" in Tatuyo is constructed from a verbal root which means to listen (*tigo*) and a suffix *ya* which indicates a reflection upon the speaker. "To think" (*tigoya*) is to listen to what speaks within oneself. Thus, at the emergence from night, silence is once more replaced by speech; but it is still not daylight, and the speech remains internal, a morbid silent speculation.

This internal dialogue which Moon holds between night and day—one is tempted to say, *entre loup et chien*[19]—shows us that the (Tatuyo) individual

18. The black dye of genipa (*Genipa americana*) appears quite explicitly as a symbol of decay and death in many contexts in Indian ritual and mythology. In particular, to signify the death of the young men at the beginning of initiation, the latter are smeared with black dye. And when, at the end of the ritual, they are (re-)born, they are covered with red *carayuru* (*Bignonia chica*) paint, the blood of the primordial anaconda, the blood of life. Another example is worth reporting since it lets the Indians do all the talking. In the myth of the imarakakana collected by M. Von Hildebrand among the Ufaina, one of them, Imarika Kayafiki, recounts a dream as follows: "I dreamed of black paint. Then I dreamed that I was combing my hair with a comb. Then I dreamed that I was shredding a liana and washing myself with it. Then I dreamed that I was washing my face with *karayuru*. The others took it back. *The black paint is someone who is rotting* (our emphasis), the comb is a *chulo* (vulture) who is coming, the liana and the *karayuru* are blood" (M. Von Hildebrand 1975, p. 336). This dream, indeed, strangely prefigures the death of Moon and the birth of Bitter, but this would take us too far afield.

19. TN: This French idiom, literally "between wolf and dog," has the metaphorical sense of "between day and night," "at dusk."

is not constituted as a monolithic block and that shame is a complex feeling. We see first of all that there are two sides to Moon, a hidden, private side, and another public or social side: there is a night-time Moon who sleeps with his sister (Moon's hidden face, as it were), and there is another daytime Moon, a Moon who presents himself to people unblemished, a "respectable" Moon, who knows his place, fulfills his role in society. This is the case up until that fatal dawn when the separation between night and day will not succeed: for on that morning, Moon's face will bear the traces of his nocturnal being: so shame is born. Shame is not born of the desire to sleep with one's sister, nor even of the fact of really sleeping with her, but rather of the fact that this ceases to be hidden by the night.

In the overture to the "Good Manners Sonata," Lévi-Strauss states that Bororo myths seem to him to display "a remarkable indifference towards incest: the incestuous person is looked upon as the victim, while the person offended against is punished for having taken revenge, or for having planned to do so."[20] It is clear in the Tatuyo myth that the one who lacks good manners is Mênê-Riyo; it is she who is the cause for scandal. In putting black genipa dye on her brother's face (through sheer "sluttishness," points out the myth—"ella sabia pero por puta"), she confuses the boundary between night and day, between the private realm of the person and his social facade: to desire one's sister is not criminal as such, but it is inappropriate, unacceptable social behavior. These prescriptions and rules of behavior thus come to be organized as so many counterpoints around a single recurrent theme, namely, that in the Tatuyo case it would be vain to look to some intrinsic quality of sex—some "nature of sex"—for the origin or motives of the interdiction of certain relationships; it is, rather, on the level of social usage or social function—that is, on the level of the process of procreation—that its codification (its repression) is founded, and where moral judgment is brought to bear.

So that morning, looking in the mirror, Moon is thinking bad things. And in the darkness which now is rapidly dissolving we see him fighting—and this internal combat is taking place upon his own body.

This episode of the myth comes from a version transmitted by Stephen Hugh-Jones. The Indian words are in the Barasana language.

Moon crushed *lini* leaves (leaves which the Indians use to wash their faces) between his hands and washed his face, but to no avail. He crushed *soma, soma, soma*, he washed himself *sina, sina, sina, sina*, nothing worked. His face was black.

He tried washing with *nyahari* but none of it went away.

He tried washing with ocra (*ewi*), in vain.

He ran off into the forest and cut into a *biti* tree and a *wasoa* tree (these two trees have a thick, white, gummy sap), he put the gum on his face and when it was dry he pulled it off, but the black didn't come off.

20. C. Lévi-Strauss (1964, p. 81).

He was still all black. He left and went to the rapids in a river and put himself under the foam on the water. The water ran *soo, sota, sota* in his eyes; he hoped the black would go away; but it stayed. He went to another rapids, then to another, and he tried again and again to wash himself but all to no avail, he couldn't get washed: "so she made me like this for what I did to her," he said. He left that place and cut *bodea* leaves.

He rubbed himself very hard, but it all stayed on.

Then he tried to turn himself yellow with powder of *bodea* ocra. He also tried with chalk, but it all stayed; the chalk just stayed white and came off. . . .

He looked at himself in the mirror, he was blacker than ever.

And, in another Barasana version of this myth, the teller adds this gloss: "If Moon had not tried to wash off the black paint which she (his sister) had spread on his face, we would all have permanent designs in black paint on our bodies, and the paint we put on today would never go away." When this is put in correlation with what we have already seen, it allows us to bring to light certain elements for an approach to a Tatuyo ethic: desires, incest, death—these are one thing; life in society, law, status, the role one plays in the social whole—these are something else. Between these two kinds of elements there is a gap, but thanks to Moon, who "washed himself well" and whose efforts, in the end, do not seem to have been entirely in vain, the decay, the shame, which everyone bears within himself, are not permanently visible to the outside.

For example: to have the desire to kill one's brother inside oneself is one thing, to live together under the shared roof of the maloca is another. This is exactly what the mythic "bird-nester" theme is telling us, through its multiple South American variants. Among the Tatuyo, its protagonists are two brothers, in an older/younger relation (the group of brothers constituting the social, political, and economic base of the local community, the maloca). The images of the myth show us how the younger brother is animated solely by the desire to kill his older brother, and the latter acts only to cause discomfort to the former; at the same time the official Tatuyo discourse allows only good relations between brothers.

Revealing itself between night and day, shame thus appears as the fundamental mechanism operating the mediation—which is at the same time separation—between private things and public things: it is the society speaking inside the individual, the silent speech that founds the social person.

But on that morning, in spite of all his efforts, Moon sees himself blacker than ever; day is breaking on the horizon and soon society will reappear in center stage as the main witness—the main actor: what has been hidden will be seen and known by all, the words spoken aloud. Moon cannot stand the idea of this gaze and this speech; the evil is irremediable. Having lost face, literally gnawed from the inside, he has only one desire—to disappear, to cease to be. Moon decays on the spot, rots, dies.

We can thus see the fundamental strategic position occupied by shame, between the transgression of the rule (committing incest) and death. For what significance can a rule—a taboo—have if its sanctions are not defined at the same time? It would have no meaning; at the limit there would be no more rule. Thus it seems that in these small Amazonian societies with segmentary structures, which lack instances external to or detached from the group to put in charge of surveillance, denunciation, and punishment, shame, with its corollary of exclusion (self-exclusion) constitutes the supreme sanction of a breach of order. These indigenous groups—the people who make them up—are fundamentally moral (or, if you prefer, religious) groups, whose morality is shared by all, and internalized by each. To behave in a moral way is not simply to reproduce faithfully, according to one's position in society (this being, in Tatuyo society, strictly determined by birth), the behavior of one's fathers, decreed long ago, in the beginning; it is also and at the same time to behave in accordance with cosmic order, an order to which reproduction and perpetuation of life on earth are tied.

To transgress the norms can thus only correspond to behavior which brings death, or to madness. For in the Tatuyo system, when all is said and done, immorality is not possible (except, probably, on the part of women, a subject to which we shall return). A character like Moon, marked with the brand of incest, and who showed himself, shamelessly, in broad daylight, could not be thought of as immoral—this would be the first step toward a system that in the end could only signify the death of the society—but as mad.

The Tatuyo express this transgression with a word, *royé-tú*, which means to ruin, to deteriorate, things, people, the world: the fundamental idea is that of disordering [*dérèglement*].[21] In our society, don't we say that a criminal, a pervert, a madman is disorderly [*déréglé*]? Moon behaves like a person who is out of order [*déréglé*] and by that alone he brings about a disordering [*dérèglement*] which in the end leads to his death.

When you ask the Tatuyo, "What does it mean to commit incest?" (you must, of course, put the question a little differently, if only because there is no Tatuyo word for incest), two answers are always given: to behave ("do it") like dogs (*yaía-re baírona*); to make "mixed people," or "mix people up" (*ka mahã ahúyári*). The Tatuyo consider dogs not to be people (*mahã*); "humans," fish, forest animals, trees, stars, etc. are *mahã*. "Humans" are simply *mahã*, fish are *wai mahã*, forest animals are *waibukɨna mahã*, trees are *yukɨ mahã*, etc.). In other words, all of these beings have the same fundamental nature (as detached pieces of the primordial sun). Each occupies a particular territory according to its own specific body, but all, in their respective ways, share the same way of life: they

---

21. The verb *royé-tú* (to disorder [*dérégler*], to ruin, to spoil) is one of the key notions in Tatuyo thought concerning the creation of life on earth. It appears in all the mythological contexts which, in the "historical" form of a passage, in fact define the gap between a full state, without faults, without pain, without work, characteristic of the earliest period of earthly life, before the exercise of any "human" praxis, and before the order of reality of present-day earthly life, which was engendered, and so signified, at every point in time and in every domain, by a first "unfortunate" practice.

are socially organized, hierarchized, structured; they live in a maloca, they have *chagras*, chew coca, exchange wives, etc. But dogs are outside the *mahã* system (they are not the only ones, by the way: the seminomadic Macu Indians, and in some contexts whites, are not *mahã*). In other words, the Tatuyo hold that the domestic dogs who live with them do not constitute an organized social ensemble, a society, among themselves. So "to do it like dogs" mainly translates this idea of behaving in a disorderly [*déréglé*] or unregulated way (especially on the level of sexuality). In this sense, this expression (used mainly by men about women) applies not only to incest but to all excessive or abnormal sexual behavior: the Tatuyo say, for instance, that a woman who repeatedly commits adultery or who is always sleeping with everybody is doing it like dogs do, or, again, that she is mad.

The second answer, "it makes mixed people," provides us with the key to the mechanism by which the specific disorder [*déréglement*] brought about by the transgression of the incest prohibition endangers society and in the end leads to its destruction. But first a brief detour through Tatuyo social structure seems necessary. Tatuyo society constitutes an exogamous social entity (all Tatuyo are consanguines, all sons of the Celestial Anaconda, the son of the Sun); within this ensemble, the social organization—the social order—minutely determines the position of everyone (individuals, lineages, clans): this is the basis of one's social being, one's social identity. And it is from this unique position, determined in its essentials by birth (based on the whole ideology of patrilineal descent), that each unit can function normally in the complex play of the social, political, religious, and other interactions of the social machine. This social order which, with maniacal care, tallies the gaps and differences among men on the one hand—older/younger hierarchization and specialization of the different segments—and between men and women on the other, is ontologically (ideologically) founded by the whole spatio-temporal process of the primordial Creation. The Tatuyo social order—the identity of each and all, and so the order of relations among individuals and between each one and the whole—appears as a particular occurrence of the cosmic order, and it is supported, reinforced, by a fantastically powerful imaginary order [*imaginaire*] which encompasses it.

Let us return to the expression "making mixed up people" or "mixing people." To mix, *ahúyá*, is a culinary term first of all, but it is applied both to good and to bad food. For good food: it is by mixing raw manioc flour and starch that one can cook the flat cassava loaf that is the basis of Tatuyo subsistence. For bad food: this occurs, of course, in myth—the discourse of myth, at least apparently impersonal, allows one to say all kinds of things. After a long and perilous voyage, the Jabiru ("dancing people") finally reach the maloca of the Shaman Woman to offer her food:

> at that place lived Headless, the husband of the Shaman Woman. . . . He was
> preparing tobacco powder, *kâi . . . kâi . . . kâi . . .* he pounded the tobacco *kâi*
> *. . . kâi. . . . "I'm going to mix poison into this tobacco* and give it to the Danc-

ing People," he said. That is how poison (*nímã*) is, so they poison people at feasts when they offer food. . . .

There is thus a cooking that gives life—reproduces the group—and a cooking that "poisons"—destroys the group. To make "mixed people" is definitely located on the side of death. If I marry my sister, is that man there my father? My father-in-law? Immediately, two (social) persons are fused into one—and who knows which one it is? This is "poisoning"! But it is also and immediately the confusing of two boundaries (boundaries which are defined in relation to each other); on the one hand, the boundary that defines kin (consanguines), on the other the boundary that creates the relation of affinity: from the individual, the corruption soon spreads to the social body as a whole, until it decomposes and we fall back into nature.

So for the Tatuyo to reproduce without a rule has the immediate and fundamental consequence of a loss of identity, loss of the discreteness of the entities (individuals, social segments) which, organically connected in and by the play of social interactions, constitutes an organized whole, the society. The rule of the incest prohibition, which in a single movement forbids reproduction among certain persons (who are thus defined as kin) and by this very fact implies reproduction with others (defined as affines—the "other people," say the Tatuyo) consists essentially in preventing confusion (not "mixing people"); in other words, in founding and perpetually reproducing as identical with itself the position, the function, or each person and of the whole. In this whole, in a constant play of coming and going between two partners (play whose rules are defined by the men), external relations (alliance) are defined by, and by this very fact reinforce, the order of internal relations (consanguinity).

By his disorderly [*déréglée*] conduct—by continuing to copulate with his sister—Moon sets off a dynamic of social confusion which, in the end, signifies the death of the group by internal decomposition; what, indeed, does Moon die of if not extreme confusion?[22]

Before pursuing this theme any further we will note that, unlike Moon (a highly moral character, in that he dies of shame in the end), his sister Mênê-Riyo, who occupies the feminine pole in the myth, never at any time feels such a sentiment; quite the contrary, as we saw at the beginning and as the course of the story confirms, Mênê-Riyo is a shameless hussy ("una sinverguenza," as they say in Spanish). Let us note in passing what a "fantastic" threat this can represent in a society like that of the Tatuyo. In this context we should also analyze how, in this society, the public (official) face of the group is represented by the face of the men.

There is, however, another context in Tatuyo mythology in which shame appears with the same amount of force and relief. In the beginning, they say,

---

22. In this way the indigenous mythology of incest presents us with an implicit theory of the continuous and the discrete, an opposition which has been shown to be at the heart of any system of signification, starting with that of exchange.

the Shaman Woman stole the yurupari trumpets from the men; after a long chase, in which the myth seeks mainly to establish the gap between the sexes in Tatuyo society, the men finally managed to catch the Shaman Woman and at the same time to get the yurupari back and to punish her (to "castrate" her? For the word used here is the same verb, *royé-tú*, which we have already seen and which means to make infirm, to deteriorate, to lessen). They opened her up: *she collapsed in shame* in the blood of her first period. (We will come back to this.)

In underlining the exemplary, the paradigmatic, character of the death of Moon, the myth invites us to a more general reflection on Tatuyo death:

Moon is the first to die, he is the one who first got sick and died.

(We should note here that death (*riá*) and sickness (*riá-ye*) have the same root); and the myth adds this "detail" which seems very important to us:

He died like that, on his own [*de lui-même*] (*ka wátóa-na*).

Wátóa means in the center, in the middle, equidistant from. And here, according to the indigenous commentary, it signifies that Moon is located at an equal distance from all external pathogenic agents and so is not subject to the influence of any of them: it is in his own heart that the source of his ill, the cause of his death, is to be found.

Through this the Tatuyo express the fundamental idea that death, finitude, is above all and essentially something that is inside people—inscribed in their lives, as it were. After this, certainly, people will die of this or that—of sorcery, disease, snakebite, falling out of a tree. But this changes nothing; in the last analysis, it is unimportant, it is contingent (although on the level of the social the death of an individual is one of the privileged sites in which the society's whole system of sociopolitical relations is expressed); fundamentally, beyond or on this side of all the vicissitudes of existence, this reality, this observation, imposes itself: man is perishable. But the myth, as we shall see, also expresses a complementary idea about human nature, namely, that death, the will for death or destruction, is an integral, constitutive part of the individual.

It is in the nature of people to be mortal: this is probably the most profound, the most constant, the most disturbing question which the Tatuyo put to themselves through their myths and their rituals; and this has been the case since *póhe*, since they were separated from the sun and born as people (*mahá*) on this earth. The sun represents the figure of the immutable, the eternal, the unalterable (the state of *póhe*). The sun does not change, but it moves, it runs along its path in the sky every day, and in this way causes changes and transformations: its heat and light are the energy which gives life to the earth and its inhabitants. But within the sun there takes place no transformation, no modification (and from this point of view it is sterile); perpetually identical to itself, it is not appropriate for thinking about the cycle of life and death. In opposition to the sun, within the moon take place all the transformations of life and death: it is born, it is young, it grows, it becomes full; then it starts to diminish, it becomes the old moon, it pines away, declines, decomposes, and dies. But the moon is reborn... and dies once more. In the myth this is clearly signified by the death of Moon, his return to life, and his death once again (cf. below).

In other words, for the Tatuyo the moon is the figure which best serves for thinking about life, death, the reproduction of life; in opposition to solar immutability, the moon expresses the essence of life on earth.

On the physiological level the female period and, by metonymy, woman (it is clear in Tatuyo thought that the menstrual period is woman, and that woman is her period), whose periodicity is in strict rhythmical resonance with the phases of the moon, represent, *are* this same cyclic process of perpetual renewal of life and death.[23] Thus it is apparent that in Tatuyo mythology the female period and the moon, the two figures which best represent the life/death cycle, the basis of human life on earth, are both marked in the depths of their being— of their flesh—with the brand of shame, decay, and death. In Tatuyo it is from a single root, *bo*, that are constructed the different ideas of death (*bori*, death in its ontological sense, also a word that signifies all the evil, negative, and destructive forces in life),[24] decay (*boa*), and shame (*bobo*). And this is probably the ultimate meaning that the metaphor of the death of Moon in Tatuyo mythology reveals; namely that in an irremediable way, in spite of the constant efforts of the shaman who struggles to protect (*wánô*), to heal, to "make live" (*káti*), in spite of his constant combat to "renew life" (*yéeri wahóa*), evil, suffering, degradation, and finally death are inscribed at the heart of human life: from the beginning, in its very foundations, there is something disorderly [*déréglé*], spoiled (*royé tú*), and finally rotten (*boa*) in the existence of earthly life. And the woman who periodically bleeds, what does she signify, if not this terribly terrestrial nature of people, their shame, their unhappiness at no longer being immortal?

The body dies, it rots. But people have in them a hard, undecaying, indestructible part that survives death: the bones (*owã̃*). When people were first born, when from being immaterial beings confused with the sun (state of *póhe*) they took on bodies (to be born is "to take on the body of a person," *ka mahã̃ rupea*, in Tatuyo), they received trumpets of yurupari (*póhe*). The yurupari are the

---

23. The Tatuyo connect menstrual periods with the phases of the moon; and the Cubeo say that when a woman has her period, the moon comes to copulate with her (cf. I. Goldman 1963). Elsewhere C. Hugh-Jones analyzes the theme of menstruation at length; she writes, in particular, that "menstrual blood is retained in the womb as if by a dam and then released. The process of release is described as skinshedding... and thus loss of old, decaying skin/blood allows the regrowth of new. It can be appreciated immediately that menstrual growth and decay are ambiguously related in the same way as life and death" (C. Hugh-Jones 1977, p. 169).

24. One of the shaman's main struggles when he "blows" is called *bori ma ta*, which literally means: to cut off or stop (*ta*) the way (*ma*) of evil, of pain, of death (*bori*).

bones of the ancestors, the bones of people who, unalterable, transmit themselves from generation to generation beyond the putrefaction of their bodies. And the first trumpets which people received, and which they still have, are (called) the "Bones of the Sun" (*mwipɨowã*). The yurupari trumpets constitute the atemporal link with the divine. Periodically, during initiation rituals (*póhe wi*), from which women are excluded under pain of death, the dream of "absolute endogamy" is relived: sexual reproduction is negated and old age and death are transcended. The young men, "those to whom you show the yurupari for the first time," are then *póhe*, and they are (re-)born as new, young, vigorous flesh in a new shedding of the body of the Celestial Anaconda, Son of the Sun, the immortal ancestor[25] of the Tatuyo.

Moon is no more; only his bones remain, scattered on the ground. But Moon's death will have repercussions; the next sequence of the myth is long, and we will summarize it:

Sun, the father of Moon, was angry: "Where is my son, what has happened to him?" he said, and went off to look for him. He said to the people of the maloca, "Stay here, don't cry" (before this crying did not exist, and the dove did not sound its sad song, huu ... huu ..., in the abandoned chagras), and he left to "blow" on Moon, to reconstitute him and restore him to life. He got there. He made a lattice which he put on the ground, then he collected all of his son's bones and carefully arranged them on the lattice.... With the "cigar-carrying fork" he remade his legs, he put the cigar into place and so remade his penis.... Then he blew, just as people would do later to blow-cure diseases. He blew tobacco powder (flesh) and rebuilt his body. With *carayurú* (*Bignonia chica*) he remade his blood, with *carayurú* liana and *ninni wê* liana he remade his veins.... In this way he rebuilt the body of his son Moon. Then Sun went all around the world looking for Moon's soul (*yéeri*).... Then he blew (*yéeri wahóa*) over the lattice, he gave Moon life (we should note that, symmetrically with the pair disease/death, a single word, *kati*, means to heal and to be alive). Moon got back onto his feet, but his legs were shaky. Sun took him by the hand and led him back to the maloca. They came to the clearing in the forest. Then Moon left the cover of the great trees and ventured out alone in the open area which surrounds the maloca. He was almost to the door of the house when suddenly a bird perched on the roof of the maloca, a "bird of ill omen,"[26] started to shout at the top of its lungs, rousing up the whole village: "Here comes Moon! But what's that? He has a tobacco penis! Look, look, there he is!" Moon tripped over a tree trunk, "Moon's evil tree trunk," fell down and fell apart. All that remained were his bones scattered on the ground. Despite all of his efforts, Sun couldn't bring him back to life. This is why Moon casts little light, why today Moon is a ghost, a reflection (*wâti*).

25. TN: The French text reads "(*anc*)-*être*," for ancestor" (*ancêtre*), highlighting the word *être*, "being." Thus the Celestial Anaconda is also the "immortal anc(ient) being" of the Tatuyo.

26. Of the *were* bird (who calls *were tsi tsi*) the Tatuyo say: it is a bird that exists, but serves no (good) purpose. It is still, at any rate, good to think.

This translation-summary of the myth hardly requires a commentary. How could one more clearly signify the scheme we have already outlined—incest → shame → death—than by the image of Moon, who dies, cut to the heart by this look and this speech, in broad daylight, in the center of the village square. According to another version, the speech is still more direct and brutal: Moon is barely back on his feet when somebody shouts "Your sister's!" [*"Et ta soeur!"*], and Moon instantly disintegrates.[27]

Then Sun, faced with the irremediable death of his son, spoke in anger: "All right, this is how it is, and it's going to stay this way. When people poison someone, the shaman comes, he blows and heals him. But the others are mad again, and they poison him again. This is how people die; there is nothing to do, inside themselves people want to die, death is inside them." And, added the narrator of this myth, this is what happens to shamans who kill too much, the evil affects them, and pretty soon they die themselves.

There follows a long sequence of lamentation, weeping, and grief. We should not forget that Moon is the first to die, and here the myth expresses all the suffering that falls upon people when a loved one dies (when a woman loses her husband, in the example given in the myth): "a cloak of grief covered the people... the people were in shock... they wept a great deal... they suffered bitterly...." The shaman blows, he drives away sadness and tears, he pacifies grief, calms suffering. At the death of a loved one you can go mad and die of sadness, say the Tatuyo.

> The people cried a great deal.... Then the Ayáwaroa arrived (these are a group of four characters who play a major role in Tatuyo mythology), they came and lined themselves up in front of the people and uncovered the ends of their penises to make the people laugh, to play, to stop the grief. The weeping stopped, then started again, then finally stopped. "Look at them," said a woman, while the *hipi boki* bird started to laugh: hî hî hî.... "Look at what those people are doing, hî hî hî...." he said. All the women looked. Even though they were all dying of grief, they looked at the Ayáwaroa and started to laugh. Life returned to them. Thus the Ayáwaroa put an end to suffering....

We should remember that everything started with the same gesture, with Moon taking out the end of his penis to satisfy his sexual desire. A decisive act, which—but if we think too much about what happened as a result we will end up going mad and dying of sadness, as the Tatuyo say. "Instead, look at those Ayáwaroa fooling around with their penises!" says the myth: the people looked, their weeping ceased, and everybody started to laugh. But this laughter that restores life only echoes that other laughter which the narrator allowed to burst forth at the precise moment when, for the first time, Moon lets himself be led into copulating with Mênê-Riyo. Here we are sent back to the beginning, the

27. More precisely, the myth says: "por que hizo con su hermana! (la luna) se deshizo de nuevo." Cf. M. Von Hildebrand, 1975, p. 348.

circle is closed, a first cycle—the periodic cycle of the generations—has been run through in its entirety.

To conclude, we will make a final journey to the realm of forbidden alliances and death by following the footsteps of Mênê-Riyo, the sister of Moon. After her brother's death she does not seem affected in the least and feels no shame; on the contrary, we see her still acting shamelessly and without discretion. But we are going to see that Mênê-Riyo is not only a "shameless hussy," she is also an "adventuress." We are getting near the end of the story. After coming back down from the sky, where her brother had sent her to be rid of her, Mênê-Riyo found the maloca empty. She went on, and when she came to the first fork in the road she laughed, but she should have acted in a reserved manner; so she was sent in the wrong direction and came to the maloca of the jaguars, the Four-Tooth Jaguars. "Hide over there" (on a shelf at the top of the maloca) "and keep quiet," the jaguars' grandmother told her. Later, the jaguars came back from the chagra, where they had been killing. In the evening they decorated themselves to dance. Mênê-Riyo lifted the edge of the basket under which she was hiding; the chief of the jaguars—in his mirror—saw her and said, "Mênê-Riyo is looking. . . . Mênê-Riyo is looking. . . ." The jaguars invited her down to dance. She thought: I am going to "make a husband" out of a jaguar; it is not good to "make a husband" out of my brother, that bum who did this to me. The grandmother suggested: you can dance with the ugly jaguars, they are good for "making husbands," but don't dance with the handsome jaguars, they will kill you and take another. She danced. . . . With the ugly jaguars I won't dance anymore, she said; and Mênê-Riyo danced with the handsome jaguars. All night they danced; the jaguars danced and sang to make her pregnant. At dawn, the jaguar chief (the worst of them all) put in his teeth, two above, two below (the Tatuyo wear this collar of four jaguar teeth) and killed Mênê-Riyo. (According to other versions, all the jaguars went to copulate with her one after the other during the night. Thus, "rotten" with lovemaking, she died in the morning.)

They went out into the open space of the maloca to broil her. The grandmother said to them: all right, broil her head but not her belly (Mênê-Riyo's head will later serve as the jaguars' football.) Then they went down to the river to skin her; their grandmother said to them: leave that to me, she's got nice fat on her, I'm going to save it, and she opened Mênê-Riyo's belly. (It is out of Mênê-Riyo's opened entrails that Bitter comes; but that is another story.)

Between the invitation to her brother, "Come and do it with me," and the Four-Tooth Jaguars, Mênê-Riyo seems to have passed from one extreme to the other in the field of sexual relations, without stopping in the middle position of alliance. If one must not marry "too close" under pain of closing the gap between the sexual drive in the raw state and its socially regulated expression, of confusing the boundary between nature and culture, and of confounding society, one must also not marry "too far"; one must remain within a limit, that of "people." (The Tatuyo cannot reproduce [marry] among themselves, but they can marry a woman from any other tribe of the Vaupés: all the Tucano are "people,"—"other people" (*ápe mahã*). We should note, however, that neighboring tribes constitute preferential groups for the exchange of women.)

With the Four-Tooth Jaguars, Mênê-Riyo, the adventuress eager for the exotic, transgresses the boundaries of the "human community" to give herself up without restraint to bestiality.[28] But while Moon's death—incest—represents a process of internal decay of the society, the death of Mênê-Riyo, on the contrary, portrays—but here we have to invent a word, for in fact there exists no term, symmetrical and inverse to "incest," which would signify "the violation of the rule of endogamy"—the violent death of the society through a brutal aggression of external origin. In such an encounter the gap between the terms is too wide, alliance is impossible: the society perishes, literally chopped to pieces, gutted, and finally devoured.

Epilogue

When he had grown up and gotten strong enough, Bitter returned and killed the Four-Tooth Jaguars who had murdered his mother. Hurled into the water of the river, they all died eaten by piranhas, except for one, the chief of the jaguars (the worst of them all) who made it to the other side of the river with the lower half of his body eaten away; he is the ancestor of the Colombians. (It seems, besides, that the Four-Tooth Jaguar women gave birth to the *Barasiderua*, the Brazilians.)

But the story has taken some strange turns, at least as it is told today by young Tatuyo: "Later, the jaguar who had half of his body eaten away, the ancestor of the Colombians, had a daughter, a pretty daughter, and when Bitter went away he went over there to live with her."

What happened to Bitter over there, among the whites? The Tatuyo don't say. However, a myth from the *Llanos*, the great plains that start where the forest ends, and where People have been in contact with the whites for a long time already, has reached the Tatuyo. This story (here highly summarized), which thus comes to enrich their mythology, constitutes for the Tatuyo a mirror in which to trace the contours of the fantastic universe of the whites.

An Indian was supposed to "make a husband" for a girl who lived with her father on the other side of the river. But since he continually deferred his marriage, he realized one day that the river had grown so much in size that it was now no longer possible to get across and that he was now unable to reach the house of his "father-in-law." So he went away with three compan-

28. It is a matter of what C. Lévi-Strauss calls "true endogamy." "True endogamy is merely the refusal to recognize the possibility of marriage beyond the limits of the human community. The definitions of this community are many and varied, depending on the philosophy of the group considered" (1967, p. 46).

ions, the cat, the rooster and the snake, and after a long journey he arrived among the whites. There was a contest, a horse race, and thanks to his magic ring he was able to beat all of his white rivals and win the prize, a bride's dress. The bride turned out to be a young and pretty (white) woman, and he married her. And he became very rich and powerful, and he had a nice house, and he bought himself an airplane and everything the whites have.

References

Bidou, Patrice. 1974. "Représentation de l'espace dans la mythologie tatuyo. (Indiens Tucano)." *Journal de la société des Américanistes* 61 (dated 1972): 45-105.

___. 1976. "Les Fils de l'Anaconda Céleste–les Tatuyo. Etude de la structure socio-politique" Thesis for the doctorate in ethnology. Laboratoire d'Anthropologie Sociale, Paris.

___. 1977. "Naître et être tatuyo." *Actes du XLIIIème Congrès International des Américanistes* Paris 2: 105-20.

Bouveresse, Jacques. 1977. "L'animal cérémonial–Wittgenstein et l'anthropologie." *Actes de la recherche en sciences sociales*, no. 16, pp. 43-54.

Goldman, Irving. 1963. *The Cubeo: Indians of the Northwest Amazon.* Urbana: University of Illinois Press.

Hildebrand, Martin Von. 1975. "Origen del mundo segun los Ufaina." *Revista colombiana de Anthropologia* (Bogotá) 17.

Hugh-Jones, Christine. 1976. "Skin and Soul: the Round and the Straight." *Actes du XLIIème Congrres International des Américanistes.* Paris. 2: 185-204.

___. 1977. "Social Classification among the South American Indians of the Vaupés." Ph.D. thesis, University of Cambridge.

Hugh-Jones, Stephen. 1974. "Male Initiation and Cosmology among the Barasana Indians of the Vaupes Area of Colombia." Ph.D. thesis, University of Cambridge.

Lévi-Strauss, Claude. 1964. *The Raw and the Cooked.* New York: Harper and Row, 1969.

___. 1966. *From Honey to Ashes.* New York: Harper and Row, 1973.

___. 1967. *The Elementary Structures of Kinship.* Boston: Beacon Press, 1969.

___. 1971. *L'Homme nu.* Paris: Plon.

Reichel-Dolmatoff, Gerardo. 1968. *Amazonian Cosmos: The Sexual and Religious Symbolism of the Tukano Indians.* Chicago: University of Chicago Press, 1971.

___. 1975. *The Shaman and the Jaguar: A Study of Narcotic Drugs among the Indians of Colombia.* Philadelphia: Temple University Press.

Torres Laborde, A. 1969. *Mito y cultura entre los Barasana un groupo indigena tukano del Vaupes.* Bogotá: Universidad de Los Andes.

Françoise Héritier

9

The Symbolics of Incest and Its Prohibition

So much has been written on incest and its prohibition, from such varied points of view, in such diverse disciplines (social anthropology, sociology, psychology, psychoanalysis, biology, ethology, etc.) that it may seem pointless to wish to add yet another stone to this monumental edifice. But it seems to me that we have not yet finished with this notion, which recent attempts seek to dilute into the more general category of prohibition as such, thus refusing it the status of a well-defined class to which a general theory could be applied (Needham 1971; Schneider 1976). The simple fact that a class of facts (for ethnological experience shows that there exists at the very least a universal tendency to regulate sexual relations among those who are close)[1] presents great diversity does not necessarily force us to conclude that it does not really exist as a class. This is throwing the baby out with the bath water. The question is rather to find out whether there exists, on one level or other, a way of approaching the phenomenon of the incest prohibition which accounts for its societally varying manifestations, its contradictory aspects, and even (why not?) its absences, if we should find proof of the existence of societies without any prohibition whatever (Slotkin 1947, 1949; Goodenough 1949).

Here I will be devoting myself to this kind of an attempt, referring to the work of Claude Lévi-Strauss, who has given the question of incest and its prohibition general value, both theoretical and heuristic.

1. TN: The phrase *entre proches*, literally "among close (people)" implies, but does not specify, what we would mean by "close kin."

As a first hypothesis, I would suggest that it is not possible to postulate any finality for the incest prohibition other than that put forward by Lévi-Strauss in the *Elementary Structures of Kinship:* women, like words, function as objects of reciprocal exchange between men, in a process that is the foundation of society. "The incest prohibition and exogamy have an essentially positive function... the reason for their existence is to establish a tie between men which the latter cannot do without if they are to raise themselves from a biological to a social organization" (p. 493). Thus, according to different modalities, it is necessary to forbid the sexual appropriation of the women of a group by the male members of the same group, defined according to its own particular rules, so as to make them available for exchange. Any union with consanguine partners, according to the local definition of consanguinity, is therefore incestuous.

While I start from the same interrogation as Lévi-Strauss (seeking the profound and omnipresent causes behind the fact that in every society and at every period of history there is a regulation of relations between the sexes) and while I accept the necessity of exchange as the foundation of any society, it does not seem contradictory to me to envisage, intimately connected to this finalistic aspect, a system of ideological explanation which would make incest and its prohibition appear in every culture as closely linked with total ensembles of representations concerning the person, the world, social organization, and the multiple interrelations among these three universes. If the incest prohibition, which establishes the social order, is culture "itself," it should also, by this very fact, be an object of representation. And if its finality is universal, despite its diverse modes of realization, why should not its representations, too, follow great universal patterns of representation? A careful inspection of this hidden part of the iceberg may perhaps have the effect of diminishing the importance of the critiques bearing on the homogeneity and pertinence of the notion; it will certainly challenge received ideas about the definition of incest, thought of as a heterosexual relationship between only two consanguineously or affinally related individuals.

Taking the *Elementary Structures of Kinship* as the starting point for any possible reflection, one can make two remarks. Lévi-Strauss based his demonstration on the functioning of these elementary structures of kinship, which have the advantage of showing reciprocity in a manifest form, in restricted or generalized exchange, following models whose general structure is easily interpretable. In addition, he insists on the "fact of being a rule" (p. 32) as the very essence of the incest prohibition; while he finds support in his analyses of specific points of the symbolic representations that everywhere accompany the rule, he does not try on the basis of these partial discourses to offer an idealogical systematic that could, like the rule itself, be universal. On this point I will ask the following question: can we postulate that there exists a guiding thread, discernible within all symbolic discourses on incest, which would on the one hand explain the various facts and beliefs cited by Lévi-Strauss, and on the other hand permit us to establish systematically the profound kinship which exists among these behind their apparent heterogeneity? Lévi-Strauss mentions, among other things, the Malagasy belief that when a couple is sterile it means that there must be an incestuous relationship between the spouses (p. 9); the Navajo belief (p. 40) in a fourth world in which the sexes are separated and monsters are the fruit of the masturbation to which both groups are reduced; the statement of a Siberian group that patrilateral marriages make water return to its source; the risk of blindness or muteness which threatens an Aleutian girl if her father looks at her at the time of her first period (p. 22); the unleashing of storm and tempest among the peoples of Malaysia by a heterogeneous assortment of actions, which includes incest, incorrect speech, noisy play, imitating birdcalls, etc. (p. 494). Lévi-Strauss analyses this set of Malaysian prohibitions and assigns them a common denominator, the abuse of language: "women themselves are treated as *signs*, which are *misused* when not put to the use reserved for signs, which is to be *communicated*" (p. 496). I would prefer to ask a different question: why in Malaysia does the abuse that constitutes incest have the power to unleash a storm, and what does this belief have to do with the Malagasy belief in the sterility of incestuous couples, and more generally with the whole set of remarkable facts associated with incestuous relationships in different societies?

I will try to offer an answer to this question, with the understanding that my aim is to draw attention to these problems rather than to provide one particular answer at this point. For the long and arduous labor of isolating the pertinent traits of the social structure, the corpus of disapproved or forbidden situations, the beliefs and representations connected with these situations, their consequences, and the sanctions they call forth, in every human society—this work has not yet been done in a systematic way. My first hypotheses come from my personal knowledge of the Samo, and they have been reinforced by facts gathered at random from other ethnographic descriptions. I must nevertheless underline two points of method. The first is the interest I have had in the series of acts which various populations designate by the same term as that which refers to what we usually call incest: certain forms of adultery between affines, or sexual relations of two close consanguines (father/son, mother/daughter, brother/brother, sister/sister) with the same partner. Evans-Pritchard (1949), for instance, describes an admirably complicated system among the Nuer. First of all, relations with the wife's sister are incestuous (*rual*) and marriage with her is possible only after the wife's death, and only if she has died childless. Evans-Pritchard analyzes this situation in terms of the exchange of cattle, but he also notes a more general prohibition which forbids a man from having sexual relations with two related women at the same time. In the same way, a man may not have sexual relations with the wife of a close kinsman during the latter's lifetime, for this would fall under the general prohibition which forbids two close kinsmen from having relations with the same woman. In an apparently surprising way, however, this strict rule is not applied to certain extremely close agnates. The wives of paternal half brothers, of half brothers, of paternal parallel cousins, of those whom the Nuer call "bulls," are legitimate partners for a man: received in exchange for lineage cattle, the wife of a "bull" is the wife of all (p. 100). In the same way, two agnates, members of the same lineage, may court and frequent the same woman, something forbidden to two cognates. Evans-Pritchard emphasizes that these agnates "have a lineage identity," which is not the case for a maternal uncle and his nephew. Still, the wives of other agnates are strictly forbidden: adultery with a wife of one's father other than one's mother is particularly shocking insofar as the father has sexual relations with both of his wives, and so transmits to the mother something of the son's sexual contact with the co-wife; nor can two full brothers share their wives, since these relations seem, as it were, to implicate their common mother sexually. For Evans-Pritchard, this whole set of rules has the function of preventing confusion between different categories of kin: thus if a man may not marry the sister of his wife who has died and left children, this is because for the children the mother's sister would also be the father's wife, a confusion of roles that is inconceivable for a Nuer. We shall see that another explanation is equally possible. But for the moment this well-known example allows us to appreciate the complexity of the category that is translated "incest," extended as it is to these various types of illicit relationships. We could describe analogous situations among the Gusii (LeVine 1959), the Baule (Etienne 1972, 1975), the Ashanti (Goody 1956), the Mossi (Pageard 1969), the Samo (Héritier 1976), and many others.

The second methodological point is that I have considered to be intimately related not only the situations, representations, and beliefs touching on incest, on the various forms of adultery between allies or illicit sexual relations between unrelated individuals, but also those that involve menstruation, sexual relations with prepubescent girls, with women during their periods, with women who are nursing, all of which involve the relations among the humors (sperm, blood, milk) and the functions of the body. I believe this attitude to be correct in that these configurations have to do with sexuality, are perceived as connected throughout the statements of informants (or so it usually seemed to me), and are generally evoked together, one way or another, in ethnographic accounts. Here again we are dealing with a class of facts, one might say a spontaneously generated class, whose content, I suggest, is only apparently heterogeneous, both for particular societies (in which case the internal coherence of the class is not problematic a priori) and in a transcultural perspective.

Durkheim, in his famous article of 1897, explains the incest prohibition as a sort of by-product of the rule of exogamy, itself based on a religious horror of menstrual blood; this horror would be part of a more general category of blood horror, which in turn springs from belief in the consubstantiality of the members of a clan with their totem. Durkheim's argument as a whole seems to have gone wide of the mark. But he raises, with admirable finesse, some very interesting points to which I will return, and above all he lays out an inventory of facts and beliefs concerning blood, menstruation, the medical cure, and power. He shows the close similarities that exist between prohibitions bearing on women during their periods or during childbirth: prohibitions explained by the fear and repulsion inspired by the impurities they give off around themselves; and prohibitions that bear on the daily lives of the most sacred sovereigns, even though nothing in them should cause such a repulsion in others. For Durkheim, the two extreme situations of disgust and veneration are comparable in that both are translated into taboos. Thus in many parts of the world, in slightly differing forms, girls in many populations are hermetically isolated during their first period, kept not only from contact with men, but also from contact with the earth and the sun, which would have "a funny taste" (p. 42) for these young mortals. In certain cases, this reclusion can last for several years. Women who are having their periods and women in childbirth are generally subjected to prohibitions, explained by the baleful influence they exercise around themselves at these times. But (p. 56) "the same rule that forbids the girl who has reached puberty to touch the ground or let herself be touched by the rays of the sun is applied in an identical manner to kings and to venerated priests. In Japan, the Mikado must not tread the ground with his feet: otherwise he would incur degradation. Nor should he let the rays of the sun reach him, nor should his head be exposed to the open air. The heir to the throne of Bogotá, in Colombia, was supposed to live in a dark room, where the sun could not penetrate, from the age of sixteen. The heir apparent of the Inca of Peru had to fast for a month without seeing the light of day." I asked above what it was that certain of the supernatural sanctions of incest—sterility here, the unleashing of a storm there—could have in common. Here again it is the content of the prohibitions rather than the fact that there is a prohibition that seems problematic: why must not a menstruating girl, or the Japanese or Inca sovereigns, or the Samo rainmaster, come into the presence of the sun? We might recall that on Samoa (Shore 1976) a man who was guilty of incest with a woman of high rank was punished, according to ancient traditions, by exposure to the sun until death; and that among the Chiricahua Apaches (Fox 1962), those guilty of incest were burned alive.

As for medical treatment, Durkheim shows that the female blood that flows so dangerously, particularly that of the first period or the first childbirth, is also endowed with exceptional curative properties. This is also attested in medieval Europe. But the list of illnesses that are treated by applications of this blood to the skin does not seem arbitrary to me: boils, scabies, impetigo [gourme], milk fever, inflammation of the salivary glands, leprosy. The inflammation of the salivary glands, to speak only of this, is the same as scrofula, or king's evil, which the kings of France treated by the laying on of hands (here again we find a relationship between menstrual blood and the sacred, no longer in terms of the prohibitions to which both give rise, but in their most profound characteristics); these are "cold humors," says Littré, arising, according to Ambroise Paré, from "corrupted and rotten phlegm." As well as designating milk crust, the French word *gourme* means a sort of equine scrofula ("the strangles" in English). Skin diseases, hot, cold, running, or dry, why is it that these diseases are treated with menstrual blood?

On Ponape, it is thought that individuals who commit incest present physical signs of exhaustion, notably large black circles under their eyes (Fischer and Ward 1976). Among the Bobo, intercourse with a prepubescent girl causes a peculiar debility in the male partner and the drying up of his virility. On Mount Hagen (Strathern 1971), menstrual blood is thought to be antithetical to masculine "grease" (the same term designates a man's semen). If a man were to take in this blood through his penis or in his food, "his skin would lose its grease and become dry and his body emaciated" (p. 162). Among the Bobo, as on Ponape, incest brings dryness—not, however, the metaphorical dryness of the body or the humors, but meteorological drought: if an incestuous couple or their children are buried after their death, the rain is supposed to stop falling in Bobo country. At Panope, a drought that occurred in 1971 on one of the islands in the district was attributed to a supernatural curse, the direct result of the incestuous practices of this island's population. Among the Palawan of the Philippines (Macdonald 1977), "the most commonly expected consequence [of incest] is the destruction of the harvest—especially the rice harvest—as a result of excessive rain or heat," a flood or a drought. In a note (p. 103), Macdonald adds that according to a number of informants incest with the mother provokes an excess of rain while incest with the sister causes an excess of heat, and any incest at all will bring floods or the dog days. The incest theme, finally, also has cosmological value in mythology. Among the matrilineal Kaguru (Beidelman 1971), the most stringent prohibition is that against sexual relations between members of the same matriclan, the next most strict being the prohibition against relations between individuals whose fathers belong to the same matriclan (they are in symmetrical positions in relation to the members of this clan). But the most common misdemeanor, *mahasa,* is a violation of the rule that two brothers of the same clan may not marry two sisters of another clan, nor may a man even seduce or court two sisters, whether or not they are unmarried. This is no ordinary adultery since, as among the Nuer, all three partners can be unmarried. For Beidelman, this unusual variety of incest is considered such because it endangers "the solidarity of matrilineal groups by setting women in competition against one another for the affection of loyalty of lovers and potential husbands." Outside the question of the likelihood of this kind of functionalist explanation, what seems important to me is that the supernatural sanction of all varieties of incest, including *mahasa,* affects the women, who become "polluted" and are threatened with sterility or imperfect progeny, and their matrilineal consanguines. "The blood of the offender's kin is disturbed, turned hot, and this may cause them illness or sterility; it may even harm their livestock or crops, for even the land itself may be so heated and disturbed" (p. 189). Simply stepping over the legs of a sexually forbidden partner, when he or she is seated with legs out-stretched, while not disastrous for the group, is so for the individuals themselves, causing sores to erupt on their bodies. Among the Muria (Elwin 1947), a girl who becomes pregnant from what the *ghotul* decides is incest with a boy of her own clan is punished by "excessive menorrhagia" (p. 417). A woman guilty of adultery endangers the year's harvest; her body and that of her partner "become covered with sores and swellings, and a watery dropsy brings a wretched death" (p. 633).

So whether it is a matter of direct consequences, inscribed on the body of the guilty parties and in their biological functions, or of disturbances of nature and ecosystems, we could pursue this ethnographic inventory of the immediate sanc-tions of incest a great deal further; these are usually details cited in passing, all of which refer us back to the same questions: that of the meaning-relations that underlie social relations, that of the possible inscription of meaning-relations in a universal logic.

I will, then, postulate that the various beliefs related to incest should not be considered absurd superstitions of no interest except, by their very foolishness, as striking illustrations of the necessity of the social rule; that every human group's symbolic beliefs concerning incest, its effects, its sanctions, are connect-ed to beliefs concerning the relationship between the sexes, biological organiza-tion and functioning, and very probably to other fields of representation, such as the ordering of the elements, the organization and functioning of the world; that every people's corpus of representations touching on the organization of the body, of the world, of society, and their manifold interrelations, can be followed back to a few fundamental, universal, and underlying laws, to what I called above a great universal scheme of organization. While such a scheme generally remains implicit, explicit fragments of it can sometimes be found in the state-ments of informants.

It would be pure presumption to attempt a full demonstration of these three points within the framework of this article, but it is perhaps not too absurd to present the general lines of the argument.

To do this I will start with semicomplex kinship systems, namely, those that have been labeled Crow-Omaha,[2] and with certain peculiarities in the prohibi-tions that characterize these systems. I will then look more specifically at the example of the Samo of Upper Volta, which falls under the rubric of Omaha systems (Héritier 1976). On the basis of a brief analysis of these peculiarities, I will attempt to show that they can be understood in relation to a symbolics[3] of *identity* and *difference.* I will then try to show that this elementary symbolics of

2. It seems useful to specify that I consider these systems to constitute a class of facts, a heterogeneous one certainly, but a class nonetheless.
3. TN: The French term is *la symbolique,* a case of an adjective (*symbolique* meaning "symbolic") turned noun. I have used the word "symbolics," in the singular (cf. Oxford English Dictionary, s.v. "symbolics"), to translate the noun, by analogy with the use of "semiotics" to translate *la sémiotique* (or "mathematics" for *la mathématique*).

the identical and the different is universal, whatever the particular trappings in which it is envisaged by various peoples, and that besides this it is the object of a limited number of manipulations whose content varies depending on the style of each people, and whose combinations allow us to follow the coherent thread of symbolic discourses about incest.

We know that Omaha systems are characterized by more or less vast bodies of marital prohibitions, involving from two to four forbidden patrilineal clans or lineages. Among the Samo there are four, the lineages of ego, his mother, his father's mother, and his mother's mother (E, M, FM, MM). The rule of prohibition speaks in the name of a masculine ego and in terms of the lineage, that is, of agnatic descent: any union of ego with female members of these agnatic groups is forbidden, whatever their real degree of consanguinity with ego.

Next come those prohibitions which are not necessarily based on the law of exogamy as understood in lineage terms. I will cite two of these: (1) the extension of the prohibition to all cognates for three generations, the common ancestor of the forbidden partners being placed in generation +4; (2) the extension of the prohibition to affines. I will return later to the first point; let us begin with the second.

A man is forbidden to take a wife from lineages from which a "father" (a man of his lineage of his father's generation) or a "brother" (a man of his lineage of his own generation) has already taken a bride. Symmetrically, it is therefore impossible for a woman to marry into a lineage into which a "sister" (a woman of her lineage and her generation) or a "father's sister" (a woman of her lineage of her father's generation) has already married. By extension this also implies (a rule explicitly formulated by the Samo) the prohibition of all adulterous sexual relations with the wife of an agnate during the latter's lifetime, the levirate being not only possible but desirable, since a woman given to a lineage in marriage is the property of that lineage. This forbidden adulterous relationship has the same name *(dyilibra)* as incestuous relations between real consanguines. By extension of the same rule, that two agnates may not court or marry in the same place, it is a fortiori forbidden for a man to marry or even to frequent a "sister" of his wife (a lineage sister), but also any kinswoman belonging to the lineages of his wife's mother, father's mother, and mother's mother, and even cognatic kinswomen attached to these lineages bilaterally to a depth of three generations. This implies symmetrically that two kinswomen whose genealogical relationship can be traced, and a fortiori two sisters, not only may not marry the same man but may not even have sexual relations with him. A woman who learns that her husband is having a clandestine affair with one of her kinswomen will leave him. We are, to different degrees, speaking on the level of sanctions and consequences, in the domain of *dyilibra* (promiscuity). These facts are clearly reminiscent of the similar ones cited above for the Nuer and the Kaguru cases. But I would like to stress one point: the principle of nonduplication of alliance which seems so manifest in the Samo rules, and which is typical of semicomplex systems of alliance (Lévi-Strauss 1969, p. xxxviii) does not exhaust the total signification of these facts, for it is not only a question of forbidden alliances but also quite simply of forbidden sexual relationships. Courting as well as copulation, with the wife's kinswomen as well as with the wives of living agnates, is as forbidden as marriage is. It seems to me that, after considering both the prohibitions and informants' statements about them, one is led to propose a second definition of incest, a definition independent of possible explanations in terms of avoidance of affective competition (Beidelman) or the need to avoid unduly mixing kinship categories (Evans-Pritchard). It is no longer a question of a relationship that unites two consanguines of different sex in a forbidden sexual relation, but of *a relationship which units two consanguines of the same sex who share a single sexual partner.* It is the same-sex consanguines, related as brother/brother, sister/sister, father/son, mother/daughter, who are in an incestuous relationship because of their shared partner, and who face the danger that this involves. In the *mahasa* of the Kaguru, the dangers of sterility and sickness through overheating affects the two consanguine women involved in the common relationship with one man, and their matriclan consanguines. Among the Samo, a married woman who learns that her husband is sleeping with one of her cousins leaves him; she leaves from fear and from anger at her husband and the kinswoman who are putting her in such danger. Among the Gusii (LeVine 1959), "when two men of the same clan have had intercourse with the same married woman, *regardless of whether or not she is married to either of them,* it is believed that a visit by one to the sickbed of the other will result in the death of the sick one" (p. 972), a fact of some importance in the daily relations of brothers, half brothers, and cousins. Here too it is not a question of either incest or adultery in the strict sense, but of the simple contact in the same sexual object of two consanguines who are in a relationship—a fact with its own importance—of siblinghood or procreation. The Baule (Etienne 1972, 1975) strictly forbid sororal polygyny and the sororate, but also sexual relations between a man and two sisters or two uterine cousins. If the affairs comes to be known, "the two girls must undergo the same rituals that sanction incest between uterine cousins. It is they who must cut the kid or sheep in half, who beat each other's naked bodies with the two halves of the animal, who are the object of the jeers of bystanders, and to whom the sacramental lustration is administered. The boy is in no way involved in these ceremonies" (1972, p. 41). Pierre Etienne is the first anthropologist to my knowledge to have suggested the hypothesis that incest is "a relationship between persons of the same sex who have possessed the same object of sexual satisfaction" (p. 106), but he seeks the explanation for this not as part of an ideological ensemble that goes beyond the local context but within the structure of relations between feminine and masculine sexuality—an area that should not be ignored, even though I have not followed this path myself. Among the Antaimoro of the lower Faraony valley (following R. Dubois 1972, cited in

Etienne 1972), the ritual of *fafy* intervenes to sanction cases of incest: its effect
is either to erase the kinship relation in favor of the sexual relation or, inversely,
to erase the sexual relation in favor of the kinship relation. Dubois shows that an
incestuous relationship exists between same-sex consanguines who have or who
have had the same sexual partner, but in this Malagasy case the same-sex consanguines are not in a relation of siblinghood, as in the Baule case, but of procreation. So if a man sleeps with his wife's daughter, the daughter by this act destroys what made her mother a mother and puts her in a situation of impurity.
The *fafy*, a lustral aspersion of blood by the daughter on the body of her mother,
has the goal of renewing the mother/daughter relationship while suppressing the
effects of the sexual relationship. But the incestuous relationship which must be
suppressed to restore former bonds is located between mother and daughter, not
between the daughter and the mother's husband.

As for our own Western societies, certain facts argue for the hypothesis that
this second variety of incest is not so foreign to our own mentalities. In the con-
fessions recorded by the inquisitor Pierre Fournier at Montaillou (LeRoy
Ladurie 1975), there repeatedly appears (pp. 79, 216, 252, 267) the story of a
man who is courting a woman who happens to be the mistress—not the wife—of
one of his first cousins, and who gives up his suit when the woman explains the
peculiar situation in which she finds herself ("even when it is through the interposed body of a common mistress, you should not touch the body of a first
cousin in a carnal way, for he already touches you naturally"). In the same way,
if we look carefully for the kinds of reasons that a sexual relationship between a
stepfather and his wife's daughter, or between a man and his wife's sister (this
was the occasion for a recent legal case of incest in England) are considered incestuous, we will probably be forced to admit the validity of this interpretation,
or at least not to discard it without further examination. And why, precisely, is
Phèdre the tragedy of incest par excellence? It is an excuse, not a reason, to say
that sexual relations with affines is incest because marriage puts affines into the
same conceptual category as consanguines, and that, because of this, sexual relations with affines would constitute a factor of disorder and role confusion. Nor
is it certain that, in the absence of any legally consecrated marriage, the popular
conscience does not consider sexual relations between a man and the daughter
of his mistress as incestuous.

I must further emphasize that this interpretation fits perfectly for explaining
why certain varieties of adultery, notably with the wives of kinsmen, are considered, named, and treated as incest, sometimes even one of the worst kinds of
incest, by many populations. It is equally adequate for accounting for the
homology of character among various forms of prohibited adulterous sexual relations. Goody (1956), contrary to the theses of Malinowski and Evans-Pritchard,
attempts a total separation of incest from exogamy. He takes as proof of this
separation the fact that the law of exogamy can in no way justify the fact that
adultery with wives of lineage consanguines should be designated and treated as

incest, since by definition the wives of these consanguines necessarily fall into the general category of permitted wives. Consequently he establishes a typology of sexual misdemeanors to account for the facts observed among various African populations:

—relations with members of the same descent group, or incest;
—relations with a wife of a member of the group, or consanguine adultery;
—relations with a married woman outside the group, or simple adultery.

This typology does not really permit him to justify the local terminological customs in any absolute way, nor to place clearly adulterous relations with the wife's mother or sister. If we look at what Ashanti informants, according to Rattray (Goody 1956, p. 305), put into the single category of *atwebeneSie*—adultery with a brother's or son's wife, with the wife's mother, an uncle' wife, the wife of a *fekuo* companion, the wife of an association mate, the wife of one's own slave, the father's wife other than the mother, the wife's sister, whether or not she is married—we find in fact that some of these are adulteries with wives of group members (in the general sense: matriclan, *abusua,* as well as patriclan, *ntoro;* and even metonymically: the wife of an age-class consanguine or a slave), while the others (with the wife's mother or sister) take place outside the group. From my point of view, however, the Ashanti informants appear very logical in giving these all the same name without worrying about the difference between intra- and extragroup adultery, since these incestuous "adulteries" all refer explicitly to the same formal situation, that of incest of the second type. In the one case, incest exists between two male consanguines, real or assimilated, who share the same sexual partner (father/son, brother/brother, uncle/nephew), since the master/slave relationship is one of paternity, and the relationship of companion-age is a fraternal one; in the other, incest exists between two female consanguines, who are sharing the same sexual partner (mother/daughter, sister/sister).

This second type of incest has a fundamental point in common with the first type, in that both are based on the opposition between the identical and the different. We may thus picture the two varieties of incest as two possible ramifications of a single ideological substratum. But we must first return to the extension of Omaha prohibitions to all cognatic consanguines for three generations, an extension we have left provisionally to one side.

A Samo ego is forbidden not only from marrying women who belong by birth, according to agnatic descent, to his prohibited lineages, but also from marrying any cognatic kin up to the sixth degree (by the civil, or Roman, mode of calculation), whatever lineage they belong to. He may not, for example, marry his MMSdd,[4] the daughter of his mother's matrilateral parellel cousin (see fig. 9.1).

This configuration is not unique to the Samo. It is attested at the least among the Mossi, the Bete, and the Baule, the Mkao Mbogendi of the Cameroons

4. I am using a conventional system of notation for kinship terms.
F = father, M = mother, B = brother, S = sister, s = son, d = daughter, ch = child.
These are read from left to right. Thus FM = father's mother; MMSdd = mother's mother's sister's daughter's daughter; MMBs(d)ch = mother's mother's brother's son's or daughter's child.

(Copet 1977), and others. It is, however, possible among most of these peoples to validate or allow the marriage when the incestuous relationship is discovered after the fact or if there is no other possible partner, on condition of performing a ritual to cut off the kinship between husband and wife, and having the couple wear a special bracelet for the rest of their lives to remind others and themselves of the peculiarity of their union. This is, of course, possible only for a certain number of positions of consanguinity, those considered the most distant in terms of the specific way the field of kinship is hierarchized.

Let me add that we should necessarily find this extension in any society with Omaha terminology and alliance prohibitions, if we also find a prohibition on marriage with the matrilateral parallel cousin. In this case the prohibition cannot be because she belongs by agnatic descent to a lineage forbidden to him; nor, in a symmetrical and reciprocal way, can it be because he belongs by agnatic descent to a lineage forbidden to her. Let us listen to the Samo's own explanation: they say that these two cousins are in contact as uterine nephew and niece of the same maternal uncles. Therefore they are forbidden to each other as matrimonial or sexual partners, because they have the same maternal lineage, and so occupy the same position in relation to members of that lineage.

If every social system must be internally coherent to the extent that it may be learned by those whose role will be to practice and reproduce it, and if the known Omaha examples attest to the prohibition of alliance between sisters' children, this means that the notion of the sharing of a common maternal lineage is relevant for the elaboration of the prohibitions (it follows from this that these systems are not dependent solely on the principle of unilineal descent). By extension, when two or more lineages or sublineages are prohibited, the same principles should apply to the group of cognatic consanguines related to these forbidden lineages through the mediation of women, by genealogical connections known to the depth of three generations (or more, if more than four

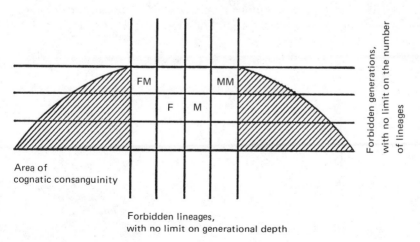

Area of
cognatic consanguinity

Forbidden lineages,
with no limit on generational depth

Figure 9.1

groups are forbidden). In this case the cognatic consanguines involved will belong to the same grandmaternal, or great-grandmaternal, lineages. The number of
forbidden lineages indicates the degree of generation that is pertinent and the
collateral categories of possible cognatic extensions: when two lineages are forbidden, the cognatic extensions go, as we have seen, only to the fourth degree;
if three or four lineages are forbidden, the cognatic extensions go as far as the
sixth degree, with the treatment of collaterals varying according to whether the
forbidden supplementary lineages are those of the father's mother *and* the
mother's mother, of the father's mother only, or of the mother's mother only.
Thus, for example, in a case in which the mother's mother's lineage is not excluded for the choice of a mate, the set of MMBs(d)ch and MMSs(d)ch should
by definition be possible spouses for ego. What is more, from ego's point of
view, it would not be necessary to establish a distinction between those who belong by birth to the mother's mother's lineage (the MMBsch, the mother's
mother's brother's son's children) and all other people who are connected to this
lineage only cognatically, for all in the same way belong to the undifferentiated
group of marriageable consanguines, divided into the various lineages.

Nevertheless, from the fourth generation following that of the common
ancestor of the two distinct lines of descent, it is not from among properly
cognatic consanguines—i.e,. those descended from two sisters of the first generation—that the Samo make their preferential choice of spouse (Héritier 1976; see
fig. 9.2); they choose a spouse, rather, among those who are cognatically connected to one of the four lineages forbidden to ego, that is, from among the descendants of the sister of a bisexual pair of siblings located in the first generation
(see fig. 9.3). It is worth noting that the choice is made, in the order of diminishing attractiveness, among the cognatic consanguines of ego's own lineage, then
among those of his mother's lineage, those of his father's mother's lineage, and
finally his mother's mother's lineage, in that order of preference. Thus it is evident that the extension of the prohibition on cognatic consanguines for three
generations is not necessary to the smooth running of a system which functions
preferentially by closing the circle every five generations, since it is not purely

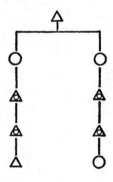

Figure 9.2

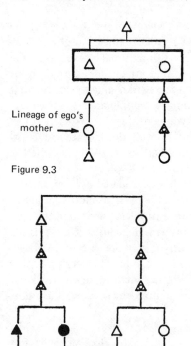

Figure 9.3

Figure 9.4

cognatic cousins of the eighth degree who marry. On the contrary, the closure in the fifth generation can be described looking only at the fact that prohibitive lineage rules are lifted after three generations, on condition that there be perfect symmetry between the situations of a male and a female ego (see fig. 9.4).

I conclude therefore that "something" passes by way of individual people, something which never disappears if it is mediated by men, which takes three generations to be diluted and disappear when it passes, even if only once, by the intermediary of a woman, something that forbids alliance between its bearers until its dissolution is complete. In the eleventh century, according to canon law, seven generations had to have passed, by way of both men and women (since this system is cognatic and not patrilineal like the one above) for the definitive extinction of this affinity between different branches sprung from a single ancestor, an affinity which Peter Damian, Father of the Church, called the "odor" of kinship: "nature herself provides that brotherly love be recognized in the human entrails up to the sixth degree of kinship and breathe forth like an odor the natural community that exists between kin." Beyond seven generations, "when the family based on kinship begins to fail, at the same time as the words that designate it, the law of marriage reappears and reestablishes the rights of the ancient love between new men" (Peter Damian 1853; translated from Latin into French by Christiane Klapisch).

Let us call another witness. Among the Samo, a woman's firstborn is not the child of her legitimate husband, who is the child's social father, but of an officially recognized lover; a child born in these conditions should never learn the identity of his genitor. The marital prohibitions that affect him come from his mother and his social father, which agrees with the Durkheimian principle that any repression of incest presupposes that relations of kinship are recognized and organized by the society itself. If, however, a young man wishes to marry (or to court as an official lover) a girl whom no marital prohibition on either side forbids to him, but who turns out to be his agnatic half sister by blood (whether she be a daughter his genitor conceived, within the bonds of matrimony or not, with another woman, or a daughter his own father engendered as lover, to another man's benefit); in this case, and this case only, the biological link that unites them is revealed to him. This obviously presents a problem: if, as appears to be the case, it is the social bond that is primary in marital exclusions, and it is the only one that counts for the recognition of kinship, why prevent this marriage, which is consanguine only in biological terms? This can only be because of that "something" which passes between individuals through descent, and whose presence even in simple procreation is signalled by a scruple, the shadow of a doubt: this is what I call the notion of the *identical.*

Two identical things have the same definition and common characteristics. For example, two matrilateral parallel cousins have a common characteristic, which is to be in the same position vis-à-vis their maternal lineage; from this lineage's point of view, they are identical. I am the child of my mother, a characteristic I share with my brothers and sisters. The criteria that serve to distinguish the identical from the different naturally vary from society to society, and each culture constructs its own symbolics around this issue. There also exist gradations specific to each culture in the definitions of identity and difference. If this is accepted, we can indicate a number of constant points, quite banal observations on the whole, that revolve around identity or difference of sex and the parallel or cross-relations that follow from this, both in descent and in collaterality.

In collaterality it is a general law, as Lévi-Strauss has noted (p. 128) "that the *brother-sister* relationship is identical with the *sister-brother* relationship, but that these both differ from the *brother-brother* and the *sister-sister* relationships, which are identical with one another." This is the principle, well known since Radcliffe-Brown, of the identity of siblings of the same sex. The strongest identity is with a twin of the same sex, then, among siblings,[5] with the sibling of the same sex, among cousins[6] with the parallel cousin of the same sex. With the impossibility of a negation of the difference between the sexes, the elementary

5. Whether or not they are full brothers or sisters.
6. Cousins are in a parallel situation when they are the children of two brothers or two sisters; they are in a cross-situation when they are the children of a brother and a sister respectively.

mark of otherness, we probably reach the core of the reflection of human groups upon themselves, from which any social organization and all ideology is constituted. This seems evident the moment one considers several curious absences from the spread of logical possibilities for the organization of kinship. Thus if we look at the determining criteria of the main types of terminological structures arising from the designation of siblings and cousins, we see that there is one, and only one, logical possibility that is missing. We find the following logical possibilities actualized, the fourth one abundantly so:

parallel cousins = cross-cousins = siblings   (Hawaiian)

parallel cousins ≠ cross-cousins ≠ siblings   (Sudanese)

[parallel cousins = cross-cousins] ≠ siblings (Eskimo)

[parallel cousins = siblings] ≠ cross-cousins (Iroquois, Crow, Omaha)

but it does not seem possible to cite an example of the realization of a general terminological structure based on the following quotation:

[cross-cousins = siblings] ≠ parallel cousins

The notion of the identical centers on commonality of gender, which in itself gives rise to the parallelism of the situations; these two traits are universally perceived as being of the same nature.

When procreation rather than siblinghood is privileged for the determination of the identical, commonality of gender still remains the primary criterion: societies more easily think of mother/daughter and/or father/son relations as privileged supports of identity than the cross-relations of father/daughter or mother/son. We should note that this identity by common gender and by descent can skip a generation among certain populations. We also observe a number of curious absences in the field of logical possibilities of the elementary modes of descent at this level. Needham (1971, pp. 10-11) enumerates six such elementary modes, four of which are definitely actualized:

m ⟶ m patrilineal

f ⟶ f matrilineal

(m ⟶ m) + (f ⟶ f) bilineal, a combination of the preceding modes in
                                              the definition of any status

m/f ⟶ m/f cognatic

but the last two:

(m ⟶ f) + (f ⟶ m) alternating

(m ⟶ m) // (f ⟶ f) parallel

"probably could not be employed socially as regular and exclusive principles of transmission and incorporation, though certain rare and uncertain approximations to them have been reported." The parallel system, while hardly convenient, still seems more viable than the alternating system, in which rights and statuses are *only* transmitted from male to female and from female to male.

It is quite evident, as we have already said, that diverse and complex patternings of the notion of the identical exist among various populations, ideological patternings that are at the very heart of the paradigmatic choices established by each society in constituting its social organization, in the broad sense of the term. But the wider interest of the lack of representation, or the very feeble representation, of formulas which do exist logically, and whose rules of functioning we can amuse ourselves trying to invent, is simply that it demonstrates, if demonstration be needed, that all human groups have thought their categories of the identical and the different along the same general lines, at the very least in a negative sense: *there is no example of the notion of the identical, as a global ideological category, being based on an absolute primacy of the similarity of cross-kin.*

We could inventory all the ethnographic reports that highlight, in a way more or less directly related to the incest prohibition, the notion of the identical. The point is raised very frequently in any case, even if only in incidental and justificatory ways. Texts do, however, exist in which the notion of the identical, in connection with the incest prohibition, is viewed more explicitly in its relations with representations of the person, especially those that involve the constitution of the individual and the respective contributions of the two parents. Thus Huntington (1978) shows the reasons why the most abhorrent incest for the Bara of Madagascar is not simply the union of siblings or other primary kin, but specifically of the children of sisters, this being the case over several generations: it is because they come from the "same heart," from the "same womb," the "same stomach." Agnatic half siblings, even though they belong to the same lineage, are only considered "almost brothers." Their proximity is more a matter of socialization than of true intimacy. The children of two brothers may therefore marry if they perform the appropriate ritual. The preferred marriage is between cross-cousins. This case clearly shows how a society constructs its own gradation of the identical seen as parallel commonality of gender, in collaterality as in this particular case, or in descent. This construction must necessarily accord with the basic traits of the social organization (descent, alliance, power...). On Tokelau (Huntsman and Hooper 1975), true siblings are also thought of as identical beings (*tutuha,* the same), and this identity involves differing attitudes depending on whether the individuals in question are of the same or of different sex. Brother/sister avoidance is complete in such sensitive domains as sharing the same residence, taking food together, or sexual joking.

This brings us to the following point. The incest prohibition generally has to be ordained as a social rule only *from the moment when the principle of identity ceases to be sufficiently strongly structured,* that is, most often, when consanguines of different sex are put into relation with each other, the strongest structuration of the identical passing above all by way of commonality of gender. This is true in the case of the first type of incest, and seems to go without saying, considering the classic heterosexual definition of incest. Still, in the second type of incest analyzed above, the prohibition concerns a homosexual relationship between consanguines, mediated through a single sexual object. Let us look more closely at this point.

In ethnological theory as in common usage, our own as well as that of other societies, incest seems to involve heterosexual relations first of all, and next heterosexual relations that involve a risk of fertilization. Thus, in French law, rape is defined as involving a forced vaginal relation; as for incest, it is considered punishable only as an aggravating circumstance in the rape of a minor: it is thus limited to heterosexual penetration such that a child might, if age permits, be conceived from the union. Margaret Mead ("Incest," p. 118) saw this aspect of the question clearly: "The prevailing emphasis on incest taboos as they are related to the regulation of marriage has resulted in an almost total neglect of homosexual incest."

I am not in a position to discuss in any depth the reality of homosexual desire in psychoanalytic terms, the frequency of the realization of this desire, whether in terms of play, fondling, or completed intercourse. Barry and Johnson (1958) say that they know of a certain number of mother/daughter and grandmother/granddaughter cases in their own files. Maisch (1973, p. 186), on the other hand, says that in his practice he has tended rather to come across cases of father/son, grandfather/grandson homosexual incest. But two things should be noted in any case: first of all that the possibility exists, that it is known, and that individual cases have been recorded; secondly and above all that there exist patent and socially recognized cases of consanguine homosexuality which are perfectly licit between certain types of kin. If it exists between certain types of kin and not among all of them indiscriminately, this is because a barrier has been put up for certain kin with whom homosexuality is not permitted. What we must investigate is the nature of this barrier.

Lévi-Strauss reports that among the Nambikwara a man's potential brother-in-law is his cross-cousin "with whom, as an adolescent, one indulges in homosexual activities which will always leave their mark in the mutually affectionate behavior of the adults." And he adds: "Brothers are closely related to one another, but they are so in terms of their similarity. . . . By contrast, brothers-in-law are solidary because they complement one another and have functional efficacy for one another . . . they play the role of the opposite sex in the erotic games of childhood" (p. 484).

What does this mean? In this text Lévi-Strauss says nothing about the status of parallel cousins; he specifies that brothers are solidary "in terms of their similarity," and he makes no allusion to possible homosexual play between them. I should add that, when questioned on this point, Claude Lévi-Strauss confirmed the hypothesis that parallel cousins have the same status as siblings, and the impossibility of any homosexual relations between them. On the other hand, brother-in-law/cross-cousins are solidary and sexually close, each one marrying the other's sister. Homosexual play seems reserved to them. This signifies, loosely speaking, that in this society individuals observe a prohibition on homosexual and heterosexual incest between partners who are thought of as identical (Lévi-Strauss says "similar"), namely, parallel cousins and siblings; the society allows, on the other hand, in different temporal patterns, homosexual play or matrimonial alliance between partners who are thought of as different, namely, cross-cousins. In this society, the most powerful criterion of the identical does not involve commonality of gender, but the parallel as opposed to the crossed, character of kinship relations.

Let us take another example from Schneider (1976, p. 151):

> The Etoro of New Guinea believe that semen is necessary to the proper growth and maturation of boys and so they are fed semen direct from its source, by mouth, as often as is deemed necessary. The ideal inseminator is the boy's father's sister's husband, but other older men may perform this function as well. Kelly says that the definitions of incest, and the prohibitions on marriage, are isomorphic with the prohibitions on the insemination of boys, except of course that in the one case heterosexual pairs are involved, in the other pairs of the same sex. Schieffelin reports of the Kaluli of New Guinea the same belief. He states that the inseminator, chosen by the father, is a man who is usually an in-law (possibly sister's husband though this is not clear) or an unrelated older man. For both the Etoro and the Kaluli such a relationship between a boy and his father or brother is considered incestuous and is prohibited.

Whether or not the father's sister's husband is the father's cross-cousin, this example clearly shows the homology of structure of homosexual and heterosexual prohibitions. Like the preceding example, it makes two definite points: that it is possible for there to be a licit type of homosexual relation; and that in this case the main criterion of the identical is displaced from that of common gender to the parallel character of the kinship relation, in descent as well as collaterality

If anthropological literature gave us only these particular examples, we could still take them as proof of the relevance of the notions of the identical and the different for understanding incest prohibitions. Certainly, these notions vary in extension, amplitude, and intensity depending on how the relation between the sexes is viewed by each society, particularly in their respective roles in the creation of a new individual. It seems, however, that beyond all of these variations, the symbolics of the identical always and everywhere presents itself in the same very simple structural patterns, in all the domains in which this symbolics is in obvious use—in medical treatment, for example, or the choice of a spouse. The only choice is between two possibilities, based on the good or bad effects which they are thought to produce: either *an accumulation of the identical will be sought* (which implies as a corollary the refusal to combine or juxtapose different elements), or else *an accumulation of the identical will be forbidden* (with, as a corollary, the systematic project of juxtaposing or combining different elements). As far as choice of a spouse is concerned, it is not rare for these choices to be accompanied by considerations of a genetic order, as among the Mkako, who "think of the mixture of identical bloods—partly or completely identical—as an incest leading to weakness and death. Inversely, the mixture of different bloods brings strength and life" (Copet 1977). We find similar considerations in our own culture.

The rules that forbid incest, that in short forbid the accumulation of the identical as each society conceives it (according to models whose inventory, or at least whose principal configurations, should be established), need to be proclaimed explicitly only when the notion of the identical wavers on the borders of difference: when the difference between the sexes intervenes at the heart of a parallel relationship of consanguinity (in collaterality or descent), as is the most frequent case, or when the parallel/cross dichotomy intervenes at the heart of a situation of common gender, as is the case among the Nambikwara, the Etoro, or the Kaluli. In this case there is a danger both for individuals and societies due to the accumulation of the identical. But outside of this kind of situation, no rule is needed to specify to a man: thou shalt not copulate with thy son, nor with thy brother, nor (for the Nambikwara) with thy parallel cousin, but only with thy cross-cousin. These are things that seem to go without saying in the social superego (we may note on this point the complete silence of the texts on any possible incestuous female homosexuality). Everything happens as if the ordering of the identical and the different, using commonality of gender and the parallelism that follows from it, acquires its full meaning in orienting sexuality towards the opposite sex for the goals of the species, and in regulating this orientation for goals of social construction.

The seeking or refusal of an accumulation of the identical can be explained by a number of formal traits.

Identical and *different,* as polar categories, are notions that bear on sets of contrasted traits which appear in the form of dualistic categories, pairs of true opposites, such as right/left, bright/dark, male/female, superior/inferior, high/low, hot/cold, dry/wet, etc., and which may also involve an organization along positive and negative poles.

To this bipolarity corresponds a balance between two ideas found more or less expressed in every society, sometimes in attenuated forms, buried within isolated beliefs (in our society, for instance, girls were formerly advised not to dip their hands or feet in cold water during their periods, or else the blood would flow back into their bodies; women who were having their periods were supposed to make mayonnaise, custard, emulsions turn sour): first, under some conditions opposites attract, under others they repel; second, a proper balance of opposites is necessary for the harmony of the world, the individual, the social order. For Greek thought, which particularly elaborated the question of the balance of the elements (Lloyd 1964), the greatest perfection lay in the greatest possible combination of opposites in correct proportions. By contrast, the accumulation of the identical always creates an imbalance, an excess. This excess may be deliberately sought, for example, in certain medical treatments or in the inverted behavior peculiar to aristocrats or sovereigns in many parts of the world (Shilluk princesses, who have free sexual relations with their kin, including agnatic half brothers, are *supposed* to be sterile, as are women of the aristocratic Vungara clan of the Zande, who are reputed to be Lesbians among other things, as are Nyoro princesses [Heusch 1959]).

I come now to the last link in my chain of reasoning: the relevance of societies' global systems of representations, organized following the canons of a very general logic whose main lines have been described above, for understanding the institution of the incest prohibition. The example for this argument will be a succinct analysis of the Samo system of representations (Héritier 1973, 1978, "Le charivari") but it could be illustrated equally well by other ethnographic materials. Needless to say, the specific content, definition, and arrangement of the pertinent ideological traits by the Samo are not necessarily the same elsewhere, whereas the general logic, based on relations of the identical and the different as these have been described, would hypothetically be invariable.

Among the Samo, the central dualistic category, which can be found in ordinary language, in discourse, myths, rituals, is that of *hot* and *cold*, with its corollaries of dry and wet. (Incidentally, judging from the abundance of literature dealing with this subject, one can say that this category appears to be equally eminent in the thought of many other peoples; one easily discovers its pertinence for our own culture by analyzing not only the ordinary discourse of the present or the past but also the scientific discourse on the sexes, the body, diseases, of the doctors and hygienists of the eighteenth and nineteenth centuries.) Bringing together two hot entities (putting hot on hot) has a drying effect; putting cold on cold causes flows, of water (torrential rains, floods), of blood (menorrhagia), of humors (dysentery). The effects of such accumulations of the identical, whatever the domain in which they take place, make themselves felt in one or another of the meteorological, biological, or social registers; a social crime, such as burying the body of a *zama*, a reputedly necrophilic pariah, which means putting hot on hot (Héritier, "Le charivari"), has meteorological consequences: it stops the rain from falling. The three registers are intimately bound together.

Man belongs to the category of the hot because, by the internal transformation of his "body waters" located in the bone marrow and the joints, he continually produces sperm, an element considered extremely hot since it is an especially condensed form of blood, which carries the heat of the body (Héritier 1977). The introduction of sperm into the female uterus brings the child, boy or girl, its necessary allotment of blood; the mother's blood, for its part, serves to build the child's body. For these reasons, the father should continue to have sexual relations with his wife up until around the sixth month of pregnancy (Héritier 1978), so that the child is provided with adequate blood. If relations continue after that date, the child risks being overheated in the womb (is this situation of being heated white-hot the reason for the existence of albinos, who, like the Samo *zama* or incestuous Bobo, may not be buried on penalty of stopping the rain from falling?). That semen carries blood or is a particularly purified and concentrated form of blood is also a popular belief in our own society (derived, perhaps, from the Greeks): for to speak of a mixture of bloods in the union of a man and woman can only imply that male semen has the power to transmit blood.

Woman belongs to the category of the cold, first of all because she does not produce blood herself: by the transformation of her "body waters" she produces milk which, like semen, belongs to the category of the hot. Milk and semen are equivalent in this sense. What is more, she periodically loses her own blood, and, once married, that which her husband introduces into her, when this is not being used to make a child. But a woman is in a hot situation during childhood, in her prepubescent state, during pregnancies, and after menopause.

These ideas about the characteristics of the vital fluids explain the prohibition on sexual relations after childbirth. Milk is hot like sperm, its homologue. The introduction of sperm into the womb of a woman who is nursing is equivalent to putting hot on hot. Its effect is to silence (dry up) the milk, to silence the male capacity to produce sperm, or to spoil the milk. There are supposed to be two cases in which a baby will refuse his mother's milk with disgust: when the mother has had sexual relations with her husband, or when she has another period while still nursing (the menstrual period can reappear after six months). Thus this prohibition, understood as for the good of the nursing infant, also serves to protect the virile capacities of the husband. Among the Mossi (Pageard, p. 128), it is thought that a drop of mother's milk falling on a boy's penis irremediably destroys his virility.

We have seen that woman, with whom cold is explicitly associated (and wet also; man is hot and dry), in fact belongs to the category of the hot during several, perhaps the longest, periods of her life. She possesses a heat of her own, which she loses periodically and which comes to her from her father and/or the lineage she belongs to (there is some hesitation on this point), a heat identical in nature and quantity to that possessed by her brothers. When she makes her baby, it is the blood she received from her father that will become the baby's body and organs: he will receive his endowment of blood, heat, and life from his own father. It will take three generations (cf. above) for this particular mark of the lineage, which her brothers transmit integrally through patrilineal descent, to disappear in her descendants who are crossed with other stocks. The contradiction inherent to the notion of the identical is that the trait of identity is passed along both by procreation and by descent, but that it must then necessarily be differentiated by sex. All, or almost all, societies have ancient fantasies of parthenogenesis.

Among the Samo, as in Madagascar, an incestuous union is a sterile one. When a couple has no children, the diviners frequently discover a forgotten consanguine relationship between the spouses, a discovery which authorizes a valid breaking off of a legitimate union. It is a sterile union because of the accumulation of two identical heats, leading to consumption, the drying up of the vital fluids. Incest heats you up, *dyilibra a fulare ma*. In the same way, copulation with a prepubescent girl, who has not yet lost her initial heat, is dangerous because it exposes one or the other of the partners to the risk of his/her vital fluids, his/her substance drying up, which can lead to death. According to the same logic, for a menopausal woman to have regular sexual relations is to accumulate hot upon hot without the possibility of a regular "cooling off" through menstruation, or a sudden and severe "cooling off" through childbirth (women in childbirth are warmed up with hot baths and a constant fire), and consequently to run the serious risk of being accused of witchcraft. A woman who is having her period, and so losing heat, attracts heat from the outside: she will ruin the cooking of poison (a hot element) if she should happen to go near the place where the men are preparing it silently in the bush. She absorbs the poison's heat. For the pregnant woman, on the other hand, the accumulation of heat provoked in her by a chance passing-by of the place where poison is being made causes an immediate miscarriage.

So there exist "short circuits" due to the simultaneous presence of two identicals, and this is not only the case in the domain of sexuality. The head and hair of the rainmaster *(lamutyiri)*, for instance, are supposed to make it rain. The person of the rainmaster is highly marked by the sign of the hot, and his heat is especially concentrated in his hair. Heat attracts the cold and wet; thus the *lamutyiri's* head of hair is supposed to carry the charge required to attract an adequate supply of rain (Héritier 1973). But if his hair, which is cut only once a year, touches the bare ground, which is hot and masculine, this produces a short circuit which unleashes drought and hot, disease-bearing winds, causes the grain to fail to germinate, etc. So the long-haired *lamutyiri* walks with care, at least during ceremonial occasions, sits by himself on straw mats, and may not wrestle during his childhood (he is chosen before birth) and adolescence, as young men traditionally do. In certain villages he may not come out during the day or bareheaded: thus he, too, avoids the rays of the sun, like the Mikado and the other princes in the examples reported by Durkheim. We may suggest that they, like him, are strongly marked by heat, and that if they exposed their bare heads to the sun catastrophic drought would probably follow for their people.

The notion of a short circuit also involves that of contagion, which we find in Durkheim (1898): "The properties of a being are propagated contagiously especially when they are of a certain intensity"; and, "we leave something of ourselves everywhere we go." Thus a man may not go down into a well, that is, into the womb of the earth, while his wife is pregnant: he would make her miscarry by contagion. Inversely, a man who dies during his wife's pregnancy, while she is retaining an unusual amount of heat, has, by contagion, all the highly dangerous characteristics of women who die while pregnant or in childbirth: he will be buried among these women, his house will be destroyed, his goods confiscated for the special gravediggers who alone may manipulate these dangerous corpses.

It may well be via these notions of short circuiting and contagion that we must understand the incestuous relationship of two consanguines through a single sexual partner, incest of the second order. This may even allow us to understand certain anomalies noted in passing above. If a Samo man has sexual relations with a "sister" or consanguine kinswoman of his wife, or with his wife's brother's wife (a double short circuit), his wife leaves him as soon as she finds out about it and will not return until all the procedures of pacification have been performed. This is not the expression of a moral reproach, but of a danger: for she has been put into carnal contact with her own substance, which she shares with her kinswoman and, just as dangerously although by way of two sexual mediations, with her brother. We have seen that among the Nuer, the most complete identity, that between consanguine agnatic men, is conceived of as perfect interchangeability. There is nothing wrong with sleeping with the wife of a "bull." But there is a prohibition on a son having relations with a father's or brother's wife. In this case, by contagion, it is a matter of the first type of incest, for reasons the Nuer explain perfectly well through their ethnographer's summary: the son comes into carnal contact with his mother if he sleeps with one of his father's other wives, since the father sleeps in the same way with both wives. If, among the Nambikwara, the relationship between cross-cousins ends after their marriage to each other's sisters, this is, of course, to avoid confusion of social roles, but it is also because each brother would, by contagion, come into contact with his own sister.

It is in terms of this problematic, understood in the sense of the logical articulations between different processes, that we can understand the disparate series of phenomena I cited at the beginning of this text, following Lévi-Strauss: they can be explained by an excess of the identical, whatever the nature of its effects. In some places the earth might be cold, hot on top of hot might give rise to floods instead of drought, another dualistic category might take the place occupied by hot and cold among the Samo, but this would not, I believe, affect the general logic that I have been trying to describe.

The sun has a strange taste for young mortal women having their periods, and they should protect theselves from it (as they should also protect themselves from cold water)—this may be because the excessive attractive power of the sun's heat would afflict them with a permanent flow of blood, or because this same force, acting repulsively, would stop their blood from flowing at all.

Masturbation is an accumulation of the identical, perhaps the most perfect of all such accumulations. In Europe, according to popular belief (and even in nineteenth-century medical discourse), masturbation causes young boys to dry up and waste away. Among the Navajo, it produces a totally abnormal fertility (monsters are born), an abnormal fertility similar to that which French popular beliefs attribute to consanguine unions, and a fortiori to incest.

It also allows us to understand the use of menstrual blood or the blood of childbirth (especially the first blood!) in medical treatments: this hot blood attracts the cold humors of scrofula; antithetical to milk, it stops it from rising in the breast; it dries up running boils or abscesses caused by heating.

If, according to Rattray (Goody 1956), among the Ashanti the rape of a married woman in the bush is classed among the most serious sexual offenses, which are judged on the tribal level and can lead to the offender's death, it is, I would readily hypothesize, because it is a hot act committed in a hot zone (the bush is hot; the village is cold), and so has climatic or epidemiological consequences that lead to trouble for the entire country. It is a crime against the group, not against a woman, nor against a man whose rights have been violated, nor even against the social institution of marriage, since it has to be committed *in the bush* to merit such a severe punishment.

The symbolics of incest, based upon the solid pillars of the identical and the different, has no necessary link with real, specifically genealogical, consanguinity; it assumes, on the contrary, a logical, syntactical relationship which unites diverse orders of representations: representations of the person and his/her parts, genetic representations of vertical or horizontal transfers that operate between individuals through channels of descent or contagion, representations of the relations between the sexes and of the world of kinship, but also representations of the natural world and the social order in their intimate relations with biological man. These relations are based on the exchange and the organic movement of flows which must be regulated. It does not, therefore, seem to me that to try to explain incest through the manipulation of the symbolic, as I have done, is in contradiction with Lévi-Strauss's demonstration. In regulating exchanges of all orders, it is still a matter of constructing society.

References

Aberle, David F., et al. "The Incest Taboo and the Mating Pattern of Animals." *American Anthropologist* 65 (1963): 253-65.

Barry, Maurice J. and Johnson, Adelaide M. "The Incest Barrior." *Psychoanalytic Quarterly* 27 (1958): 485-500.

Beidelman, Thomas O. "Some Kaguru Notions about Incest and Other Sexual Prohibitions." In R. Needham, ed., *Rethinking Kinship and Marriage*. London: Tavistock, 1971, pp. 181-202.

Bischof, Norbert. "Comparative Ethology of Incest Avoidance." In Robin Fox, ed., *Biosocial Anthropology*. New York: Wiley ASA Studies, 1975.

Bobos-Oulés (Les). I Droit civil. II Droit criminel. Coutumier anonyme. No place or date. 47 pp. MS (on deposit at the C.V.R.S., Ouagadougou).

Cooper, J. M. "Incest Prohibitions in Primitive Cultures." *Primitive Man* 5 (1932): 1-20.

Copet, Elizabeth. "Nguelebok, Essai d'analyse de l'organisation sociale des Mkao Mbogendi." Mimeographed. Thesis for the doctorate of the 3d cycle, E.P.H.E., 5th section, Université de Paris X, 1977.

Coult, Allan D. "Causality and Cross-Sex Prohibitions." *American Anthropologist* 65 (1963): 266-77.

Damian, Peter. *De parentelae gradibus*. In Migne, *Patrilogia latina* (Paris, 1853), Vol. 145, cols. 191-208.

Dubois, R. P. R. "Fihavanana. Approche de la spécificité malgache." Mimeographed, 1972.

Durkheim, Emile. "La prohibition de l'inceste et ses origines." *L'Année sociologique* (1898): 1-70.

Elwin, Verrier. *The Muria and Their Ghotul*. Bombay: Oxford University Press, 1947.

Étienne, Pierre. "Les interdictions de mariage chez les Baoulé." Mimeographed, 1972.

___. "Les interdictions de mariage chez les Baoulé." *L'Homme* 15, nos. 3-4 (1975): 5-27.

Evans-Pritchard, E. E. "Nuer Rules of Exogamy and Incest." In Meyer Fortes, ed., *Social Structure. Studies presented to A. R. Radcliffe-Brown*. London: The Clarendon Press, 1949.

Fischer, H. T., Ward, Roger, and Ward, Martha. "Ponapean Conceptions of Incest." *The Journal of the Polynesian Society* 85, no. 2 (1976): 199-207.

Fortune, Reo. "Incest." *Encyclopedia of the Social Sciences*, vol. 7, pp. 620-22. New York: Macmillan, 1932.

Fox, J. R. "Sibling Incest." *British Journal of Sociology* 13, no. 1 (1962): 128-50.

Freud, Sigmund. *Totem and Taboo*, 1913. *Standard Edition*, vol. 13. London, 1953.

Goodenough, Ward H. "Comments on the Question of Incestous Marriages in Old Iran." *American Anthropologist* 51 (1949): 326-28.

Goody, Jack. "A Comparative Approach to Incest and Adultery." *British Journal of Sociology* 7 (1956): 286-305.

Harris, Grace. "Furies, Witches and Mothers." In Jack Goody, ed., *The Character of Kinship*. Cambridge: Cambridge University Press, 1973.

Héritier, Françoise. "La paix et la pluie. Rapports d'autorité et rapport au sacré chez les Samo." *L'Homme* 13, no. 3 (1973): 121-38.

___. "Contribution à la théorie de l'alliance. Comment fonctionnent les systèmes d'alliance omaha?" *Informatique et Sciences humaines* 29 (1976): 10-46.

___. "L'identité samo." In *L'Identité. Seminaire dirigé par Claude Lévi-Strauss*. Paris: Grasset, 1977, pp. 51-80.

___. "Fécondité et stérilité. La traduction de ces notions dans le champ idéologique au stade pré-scientifique." In Centre Royaumont pour une Science de l'Homme, *Le Fait féminin*. Paris: Fayard, 1978, pp. 387-97.

_____. "Le charivari, la mort, la pluie." In the collection *Le charivari*, forthcoming.

Heusch, Luc de. *Essais sur le symbolisme de l'inceste royal en Afrique.* Brussels: Institut de Sociologie Solvay, 1958.

Hooper, Antony. "'Blood' and 'Belly': Tahitian Concepts of Kinship and Descent." In Jean Pouillon and Pierre Maranda, eds., *Echanges et communications. Mélanges offerts à Claude Lévi-Strauss.* The Hague and Paris: Mouton, 1970, pp. 307-20.

_____. "'Eating Blood': Tahitian Concepts of Incest." *The Journal of the Polynesian Society* 85, no. 2 (1976): 227-41.

Huntington, Richard. "Bara Endogamy and Incest Prohibition." *Bijdragen tot de Taal-, Land- en Volkenkunde* 134, no. 1 (1978): 30-62.

Huntsman, Judith, and Hooper, Antony. "Male and Female in Tokelau Culture." *The Journal of the Polynesian Society* 84, no. 4 (1975): 415-30.

_____. "The 'Desecration' of Tokelay Kinship." *The Journal of the Polynesian Society* 85, no. 2 (1976): 257-73.

Huth, Alfred Henry. *The Marriage of Near Kin Considered with Respect to the Laws of Nations, the Results of Experience, and the Teachings of Biology.* London: Churchill, 1875.

Kelly, R. *Etoro Social Structure: A Study in Structural Contradiction.* Ann Arbor: University of Michigan Press, 1977.

Kiste, Robert C., and Rynkiewich, Michael A. "Incest and Exogamy: A Comparative Study of Two Marshall Island Populations." *The Journal of the Polynesian Society* 85, no. 2 (1976): 209-26.

Kroeber, Alfred L. "Totem and Taboo: An Ethnological Psychoanalysis." *American Anthropologist* 22 (1920): 48-55.

Labby, David. "Incest as Cannibalism: The Yapese Analysis." *The Journal of the Polynesian Society* 85, no. 2 (1976): 171-79.

Le Roy Ladurie, Emmanuel. *Montaillou, village occitan de 1294 à 1324.* Paris: Gallimard, 1975.

LeVine, Robert A. "Gusii Sex Offenses: A Study in Social Control." *American Anthropologist* 61 (1959): 965-90.

Lévi-Strauss, Claude. *The Elementary Structures of Kinship.* English translation of the 2d ed. Boston: Beacon Press, 1969. Modified to fit the text.

Lloyd, G. E. R. "The Hot and the Cold, the Dry and the Wet in Greek Philosophy." *Journal of Hellenic Studies* 84 (1964): 92-106.

Macdonald, Charles. *Une société simple. Parenté et résidence chez les Palawan (Philippines).* Mémoires de l'Institut d'Ethnologie, 15. Paris: Institut d'Ethnologie, 1977.

Maisch, Herbert. *Incest.* English translation. London: Deutsch, 1973.

Marshall, Mac. "Incest and Endogamy on Namoluk Atoll." *The Journal of the Polynesian Society* 85, no. 2 (1976): 181-97.

Mead, Margaret. "Incest." *International Encyclopaedia of the Social Sciences*, vol. 7, pp. 115-25. London: Macmillan.

Middleton, Russell. "Brother-Sister and Father-Daughter Marriage in Ancient Egypt." *American Sociological Review* 27, no. 5 (1962): 603-11.

Monberg, Torben. "Ungrammatical 'Love' on Bellona (mungiki)." *The Journal of the Polynesian Society* 85, no. 2 (1976): 243-55.

Needham, Rodney. "Remarks on the Analysis of Kinship and Marriage." In R. Needham, ed., *Rethinking Kinship and Marriage*. London: Tavistock, 1971, pp. 1-34.

Pageard, Robert. *Le droit privé des Mossi. Tradition et évolution*. Collection Recherches voltaïques, 10 and 11. 2 vols. Paris and Ouagadougou: C.N.R.S., C.V.R.S., 1969.

Parsons, Talcott. "The Incest Taboo in Relation to Social Structure and the Socialization of the Child." *The British Journal of Sociology* 5, no. 2 (1954): 101-17.

Reynolds, V. "Kinship and the Family in Monkeys, Apes, and Man." *Man* 2 (1968): 209-23.

Rose, Frederick. "More on the Origin of Incest Rules." *American Anthropologist* 53 (1951): 139-41.

Sahlins, Marshall D. "The Social Life of Monkeys, Apes, and Primitive Man." In J. N. Spuhler, ed., *The Evolution of Man's Capacity for Culture: Six Essays*. Detroit: Wayne State University Press, 1959, pp. 54-73.

Schapera, I. "The Tswana Conception of Incest." In Meyer Fortes, ed., *Social Structure: Studies Presented to A. R. Radcliffe-Brown*. London: Oxford University Press, 1963, pp. 104-20.

Schieffelin, E. L. *The Sorrow of the Lonely and the Burning of the Dancers*. New York: St. Martin's Press, 1976.

Schneider, David M. "The Meaning of Incest." *The Journal of the Polynesian Society* 85, no. 2 (1976): 149-69.

Seligman, Brenda Z. "The Incest Taboo as a Social Regulation." *The Sociological Review* 27, no. 1 (1935): 75-93.

_____. "The Problem of Incest and Exogamy: A Restatement." *American Anthropologist* 52 (1950): 305-16.

Shore, Brad. "Incest Prohibitions and the Logic of Power in Samoa." *The Journal of the Polynesian Society* 85, no. 2 (1976): 275-95.

Slater, Marian K. "Ecological Factors in the Origin of Incest." *American Anthropologist* 61 (1959): 1042-59.

Slotkin, J. S. "On a Possible Lack of Incest Regulations in Old Iran." *American Anthropologist* 49 (1947): 612-17.

_____. "Reply to Goodenough." *American Anthropologist* 51 (1949): 531-32.

Smith, Alfred G., and Kennedy, John P. "The Extension of Incest Taboos in the Woleai, Micronesia." *American Anthropologist* 62 (1960): 643-47.

Strathern, Andrew, and Strathern, Marilyn. *Self-Decoration in Mount Hagen*. London: Duckworth, 1971.

Wallis, Wilson D. "The Origin of Incest Rules." *American Anthropologist* 52 (1950): 277-79.

White, Leslie A. "The Definition and Prohibition of Incest." *American Anthropologist* 50 (1948): 416-35.

Alfred Adler

10

The Ritual Doubling of the Person of the King

Three great festivals mark the yearly ritual cycle among the Moundang of Léré (Chad). The first corresponds to the time around the middle of October when the maize and red millet are getting ripe, and is called "the month (or the festival) of the Moundang" *(fing-moundang):* it is the most important of the three and lasts for four days. The second is that of "the Soul of the Millet" *(cié sworé)* and corresponds to the end of the harvest of all the millets (end of January): its participants witness the deposition in the great royal granary of the last sheaf made up of the main varieties cultivated by the Moundang. The last, called "festival of the guinea fowl" *(fing-luo),* takes place when the dry season is near its end around mid-April, and is devoted to propitiatory rituals for rain. The sacrifices of guinea fowl and other animals are preceded by a great collective hunt, in which the king himself participates. The trait common to these three festivals is that the privileged setting for the ceremonies is the palace and the courtyard that stretches in front of its single southern gateway, and that the king himself plays the central role in them. He is the provider of oxen for the sacrifices, of jars of millet beer for the libations, and of all the food and drink that the population assembled at his palace consumes on these occasions. All the arts practiced by the Moundang—music, song, dance, and poetry—are put to work to exalt his glory alone, as if he were the source of all the good things he lavishes. Still, the obligation to provide sacrificial meat and drink; the fact that his dwelling is the place, even, to a certain extent, the object of worship; finally, the imperious necessity to regale his people with generosity essen-

180

tially define the religious functions of the king. But these functions are not attributed to him solely by virtue of a particular distribution of roles in the religious organization of society, for the king is not one of, or the first among, the religious dignitaries but rather, one might say, the minister of a cult whose object he himself partially incarnates. More precisely, it is the invisible force, the beneficent and maleficent power which the reigning sovereign is supposed to have over nature, and on which the regularity of the seasons, the fertility of the fields, etc., depends, that puts him on the level of powers which human rituals and prayers must influence to keep away drought, famine, and epidemics. This form of royalty, which ethnologists have called sacred, or, more hesitantly, divine kingship, following Frazer's expression, thus implies a radical division within the person of the king: on the one hand, he is the receptacle of an atemporal power that fell first upon the founding hero of the dynasty and has been passed down to the present king via all the sovereigns who have preceded him; on the other hand, he is the possessor of a temporal and temporary power whose enjoyment has no other justification—even though it has other effects—than to put this power in the service of the society. The innumerable prohibitions, but also the enormous privileges—matrimonial and economic—which turn the person of the king into a being completely separated from the rest of the social body are the means of establishing this division within the king himself and, at the same time, of protecting him from its destructive effects, or at least slowing them down. Elsewhere I have sought to show (Adler 1978, pp. 25-40) that one modality or the other of ritual regicide—killing the king to save the kingship—is inscribed in the logic of this type of politico-religious institution. While the actual performance of this custom is difficult, if not practically impossible, to prove, and researchers such as Evans-Pritchard (1948) have been tempted as a result to seek a sociopolitical explanation for a "religious dogma" that nothing forces one to take literally, still its existence can no more be rejected than it can be accepted as self-evident. Certainly, historical criminal investigations (such an investigation was in fact once undertaken by the Nigerian colonial administration in an unsuccessful attempt to verify rumors surrounding the death of the king Jukun of Wukari [cf. M. Young 1966]) are quite incapable of establishing the materiality of an act that is surrounded, by its very nature, by the deepest mystery. It is clear, nevertheless, that an analysis of royal rituals that may still be observed today reveals a symbolics,[1] that would be indecipherable without the "dogma" of ritual regicide. My purpose is not to assemble facts and arguments in favor of the thesis of the *Golden Bough,* which I consider proven, but rather to start from this thesis and go further into the function of sacrifier and, in the last analysis, of sacrificial victim, that falls to the king in the political and religious system of the Moundang.

1. TN: For "symbolics" (translating *la symbolique*), see above, Chap. 9, n. 3.

The sacrificial rituals performed at the palace during the festival of *fing-moundang* are the subject of long divinatory consultations: these involve examination of the favorable or unfavorable dispositions of the chthonian powers and the local spirits who, in the Moundang phrase, "own and command all the territory of Léré"; the scrutiny of the states of persons and the various social categories (age and sex classes and group of dignitaries) who participate in the ceremonies in various ways. But above all quite a considerable place is devoted to all that directly involves the king: his souls or spiritual principles, and the signs that manifest them: his bearing, for instance, his palace and the great many wives who inhabit it (it is these who prepare the beer for the libations), and, finally, the various places, inside and outside the royal enclosure, where the agents of the ritual are located. As I was able to observe repeatedly, the people involved pay the greatest attention to the diviners' oracular statements and scrupulously follow the prescriptions they lay down. The immense collective purification which then takes place constitutes the preparatory phase of the ritual of *fing-moundang*. But, quite significantly, no mention is made of an essential rite which immediately precedes the official opening of the public ceremonies and is closely related to the sacrificial function of the king. This is the rite of *gõ-pekworé*, "the chief of the seko," or screen of plaited straw: this rite is not absolutely secret, but it is so discreet as to be almost unknown to those who are not involved in it.

The *gõ-pekworé* is a man from the clan of the chief of the earth *(pahseri)* in Léré and, in principle, he is chosen from among the close younger kin of the holder of the office whose representative or rather, as we shall see, whose sacrificed replica he is. The day before the beginning of the festival, toward the end of the morning, the *gõ-pekworé* enters the palace courtyard. This immense Moundang farm, the palace of the *gõ-léré*, appears to the foreigner as a fortress of some 450 meters in circumference. The thick wall of beaten earth which forms the castle bristles, at regular intervals, with squat turrets and keeps—kitchens and granaries adjoining the chambers of the royal wives. These dwellings, disposed all around the castle wall (and formerly the palace included not only an external wall but also an internal concentric circle to accommodate all of the king's wives, who numbered more than three hundred at the beginning of this century) are arranged according to the orientation of the quadrant they occupy. To the south and east from the vestibule that constitutes the only visible entrance to the enclosure live the chief wives, the real mistresses of the house, who rule over the domestic and ceremonial life of the palace. Upon the northern half-circle, an inauspicious direction in opposition to the south, which is turned toward the good rain-bearing winds, dwell the old wives the king has inherited from his predecessor(s). In the middle of this facade there is a narrow opening masked by a mat. Through this opening the body of the dead sovereign, whose death is kept secret, is passed, wrapped in the mat. Near this opening—and so constituting the "last one" on the semicircle of great women–lies the dwelling of a wife who bears the title "mother of the house" *(mah-mur-yã)*, the only wife whom interpreters designate with the name of queen. This mother is, in fact, quite separate from the rest of the king's consorts, who were all married without the king paying any kind of marital compensation (brideprice). She alone is given by a particular clan, which receives a horse in exchange. Her marriage is an integral part of the enthronement process, for no matter how many wives he had during the time he was a mere prince, and whether or not they have borne him children, the king becomes master of his house and may have legitimate heirs only after his *mah-mur-yã* has been installed in the palace. She is a sort of priestess in charge of the regalia, which she hides in one of the chambers of her residence. The regalia include various objects (jet knives, pipes, assagais, a double clock made of copper, etc.) which are supposed to have belonged to Damba, the founder of the royal lineage. The Moundang call these objects *fa-syĩn-gõae*, which can only be translated as "the king's fetishes," fetishes which the king himself may not see without mortal danger. It is her responsibility for this secret store which she lives in contact with that transforms *mah-mur-yã* into a being set apart, vested with forces that raise her to the same level as men holding the highest religious responsibilities: those connected with initiation and with the masks.

When the *gõ-pekworé* enters the palace courtyard, he carries a freshly plaited seko to offer to *mah-mur-yã*. The latter pulls down the old seko which has been serving as the curtain for the door of her hut and gives it to her guest in exchange for the new one. The used curtain is put up as a rounded screen with an opening facing the masked hole that contains the regalia. As discreetly as possible, *mah-mur-yã* takes the regalia out of their hiding place and puts them on the ground behind the screen. At this time the sacrificer-slave who officiates in the palace comes forward with the sacrificial ox; he is followed by serving women carrying pots [*canaris*] of millet beer which they have prepared themselves under *mah-mur-yã's* roof. The sacrificer kills the ox and pours a little of the blood onto the regalia while the *gõ-pekworé* invokes the spirits *(mezuwũnri)* of the earth, the local spirits and the paternal and maternal ancestral spirits *(mezunpame* and *mezun-name)* of the king of Léré. After the blood, the serving women pour sweet beer (beer which has not been allowed to ferment) while addressing the same spirits. Meanwhile the sacrificer and his numerous helpers hurry to skin the slaughtered ox, and soon little pieces of grilled meat are thrown in all directions to keep evil away from the place of the regalia. The *gõ-pekworé* is now installed in his little straw enclosure *(pekworé)* which he must remain inside until the following dawn, at which time, since the entryway is forbidden to him, he will exit by breaking through the wall. The seko will be thrown into the river where he goes to purify himself, and he will receive the skin of the ox. His "work" is to remain completely enclosed, hidden from all eyes, and to await the dawn, but he may communicate with the outside through the mediation of his uterine nephew, who accompanies him during the first part of the ritual. Their communication, however, is limited solely to questions of food and drink, the unfortunate substitute for the chief of the earth having only one thing to look forward to: that he be served the cuts of meat (the right foreleg) of the ox sacrificed in his name that are his by right. In the words of the Moundang who, as is their custom, enjoy making fun of the most sacred activities: "*gõ-pekworé*'s only work is to beg for food and drink." People going by the seko salute him and call him king. The real king can no more see the regalia than can their one-day owner: what is more, he should not even go near this northern part of his palace, in which someone who could be called his double negative is reigning. Things happen on this occasion as they do on the day of enthronement, when the whole palace courtyard is cut in two by an east-west pallisade: on the southern side, the newly anointed chief of the earth celebrates his entry into the kingship with his young brides; on the northern side, the old widows are in mourning for their late husband. *Gõ-pekworé*, certainly, does not represent the dead king, but rather, for the king and in place of the king, confronts the deadly danger that threatens anyone who has anything to do with the regalia. In any case the *fwoké*, the misfortune or bad luck provoked by the king's impurity, will fall upon the *gõ-pekworé*, and will not fail to kill him sooner or later. The various objects which, when brought together, make up the regalia, have no power in themselves; it is, they say, "the power of the cures that holds them together" *(gbe ne syĩnri)*, cures which the king holds in his hand. But this force is inert unless it receives the blood of the sacrificed ox and the unfermented beer, in other words the "cures" of the chief of the earth. The *gõ-pekworé* thus sacrifices to renew the strength and life in something which represents the principle of the kingship itself, and in so doing arouses the force that will kill him. The king does not touch the flesh of the immolated animal, nor does he taste the millet beer for the libations. Since he does not consume the sacrifice, it must be said that the king, from an immediate, sensory point of view, is not a sacrifier; his mode of being himself forbids him to take communion, or, more profoundly, to communicate, in a manducation that involves a substance shared by commensals. He gives, he allots to the ritual's agents animals and millet that belong to him or which he has gotten from a particular village or clan as prescribed by the diviners; he plays the role of a kind of exchanger, as it were, of sacrificial substances, but he himself is outside the circuit. He cannot participate in the demand put forth by the sacrifice, since he himself participates in the nature of the object invoked. This is why he must become two instead of one, and why he finds in the deputy of the chief of the earth, the deputy, that is, of one who holds a piece of the power that made him king, the sacrifier-sacrificed[2] that he could not be himself without the system foundering on contradiction.

2. TN: For "sacrifier" (translating *sacrifiant*), see above, Chap. 3, n. 1.

Fing-moundang is a festival of the firstfruits, a festival of the renewal of vegetation; and while the lifetime of the king's person is intimately associated with the cycle of vegetation, the day is still far off when, in the Moundang expression, "death will come and eat on his head." Thus the *gõ-pekworé* incarnates a death deferred, a death by wearing down with the repetition of the rite over the years. This relative putting off of the effect of the rite should be set in relation with the structural distance that separates the king of Léré from the chief of the earth. The chief of the earth holds his function of sacrifier in the agrarian rituals by virtue of his clan which, locally, happened to have been the first to "cut wood for construction" and to have planted the wild onions *(kuli)* which made the earth habitable and cultivable and allowed the village to be built. He is not the master of the earth (the local spirits are the real masters of the ground and the underground), and if it is possible to speak of ownership in a way appropriate for this kind of society, then we must say that the land of the Moundang *(ser-lere)* belongs to the set of clans represented by the college of the *zah-sae,* "the excellent ones," or the *zah-luri,* "the great ones of the earth," who are, strictly speaking, the kingmakers. The *zah-sae* are a continuation of the elders who, at the beginnings of Moundang history, gave the kingship to the foreign hunter Damba, the generous giver of meat, and drove out the chief of the clan of "pockmarked legs," who gave nothing but beans for the celebration of *fing-moundang.* While they do keep something of their inalienable sovereignty over the land they gave to the king, whose status as a foreigner is never forgotten, the *zah-sae* constitute the essential part of the state apparatus with which the Léré sovereign "works," and are, consequently, closer to him whom they serve than to those they represent. The chief of the earth is simply the representative of a clan on village land or a piece of village land, and, however modest his responsibilities, they confer on him an authority that owes nothing to the power of the king. On the contrary, the enthroning of both the central power of Léré and of the princes of Léré assigned to rule villages of the brush *(gõ-zalalé),* is conceived of as an alliance with their symbolic spouse, the chief of the earth. The reigning lineage is of foreign origin, those called upon to take command over a village were rarely born in that village, and in any case have never been brought up there: they are mobile, like women in the matrimonial exchange, while power is, as it were, virilocal. This is why I have spoken of structural distance to oppose the king and the chief of the earth not as statuses located at two extremes of a hierarchy—something that would establish a social distance—but as polar terms possessing the greatest independence in relation to each other in the symbolics of Moundang power.

We will better understand the signification of this distance between the king and his double by examining its place in the ritual of the Soul of the Millet. Whereas *fing-moundang,* placed under the sign of the inaugural alliance between the earth and the kingship, is the affair of the *zah-sae,* the festival of the Soul of the Millet falls under the responsibility of the second college constituting the governmental apparatus of Léré, that of the *we-puliã-gõae,* which may be approximately translated: "the children who serve the king." The Moundang consider them the lackeys and thugs of the king of Léré, who puts them to work at "noble" tasks of repairing the thatched roofs of the palace, the plaited sekos, and the posts that hold up the gate of the entranceway, and also entrusts them with punitive missions against those who, deliberately or not, have offended him. The *we-puliã-gõae* are great dignitaries, and their ritual role is equally considerable, particularly during royal funerals. While today they are mostly recruited by cooptation, formerly they were chosen from among the young servants of the palace, of free birth, "the children of the king's roof." These children were given to the king by heads of families who in this way lost authority over their sons but gained the assurance that the latter would receive a wife "dowered" by the king. At the festival of the Soul of the Millet, it is from among these "children of the king's roof" that the elders choose the person who will carry the sheaf into the royal granary and thus become a member of the group of *we-puliã-gõae.*

The young man chosen in the bush, in the field where the sheaf is made ready, undergoes, in a lightning-like abridgement, a repetition of the circumcision rite. *We-puliã-gõae* hurl themselves upon him, strip him completely, and one of them, knife in hand, after imitating the movement of the crocodile (metaphor for the circumciser) for a few moments, takes hold of the young man's penis and pretends to circumcise it. While his age mates watch the scene, dancing and singing songs they learned in the initiation camp, another dignitary anoints his body with a mixture of oil and ashes, then puts a penis sheath on him, which will be the only clothing he will wear throughout the course of the ceremony. This phase of the ritual precisely reproduces that passed through by the heir during the funeral of his father.

Next comes the delicate operation of depositing the sheaf (which can weight more than twenty-five kilograms) on the head of the young man. The burden is secured solidly with ropes that encircle the trunk tightly to prevent unbearable strain on his neck during the long journey that lies before him. But first some of the regalia have been passed over the sheaf: a hoe, a small jet knife, and a sickle. Against these regalia, which are also said to be *ke,* objects which allow the king to cause or stop rainfall, the bearer is protected by "medicines" *(fasãné)* materialized in traces of red clay on his forehead and temples. When these preparations are complete, a major procession hurries off, the chief of the *we-puliã-gõae* riding at the head followed by the bearer of the Soul of the Millet whose movement, while careful, is swift. There follow the dignitaries—on horse and on foot—and the crowd of the people of Léré, without the women. Following an itinerary prescribed by the diviner, all these people go along until they come in view of the palace of Léré.

Meanwhile the king is standing alone before the gateway to his palace, gazing at the point on the distant horizon where the procession is to appear. His face, too, is marked with traces of *fasãné*, and in addition he holds pebbles in his hand which are another vareity of *fasãné*. As soon as he spies the procession of *cié-sworé*, he throws three pebbles in the direction of the bearer and pretends to flee inside the palace. A short time after this, the same gesture and the same pretended flight are repeated. Finally, when the procession is clearly in sight, except for the bearer, whom the king is not supposed to see, any more than he is supposed to see the *gõ-pekworé*, he hurls his last three pebbles and disappears into his residence once and for all. The sheaf-bearer arrives, crosses the threshold of the entryway, and approaches the great royal granary *(cel-damé)*, which is almost three meters high. It is breathtaking to see a rather frail adolescent scale a ladder made of uneven steps cut into the forked trunk of a palmyra palm and deposit his precious and terrible burden in an opening made in the top of the cone. If he stumbled, the dignitaries behind him would not hestitate to kill him on the spot.

The contrast of this rite with the one preceding the opening of *fing-moundang* is striking: *gõ-pekworé* was an immobile and hidden duplicate, the bearer of the *cié-sworé* is excessively mobile and completely visible. The former remained confined near the masked hole in the north wall, the latter "gloriously" enters by the entryway and reaches the place that best symbolizes the wealth and strength of the king. The *gõ-pekworé* was protected from the regalia by the blood of the sacrificial animal; the bearer of the sheaf does have his forehead and temples smeared with *fasãné*, but he is threatened with immediate death. *Fing-moundang* celebrated a new beginning, while with the return of the Soul of the Millet, which corresponds to the purification of the seed for the next season, it is already the end of the cycle that is being announced.

Formally, the sheaf-bearer appears in a filial position in relation to the king: as a child of the king's roof, he receives a wife from the king and, in the very act of laying the millet in the granary (the central granary of the enclosure, the one belonging to the family head, not the women's granary), he fulfills the duty of a firstborn son. But the initiatory and funereal symbolism whose importance is evident in the description of the rite that has just been presented suggest a much closer relationship between the two protagonists. First of all, the repetition in the brush of the circumciser's gesture—a gesture which, say the Moundang, definitively expels the individual's "crazy soul" *(cié tegwi)*, which resides in the foreskin—identifies the sheaf-bearer with the king as, in mourning, the heir apparent, in principle the firstborn son, is identified with the father whom he replaces, following the system of total succession. But above all, the death which haunts his every step makes him the equivalent of the *gõ-tau;* this twin name is given to the child who must necessarily die in the bush so that the initiatory ritual may be successfully completed, so that there is no massacre among the novices. The sheaf-bearer and the king form a set of twins (twins bear the names of kings [Adler 1973, pp. 167–92]): the first, *gõ-tau,* "the chief with a huge head," is doomed; the second, *gõ-comé,* the "sun chief," reigns (his name is an allusion to a strophe of the royal slogan: the burning sun found him, the cold moon guarded him). If we return to the notion of structural distance, this distance appears to be the smallest, and so corresponds to a maximal interdependence of the two terms. We know that the *we-puliã-gõae*, among whom the sheaf-bearer will take his place, form a political body that owes everything to the king; the king picked them out, extracted them from the sphere of kinship, not only to "help him" in prestigious corvées and to do his dirty work but also to take upon themselves a part of what Frazer so justly calls "the burden of kingship." What more profound image could be found to symbolize this mutual dependence than the relationship between twins, which exceeds any kinship relation and even, at the extreme, any possibility of relation, since one of the two terms ceaselessly threatens the other with destruction.

For the idea of twinship in Moundang thought implies the idea of an excess of fertility, an excess of being, from which the Moundang draw what is for them the obvious conclusion that, when there is a pair of twins, both cannot survive for long. It is one or the other. This either/or formula appears as the law that rules the pair formed by the king and his twin-double. It would, of course, be completely specious to force this evidence by seeing the *cié-sworé* ritual as a kind of human sacrifice disguised in a mock ordeal from which the sovereign always emerges victorious. It remains the case, however, that certain aspects of this ritual raise questions that my inquiry leaves entirely open. Unlike the two other festivals of the Moundang calendar, *cié-sworé* is only celebrated at Léré, and only for the king. There is no blood sacrifice, of cattle or even of fowl. The only sacrificial elements of this festival are precisely the initiatory costume imposed on the sheaf-bearer and the mortal risk he runs as long as he is in that state. This was the Moundang's response when I expressed surprise that such an important ritual manifestation should be unaccompanied by any sacrifice, in the ordinary sense.

Perhaps considerations of another order, touching on the character of the agrarian calendar itself, might enlighten us. One cannot fail to observe, for instance, that between the celebration of the firstfruits at the end of the rains during *fing-moundang* and the *fing-luo* ritual that just precedes the first showers after which sowing begins, the festival of the Soul of the Millet occupies a place that is far less marked in the seasonal and meteorological order. It is isolated in the middle of the dry season, in a period of agricultural and ritual rest for the specialized clans who, all during the rainy season, punctuate the villagers' labors with special ceremonies that "help" the crops to mature. *Cié-sworé* thus appears as an agrarian festival tied less to the natural rhythm of the seasons than to a more specifically sociological rhythm determined by the institution of kingship and its specific temporality. When they say that they count the years of a reign by the number of *cié-sworé,* the Moundang are thinking of this temporality, which ritual regicide allows us to grasp in its most intimate essence.

The theme of the ritual doubling of the king, as I have been examining it, seems absent from the *fing-luo* ceremonies, in which no one plays the role of an emissary victim. But actually it is in this closing festival of the annual cycle that it finds its strongest expression; it is only that the external double, who drew danger away from the king, has disappeared, leaving the king alone with his double in himself.

A great collective hunt in which the sovereign participates constitutes the central manifestation of the festival of guinea fowl. All the men of the village, from children barely able to find their way in the brush to old men, go into the brush with assagais, bows and arrows, and clubs, to kill as much game as possible since, naturally, they are not content with mere guinea fowl. These birds, but also the rest of the catch, will be deposited together at the foot of the great war drum *(damé)* set up before the threshold of the palace where the chief of the we-puliã-gõae, grand master of this festival, is waiting for them. He then will preside over the distribution of the meat among the hunters and distribute the guinea fowl among the chiefs of the earth of Léré and neighboring villages. The latter, with the slaves whose job is to "wash" and manipulate the rain stones, will perform the sacrifices custom calls for in various locations. The departure for the hunt takes place late in the morning, when the entire populace has assembled in front of the palace. Meanwhile a feast is served in the palace courtyard, to which only people from the village of Fouli are invited. *Fouli* means "abandoned village"; in this case, it is the name of the last royal capital before the present Léré, and its site is only a few kilometers from Léré. When a new king takes the throne, it is customary for his mother to leave the palace and be installed in Fouli, whose symbolic ruler she becomes. This village is also called Fouli *mah-gõae*, "Fouli of the king's mother," and the people of this village are *nan-gõae*, the maternal kin of the king. The maternal kin come, then, according to custom, to "beg" food from their uterine nephew: insults and obscenities are exchanged, not with the king himself but with his wives, who do not deny themselves vigorous replies. While this ritual exchange, which the Moundang explain is a purification of the king before he goes hunting, is taking place, the latter is dressed in his most splendid garb. When he appears on his terrace, his sumptuously caparisoned horse is waiting for him, surrounded by parasol bearers and his personal guard. He is hoisted onto his horse, not without difficulty, due to the weight of his outfit, and, followed by all of his wives with the four chief wives at their head, he goes out of the palace in a din of drums and cries of adulation from the *bambaro* (Peul and Hausa griots). Outside, the whole mass of the people is in arms. In a disorder that is indescribable and even dangerous for the horsemen, this crowd advances as far as the eastern gate of Léré, where they suddenly stop. The wives head back home, with the exception of the four chief wives, and a rigorously ordered procession takes shape: the chief of the *we-puliã-gõae* and his men ride on ahead; next come the other horsemen (dignitaries whose titles are borrowed

from those of the entourages of the *lamibé* of Adamawa), the king closely surrounded by his guard of assagai carriers, the four wives, and finally the compact
mass of "infantry" *(mwena)*. The chief of these last, *puliã-mwena,* is already in
the brush where he has performed the many magical rites that are his responsibility for ensuring a successful hunt.

The procession arrives at a place called *tekaluo,* "the place where the guinea
fowl live," about two kilometers from Léré. A place is quickly cleared to prepare
for the king's dismounting, and a stool is put in place for him. Then his four
wives start to undress him. Formerly, he wore nothing but a kidskin around his
waist; today he wears a pair of cloth breeches resembling English shorts, and the
short tunic of the peasant. He sits on the stool, and his wives, who have brought
a great enameled basin and gourds full of water, wash his feet. This ritual of purification is required because of the prohibition against the king treading the
ground with his bare feet. One more modification of the custom: the king hunts
in a pair of shoes with the laces removed. Thus purified, the king stands up, and
the signal for the hunt is given by the whistling of the *gauw* (professional hunters)
and the cries of the horsemen. The wives, carrying their husband's carefully fold-
ed clothing, return to the village. At the end of the hunt, they will once again be
at the east gate of Léré where they will wait for the king, whom they will dress
and lead back to the palace in triumph.

Barefoot and dressed (in principle) only in a kidskin, lost amidst the mass of
the "poor" *(zah-shakre),* the king hunts with his bow and a club. At this time
custom authorizes anyone who wants to, to make fun of him, insult him, and
even strike him. "You're king in the village," somebody cries, "but here in the
bush you're nothing." Today, the sort of ritual mutiny that the hunters perform amounts only to simple verbal license and feigned blows. Things used to be
different, far more serious, it seems, and real mutineers (junior men, but of a
high enough rank to think about legitimately succeeding the reigning sovereign)
could try their luck in provoking an accident that would get rid of their brother.
Those days are definitely gone, but not in the mind of the present king, who
tries each year to delay as long as possible, if not to cancel, a festival for which
he prepares as one would prepare for war. We can imagine his relief when, at the
end of the hunt just before nightfall, he leaves the hostile brush of men to return,
at the gateway of Léré, to the feminine universe that protects and accompanies
him in his glorious raiment back to the palace. For it is the women who welcome
him, not only the four chief wives but all of his wives and the women of Fouli.
During this time all the hunters have left for the river to purify themselves, and
when they come back they join the procession which is now constituted as
before. The few hundred meters of return are traversed slowly by a people over-
flowing with joyfulness. Only the king maintains a serious face; he stares at the
palace toward which he is being led, and he is rigorously forbidden to look behind him. This prohibition on looking toward the bush where he was exposed
to mortal danger belongs, no doubt, to the same category as the prohibitions on

looking that involve the *gŏ-pekworé* and the bearer of the *cié-sworé*. In all these cases it is a question of avoiding an impossible face-to-face meeting with the emissary victim, a part of oneself. In the rite I have just been describing, it is hard to imagine how any other image could draw a backward look than that of the king himself, naked in the brush, jeered at by the hunters. The analogy is striking: for one of the things the king is blamed for in the ceremony of the Millet Soul is the nakedness imposed on the sheaf-bearer during his journey to the granary. The nakedness of the hunter, all the more marked in that it contrasts with the extraordinary vestmental overload which prevails up to the last moment at *tekaluo*, is just as blameworthy as that of the initiate, even if this time the victim is the person of the king. The problem is evidently to know whether there can be a victim without a guilty party, in other words one must ask what is the nature of the doubling in the ceremonial of the guinea fowl hunt.

In the two earlier cases I made use of the notion of structural distance to distinguish a pair of terms excessively close to and dependent upon each other; the terms in question are on the one hand the king and the clans, and on the other the king and a part of his governmental machine. In the *fing-luo* ritual, we seem to pass to another level of the structure: it is no longer a question of the king's relationship with constituent parts of the political body of the society, but of the relationship of the kingship, or the symbolics of power, with the division of the sexes.

This extremely complex relationship has a very simple but suggestive illustration in the order of march of the royal processions that I have described. In the procession to *tekaluo*, as in the return procession, the king in all his majesty rides in the middle, with the men always on the side of the bush and the women on the side of the palace. Men and women, each group on its own side, constitute masses without social distinctions. Since the hunt is assimilated to war, the men know no order but the order of battle: "in the bush," they say, "no one asks your clan, it is only bravery that counts." The women, palace women, village women, and women of Fouli, are all mixed together, all assimilated to the palace wives; they are on the side of the king and his machinery of production, thanks to which he can fulfill his priestly functions. This separation of the sexes has nothing to do with the social division of tasks and roles according to sex, for it implies no complementarity. What we have, on the contrary, is a rite which should be interpreted as the symbolic manifestation of the sexual duality of the sovereign. It is important, furthermore, not to misunderstand the meaning of this duality. When the "great ones of the earth", *zah-lu-seri*, the *zah-sae* I have already described, the *pah-yāné*, "masters of the sacred wood" (who keep the masks), the *pah-cuki*, "masters of the bush" (who perform circumcision and direct the initation camps), say that, faced with the elements that they represent, the king is a woman, they are stating, in the form of mockery, a religious and political truth. This truth is that the king has a master, the only master they recognize in the forms of the earth, the ancestors, and the masks: this is death.

Thus the sexual duality within the king does not involve sexual reality, but serves for thinking, if one may say so, the division of the person of the soveriegn within himself.

If one were tempted to interpret the ritual doublings incarnated in turn by the *gõ-pekworé* and the bearer of the Millet Soul as freeing the king from the mystical servitudes and dangers inherent in his priestly office, the ritual of *fing-luo* shows us that what is going on is something else entirely. Moundang kingship is not the illustration of one phase in a process of dissociation of the religious and political functions which is supposed to accompany the development of the state. Ritual doubling, in the three increasingly interior forms we have looked at, reveals, rather, the radical nature of the subjection of the king's power to what are truly sovereign powers. There is no festival in the year's ritual cycle that does not remind the king that the end of his reign is nearly at hand.

References

Adler, A. "Les jumeaux sont rois." *L'Homme* 13, nos. 1-2 (1973): 167-92.
___. "Sexe et souveraineté." *Nouvelle Revue de Psychanalyse* 8 (1973): 115-39.
___. "Le pouvoir et l'interdit." In *Systèmes de signes*. Paris: Hermann, 1978, pp. 25-40.
Evans-Pritchard, E. E. *The Divine Kingship of the Shilluk of the Nilotic Sudan*. Cambridge University Press, 1948.
Young, M. "The Divine Kingship of the Jukun." *Africa* 36, no. 2 (1966): 135-52.

Patrick Menget

11

Time of Birth, Time of Being
The Couvade

It was the height of the rainy season, when the waters are stirred up and fishing is difficult. The inhabitants of the house of Opote, the village chief, had not eaten fish for several days. Maize cakes, manioc cakes, maize gruel, and caterpillars didn't do very much for the hunger of the Txikáo. At the end of a rainy afternoon, Opote came back home carrying a fine *matrincháo* fish he had caught in his nets. He put it down without a word next to Tubia, one of the four family heads of his house. Tubia cleaned it and put it on to smoke. Until the fall of night he ate it, by himself, in small mouthfuls, under the interested eyes of the other inhabitants of the house. No one else touched the *matrincháo*, nor showed any desire to have some of it. Yet the hunger was universal, and the flesh of *matrincháo (Brycon brevicaudus)* is among the most highly prized. Why this general abstention? The fisherman, Opote, possessor of fishing magic, could not consume his catch without the risk of damaging this magic. The other family heads avoided the flesh of the *matrincháo* for fear of endangering the health and the lives of their young children, or their own health. Since their wives were nursing, they had to abstain for the same reason. The children, finally, would have absorbed the particularly dangerous spirit of this species. As for the five bachelors of the house—all adolescents—they had nothing to say. The next day, with a certain amount of reticence, two of them quietly admitted that they had been having sexual relations with mothers of the families of the house, and did not want to hurt their children; the others, even more discreetly, told allusively how they had been occasional lovers of a woman from another house, who had just given birth to a daughter. If anything happened to the child, the mother

193

would know perfectly well who had broken the couvade taboo, and would hold it against him for a long time, not to mention the personal risks run by those who eat a forbidden fish during the couvade. In brief, out of the twenty or so people living in this house, only one could satisfy his hunger for fish; the others were all held back by their observance of the couvade.

Among the Txikáo Indians of the Xingu National Park (Mato Grosso, Brazil), a small group of slash-and-burn cultivators who speak a Carib language, originally from the Lower Xingu region,[1] the couvade is thus not a mere question of belief, but a strictly respected taboo which seems to involve a much wider circle of near kin than in those South American societies in which the custom has usually been described. Generally speaking, there is hardly an indigenous society of South America in which restrictions and prohibitions have not been described that bear on the activity, diet, and sexual life of parents at the time of a birth (Métraux, pp. 369-74). The interpretation of this set of beliefs and rites has given rise to many misunderstandings, well summarized by Peter Rivière in a recent article (Rivière, pp. 423-26): the historiography of interpretations of the couvade reflects more the evolution of ideas in anthropology than the ripening of a solution to the problem. The difficulties begin with Tylor's baptism of the institution in 1865 (Rivière, p. 423). Tylor probably borrowed the term from the French chroniclers who, in describing the beliefs and attitudes of fathers after the birth of a child, particularly in the Caribbean, did not fail to be struck by the resemblance of these beliefs and attitudes with a European custom, once well attested in Béarn and the Basque country, and locally called "couvade" or "covada," "according to which the father takes the mother's place in bed, is taken care of in her place, and plays the role for a varying length of time" (Van Gennep, p. 121). This symbolic substitution of the father for the mother, which constitutes the custom in Europe, is, however, rare or absent in the American data. Only two examples are presented by Métraux, and he correctly points out that these are really interpretations rather than descriptions (Yves d'Evreux and Dutertre, in Métraux, p. 369). We forget too often that for a forest Indian the fact of lying in a hammock is not necessarily the result of a disease, not even a psychosomatic or symbolic one, but can more naturally result from the obligation to cease all physical exercise and from a very meager diet, which sometimes restricts one to fasting: there is almost no other place in an Indian house where a man could rest. In fact, a large proportion of the misunderstandings and unfortunate explanations, from Bachofen to Schmidt (cf. Rivière), come from this initial confusion between the European rite, which itself is described quite

1. I studied the Txikáo group from the time of its arrival in the Xingu National Park in 1967 through 1977. My total time with the Txikáo amounted to twenty-four months. My different missions were made possible by a grant from the N.S.F. (1967-69) and research credits from L.A. 140 of the Université de Paris—X, Nanterre (1972 and 1975).

sketchily, in which incontestable psychosomatic elements seem linked to a brief imitation of the mother's role by the father, and the more complex and widespread set of South American practices. Lévi-Strauss, in *The Savage Mind*, had the merit of first posing the problem in its generality:

> It would be a mistake to suppose that a man is taking the place of the woman in labor. The husband and wife sometimes have to take the same precautions because they are identified with the child who is subject to great dangers during the first weeks or months of its life. Sometimes, frequently for instance in South America, the husband has to take even greater precautions than his wife because, according to native theories of conception and gestation, it is particularly his person which is identified with that of the child. In neither event does the father play the part of the mother. He plays the part of the child. Anthropologists are rarely mistaken on the first point; but they yet more rarely grasp the second (p. 195).

Lévi-Strauss thus once and for all finishes off the explanations that saw the couvade as a "masculine hysteria," in F. Max Müller's felicitous expression, and calls attention to the fundamental link between the parents of the child. For the couvade must not be limited to the father, even if he is often the subject of the most visible taboos. I will show that the couvade is a system of taboos that bear on a social ensemble, and not a collection of rules affecting the status of an individual. It is quite possible that maternal "fullness," in the sense of the cumulation of a manifest biological function and a recognized social role, should cause the father to have confused attitudes and emotions in compensation, as it were. It is told, for example, how formerly in East Anglia in a household expecting its first child it was customary for the husband to complain of a toothache, and it was a ritual to pity or tease him about it *(Encyclopaedia Britannica,* 11th ed., S.V. "Couvade," p. 338). It is not adventuresome to see a theme of extraction implicit in this; but such facts, whose distribution seems to be more or less universal, can in no way account for a ritual complex that is as distinctly defined as that of South America. I have limited my analysis to this part of the world not because the couvade, or rather certain of its elements, have not been attested elsewhere, but because the American facts form a unique system of rites and conceptions that is both coherent and subject to variation from culture to culture. It is on the basis of this system that facts of the psychosomatic order may one day be explained, and not vice versa, as Rivière has already remarked (p. 425).

Beyond this, it appears in the analysis of Txikáo ideas and prescriptions that the system of the couvade is not an autonomous reality. It is a difficult institution to discern and to understand, for two reasons. In this society, as elsewhere in South America, the couvade is a ritual period that can be separated out from within a sequence of perfectly comparable acts and precautions which mark changes of biological state, whether evolutive or catastrophic. Birth, growth, pregnancy, sickness, murder, natural death form a series that gives rise to rites of one nature, organized according to a single logic. It is clear that the schema of rites of passage proposed by Van Gennep is both too formal and too mechanical to account for this ritual sequence as a whole, permitting at most a periodization of part of it. But in addition to this, the couvade is also a system of taboos whose social extension largely overlaps that of other systems. The interest of the Txikáo example lies in the fact that it shows the close relations between the couvade taboo and the incest prohibition, in relation both to their field of application and to the consequences that result from failure to observe the former and from violation of the latter.

The Txikáo are a tribe of around eighty persons, reduced by half since 1960, following murderous reprisals from their neighbors in the Upper Xingu, and particularly because of viral diseases contracted from the whites. From 1967 on, they have had to give up the permanent war they waged with their neighbors and have accepted living in the Xingu National Park, where they fairly quickly reconstituted an autonomous village. Their material culture is of the Amazonian type; they grow crops of bitter manioc, maize, and some other cultigens in clearings in the jungle; in their former habitat hunting was generally more important than fishing for the acquisition of animal foods. Today fishing is predominant because of the abundance of fish in the rivers and lakes. They fish by bow with traps and weirs, with fish-poison, but mainly with manufactured hooks obtained from the reserve's Brazilian authorities. They do not have unilineal descent-based corporate groups, nor global divisions of society. Descent is cognatic, and the kindred group varies in extent from the nuclear family to the whole of the tribe. Several nuclear familes, with some dependents, siblings of one spouse or the other, live together in a large house; the latter is a flexible unit of cooperation, especially in women's tasks (preparation of the vegetal staples, manioc and maize, for eating). The principle of aggregation of these families is the rule of matrilocal residence, but changes in household composition are fairly common. The number of households varies, depending on the circumstances, from one to four or five. War, fundamental in the ideology and values of this society, had the principal goal of taking children (of both sexes) from the enemy; these children replaced those who had been killed by the sorcery of strangers/enemies. Adoption and marriage of captives thus represented one of the modes of social reproduction. Small as the numerical importance of this incorporation of foreign elements was, it was of great symbolic importance, for the adopted individuals, from the time of adolescence, became the privileged name-givers for children born of Txikáo parents. In conferring names of foreign origin on the Txikáo, they increased the stock of identities at the group's disposal; they themselves received Txikáo names, while keeping ethnic nicknames (Menget, 1977, passim).

Natural reproduction, which ensures the basic perpetuation of the group, is the object of a discourse that at first sight appears contradictory. On the one hand it is stated that men succeed men and women succeed women, as is also the case for animals. There is even a tendency for a son to look like his father and a daughter to look like her mother. In a litter of six puppies, three were light and uniform in color, three dark and spotted: for the dog's master the first three were "from the mother," who in fact had a light coat, the others "from the father," who was absent from the scene. This homo-sexual succession is called *eru*, a very general term that also designates the succession of days and nights, as well as the reserves of maize seed that are kept for the next planting, or the cuttings of manioc removed from the stem to produce a clone. But at the same time conception is an exclusively masculine affair. Semen (*imoru:* semen, penis) is the sole constituent of the embryo. To assure its growth it is necessary to practice repeated copulation, and one man, even if he is the legitimate husband, is rarely enough. So a woman reactivates her illegitimate relationships during her pregnancy, instigating new ones if need be. There is not generally one genitor for the Txikáo, but a small group of associated genitors, of which the husband is almost always a member. There is therefore a logical difficulty in reconciling the notions of parallel succession and resemblance and this hyperbolic affirmation of physiological paternity. But the contradiction exists only if we assume, in a perfectly ethnocentric way, that the human being is formed at birth. For the Txikáo, it is clear that a newborn person is still incomplete. The newborn child does acquire a soul (*egaronpun:* the cast shadow, the reflection) in the first hours of its existence, but it is not yet a person, nor even a biologically complete being. It is, first of all, equipped with a swollen appendage, the end of the umbilical cord, which falls off in about a week. This moment is not marked by the Txikáo, although it frequently is among other American tribes (Karsten, chapter 14, and A. Butt Colson, concerning the Akawaio, p. 289) for whom it signals the end of the most rigorous restrictions and fasting. But above all the new baby does not "hold," its substance is not formed in such a way that it can hold itself up. Just as the Akawaio name the newborn child at the fall of the umbilical cord, the Txikáo do so when the baby is able to hold its head upright, at around six or seven weeks of age. Whether or not the umbilical cord is the trace of the link with the father's substance (rather than with the mother's placenta) seems to be a secondary question: its persistence is the sign of incomplete formation, just as, for the Txikáo, the inability to raise the head is proof by default of the child's incompleteness. Between birth and naming, suckling fills out the human being's substance, and evidently extends well beyond what is considered the minimal threshold of socialization by naming. It is through mother's milk that a child acquires a resemblance to its mother. One informant, who may have been sensitive to the contradiction, even declared that girls "took more milk" than boys, probably to make up for the initial opportunity lost; a woman, probably using her sense of observation alone, added that this was not true at all.

It was formerly thought desirable to interpret this exclusively physiological paternity, common among the ancient Tupinamba as well as among more recently observed forest tribes, as the very root of the couvade[2] (Von den Steinen, pp. 337-38). This is to forget all too quickly that the child's only food after birth comes from the mother—a fact that cannot be missed by observation—and, therefore, that the taboo concerns both the father and the mother. From the time of her pregnancy, the mother is subject to food restrictions which the couvade prolongs and amplifies. The physiological explanation completely misses the complementarity of the parents in their substantial and spiritual contributions to the child and arbitrarily isolates acts and rites that are really interconnected. In Txikáo, a series of terms, literal and figurative, clearly reveal the sexual complementarity in conception and gestation. The fetus is *tenpano* (human being, Txikáo) and the womb is the *tenpano euru* (the house of the fetus); in masculine speech, the vagina of a wife or a girl friend is *geuru* (my house) whereas in feminine speech, the penis of a regular partner is *gagwep* (my pestle) or *umtagli* (my food). There is both a relationship of container to contained, which means that a woman may not ingest certain dangerous foods during her pregnancy, and an obligatory one-way relationship of "seminal food," without which the child could not "hold up," as the Txikáo put it, which is to say that there would be a spontaneous miscarriage.

Birth properly speaking is the occasion for activities that are more technical than ritual. The child's father is not formally excluded from these, but he does not participate in them directly. It is a woman's affair, in which the oldest women assist the mother. The latter is seated in a hammock hung quite low to the ground, and she holds onto a hammock hung at the level of her shoulders. The child is born and passes between the meshes of the hammock, the placenta falls into a hole that has been dug under the mother, and in the next few days residual blood is buried in the same way. We should note that the birth and the burial of the afterbirth take place in the house, as does the burial of the dead, except for those who die in wars far from the village. A man is buried under his hammock, under the place where he always hung it up. There is, however, one difference: a woman does not give birth at her usual place in the house between a central housepost and the outer wall, but along the wall, and so in the back of the dwelling and in its darkest part. Women say that they are ashamed, and that they cannot go back to their customary position (under their husband's hammock) until the flow of blood has stopped. The umbilical cord is cut by a real or classificatory grandmother, with the help of an Indian razor (a splinter of bamboo). They say that there are songs which the shamans can sing in case of a dif-

2. Von den Steinen notes that in Bakairi, as in Carib languages generally, the terms "father," "egg," and "child" (male speaker) have the same root. He adds, "the father is the egg and the child is the little father." In Txikáo the three terms—*imú, mumú, imun*—seem to be related, but the last one simply signifies "son" (male speaker). This relationship confirms Txikáo notions about the nature of the fetus, but this does not mean that the substance of the being who is biologically complete, some time after birth, is of exclusively masculine origin, as Von den Steinen would maintain.

ficult birth, and that these are songs "of spirits." As soon as the child is born, it is bathed in lukewarm water and dried over the fire, then immediately given the breast. A little while later the mother is also bathed in lukewarm water, and she lies down with her baby; she may take a very runny porridge of manioc flour, lukewarm or cold, but nothing else the first day. During this time the father is not necessarily confined to his hammock; he apparently feels neither pain nor fatigue. He is simply measured and discreet in his words, usually stays inside the house, and often takes care of the other children if there are any. The associated co-genitors are even less visible; they avoid hunting, fishing, violent physical activities and baths.

Until the umbilical cord drops off, restrictions on activity, dietary restrictions, and sexual continence are very strictly applied both to the father and the mother. Associated genitors are in principle subject to the same rules, but these persons are looser about the rules as far as physical activity is concerned. They still, however, will not bathe in the river. During the following month, or until the baby can hold its head up by itself (and it has received a name from its father, or from its grandparents if they are still living), there is a steady loosening of the prohibitions, with a greater latitude for the co-genitors. It is permitted to go hunting and fishing, although only nondangerous species are killed, i.e., those that the parents may eat in the following phase. Dangerous species are strictly forbidden to the parents and other genitors until the child is able to walk. Following this, father and mother continue to abstain from these same species as long as nursing continues, for two or three years. Associated genitors may resume sexual relations from the time of naming; the parents may do so a little later, depending on their desire—that is, depending on their fears. What characterizes this system, as Rivière has pertinently noted (p. 428), is its flexibility and its plasticity. The stages of biological development (dropping off of the cord, raising of the head, crawling, first steps) are not automatically accompanied by ritual changes. It is a question of circumstance, depending on the state of the child, the state of the family, the fears people have, the number of previous births. Thus it is true, as is often the case elsewhere, that the first birth gives rise to a far stricter couvade than do the following ones. Among the Yawalapiti of the Upper Xingu, the father of a firstborn child stays in his hammock for the first month "because the child is too fragile." One cannot, then, reduce the couvade to a set of rites of passage; it is, rather, a system that encompasses rites of passage, according to modalities that vary from society to society, but also from individual to individaul.

The Txikáo put the main emphasis on the violent aspect of forbidden physical activities. Nothing that is done in this period should cause excessive fatigue, which rules out long hunting expeditions, cutting down trees and brush to prepare plantations, building a house or a wooden canoe, nighttime fishing, making hunting traps, and even extended walking in the sun, i.e., in the grass-savannah. A fortiori a new father may not go on a war expedition. Within the women's domain the prohibitions are equivalent: no shredding and pressing manioc, no pounding maize, although they do continue to carry quite heavy loads, particularly baskets of manioc roots, which they look for in the clearings after the second or third month. If a man or woman failed to respect these prohibitions, the child would be seized with convulsions, and might even die. More curious at first glance is the prohibition on bathing in the river, which holds both for the men involved (the associated genitors) and the mother, and lasts from two to four months, sometimes longer for the mother. It is explained in many different ways. The consequences of a bath—taken several times a day in ordinary times—during the couvade affect both the child and the adult, since the former risks convulsions and vomiting, and the latter's body, particularly the feet, risks swelling up. One of the adolescents mentioned above took his first bath three weeks after the birth of his friend's child, and developed a spectacular abscess on his foot. A week later his foot was cured, but an old woman of his household passed a stone heated on the fire over his feet "so that he can go back and bathe without his foot swelling up, and to protect him from the *imele* spirit" (the thunder). This rationalization recalls the sanction risked by a woman who bathes during her period: she will be paralyzed, and will bring hail (the spirit *Memat*). I should emphasize that transgressions of the couvade taboo are not only harmful to children but can also affect the transgressors, father or mother, in return. The baby's state of weakness is thus not the mystical "cause" for the parents' precautions: it is also the state of the parents themselves.

The food prohibitions involved seem disconcertingly complicated if one seeks to discover their rationality on the basis of taxonomic criteria of the classification of species; if, on the other hand, we try to grasp the generic mode of action of bad foods on the basis of the consequences that violation of the taboos bring, then a coherent tableau appears, with a few residual elements left over. In the vegetable domain, flour and water preparations (the *eau blanche*, "white water," of French chefs) are the main element of the diet, then flat manioc cakes. On the other hand, soup of bitter manioc with the poison evaporated off, which is usually eaten lukewarm, cold, or reheated the next day, is totally forbidden for a long time. It is *wonkinpe*, accompanied by (or endowed with) an evil spirit. Even more forbidden are fermented preparations of manioc, maize, or both (indigenous beers). Here the implicit opposition clearly lies between the inert (bland to the taste) and the active or potentially active. If manioc soup is kept for a long time it ferments, since it contains sugars; "white water," on the other hand, remains neutral. Things made out of maize are opposed in the same way: cornmeal mush is allowed, while the cake that is baked and served sticky is forbidden. In most cases game is considered *wonkinpe*, not because of the spirits who are masters of species (who are not designated as *wonkin* but as *x-yum*, father of the species *x*), who do not intervene in the couvade, but because they have a harmful "charge." What is the nature of this charge? It seems to me that it is above all a question of humors (blood, fat), since their ingestion causes an internal "hurly-burly" (evoked by very convincing Indian onomatopoeias: *tolok-tolok* or *tik-tik-tik*, when they are sick), a hurly-burly that causes vomiting, swellings, and sometimes death. This kind of disease is called *ibarantet* in Txikáo, which comes from the root *ibarap*, "it is inside." The only species that may be eaten in the last stages of the couvade are some white- or gray-fleshed birds, which have a delicate flavor but tend to be rather lean food.[3] As for fish, most species longer than fifteen centimeters or so are *wonkinpe*, and so forbidden. However, a curious peculiarity of fish nomenclature deserves attention: most species commonly available in the Upper Xingu (there are around fifty of them) are designated by two different terms, often with different roots, depending on whether what is meant is a young fish or an adult. It is certainly true that important variations in pattern and appearance could sometimes justify this terminological refinement, but it is more likely that the Txikáo make the distinction on the basis of "spiritual" condition. The young fish may generally be eaten during the couvade (and other periods of dietary taboos), but not the adults. So it is the small species—preferably those with bony plates ("women's fish")[4]—and the young of larger species that may be consumed without danger. Two exceptions, which I cannot explain, the piranha *(Pygocentrus piraya)* and the tucunare *(Cichla ocellaris)* are eaten with impunity. Eggs, finally, of any species, are generally forbidden to people who are still growing and people of reproductive age; they make them sick. Insofar as the embryo of an egg is called *tenpano*, like a human embryo, it is difficult not to see in this the fear of an overload from the mixing of identical substances. Thus most alimentary prohibitions follow a logic of harmfulness that opposes inertia to activity as it opposes lean meat to the humors, a logic that lies in the food itself far more than in the living being, and in its physiology more often than in its morphology. This logic is to be found throughout all the ritual prescriptions, from birth to death, through periods of adolescent seclusion and the stages of "decontamination" that follow a murder. Certain prohibitions, clearly of a secondary order, are based on a logic of the identical, in which an external quality of a natural species can transmit itself to the child (sweet potatoes, for example, which in this region are the color of beets, are forbidden because they make the child's face turn reddish). This logic of the transmission of the identical from animal or vegetable to the human being is subordinate to that of opposites: as long as a functional balance has not been achieved between the dangerous humors and the other constituents of the biological being, one runs the risk of these "naturalistic" transformations of the human appearance or human activity.

Sexual continence, which has been talked about much less than restrictions on activity and diet (see, however, Lizot p. 22, who notes the Yanomani taboo

---

3. Among the most often cited are the *tinamidae, tongyo,* macuco (*Tinamus serratus*), *pongo* (*T. ato*), and certain parakeets.
4. For example the small *cascudo* (many species of the group *Otocindus*) which seem to be remarkably lean.

on copulation with a nursing mother) does not only involve the mother and the genitors. It applies to the whole of the genitors' sexual activity, including that with other women. If this rule is violated, the child will start to vomit, until it empties itself out and dies. It is also said that the child will not be able to walk, that is, that its development will be arrested. Here again the father cannot "empty" himself of a humor analogous to the maternal milk that nourishes the child without the child in turn losing its substance. It takes a certain time for the mixture of the two substances to cohere, and the development of a child requires maximum cohesion of the father. In other words the father does not imitate his child but rather affirms their substantial similarity. The progressive relaxing of the couvade is thus the sign of a gradual differentiation of substance, and the child's eventual acquisition of a separate identity.

The Txikáo do not say very much about the dangers that threaten the souls of young children. Still, there are circumstances in which the *egaronpun* (reflection, shadow) of human beings can be taken away by spirits, during certain festivals (funerals, initiation of children, particularly at the equivocal ritual moment between sunset and the fall of night), during solitary nighttime hunts, and especially in dreams. The consequences are a progressive diminution of bodily substance and, if a shaman does not succeed in finding the stolen soul, death by wasting away. This can happen to a baby, but seems rare. A child is not, of course, exposed to what are known to be dangers, but the more profound reason for this is rather the Txikáos' uncertainty about the exact function of the soul, its origin, and even its fate after death. They say that souls become bats, *Morfo* butterflies, and some other floating aerial species of little consistency. Souls can also turn into harmful spirits, particularly those of enemies. In general the soul is more a reflection of the body than a constituent part of the person, and as such symbolizes the unstable equilibrium of the substances of one's being. A child "without a soul" is suffering from a lack, in that he either has lost substance (diarrhea, vomiting) or that he does not "hold" well, does not develop normally. The Txikáo ideology of the couvade does not deny spiritual realities but subordinates them to a theory of substance; it is usually by the ingestion of a *wonkin* (evil spirit), who characterizes an active, effervescent, or rich food, that one falls sick and dies.

This ideology, as we have seen, is not limited to the couvade. An adolescent who "abuses" sexual relations before he is fully grown (the old people go so far as to declare that he should have no sexual relations at all) wastes away and ages prematurely: he even turns whitish. Grown men who take part in a murder during a war expedition and drink hot manioc soup on their return become fat and potbellied: the enemy's blood has entered into them by splattering or simple inhalation (one always spits when there is a bad smell: the blood of foreigners smells bad), and they must stringently restrict themselves to a "white," neutral, lean diet. In brief, everything happens as if two antagonistic principles ruled over the life processes, in a dynamic that finds a balance only to lose it again, tries to reestablish it and loses it in the end. A strong principle, tied to blood, to fat, rich meats and fermentation results from the constant somatic transformation of weaker substances, water, milk, sperm, white flours, lean meat. But inversely, the human body, in rhythms that vary with age, sex, and condition, anabolizes the strong substances and neutralizes their danger. These two antagonistic principles are not equivalent, since the first always contains a potential danger, and the second serves to correct the excesses of the first. So in a disease it is generally the strong principle that is excessive, and health is restored by treating the sick person with a "white" diet and lukewarm washings; he must swallow emetic drinks for relief and drink decoctions of medicinal plants, *Pfugu*. It is difficult to characterize these plants in general, since they make up a functional rather than a botanical class; but all those that I was able to taste had a strange, rather bland taste, sometimes sweetish, sometimes slightly aromatic, sometimes a bit tart. While it is possible to die from the action of the second type of substances, this is always by loss and never by excess. In the couvade, the whole set of occupational, alimentary, and sexual taboos comes down in the end to avoiding either an excess of strong substances whose nonassimilation leads to swelling diseases, or a loss of the weak and somatized substances, which appears in diseases of desiccation, of drying up, and leads to a death analogous to dying of old age. The creation of a new human being activates the whole universal process of transformation of substance, but also the separation of a part of the somatized substance of the parents and the initiation of an individual cycle. It thus involves both the division and the fusion of analogous substances from the two sexes.

A similar model has been suggested for the Carib Indians of the Caribbean Islands, on the basis of old chronicles (Taylor 1950), and also for the Bara Maku of the Columbian Vaupés (Silverwood-Cope 1972). In the first case, Taylor denies any specificity to the institution of the couvade, which is only one of "life's critical corners" among others. For the Maku of the Vaupés, a group of hunter-gatherers with relations to sedentary riverine peoples, there exists an explicit link with a cosmogony which assigns a celestial origin and a mythic history to these principles. In both cases, these principles are labelled "hot" and "cold."[5] In both cases the same fundamental system is involved, seen in its thermodynamic and energetic aspects. The Txikáo do sometimes describe certain remarkable physiological states as particularly "hot" (menstruation, pregnancy during which a woman is *urup,* burning, smarting), and *Pfugu* remedies are called *Abianke* (cool and pleasant); we have also seen the disastrous effects that river water, which is cold in comparison with the water in the house's calabashes, has on those who are undergoing a particularly active phase of growth, which we

---

5. In a recent publication which I have not seen, Audrey Butt Colson emphasizes the association hot, bitter / cold, sweet in South America north of the Amazon, as well as a mediating category, lukewarm (summary in Polgar 1978).

could analyze as too sudden and severe a chilling of an active and "hot" body. We should remember, too, that during the only important occasion in which men seek out and eat the most *wonkinpe* foods, namely departure for war, they also drink burning hot manioc soup (something that makes one's teeth fall out in normal times): this is a case of making oneself dangerous, possessed by a warrior's frenzy, "burning" with anger to avenge and kill. This is the exception of the food taboos that proves the rule, proving the model's relevance for the Txikáo. Still, bringing to light this dynamic of substances (the "physiological model," according to Rivière), which may characterize Amazonia as a whole, has the primary effect of making the institution of the couvade disappear. It becomes nothing but a moment in the general process.

In his Malinowski memorial lecture, Rivière reaches an analogous result, even though he proceeds from a different hypothesis. For him, the couvade is an attempt to resolve the universal problem of man's duality (body; soul) and "the explanation of such institutions as the couvade and the *compadrazgo* does not exist at the level of the institutions themselves, for they are merely the manifestations of deeper and more intractable problems" (p. 434). But it has not been proven, first of all, that the multiplicity of components of the human person are everywhere reducible to a duality, and it is possible that what we have here is a problematic stained with ethnocentrism; but, most important, half of the problem has remained in shadow: that of the social extension and configuration of the couvade.

The couvade concerns the nuclear family above all; this is a piece of evidence that seems to have imposed itself on observers, but that seems to allow only an explanation of the functionalist type. The couvade is neither a rite of legitimation of the social role of the father, as Malinowski held, nor even a way of reinforcing conjugal bonds in societies in which the marriage bond is weak or unstable, as Mary Douglas maintains (both cited in Rivière, pp. 423 and 426). For the father's legitimacy is given in the character of marriage itself, and not by the physiological theory of conception or the practices following a birth. There do exist societies in which the genitor's status as father is validated by the couvade, but in general paternal legitimacy precedes the birth and does not arise from it. As far as the symbolism of the conjugal bond is concerned, the postulated relationship is not verified by the South American data, and it is not clear how the association of two adults in the creation of a new human being and the ritual expression of this cooperation for a limited period of time would necessarily lead to more lasting legitimate unions. Alliances, even when prescribed, follow considerations of choice and are subject to the vagaries of compatibility and incompatibility; the couvade orders natural phenomena (i.e., phenomena that are thought of as natural) which it cannot modify at will, even if it is able—however little—to correct for the effects of violations of the rules. It is worth the trouble to look more closely at this anchoring of the couvade in the nuclear family. The Txikáo, as we have seen, take the biological model seriously in that they associate genitors and parents. The social circle affected by the couvade is thus distinct from and wider than the nuclear family. Among peoples of the Gê language group, it is not rare to see other consanguines involved in ritual prescriptions. Among the Xikrîn (Kayapo of Brazil), the kin of a newborn child belonging to the categories of *Ĩnget* (MB, MF, FF, FZH, MBS...) and *Kwatui* (FZ, FM, MM, MBW)[6] are subject to some of the restrictions, particularly the ban on body painting, "when they love the child" (Vidal, p. 90). These two categories are also the preferred name-givers in the naming ritual. Among the Apinayé, in case of illness—things are less clear for the couvade—the brothers and sisters of the sick person abstain from dangerous foods (Da Matta, p. 92). The author adds that the notion in the *resguardos* is that of gradation: appreciation of the bonds of substance allows the social classification of kin closest to or on the edge of the nuclear family to be manipulated. These examples, which could be multiplied, show that the social functions of the couvade taboo are not limited to the vertical bond of father, mother/son, and that its graded character allows reformulation or adaptation of the elements of the classification system. The couvade no more "marks" the legitimacy than it punishes the illegitimacy of births; it is a way of publically confirming, denying, or creating classificatory relationships, or rearranging the cognatic universe in the idiom of substances. This language, which can be combined with or opposed to a kinship classification, is the first precondition for the latter: there is no kinship system without a theory of conception, just as there is no kinship system without an incest prohibition. Incest and the couvade are thus preconditions for the language of kinship, and it is interesting to pose the question of the forms that the incest prohibition, which is universal, takes in societies in which one finds the couvade, which is not universal.

In South American societies that have the couvade, incest is generally regarded as an antisocial act: "marrying like monkeys and toucans" (Txikáo), "like tapirs" (mother-son incest among the Maku [Silverwood-Cope, p. 176]), "like wild pigs" (idem, brother-sister incest). A Txikáo myth tells of father-daughter incest:

> Mongat liked looking at his daughter's vagina; he looked at it a lot. One day, on the road, since he wanted to marry her, he said: "I dreamed that I was going to die, you wept over me; after you have wept over me, you will marry my brother. I walk exactly like him [that's how you'll recognize him...]."
>
> He went off looking for jatobá bark *(Hymenaea Sp.)*, put his ladder up the tree, broke the ladder and threw tapir bones under the tree, then went away to another house.

6. TN: For the abbreviations for kinship terms, see above, Chap. 9, n. 4.

"My father has fallen down!" said his daughter. "He is dead! I always cried on his shoulder!.... He was the one who wiped me! He was the one who kept me warm!"

Mongat came there, he looked at the grave of his elder "brother," wept, lay on the ground for a little while, poured a calabash of soup of the dead man's manioc on the ground, then went off to sleep with his daughter.

Whenever he went to his clearing, all the others said to the daughter, "But he is your father!" He was fed up with hearing this all the time, really fed up. During a festival he started to dance, he danced with Jaguar. Then he disappeared with Jaguar. Today he is *mongat*, he turned into the *mongat* owl (an unidentified estriligid).

Today a song recalls this primordial incest, whose punishment is transformation into an animal. A shorter myth tells of Lele's transformation into a bat after he cut out his mother-in-law's vagina and decorated and painted the organ to make a pendant for a festival. Another, very brief, tale tells of an attempted rape of a woman by her brother; she punished him by tearing off a bit of his scalp in her teeth. He fled, but there was no supernatural punishment. These mythical references distinguish two types of incest, since one leads to transformation into an animal and the other brings shame, flight being only a result of the victim's reaction. In practice, the Txikáo condemn any incest between parents and children, parents-in-law and children-in-law, as "ugly" and shameful, and say that brother-sister incest is equally reprehensible, but that the parents may authorize marriage when half-siblings are involved, or when the relationship is classificatory. As in the myth, then, there is a difference of intensity for the prohibition of incest between parents and children and the prohibition of incest between siblings. The association of parents-in-law with parents poses an interesting problem: for relations with this last group, the punishments are both natural and social. If a man has sexual relations with the wife of his son, he will be ashamed "because she will tell his son," and the whole community will find out and make fun of him. We can put the three types of relationships forbidden by the Txikáo in order of their seriousness:

1. Relations between (biological) parents and children.
2. Relations between parents-in-laws and son- or daughter-in-law.
3. Relations between siblings.

The first two types represent acts that are supremely antisocial, as is confirmed by their mythical punishment. The ideology of the couvade allows us to understand the relationship between these two prohibitions: for if this ideology expresses the gradual separation of what was originally a shared substance, then father-in-law—daughter-in-law incest, like mother-son incest, would join again what had been irreversibly divided; whether toward the top or toward the bottom, the joining of the substance of father and son would invert the temporal direction stamped on the person by the couvade. The couvade forever divides persons of the same sex, just as it forever unites substances of opposite sex. Incest between siblings is different, since the two biological beings, while of common origin, have never been in communication through the rites of the couvade. But here a complicating factor enters in, namely, the practice of associated genitors. Once their contribution has been recognized through the couvade, their own children, by their own wives, are considered classificatory brothers and sisters of the newborn child. They are thus in turn subject to the incest taboo, although to a weakened version of it. Everything happens as if the quantity of substance contributed influenced the *degree* of prohibition. As soon as a conception is shared, it involves a moderation of the taboo between the children of the genitor and those of his lover. Inversely, children who know that their father had nothing to do with their conception can marry "sisters" who are daughters of their father with another woman without violating the prohibition. In principle, the whole set of people who have undergone the couvade for a child engender children who are siblings to each other, and so may not be united under pain of incest. If the system were rigorous, it would lead to a multiplication of marital prohibitions. (We should note that in this society, sexual prohibitions and marital prohibitions overlap perfectly.) In fact, just as the couvade is gradual and adapts to individual conditions, the incest prohibition, too, establishes degrees which go from absolute prohibition to tolerance.[7] This would be a paradoxical definition of prohibition, if the dominant idiom in which it is expressed were not that of the indigenous physiology.

For the natural punishments for incest, in the three cases ordered above, are of two kinds: the most numerous involve the child to be born (and the mother as accessory), and sometimes also affect incestuous men. The most common consequence is a monstrous birth, either inverted (a breach birth), or with a fault in the child, characterized by the rigidity of a limb or of the head, already present while inside the womb. A breach birth almost always, and a paralysis of a limb always, cause death, sometimes, *in utero*. The logic of opposites, which I have pointed out in the system of food prohibitions, is also at work here. We have seen that the substances that make up the newborn child, the sperm accumulated during pregnancy, then the mother's milk, hold together in a coherent way only after several weeks (there is also a progress in the ability to hold up the head), as long as certain precautions are respected; when there is incest, everything happens as if the identity (or the similarity) of the substances put together (in a container/content relationship) brings about a prematuration, an acceleration of the constitution of the human being. The long period of biological

7. Reclassification of forbidden kin as marriageable kin is a common trait of many Amazonian societies. See, for example, Lizot, p. 66. This must be seen as being, besides a formal property of extremely intricate cognatic networks, an effect of the extreme proliferation of "extensions" of kinship which are continually being provoked by the ideology of substance and marked by the couvade.

maturation which is patterned by the rigorous and gradually decreasing restrictions of the couvade is opposed to the quasi-instantaneity of the conjunction of human beings with substances that are too similar because of common origin. The disease of incestuous people is wasting away and drying up, as if excess in copulation provoked a too-rapid growth that decomposed their somatic balance. Breach birth, on the other hand, depends on the logic of the identical, on inversion as sign of the antisocial. There is both a relationship of continuity between the couvade and the incest prohibition, since the latter keeps separate what the former had separated out of a common substance, and a functional complementarity, insofar as the couvade orders a communication within the social group which allows its diversification, and the incest prohibition establishes its external communication. While both of these are expressed through the physiological model, incest also gives a foundation to social circulation, in a break with natural processes.

By paying attention to the field of application of the couvade as well as to its normative content, analysis reveals the complexity of the institution. The couvade does express the universal problem of the composition of the human being and patterns his earliest development, but to look only at this aspect of it would be to miss the singularity of the institution. It belongs, in fact, to an ordered and coherent series of taboos that accompany and guarantee the development of individual biological destinies, while demarcating and initiating commonalities of substance within society, whether nuclear families or not, which the incest prohibition destroys in that it forces them to break apart. The power of the couvade lies in its articulation of a logic of the natural qualities of the human being and a problematic of succession, and in signifying by its progression and duration the irreversibility of human time.

References

Colson, Audrey Butt. "Birth Customs of the Akawaio." In *Studies in Social Anthropology. Essays in Memory of E. E. Evans-Pritchard*. J. Beattie and G. Lienhardt, eds. Oxford, 1975.

Da Matta, Roberto. *Um mundo divido: a estructura social dos indios Apinayé*. Petropolis, 1976.

Encyclopaedia Britannica. 11th ed., s.v. "Couvade." New York, 1910–11.

Karsten, Rafael. *The Civilization of South American Indians*. London, 1926.

Lévi-Strauss, Claude. *The Savage Mind*. Chicago, 1966.

Lizot, Jacques. *Le Cercle des Feux*. Paris, 1976.

Menget, Patrick. "Au nom des autres: classification des relations sociales chez les Indiens Txikáo du Haut-Xingu (Brésil)." Thesis for the doctorate of the 3d cycle, E.P.H.E., 1977.

Métraux, Alfred. "The Couvade." In *Handbook of South American Indians*. J. Steward, ed. Vol. 5. Washington, 1949.

Polgar, Stephen. Review of *Social Anthropology and Medicine*, ASA Monograph 13, New York, 1976. In *Man* 13, no. 1 (1978).

Rivière, Peter. "The Couvade: A Problem Reborn." *Man* 9, no. 3 (1974).

Silverwood-Cope, Peter. "A Contribution to the Ethnography of the Columbian Maku." Ph.D. dissertation, Cambridge, 1972.

Taylor, Douglas. "The Meaning of Dietary and Occupational Restrictions Among the Island Caribs." *American Anthropologist* 52, no. 3 (1950).

Van Gennep, Arnold. *Manuel de folklore français contemporain*. Vol. 1. Paris, 1943.

Vidal, Lux. *Morte e vida de uma sociedade indigena brasiliera*. Sao Paulo, 1977.

Von den Steinen, Karl. *Unter den Naturvölkern Zentral-Brasiliens*. Berlin, 1894.

Michel Cartry

From the Village to the Bush
An Essay on the Gourmantché of Gobnangou (Upper Volta)

12

In a very valuable study devoted to the village/forest opposition in the "ideology" of Brahmanical India, Charles Malamoud[1] recalls that the Sanskrit word *araṇya*, which is commonly translated "forest," is derived from *araṇa*, "strange,"[2] "which in turn is related to the Indo-European root *al-*, *ol-*, itself the source of the Latin words *alius, alter, ille.*" The *araṇya*, before defining a territory distinguished from the village space by a certain number of material traits (a zone without agriculture, covered with trees), "designates" in these societies "the other of the village." The other of the village, specifies the author, is what is beyond the village boundary, with the understanding that "it is not the boundary that defines the village," but "the village that engenders . . . the boundary."

While my researches on space concern societies in which the opposition between the village and "the forest" appears in a quite different form than in Brahmanical India, these remarks of Malamoud's are valuable because they invite us to reexamine the notion of projective space. Is this notion sufficient in itself to account for the tendency, attested by many ethnologists, which leads numerous societies to expel into the wild and uncultivated space that stretches beyond the boundary (here the forest, there the bush, elsewhere the desert) everything within the village scene that puts one in the presence of the strange, the abnormal, the preculiar? Among the Gourmantché of Gobnangou (a society of farmers-

1. "Village et forêt dans l'idéologie de l'Inde brahmanique," *Archives européenes de sociologie* 17 (1976): 3-20.
2. TN: The word *étrange* can mean "strange" or "foreign."

hunters-gatherers), the wild and uncultivated space appears rather as a sort of necessary referential space, which we could say is introduced as a third party between the "being" of the village and its question, whenever this question imposes itself as an enigma. But it is not, for all that, the place of the answer, but appears as a sort of logical operator authorizing a certain permutation of terms within the structure of the enigma itself. It is this provisional hypothesis, which suggests that we reexamine certain correlations which the Gourmantché establish between the bush and the village, that will serve as our guiding thread.[3]

How does what is generally called the space of the bush appear in the region of Gobnangou? What traits characterize it as a physical and geographical reality? What mode of occupation of the land is characteristic of the Gourmantché villages of this region? What is the layout of the dwellings? Some elements of an answer to these questions will allow the reader to picture the general geographical environment in which bush-related rites and activities take place.

The Gourmantché house *(diegu)*[4] looks like a little circular village built around a central plaza. It is not the construction of a single tenant but a set of small circular buildings (minimal units of habitation, currently called "huts") arranged side by side along a circular or elliptical path. Little fences of millet twigs—sometimes covered with sekos—wall up the gaps between these neighboring huts, thus delimiting an almost entirely closed space. The opening to the outside is by means of a vestibule with two doors, one for entering the vestibule from the inner courtyard, the other giving onto the outside. The fence is often damaged (by animals); one can sometimes go out through these accidental breaches.

Here the habitation is directly inserted into a rural landscape. In the space separating the different enclosures of one village (the dimensions of this space vary from 10 to 15 meters), almost no territory remains uncultivated; "hut gardens" and fields are everywhere, growing a highly diversified range of plants. At the end of the rainy season, a veritable forest of millet has grown up between the houses, and each enclosure is so shut in that it is no longer possible to see the neighboring one. At harvest time this forest of millet gives way under the blows of the axe to a bare space, covered only with stumps of millet, and crisscrossed by a network of small, ill-defined paths.

While variations can be observed from one agglomeration to another, a single general scheme orders the laying out of a village territory. If we use a coefficient of occupation of the soil as our criterion, three large, fairly well differentiated

3. This study discusses, in a slightly different perspective, a theme I first dealt with in 1975–76 in seminars at the E.P.H.E. (see the summaries of the year's conferences for 1975–76, pp. 79–94, in the *Annuaire de l'Ecole Pratique des Hautes Etudes, 5ᵉ section*, vol. 84).
4. For the sake of convenience, I usually cite Gourmantché nouns without their prefixes. In place of *u-die-gu* I transcribe *diegu*. I have generally followed the rules of transcription proposed by the Subcommission for Gourmantché of the National Commission on Voltaic Languages.

zones can be distinguished.[5] On the one hand the space occupied by the village houses, and on the other the space occupied by "hut gardens" and fields lying between the houses, constitute the main elements in the first zone; to this we should add the cultivated space in the area immediately surrounding the village. This territorial ensemble is the object of intensive and continuous occupation. Going away from the village, one enters a zone in which the occupation and exploitation of the land are only temporary. Here space, which is discontinuous, appears in the form of a number of cultivated clearings in the midst of "the bush." In these clearings, "farm houses" *(kua'diegu,* "field houses," say the Gourmantché) are scattered among "temporary" fields. There is, finally, the zone of fallow land, within which two types of territory can be distinguished: (a) land that was "once cultivated, then abandoned, and which will be put to use again"; (b) territories that have never been exploited. The vegetation characterizing all of these fallow lands is typical of what are called "wooded savannah" regions (scrub, bushes, very large trees in places). A lesser density of large trees, a heavier growth of grain-bearing plants, finally the presence of the African locust tree *(Parkia biglobosa)* indicate that a piece of land, today lying fallow, is in fact an ancient field (it is by the planting of the African locust that the man who first clears a piece of land marks his ownership rights).

It is to this land that has never been exploited, or that has not been used for very long, that one would tend to apply the term "bush." In Gobnangou, this kind of bush is usually located at a very great distance from the village. But bush zones do exist quite close, particularly on the plateau of the Gobnangou cliffs.

To designate what we call "bush," the Gourmantché have two terms at their disposal. The term *moagu* (lit. "where there is grass or straw") serves to designate places where the vegetation is marked by the presence of grasses, scrub, bushes, but also by burned tree trunks, indicating that this is land that has been left fallow. While *moagu* is primarily a descriptive term, the word *fuali* is something quite different. It is true that this word can, in certain contexts, be used to speak of pieces of territory that have never been or never could be exploited, whether this be dense forest land or, on the contrary, an enormous natural clearing unsuitable for agriculture. When you ask them to be more specific, the Gourmantché sometimes say that "real *fuali*" means those stretches of savannah in which there is no longer any trace of African locust trees. Since it is from the fruit of the African locust that women make soumbala, a highly prized condiment that accompanies all sauces, the tree that produces these fruits is associated with woman, woman as wife, the purveyor of cooked food. Where there are no more African locust trees, there are no more women. What is a land without

5. The citations and references that follow in the text, concerning the organization of the soil [*terroir*], are extracted from G. Rémy's study of one of the major villages of Gobnangou. See G. Rémy, *Yobri, Etude géographique du terroir d'un village Gourmantché de Haute-Volta,* Atlas des Structures agraires au sud du Sahara, vol. 1 (Paris: Mouton, 1967).

women? It is a "male land," say the Gourmantché, a land marked by a certain kind of sterility.

As this last metaphor already indicates, the Gourmantché notion of *fuali* cannot be translated in terms of physical or geographical reality. While it serves to take in the domain of wild animals and plants, we shall see that it is not sufficient to say that the space designated by this term is one that is not humanized, not tamed, not worked by the hand of man. Sometimes it is spoken of as that toward which one goes when one goes away from the village. It is over there, far away, always farther away. But far away does not just mean "situated at a great geographical distance." What is far away can be next to you. *Fuali* is not a surveyable territory but a space with shifting boundaries, its boundaries varying notably as a function of time. At night the space of *fuáli* advances into the village up to the space marked by the habitation's enclosure, sometimes even penetrating its interstices. When the sun is at its zenith, the village territory seems to be dotted with little islands of bush into which it is dangerous to penetrate. *Fuali* implies indistinction, the absence of differentiated contours, the evaporation of boundaries. Thus at night any space outside that of the house tends to turn into "bush"; the way the landscape looks in the raw light of noon, when things seem to return to a state of indifferentiation, is equally the bush.

The root *fua*, from which *fuali* is derived, is opposed in certain contexts to the root *do*, which provides the basis for the word "village" *(dogu)*, these two roots serving to form a long series of pairs of contrasting terms.[6] For one of my informants, the semantic field covered by the root *fua* included the notion of a space affecting the human body in a specific way: if you stay *fuali-ni* ("in the bush") for too long, he said, or find yourself in certain situations, it is as if you were "emptied," "pumped out," "pressed," "flattened," to the point of "evaporation." Whether this etymological reconstruction is "ture" or "false," it does not express a personal interpretation but evokes the idea of a relationship between the body and the "bush," so that, at the extreme limit, the intervention of the bush on a body leads it to being confounded with the indifferentiation of the bush. We will see that this apprehension of limits, of the body as well as of the territory, always problematic, cannot avoid some reference to the bush.

Van Gennep was able to circumscribe a class of rituals whose only words, gestures, objects are those mobilized to deal with a problem of space. In what he called "rites of passage," we find always, and everywhere, thresholds, gateways, apertures. It is certainly the case that among the Gourmantché the necessity for an intervention of the bush as third party is most easily grasped in rites of passage. But rites of passage have no monopoly on references to the bush. We shall see that in ordinary times, and not only at moments of passage, the bush is

6. Examples: *do'yanga/fua'yanga* (domestic animal/wild animal); *do'tielo/fua'tielo* (village being/bush being), etc.

there, ever present, more diffuse, certainly, in the village, but always discoverable in words and actions.

A baby is expected. What presided over the production of the "child of the womb" (the fetus)? What sex will the new arrival be? This "kinsman of the earth" (ancestor) whom the woman is "bearing," who is he? This "stranger" who is announcing himself, where did he come from? What does he want? What is he going to "put between" the husband and his wife? The Gourmantché put these questions—and many others—to diviners. To formulate them, they use a group of extremely complex notions, which we will not be able to analyze here. What is procreation? Where could the child have come from? It would be naive to think that the repetition of this question before the diviner, the displacement of terms in the order of questioning, originate in the ignorance of a population that has not yet attained a knowledge formulated in the terms of a scientific genetics and embryology.

When the question is put to him, the diviner gives the earth's answer; he knows that this answer will lead to other questions. He also knows that the desire to know about the origin of a child involves far more than a request for an explanation of the "causes" of a phenomenon. God *(tienu)*, a particular ancestor who has manifested himself in one of his descendents (*ngaali*), the preexisting part of a man (his *cicilga*), the prenatal choice of the mother or of an "ancestress" *(yemiali)*, the bush, all of these elements are mobilized to say something about the arrival of a child.[7] If they can be deployed simultaneously in one discourse, this is because the latter never takes the form of a body of propositions distinguishing between first and second causes. In spite of the subtlety of the connections they establish between these elements, the Gourmantché accept that something will be left over.

The child has arrived. Let us suppose that it is the child of a single birth, with no culturally noteworthy mark on its body to suggest an unusual destiny. Let us insist on this point. Although the child seems destined to the life of a human being, in these first days of life a durable inscription into the village space is still in no way assured. The child comes from somewhere else. They say first of all that it is a water being. The study of birth rituals shows that the human fetus is assimilated to a catfish, this assimilation being based on a common aquatic situation: the catfish lives and develops in the water of marshy country, and in the same way the fetus develops in the liquid of the amniotic sack, another marsh. Within the waters of the mother, he "breathes," thanks to his fontanelle (called "the fish of the head"), like the fish breathes in the marshes by means of its gills. Outside the mother's womb he will continue to share in the nature of the catfish, and this will continue until his fontanelle has completely hardened. The fact that he is fed only on liquid (milk and gruel) for the first few months of life is, for the

---

7. Some of these notions have been analyzed elsewhere. See M. Cartry, "Le lien à la mère et la notion de destin individual chez les Gourmantché," pp. 255–82, in *La notion de personne en Afrique noire*, Colloques internationaux de C.N.R.S. (Paris: C.N.R.S., 1973).

Gourmantché, not merely an anatomical detail, but the sign that he is still marked by the nature of the fish.[8]

But on the young human's road to humanization,[9] the threshold between water and earth is not the only one he must cross to become a being of the village. A ritual performed after the birth, certain daily gestures done by those around the newborn child, the interpretation made of certain of the child's behaviors indicate that the elsewhere out of which the child must be drawn is also the elsewhere of the bush. Geomancy—the dominant form of divination among the Gourmantché—yields material on this subject which leaves no doubt about the fact that the elsewhere of the aquatic world and the elsewhere of the bush occupy different topological positions. To the client who has come to consult about his child, the diviner may say that the child "is still in the water" or that he "has not come out of the womb yet"—a bad sign for the child, and also for the couple, and it may lead to divorce. If we analyze the geomantic manipulations on the basis of which the diviner produces this kind of statement, we notice that the child, for all that he is still in the water, still where "all that is hidden has not yet come out" (the house of "hiding"), is still not located in an outside (house of the "outside"). The elsewhere of the bush, on the other hand, is almost always related to this "house of the outside." It is when he is taking the bush into consideration that the diviner will produce statements that involve an "outside," an "exterior," an "abroad" of something appearing from a far-off place. The child is "a foreigner" [étranger], the Gourmantché say freely. We now know that the child's foreignness is conferred on him by his relationship with the bush. But in what way is a child of a single birth a being of the bush?

The new mother is isolated for three or four days (depending on whether her child is a boy or a girl). On the first day after she emerges from isolation, and on the days following, she must attach a knife to her back, adjusting it in such a way that it can cut the child she is carrying. This knife should be with her when-

8. See M. Cartry, "La calebasse de l'excision chez les Gourmantché," *Journal de la Société des Africanistes* 38, no. 2 (1968).

9. TN: The use of the phrase *le jeune d'homme*, "the young of man," to indicate a small child, alludes to some of the central ideas of structuralist thought. It points to the notion that "the young of man" is not so different from the young of other animals, except in having a potential for becoming part of specifically human linguistic and cultural systems—this potential being the "symbolic function" talked about in the preface to this book. The symbolic function is not actualized by simple biological maturation but through interaction with other human beings and with the linguistic and cultural system as a whole. Western common sense tends to see the transition from the state of the infant to that of a speaking human being with a name and a specific social role in terms of internalization: the child learns how to talk and behave by internalizing knowledge. Structuralists, on the other hand tend to view this transition as the insertion of the "young of man" into an always-already-present linguistic and cultural system, in which (if the child is lucky) she or he finds a relatively stable place, "a name to call my own." This approach underlies the basic argument of Lévi-Strauss's *Elementary Structures of Kinship*; but the allusion here is to the work of the psychoanalyst Jacques Lacan, who has emphasized the dangers that beset the "young of man" on this road to humanization. This aspect of Lacan's work is brought out clearly in Louis Althusser's article "Freud and Lacan" (reprinted in his collection *Lenin and Philosophy and Other Essays* [New York, 1972]).

ever she moves about. This is a rite of protection against the *pola* (singular *poli*), one of the categories of beings that populate the bush. The knife discourages the *pola's* attempts to come near, for it is said that if they managed to get close they would try to steal the child away. What is the nature of this abduction? It is still too soon to answer.

Here is an ordinary scene from daily life. The child has grown and can move about on all fours. It often happens that the mother, busy with something, leaves her child alone in the hut for a few moments. If the child does not yet know the language of men, this does not mean that he cannot speak. His babble is taken as a real language, a nonhuman language he shares with certain domestic animals (cat and horse) and with the *pola* of the bush. Even when his mother has left him, the child is not alone. People think he is talking and laughing to himself, but he is really talking and playing with the *pola*. His mother is well aware of this. When she comes back, she pauses a moment on the threshold of her hut, claps her hands and says *gafalla*, a polite gesture and formula that are reproduced every time one is about to enter someone's hut. When the mother has signalled her arrival in this way, the *pola* will leave the home.

We can see that a kind of understanding, a sort of complicity exists between the *pola* and young children who cannot yet either speak or stand up. For the parents, the fear of an abduction lessens as the months pass. But it does not quite disappear, and certain precautions must be taken. The mother never leaves her child alone without leaving some *sagbu* (millet cake) nearby. The spirits are extremely fond of cakes made in the village, and leaving them some is usually enough to make them forget about stealing the child.

An old custom that is no longer practiced today allows us to define more precisely the relationship between the newborn child and the *pola*. Formerly the midwife, immediately after a birth, would procure a chicken from the child's genitor and then go back into the birth hut and gut the animal, spilling the blood onto the earth of the "birth hole."[10] She would then make a dish of a mixture of millet cake and pieces of the meat of the sacrificial chicken. In order to reach the *pola*, the dish was then put on the roof of a *ciiagu* (a shelter called a "hangar" in colonial jargon). This elevated food was visible to *pola* for a great distance. The next day the cake could be seen to be "wet" and, as it were, "emptied" of its substance. A *poli* had come and eaten it during the night. This sort of cake was called *cyan'dugu*, the "foreign companion." It appears from this custom—to which we shall return—that from the time it is born the child of a single birth is paired with a *poli*, thus reproducing, as it were, a particular modality of twin birth. The Gourmantché make almost no comment on this point. Unlike their Mossi neighbors, they do not say that to every human birth there corresponds

---

10. Certain sequences from birth rituals have been described in detail in my article, "Les yeux captifs," pp. 79–110, in *Systèmes de signes, textes réunis en hommage à G. Dieterlen* (Paris: Hermann, 1978).

the birth of a *kinkirsi* (the equivalent of the *pola* in Mossi culture), both beings having interlocking destinies.[11] We should, however, remember this idea of a "companion from the bush" paired, from birth, with the child of a single birth.

When the child grows, the mother intervenes to end this relationship of complicity with the "companion," as well as with the whole group of *pola*. It is now time for the child to cross the threshold and enter the village once and for all. This passage implies, as it were, a change in the level of view. Except in certain circumstances, the *pola* are invisible to most people. But in the presence of very young children they are said to lose this invisibility. Children can see "into the bush," but they cannot keep this "gift" beyond the time when they begin to walk or to talk like adults. If a child continued to see "far away," he would sooner or later provoke suspicion. If her child is too content with going on all fours, the mother should wean him. She will strike him lightly on the head "to make him blind for the bush."

I have offered the hypothesis that the intervention of the bush as a third-party space is made necessary by a kind of enigma posed to the village. We have seen that the child of a single birth is related to the bush. More clearly still, certain rites have shown us that a bush being of the *pola* category was paired with each of these children, and in such a way that it could evoke a relationship of twinship. The occurrence of a single birth involves, beyond any doubt, the intervention of the bush as a third party. What, then, is this enigma posed by a birth which, after all, is perfectly ordinary and usual? We could, of course, content ourselves with this as the enigma posed by the arrival of a stranger, certainly not an unimportant factor. But, as we are going to establish, the enigma takes on meaning only by reference to other enigmas. When one enigma is posed, a part of the veil is lifted only by the intervention of the bush as a third party in another enigma which, in turn, draws part of its answer from a third enigma. The numerous cross-cuttings that could be performed here introduce a sort of spiral logic that is impossible to follow merely by making one-to-one correlations. From the treatment of twin births we can draw some supplementary elements for the question posed by the arrival of children of single births, as well as for questions which grow out of the study of rituals involving the bush.

Rites performed for the birth of twins refer explicitly to the bush, situating it first of all as the probable place of origin of the two newborn children. Like children of single births, they too are linked to the *pola*, but the bond that is established here is a far more intimate one. That the very word *pola* is also applied as a generic term to twins is a fact that is already an index of this kind of ontological proximity (the distinction can be marked by speaking sometimes of *fua'pola*, "*pola* of the bush," and sometimes of *nu'pola*, "human *pola*").

---

11. The nature of this bond has been studied in a very interesting way by Pierre Vogler. See "Structuralisme et théologie. La divinité chez les Mossi," *Annales de l'Université d' Abidjan*, Series F, vol. 3 (1973).

The lineage elder, who has "the medicines" associated with twins, is called to the mother's hut.[12] These medicines, as well as the incantations associated with them, are generally transmitted within a lineage, or a clan, of hunters. This old man, a specialist in rites concerning twins, is awaited anxiously. It is known that his ritual intervention will make possible the symbolic mastery of an event which, however it is lived by each person, remains, for everyone, the problem of his own origin.

As for an ordinary birth, the midwife will await the expulsion of the placenta or placentas before cutting the umbilical cord. The rite of *kimi,* which is done by the specialist, immediately follows the expulsion of the placenta. When this rite has been completed, it is time for the midwife to separate the children from the placenta. The specialist begins by invoking the name of the ancestor (man or woman, more usually woman) who was at the source of the power that has been transmitted through his or her lineage, asking this ancestor, "so that he does not bump into anything," to precede him on the "path" he is preparing himself to follow. In all the invocations that precede the performance intrusted to a specialist in a particular rite, we frequently find the metaphor of the path. The allusion to the dangers of stumbling on the path suggests that the twin specialist will be going into that bush in which so many hunters have lost their way.

Armed with a small broom, he dips it several times into a vessel containing a decoction of vegetal medicines *(boroda)* and, several times in a row, sprinkles the twins, who remain in the "hole of childbirth." We have collected two variants of the ritual words he pronounces during the aspersion:

First variant: "We want to know where you come from. If it is because you have smelled the aroma of the millet cake that you, *pola,* have come, then tell us so. Whether you have come from the south, from the east, from the north or the west, you should know it all. What time did you come? Was it at midnight or in the morning, at cock-crow? Did you come toward evening?"

Second variant: "Today, Saturday, I want you to remain people like us. I make you blind for the bush. I do not want you to go back there. I want you to have our eyes. I want you to see as we see."

The twins' reaction to contact with this medicinal water serves as a forecast of the future. They are good twins, human twins, if they weep or cry out; they are evil twins, a pair of bush *pola* who have entered the village through a woman's womb, if they remain silent. If only one of them cries, this will be seen as a sign that he does belong to the village. The one who remains silent, they say, might well kill his father or mother. If two twins of the same sex remain silent, it is feared that they will endanger the life of one of their parents, the one who is of opposite sex from them. The words cited in the first variant indicate that to each aspersion corresponds a new test, and that the manner of testing becomes more

12. Whenever I speak of "medicine" in this article, I am referring to the Gourmantché idea of *nyoagu,* a term that is untranslatable since it designates medicines, poisons, spells, charms, talismans, and potions at the same time.

and more urgent. It is not enough for the twins to have cried out once; they must cry at the right time. It is towards the fall of night, when the women light their cooking fires, that the *pola* of the bush approach the houses in search of millet cakes. If the twin who has just been born has come only to "beg for cake," he will, without knowing it, reveal his true identity by crying, i.e., making an affirmative answer, immediately after the aspersion of water which accompanies the question, "Towards the evening?"

In comparing the two formulas, we note a difference of perspective in regard to the way of apprehending the nature of the difference that separates the "good" twin from the "bad" twin. In the first variant, it is accepted that conceiving twins can also be a human phenomenon. The aspersion will allow a recognition of which category of twins the two present children belong to. If, by their tears, they react at the right time to contact with the cold water, they will be identified as *nu'pola*, "human *pola.*" "This," they say, "this comes from men." If they react badly, they will be taken to be *fua'pola*, "*pola* of the bush," who have intruded into the world of men. In the second variant, we feel touched by the conviction that all twins are *pola* of the bush. The aspersion rite still serves as a test, but what is being tested is quite different: are these creatures of the bush going to attain to the existence of village beings? This is the question of the second variant. If the children do not cry, it is the sign that they will never reach this state. Contact with cold water should be enough to make any newborn human baby yell; if, after several sprinklings, they remain imperturbably mute, this shows that they are beings of the bush to such an extent that it would be best to let them return to the bush from which they come. Letting them return to the bush is equivalent to deciding not to intervene to permit them to survive. Everything happens here as if what we are looking at is a test that provides a way of allowing those that already present signs of death to return to the bush. For we might suppose that children who do not cry at all after such an ordeal are either already dead or would have little chance of survival.

We have seen that these two ways of apprehending twin births are not fundamentally different. Even if the twins have gotten over the hump of the birth rituals, the village will treat them as beings apart, will point them out to each other by all kinds of emblems, distinguishing marks, rites, attitudes, ways of speaking, as beings forever marked by their bush origin, destined always to remain intimately associated with the *pola* of the bush. We shall give two examples of the way they are treated as set apart.

Twins' hair, like that of their "companions" of the bush, must remain uncut for a long period. A person of the village is called *nu'salo*, someone who is smooth and hairless, and for the Gourmantché, the fact of having no hair is an essential attribute of the category of human being of the village. Performed three or four weeks after birth, the shaving of a child of a single birth is a fundamentally important rite of emergence into the human order.

As is the case for children of single births, but in a far more marked way, twins are presumed to have the ability to see into the bush. This faculty, indeed, is never lost entirely. Faced with this "power," parents of twins will typically show ambivalent behavior, vacillating between the desire to make them, "blind for the bush" and the fear of taking the ritual initiatives necessary to reach this goal.

At the birth of twins, the *pola* of the bush will try to get close to the birth hut, all set to intervene to take away one of their own. To keep them out, an old woman, a specialist in twin rites, will go slowly around the house; at each step, she will sprinkle the ground with medicinal water mixed with sand from a termite mound. For the Gourmantché, the termite is the main emissary *(tiendo)* of the bush. They say that termites would come to bite any bush *pola* who try to cross this magic circle. This rite verifies what we have already said about the indeterminacy of the boundaries separating the village from the bush. For what is it that the old woman does? Inside the birth house, one would assume that one was in the middle of the village. What does the ritual say but that, even in these circumstances, it is necessary to mark off—inside the village—a territory which is outside the bush? In relation to what is already inscribed, this new inscription could only be a kind of redundancy. We should, rather, turn the proposition around and say that it is because the bush invades the village at this time that it is crucial to mark off a prohibited space within this bush.

Once the twins have passed through the period immediately after birth, during which the danger of death is greatest, the frequency of rituals or ritualized attitudes marking their singularity diminishes. By succeeding in surviving, they show that they are achieving the existence of village beings. But during the periods of transformation dealt with in rites of passage, it is always believed that their true nature as beings of the bush is likely to reassert itself. This appears clearly in the simulacrum of flight into the bush performed by every female twin on the day of her marriage. On that day, she is shut up inside a hut along with her mother and a specialist in twin rituals. All the openings of the hut, all apertures, all holes, even the smallest, are closed up, including cracks in the roof. Around the hut people are gathered to guard all possible exits. It is the administration of her "medicine" that is believed to terrify the twin. She breaks free of human hands, runs in all directions, ends up finding a way out, breaks through the barriers of the crowd, and tears off towards the bush. That day, young men "gird up their loins" and take off after her, and finally catch her. The mother of the twin has followed them and comes to take her daughter back. They say that if the specialist in twin rituals had not succeeded in giving her his "medicine," she "would have gone back to the *pola*" ("she would have run into the bush and that would have been the end of it"). In this ritual, the bush as a third-party space no longer appears only on the level of representations, for it is indeed toward the border area between the village and the bush that the twin flies.

Let us stop for a moment at this point in our argument to ask whether the facts that we have been presenting have a relationship among themselves other than that which each of them, taken individually, has with the bush. Everything happens as if every village event that we have been considering, while it is questioning the bush, also questions every other event that is connected to the bush. Thus the bush seems to act as a prism sending a refracted answer, whose elements are so many new questions, back to the village. This would not be a matter of an exchange between the bush and the question of the village, an exchange such that, passing from one complexity to the next, some more precise response could eventually be reached. On the contrary, the refracted elements, bounced back by the bush, seems to infiltrate the questions posed by other events of the village.

What supplementary relationship exists between data as apparently heterogeneous as a newborn baby considered as a "beggar of cake," hitting a crawling child on the head to "make him blind for the bush," and finally, a female twin trying to escape from the village?

In all of the three cases, what is involved is, I believe, a matter of territory. We know today that the notion of territory does not refer only to an area outlined on a piece of land, but to a space that has been marked out in such a way that, recognizing it as one's own, one can move about on it without danger. Every foreign incursion inside this space, and any movement outside its bounds, are felt to be dangerous. It would take long arguments to show that this feeling of insecurity is not unrelated to the problem of the boundaries of the body itself, the appropriation of a territory necessitating, beyond the apparent bodily boundary represented by the skin, the marking out of a body-space. There is a great deal of evidence that the Gourmantché conceive of the village territory as a body-space. The *dogu* (village) is a *tin'gban'yendo*, a single "earth skin" (lit. "earth skin one"), which means that the unity of the village is thought of on the model of a body, the great spatial divisions (what are mistakenly called the four quarters of the horizon) being sometimes designated by reference to the presumed organs of the "body earth one" ("toward the mouth of the earth," "toward the anus of the earth," "in the belly of the earth" are the ways people express themselves to indicate an intention to move towards the west, the east, or the middle of the village respectively). This way of conceiving of the village territory as a body says implicitly that this "pumping" bush is not itself a body. The three examples of ritual attitudes that we have selected all fall under the following axiom: for every new arrival, for every individual "on the margin," there is no way to escape this necessity of integrating to their own body that other body that is the village.

In signaling by his tears his membership in the bush, the "cake-begging" twin at the same stroke designates himself as a being without a territory. What can be done with such a twin? What is the source of his body? If he is a being of the bush, his attempt to come and live in the body of another still does not mean that it is possible for him to integrate the limits of the village body. There is no choice but to let him go back into an extraterritorial elsewhere.

Even the child of a single birth remains in a relationship of proximity with the bush. By continuing to crawl, he signifies that he is still marked by the absence of a territorial limit, characteristic of the space that he has come from.

Hitting him on the head marks that the time has come to establish the boundaries of a territory. Limited in his field of vision (made "blind for the bush"),
made to give up his language, he will be forced to learn about his own limits,
starting with these elements of his body.

The flight of the female twin towards the edge of the bush marks her uncertainty about the limits of her body. It does not seem surprising that the situation
of twinship should make this understanding of limits more difficult. The fact
that this flight is organized for the day of her marriage indicates that she is going
to be confronted once more and in a different modality with the need to integrate the limits of her body (and, through modifications yet to come, both the
limits of her own body and those arising from the change in territory involved in
the passage from her parents' house to that of her husband). In this ritual,
society tries to save the twin from this vain attempt at flight: for it is not a body
that she would find in the bush, but the space of wandering.

We must now approach and try to get to know these bush *pola* whom the
twin is so eager to rejoin. Like the Gourmantché hunter, we will have to put
them to the question.

The *pola* are not the only bush beings that offer resemblances with the humans of the village. In this bush live other "powers," distributed into three other
"families": (1) the *fuatieba* (sing. *fuatielo*); (2) the *jiindi* (sing. *jiingu*); (3) the
kpankpa amu (sing. *kpankpaaga*). To each family of the bush corresponds a
typical picture, but there is a remarkable similarity among these different pic-
tures. All of them appear as mirror images of the human body, images corresponding to different types of distorting mirrors.

While they are sometimes described in great detail, all of these bush beings are
"essentially" invisible. It is only those village humans who are in league with the
bush in one way or another who can see them under certain circumstances. Their
invisibility confers on them a power over men, all the greater since they are seers
themselves ("we don't see them but they see us", say the Gourmantché). Not
only do they see men, but they also foresee what is going to happen in the
village.

The beings come out of their bush domain periodically to make incursions
into the human realm, but the times they choose for these visits vary with the
different categories of beings. Their ways of life, and the ways in which they
intervene in human life, also differ. The *kpankpaamu* and the *jiindi* are solitary,
whereas the *pola* and the *fuatieba* are attached to particular places, where they
are supposed to be organized in a kind of village community of the bush.

The bush spaces in which these two "families" of beings are located are quite
distinct in terms of vegetation, flora and fauna. It is said that the *futieba* and the
pola have remarkable knowledge of the "medicinal and magical" virtues of the
various plants that characterize their respective environments. It is added that
they are the "owners" of certain species of wild animals (buffaloes and various
kinds of antelopes).

Keeping in mind only those traits that are directly relevant to us, we can try to isolate the main characteristics of the *pola*. The stature of dwarfs, long hair, reversed feet as if they walked with their feet crossed,[13] are the most commonly mentioned traits of their physical appearance. Portraits of them also share three other points: (1) like twins, they always go about in pairs, either side by side or one behind the other (the question of whether the pair includes individuals of opposite sex does not seem to be very pertinent); (2) each of the partners holds in his hand a calabash gourd without a neck and with a cover; (3) both of them are covered with a sort of net-bag, with their head and part of the body closed up inside it. This net, which looks like the nets women use to carry their calabashes, also contains medicines.

The bush space in which their habitat is situated corresponds to a type of savannah landscape that is to be found fairly commonly in this region of Gobnangou: it appears as an immense clearing with small trees growing on its edge. The characteristic trees are the *natombu* and the *diabougli*. It is in these areas that the *pola* have their houses ("they are there, invisible, in the clearing," some say; others say, "it is the trees on the edge that serve for their house").

There are many occasions for meetings between *pola* and humans. These meetings can be good or bad. Encounters with women, pregnant women, or women who have young children are thought of with a certain ambivalence. Things seem to happen differently depending on whether the meeting takes place in the bush or in the village.

Because of its *pola*, the bush is full of dangers for a pregnant woman, especially after the fifth month. Here are some of the things that are said about this. A pregnant woman who goes away from the village to do something in the woods is advised to "hold her garment high on her chest and never leave her belly uncovered." By "the feeling of a caress" on her belly, an imprudent woman knows that a *poli* has come to take away "what is, after all, his child," removing "the best part" of the fetus, leaving only "the shadow." A woman who is "besieged" in this way risks miscarrying, or even of giving birth to a deaf-mute or an idiot. The *poli* takes the "best part of the child" off to his own domain to "strengthen" a fetus of the bush.

But the *pola's* anxious quest is also directed toward young children. In the bush, a woman must keep her child continually on her back. If the child is left alone for a single moment, the *poli* will come to steal it away on its own back.

Encounters with *pola* in the village usually take place at dusk, when the women are preparing the meal. At this time the *pola* arrive in great numbers, attracted, as we have seen, by the smell of the millet cake they are so fond of. Some come into the house, but most stick in a mass onto the fence. The fear that they inspire at this time is not quite the same as that which they provoke if encountered in the bush. For to the fear that they have come to steal fetuses and

13. Feet crossed or backwards?

young children in or near the house (when evening falls, a pregnant woman is supposed to avoid going out, even to wash in the nearby well), is added the anxiety that they have come to stay, in the form of twins who will soon be born from the women of the area. Explanations of the mechanisms of production of twin births vary,[14] but out of all that is said, prescribed, or forbidden it is always clear that between *fua'pola* and *nu'pola* there lies woman and the womb, thought of as the necessary place of passage between the space of the bush and the space of the village. The risks or the chances of a woman being taken in this way are not distributed at random, but especially concern pregnant women or women who go out at night, not by the normal route, the vestibule, but through a hole in the enclosure. Among the motives for fear we should, finally, recall those concerning newborn twins. We have mentioned that on the day of their birth an old woman tries to drive away the *fua'pola* by tracing a magic circle around the house in which the birth has taken place. On the place where the placenta(s) of the twins is (are) buried on the appropriate day, protective medicines are laid. In this ritual, it is the twins themselves, and not the placenta as such, that the participants are trying to protect (from the *pola).* At the time of the treatment for the placenta of the child of a single birth no protective ritual of this sort will be performed. When they are neither at home nor in the homes of men, the *pola* hop around tirelessly in clearings in the bush. They never hold still. Incessantly shifting, they are continually bending over to gather up wild seeds, which they store in their gourds. Like their bush homologues, village twins are also given gourds, on the very day they are born. It is the specialist in twin ritual who goes into the bush himself to cut these gourds; the mother has the responsibility of putting a mixture of domestic and wild seeds into them the same day. On the first day of the month and on festival days, she takes seeds out of these gourds, scatters them to the *pola* of the bush, and throws some under the enclosure of the house. Once the gourd is empty it will be refilled. They say that a twin never goes anywhere without his gourd, and it is with this gourd that a female twin goes to join her husband's house. The day a twin dies, the gourd is put into his grave.

So the *pola* keep on moving, never still, always looking for food, always wrapped up in their nets. The informants are unanimous: these strange nets are what make the *pola* invisible. What is more, while this is never said per se, this net is in itself invisible: it acts neither as a mask nor as a veil, which are there to be seen in place of what they hide. The *bu-gambu's* function of rendering invisible does not make it visible itself.

There does exist, however, a situation in which both the *pola* and their nets simultaneously lose their invisibility. They say that before going into the water, the *pola* take off their nets and hang them on the *diabougli* tree (the species

14. Sometimes they say that two *fua'pola* enter a woman's womb during the gestation period, but certain informants propose another schema: one of the *fua'pola* intervenes in the woman's womb in the same way as a *jaali* type of ancestor, that is, by "putting the womb in place" in such a way that it must necessarily bear twins.

characteristic of their ecological zone); when this has been done, they spring forth, suddenly visible to the hunter's eye. The evocation of this scene clearly indicates that access to the visible arises from a separation of two indissociable entities; it is through this separation that a man is able to see the *pola* and their nets hung in the tree. The hunter may now take hold of this net and pull it to the ground at the bottom of the *diabougli.* The moment the *bu-gambu* touches the ground, the hunter has the *poli* at his mercy. The *poli* has no alternative but to answer any questions the hunter asks him, yielding to the hunter everything he knows about the magical virtues of plants of the bush and about the "medicines" contained in the wrapping the hunter has laid on the ground.[15]

While investigating the *pola,* I was particularly intrigued by the existence of this *bu-gambu* but was far from suspecting its true nature—which was, however, known to everyone else. I finally found out from the old women that it was understood as a placenta of twins (same texture, same color). To understand this correlation between the *pola's* net and the placenta of human twins, I will briefly outline how the Gourmantché think of the relationship between the child of a single birth and his placenta.[16]

The Gourmantché call the placenta *o-lielo,* "the second one," "the companion," "who is more yourself than you are yourself." This second one will be separated from the child only as a last extremity, for the umbilical cord will not be cut until the placenta has joined the child lying "in the hole of childbirth." For the Gourmantché, all births take place in pairs, and they say this clearly in comparing the placenta to a twin. But it is not possible to stay paired for long, and the midwife's knife must soon make the separation. The placenta is, to be sure, the object of rites meant to provide it with a sort of perennity (it is put into a pot of water, soon provided with a cover; the pot itself will be buried near the threshold of the new mother's hut). But it is clear that the life that is thus granted to the placenta is not the same as the life that it shared with its "companion" while still in the womb. Denying that the placenta can die in its pot full of water amounts, in fact, to saying that it has been given over to a certain kind of death. On the level of what ought to be done, the question of leaving the child with his placenta does not arise. But these beings who live in the bush, wrapped up in their placentas, bear clear witness to the fact that the effects of this separation remain no less an enigma for mankind.

In search of a solution to the enigma posed by the fact that the birth of a single child necessitates the intervention of the bush as a third-party space [*espace tiers*], we have gradually been led to reexamine the notion of village territory. Suggesting the idea of a body-space on this subject, we tried to show that to attain the existence of a village being, one could not escape the necessity of having to integrate into one's own body that other body that is the village territory. In relation to this necessity, we have sought to outline the respective

15. It is likely that the *poli* also reveals the way to "see" wild animals.
16. For a detailed analysis of this question, see "Les yeux captifs."

positions that are occupied by the newborn "bad twin," the child of a single birth hesitating to cross a threshold, and the adult female twin about to be married. Since the description of certain rituals connected with twins has seemed constantly to evoke the figures of the *pola* of the bush, we tried to read their specific traits as so many signs bearing witness to the question put by the village. It was one of these traits, the mysterious *bu-gambu* net, that suddenly gave rise to the question of the placenta. The placental problematic which we have briefly redefined will now allow us to specify the problem of limits, both of the body and of the territory.

These *pola*, whose body-space does not go beyond the limits of their placental envelopes, I would hypothesize, have no other territory that that whose boundaries are marked by the net that enfolds them. A number of their characteristic traits lend support to this hypothesis.

Unlike men, who "confirm" their territory by surveying it step by step, the *pola* walk with their feet crossed, always hopping, never marking the ground with a print the length of a foot. Nothing in the movement of the *pola* suggests that they have their own specific territory; on the contrary, they are said to be always unstable, always moving, and that they meander in all directions through the bush. Village people do, to be sure, assign them places in which they are believed to be met with most often (clearings in the bush). That such places do not constitute a territory can be deduced from the fact that these *pola*, even though they are so unstable, can go from this place to another, from the bush to the village and from village to bush, without, it seems, any peril to their power—as if they were at home in any place, carrying along with them, wherever they might go, the space of the bush.

The only place outside of which they lose their invisibility and thus come under the power of the human eye, is their *bu-gambu*. Outside the *bu-gambu* they are vulnerable, defenseless, and must give up their secrets. This clearly suggests that it is really the *bu-gambu* itself that represents what is usually called a territory.

We might think that the *pola* would lose their power upon entering a village. The facts that we have reported show that this is not the case at all. That their power remains unimpaired even within the village territory is perfectly well known to the women who, instead of driving the *pola* away, save them a piece of the cake. Because he has entered a territory which by definition is alien to his own, an intruder is always vulnerable, from one side or the other. He can be driven out. But the *pola*, creating a veritable territorial enclave inside a foreign territory, cannot be driven out. The fear they inspire in women is linked to the recognition of the *pola's* faculty of "settling in" at a place they like. Once established in these places, the *pola*, as we have seen, are securely in their own territory wherever they might be, and cannot be dislodged.

The most widely feared intervention of the *pola* is a kidnapping, which can take a number of forms. What is the nature of this kidnapping?

They say that after the *pola* have gotten hold of the "best part" of a fetus in the womb, or the little bit of life left to a sick person of the village, they go off to feed this to their children.[17] But what kind of children could these be, the children of beings that have never been separated from their placentas? What are they themselves in relation to the child? And so what are they looking for when they practice their other forms of capture, the abduction of a child already born, or the usurpation of the place in the womb of a child to be born?

These questions are too complex to be answered here. We will simply outline two hypotheses.

The existence of placental beings in the bush bears witness to the fact that the separation of the child from his placenta has lasting effects. For the child there was a loss at birth, an irreparable loss since it involved "a second self," "more yourself than you are yourself." When a child is amputated from his second self, has he not been so weakened that his life must be feared for? In this abstract form, the question would probably never arise. But it arises nonetheless, for twins, through the mediation of *pola,* serve, as it were, as silent bearers of the question. A child is dead, and the cause of death is attributed to a kidnapping by the *pola.* Something happens in this situation which comes like an echo of what happened at birth. It is as if the *pola* had just said to the women whose children they had taken: by amputating from them that net from which we are never apart, you have caused the death of these children.

But another interpretation is possible. What does the *poli* who has come to steal the child wear if not, as it were, the emblems that the child he has come for lacks? We say emblems, for while he is the bearer of the placenta, the *poli* is also the bearer of the number 2, a number forever lost to the child of a single birth. Separated from his placenta, the *poli* falls to the mercy of the hunter. In coming to take a child, what is this being of the bush doing but seeking to remove the risk that the secrets still held by the child (who is still so close to placental life and to his correlate, the "2") might be divulged?

While it is difficult here to prolong this reflection on the *pola's* kidnappings, as well as on the "lust for life" so apparent in these beings who are nevertheless endowed with the extraordinary life-power represented by the *bu-gambu,*[18] the placenta, on the other hand, introduces us to the other fundamental aspect of these dwarfs of the bush, which makes them doubly twins: every *poli,* paired with his placental net, is also twin to another *poli.* This reduplication of duality is found in the village in the form of twin births. In this case, instead of an

---

17. At the fall of night the sick are brought out of their huts, to prevent, they say, the *pola,* who are numerous at this hour, from taking away their lives.

18. The *jiindi* (another category of bush beings) are taken to be young men who have died before having sexual relations. I do not exclude the hypothesis that the *pola* are children who have only known intrauterine life. These children, buried with their placenta, cannot be said to have come to life, as children, in the village. Nor can they be said to have died as children.

organism divided in two (the child of a single birth and his placenta), we find two separate organisms. After the cord has been cut, there will still be two of them there.

The *bu-gambu* is compared not to the placenta in general but to the placenta of twins. Without going into details, I will simply say that a placenta of twins is not treated ritually in the same way as the placentas of children of single births. It is lodged between two forked sticks, as if it were supposed to be hung up in the pot that receives it. It is when the *bu-gambu* is hung in the *diabougli* tree, as has been mentioned, that the hunter suddenly catches sight of it. If, through the hunter's intervention, the net touches the ground, then the *poli* must reveal his secrets. If the midwife commits some error in treating the placentas of twins, then the twins will become "blind for the bush," and will themselves strike the midwife blind.

Twins reveal at least "one" of the emblems that characterize the *pola,* the emblem that we have called the "2." Twins go in pairs. Both of them have, of course, been separated from their placentas, but the power that is attributed to them (the ability to see into the bush, etc.) is reminiscent of that which is attributed to the little people of the bush, as if living with one's twin meant living, as the *pola* do, with the representative of one's placenta. This is something we have been expecting. The *pola's* intervention in the case of twins cannot be in the form of a capture. Rather than a taking of life, it is a case of the *pola* taking on life within the "body-space of the village."

This power of having been able to escape placentary mutilation which village people attribute to the *pola,* leaves them no less shiftless and greedy. In seeking to come to life as twins, aren't they saying as well that the instrument of their power is also the instrument of their alienation, and that they are quite ready to sacrifice it?

So the question is turned back. In the village, no one has the right to keep his placenta. And as for the beings that seem to have a choice in the matter, nothing gives us any assurance that they are really quite alive.

And it could be shown that this return of the question implied in the intervention of the bush reappears in all the situations in which the inscription of a territory again poses the problem of the boundaries of the body itself.

Michel Izard

	Transgression, Transversality,
13	Wandering

In the Mooga (or "Mossi") kingdom of Yatênga (Upper Volta) there are people called *yaralentîise* (singular *yaralentîiga*), a word that can be translated fairly closely as "they who are hung in trees." Who are these people?

The immediate answer is: they are people who have had sexual relations with animals, the act of bestiality being envisaged only as the copulation of a man with a female donkey. Whatever the case for this reference to bestiality, the state of the *yaralentîiga*, the result of a singular event, is presented first of all as an individual state. To be a *yaralentîiga* is to have become one, not to have always been one; someone who is not a *yaralentîiga* has not become one, but could still do so. But the passage to the *yaralentîiga* state can also be effected by the transmission of a trait, a sort of social gene, following two main modalities: by sexual contact between a man and a woman; by undifferentiated descent. One becomes *yaralentîiga* by having sexual relations with a *yaralentîiga;* the children of a *yaralentîise* couple are *yaralentîise.* If someone becomes *yaralentîiga*, his/her sexual partner(s) do not also become so because of having had sexual relations with him/her before the event marking the change of state, but they do if they continue to have relations after this event. The children born to someone before he or she becomes *yaralentîiga* are not *yaralentîise,* only those born after the event, during the same period that there will be transmission of the *yarlentîiga* "trait" through sexual relations.

An earlier version of this text served as the outline for a presentation in Claude Lévi-Strauss's seminar on "Ethnological Considerations on the Idea of Prohibition" at the Collège de France, under the title "Les mauvais morts" (November 1976).

229

The notion of a transmission of the *yaralentīiga* trait both horizontally and vertically takes us a considerable way from the first reference to the *yaralentīiga* as an individual freely engaging in a real sexual transgression. For everything happens as if a single act of bestiality was, certainly, necessary, but also sufficient to found the existence of a population of *yaralentīise* from a source in a single person. A distinction should, however, be introduced into this population between transmission through sexual relations, which involves no diminution of the *yaralentīiga* trait's substance, and transmission by undifferentiated descent, which is accompanied by such a loss; this would lead one to think that vertical transmission would lead to the extinction of the trait as society's memory for this type of transmission weakens progressively (and provided that no mutation causes this mechanical course to change). To mark this difference, the Moose distinguish "black" *yaralentīise* (the first mode of transmission) from "blue" *yaralentīise* (the second mode).

There is now almost nothing left of the first definition I gave of the *yaralentīiga* state; to speak only of black *yaralentīise*, I will simply say that this state comes from sexual contact with another *yaralentīiga*, whatever the nature of what is transmitted in this contact. Let us imagine then that someone becomes *yaralentīiga* through this latter process. He cannot know what has happened to him, for this would mean that he knows how it happened and from whom he got the *yaralentīiga* trait: an impossible hypothesis to maintain, for if you know the identity of a *yaralentīiga* you carefully avoid all contact with him or her, not only all sexual (male/female) contact, but any relationship that might directly (male/female) or indirectly (male/male or female/female) leave one open to the accusation of sexual contact, since any *yaralentīiga* may have "contaminated" those close to him or her, of the same or the opposite sex. For fear of an accusation of sexual contact, one avoids spending the night under a *yaralentīiga's* roof, that is, under the roof of a family of *yaralentīise*, or even going into the courtyard of the family residence. Here then is a trait that is transmitted unbeknown to at least one of the partners involved in the relationship of transmission, namely, the partner who was not a *yaralentīiga* to begin with but who is going to become one. But since someone who has become a *yaralentīiga* without knowing it can transmit the trait in turn, it is evident that it is the others who manipulate the transmission of the trait in question. One always becomes *yaralentīiga* without knowing it, wherever in the chain of transmission one finds oneself. And it is all the more difficult to be sure of the moment when this mutation occurred in oneself since the justification of the transmission is finally constituted only through public rumor. One is rumored to be a *yaralentīiga* within a society whose ability to create an infamous reputation is all the more complete since such a reputation is not usually based on any proof; the group does not need proof and does not bother to look for proof to sustain a conviction which it forges for itself in the imaginary.[1] Since the group manipulates the supposed

1. TN: *L'imaginaire* is a concept borrowed from recent French psychoanalysis; see J. Laplanche and J. -B. Pontalis, *The Language of Psychoanalysis* (New York, 1973), p. 210.

facts of transmission, it follows that the group as a whole holds the means of reproduction of the smaller group, unconscious of itself, of the *yaralentīise* of the kingdom.

A *yaralentīiga* does not usually know that he is becoming one at a particular moment; instead he ends up finding out that he has become one. A man is reputed to be a *yaralentīiga*. No integral system of social avoidance is put into place around him, but the surrounding group makes sure that he does not get a wife, that old marital agreements are broken, that no more women visit his courtyard or maintain relations with his wives, etc. After a certain period of time, which evidently varies depending on the avoidance procedures used, the unfortunate fellow understands what is happening to him and so can only choose between confrontation—to attempt to prove that he has been outlawed unjustly by society—or renunciation. Among the Samo, western neighbors of the Moose of Yatênga, where the institution of the *zama* is exactly homologous to that of the *yaralentīise*, to prove one's innocence means submitting to an ordeal specifically for *zama*, the results of which count as absolute proof of the total guilt or innocence of the plaintiff. As far as I know no such thing exists in Yatênga, and trying to prove one's innocence there means getting the lineage to sponsor a trial in public view and public knowledge. With the ordeal we are in the realm of belief: the imaginary of suspicion or rumor and the violence of the rite are logically articulated. To conduct a trial is to try to put back into doubt a conviction that is a conviction solely as the effect of a preverse consensus. The enterprise is usually so difficult that even the most determined give up, shaken from the first, as they are, by the very fact of the accusation. The *yaralentīiga* person has, for himself and others, become a *yursoba*, someone whose name is "spoiled." Someone who learns that he is reputed to be a *yaralentīiga*—that he is a *yaralentīiga*—is socially a dead man, one who knows he is dead but cannot kill himself, since he knows the treatment that would be in store for his corpse. This living dead man who will not let himself die for fear of what will happen after his death has no choice, for fleeing from an unliveable world, other than social death: eternal flight toward some place where no one knows who he is.

There is, then, one event that irreversibly reveals the *yaralentīiga*: this is death. Two cases should be considered. Nothing stops us from supposing that a man may live out his destiny as a *yaralentīiga* to the end, even if the group maintains perfect silence about his state; the man dies and silence has to be broken, since even if it is possible to let a *yaralentīiga* live more or less normally, it is not possible to bury him where he lived, in the earth where the people of his village are buried: the earth does not accept the corpses of *yaralentīise* and punishes the group that, deliberately or not, would transgress its commandments, by calling down an endless drought upon the cultivated land. The presence of a *yaralentīiga*'s corpse in the earth stops the rain from falling. The *yaralentīiga* who has lived in ignorance of his state becomes an accursed corpse, like any of the *yaralentīise*, with the added burden that the lateness of the revelation will have a chain of effects on all those close to him, first of all his wives and children, who, if the group's silence also included them, have waited until the moment of this death to find out what they are. A different situation is that of a man on whom no suspicion has ever fallen. He dies and is buried normally. But suddenly the rains burst forth disastrously, the crops are destroyed. Earth masters and diviners are consulted to find the reasons—they can be quite diverse—for the disaster that has fallen upon the village. In the end, a consultation reveals the cause of the calamity: a *yaralentfiga* has been buried without the knowledge of the people of the community. Once the *yaralentfiga's* identity has been discovered, his corpse must be disinterred and subjected to the fate it should have undergone at death. Shame and scandal come to the family, for this postmortem revelation may well reveal to the group a whole series of living or dead *yaralentfise:* for example, the dead man's widows, and so those who have inherited them, etc. Among the Samo, as Françoise Héritier has pointed out, those who find out that they are *zama* in this way may not have recourse to the ordeal.[2]

So the body of a *yaralentfiga* is not buried. Without any preparatory treatment (mortuary washings, shaving of the hair, etc.), the corpse is wrapped in a used mat and carried by young men as far as the edge of the village lands (the territory within which there is obedience to the earth master of the locale), toward Renea, the village of the *yaralentfise* (in the northwest of the kingdom, near the border with Samo country). The transportation of the corpse takes place in a great uproar. When they reach their destination, the bearers put the cadaver on the ground and call the young men of the neighboring village on their small arm-held drums; they they run away, without looking back, and return to their village. New bearers arrive and take the body on another stage of its journey toward Renea. In the end the *yaralentfiga* reaches his destination.

Renea, which means "meeting," is a large village, very long established on relatively rich soil; a prosperous village, with a reputation for beautiful and fertile women. Renea is located in a small region of Yatênga inhabited by Kalamse, who are culturally closer to the Dogon than to the Samo. An examination of the "ethnic" composition of the village shows it to contain Silmîise (Peul) who have "become" Kalamse, Moose who have kept their original (?) identity, and Kibse (Dogon). The village is under the command of an earth master, who bears the title of "chief gravedigger" *(laraad naaba)*. One of Renea's five wards, called Lo, is inhabited by Kibse. Here is what they say about it:[3]

A man from Renea had two wives. When the rainy season was approaching, the man's first wife sowed gourd seeds in his maize field. When the maize

2. The Samo data concerning the *zama* have been presented by Françoise Héritier in *La charivari, la mort et la pluie* (Paris, 1977), text of a presentation made in April 1977 in the context of a roundtable discussion organized by the Ecole des Hautes Etudes en Sciences Sociales, on the theme: "Social Tensions and Age Classes: the Charivari." Cf. the same author's "La paix et la pluie. Rapports d'autorité et rapport au sacré chez les Samo," *L'Homme* 13, no. 3 (1973): 121–38, especially p. 132, n. 1.

3. On the village of Renea and the tradition of the ward of Lo, cf. my work in preparation, "Les archives orales d'un royaume africain. Recherches sur la formation du Yatênga."

was harvested, the animals trampled on the gourds, so the wife asked her co-wife to give her a canari (container) with holes in it to protect her plants. Soon the fruits appeared and the second wife asked the first to give back her canari with holes in it. The first wife said to her, "I can't give back your canari with holes in it, since I cannot take it off without tearing out the bottoms of the gourds; after I have harvested the gourds I will give it back." The second wife kept on asking for her canari; the first wife offered to give her a new canari, but she refused. In the end the first wife had to tear out the bottoms of her gourds to give the canari with holes in it back to her co-wife. When she gave back the canari with holes in it, the first wife cursed her co-wife, so that ever since then her descendants have been *yaralentîise*.

Another version of this story specifies that the first wife had the inhabitants of the village intercede with the co-wife to convince her to accept a new canari.[4] This attempt at mediation by the people of the village remained without result, the first wife gave back the canari with holes in it and "accused all the people of complicity with her co-wife, declared that such an act had never before been seen, and that in fact the whole village had violated custom, (and so) its inhabitants should be treated as *yaralentîise.*" "Word spread around Yatênga and since then the inhabitants of Renea have been (considered) *yaralentîise* and condemned to marry only among themselves. From that time on, no Mooga[5] of Yatênga has been willing to spend a night in Renea, for fear of being accused of having (had) sexual relations with an inhabitant of the village."

What relationship can be established between the external *yaralentîise*, whose social status is linked to the real or imaginary accusation of bestiality, and the *yaralentîise* of Renea, victims of the gourd woman's curse? To try to clarify this problem it is worth making a brief detour through Samo country. The *zama* are comparable to the *yaralentîise* except for the fact that for the Samo necrophilia plays the role which the reference to bestiality plays among the Moose of Yatênga. *Zama* corpses are brought to the village of Turu just as those of *yaralentîise* are brought to Renea, and just as the inhibitants of Renea are assimilated to the *yaralentîise*, the people of Turu are assimilated to the *zama*. However, the curse upon the inhabitants of Turu ("gravediggers") does not give the same source as that of the people of Renea, and it is this difference that matters to us here. Here is how Françoise Héritier sums up the Samo myth in question:

Men came down from the sky, which was stricken with overpopulation, onto the earth, led by the gravedigger, by means of a chain forged by the blacksmith, whose incandescent hammer attached to the end of the chain dried off the earth which had previously been covered with water. God, who had shown men the path to follow, had specified that all unknown things should go to the blacksmith in recompense for his labor. The earth was by definition something unknown, but the gravedigger, seeing what he could get

4. The variants given here have been drawn from Seydou Ouédraogo's unpublished work, "Note sur les yaghlen-tissé au Yatenga," (Ouagadougou, n.d.), p. 2.
    5. The singular of Moose.

out of it once he was on the ground, decided to take it for himself. For this he used a trick. He told the people, contrary to the blacksmith's assurances, that God had given *him* the earth and suggested, to decide the matter, to leave the judgment to the earth itself. He had previously put his younger brother in a covered pit, dug at the spot where the chain had touched the ground. When the questions were asked . . . , the gravedigger's younger brother, speaking for the earth, lied, agreeing with his elder brother and disagreeing with the blacksmith. The elder brother came to dig his younger brother up the next night. But the latter refused to live with him any more, and decided, having experienced to his great discomfort and horror *the heat of the earth* [Héritier's emphasis], that he did not want to be buried after his death. He wandered from village to village in Samo country and finally settled [in] Turu.[6]

The gravedigger's younger brother was thus the first *zama*. The origin of the curse on Renea is a failure of the given word, a veritable false oath by Mooga ethical standards; the origin of the curse on Turu is a lie, here too put to the service of a false oath. In both cases we are dealing with a serious moral fault, a transgression of the social order that, in both cases, was grafted onto the order of the world by, precisely, the mediation of the earth. In the Samo myth, the role which the gravedigger makes the earth play, the way in which he uses the earth, are clearly indicated. The earth was offended, it reacted to the violence that had been done to it by releasing a heat which the gravedigger's younger brother interpreted as a rejection, a refusal to welcome him into the earth; in this respect, trees, in relation to the earth, hold in their branches a kind of antitomb capable of receiving those whom the earth does not want. At Renea, the story of gourds and pottery, far less immediately dramatic than the events of the Samo tale, may also involve the earth in a very direct way. We should remember first of all the nature of the foundations of the land law that prevails in the West African regions we are considering. (1) There is no territory over which no mastery of the earth is exercised. (2) Several distinct rights may be exercised over a single territory, from the most ancient and most eminent (mastery of the earth) to the most recent (right of most recent effective usage). (3) All rights in land are transmissible, but only within descent groups, each of which is the holder of one such right: these rights are thus inalienable, with the exception of individual rights of effective user, which are alienable in principle but in fact are the object of transmission from person to person within a restrained segmentary group which holds the immediately anterior right of user. (4) The death of a segmentary right-holder means the reversion of the right he held to the immediately superior segmentary unit. (5) In principle, all rights of user are erased at the end of a cycle of exploitability of the land (the maximum interval between two long-term fallow periods); in fact, putting land into fallow maintains a priority for the segmentary group which formerly held rights of user in case of con-

6. Héritier, *La charivari*, pp. 4–5.

cession of a new right of user after the fallow period. (6) The earth does not refuse itself: this principle founds the tacit contract between the effective user of a piece of land and the holder of the immediately anterior right, and more generally is the basis for the articulation between the two different rights to which the earth is subject. (7) The earth does not take back its own, which follows from the preceding principle.

The co-wife of Renea holds a first right over the pot she gives to the first wife, to whom she grants a right of user. The co-wife cannot refuse to give this pot to the first wife and, having given it, she cannot take it back, which does not mean that the first wife cannot consider giving it back, thus annulling her right of user. If we leave aside the question of the gourd seeds, the first wife cannot refuse to give this same pot to a third person, as long as she informs her co-wife of the fact: a pot, like any other object, and like the earth, can thus be the object of successive rights, without the accumulation of these rights having the least effect on the free use made of the object by the last holder. At Turu there is a misappropriation of the universal mastery over the earth; at Renea there is a demand for inverting the direction of the transmission of rights. In both cases there is transgression of the world order and/or the social order. The earth intervenes in human lives in two ways. It intervenes first of all as guarantor of the social order, as the supreme juridical authority to decide on good and evil: the earth judges, punishes, and may kill. It also intervenes as guarantor of human prosperity, as the cosmic force that fertilizes cultivated soil with rain, and, being itself this soil, as the bearer of cultivated plants. At Turu, the presence in the earth's body of this untruthful young gravedigger is a presence refused by this supreme authority, judge of men; at Renea, what the earth contains—the seeds, then the bottoms of the gourds—is accepted by the earth as congruent with its practical vocation, and it is the uprooting of these plants that is refused. At Turu as at Renea, the earth is insulted.

At Turu, a living man is put inside the earth; he takes the place of a dead man. From this substitution, identification, or even negation of the division between the living and the dead is born a first subversion of the world order and the social order: the gravediggers take the place of the blacksmiths. If there is an identification living=dead, the living/dead pair is formerly equivalent to the pairs living/living (couple of procreation) and dead/dead (a "couple" that is unmarked in sexual terms). The reproduction of the human community, which the Moose associate with the unity of mastery over the earth or *tênga*, marked by the presence of an earth altar (also called *tênga*), requires both the separation of the world of the dead (*kĩimse*, "ancestors") from that of the living, and the existence of a ritual mode of articulation between these two worlds (funerals, regular sacrifices in "ancestor sanctuaries," *kĩims roodo*, on tombs, and on individual altars dedicated to the ancestor from whom one gets one's name, the *sigsoba*). Insofar as the act of necrophilia establishes a practical (sexual) conjunction between a dead person and a living person, it upsets this dialectic of continuity and rupture between the dead and the living; it causes an inversion of the biological process of the community's reproduction by a negation of the necessary link between copulation and procreation; it plunges the ancestors into social nothingness. This is a second subversion of the order of things, which we have tried to show has profound affinities with the first.

At Renea, it is seeds that are put into the earth. The territorial space called *tênga* is divided into a human space and a wild space. The first is that of men, domestic animals, and domestic plants; the second is that of the *kinkîrse*—small invisible beings whose society duplicates that of men—wild animals, and wild plants. Humans and *kinkîrse,* domestic and wild animals, cultivated and non-cultivated plants are not opposed in the same way as are the living and the dead in the human world. Here space replaces time as referent. With one exception, we discover a dialectic similar to the preceding one, separating and associating connected universes which partially interpenetrate: certain men can "see" the *kinkîrse;* a *kinkîrga* can penetrate a woman's womb in place of a human child; hunting and gathering are human interventions into wild nature. The relationship between man and domesticated nature grounds the economic order of the community, whose main constituent elements are pastoralism [*élevage*] and agriculture. The co-wife of Renea, by forcing the first wife to pull up her gourds, introduces a subversion into the human treatment of domestic plants; she inverts the relationship of man to domesticated nature. The act of bestiality introduces a comparable inversion. With necrophilia we had a biological antireproduction; now we have an antipastoralism (bestiality as the negation of animal reproduction) which is articulated with the biological antireproduction of the group to the very extent that, in order to reproduce itself, the human species must have both procreation and a social harnessing of nature, from which it draws its subsistence. If we provisionally accept the hypothesis of a permutability of the human treatments of domestic animals and domestic plants, we may pass from the vegetal crime of Renea to the bestial crime of the *yaralentîise*. Here we have indifferentiation between the living and the dead, a doubly negative articulation of the relation of man to nature: necrophilia and bestiality mark two inversions, that of the passage from the world of the sky (living/dead indifferentiation) to the world of the earth (living/dead distinction and articulation), that of the passage from nature (separation between humans, on the one hand, wild animals and plants on the other) to culture (separation and articulation between humans on the one hand, domestic animals and plants on the other).

In an articultural society, the agents of the continuous passage from nature to culture are the holders of mastery over fire: blacksmiths, ironworkers, whose women, in Yatênga, are potters. In a pastoral society, as among the Peul of Yatênga, there corresponds to this group of blacksmiths that of woodworkers, called *laobe* in Fulfulde or *setba* in Moore. Blacksmiths make the tools necessary for working the earth (hoes), for cooking and eating foods (baked earthenware containers); they also make the tools for the "struggle" against "wild" men (war) and wild animals (hunting)—spears and arrowheads; and against wild plants (land-clearing)—axes. The *laobe* make the tools for milking and making butter. These people, blacksmiths and *laobe,* form endogamous groups in the society we are considering, and it is germane to note that those who do not belong to these groups but have sexual relations with their members are considered *yaralentîise.* This is not, however, the case for members of the royal lineage, the *nakombse.* Everything happens as if respect for the right direction [*le "bon" sens*] [7] of the passage from nature to culture went along with a concern to close up into its own historical destiny the group of people who ensure that passage. We could further develop this theme of the blacksmith's place in society, noting that he alone may dig the earth to bury the dead (a perpetuation of the passage from sky to earth, when the fall of the iron chain forged by the blacksmiths hollowed out a hole in the ground) and that the blacksmith's space (mines, high furnaces, forges) defines an intermediate space between human and wild space, since, while it is indeed a human space, it is neither inhabited nor cultivated. [8]

Our first questions about the nature of the *yaralentîise* have led us to a reflection on the passage from nature to culture and the construction of social space. But why does the opprobrium that weighs on *yaralentîise* take the form of an accusation of sexual transgression, even if only in a metaphorical sense?

One should not copulate on the ground: this is one of the cardinal prohibitions of the Mooga social code; in this regard the *yaralentîise* are transgressors even in transgression itself. In plain language: one must make love in one's bed. Everything suggests that one should also die in one's bed. The transgressor par excellence, the *yaralentîiga,* copulates on the bare ground and dies outside his home, whether he is exiled for life or, dying in his own village, his corpse is denied the care customarily due to the dead. If the *yaralentîiga* has not left his village while alive, he will leave it after death, for Renea. Here we can see in outline a generalization of the socialization of space. The human space/wild space opposition does not intervene in the closed framework of a village territorial unit but involves the whole world, centered on a given village, in such a way that the "wild" earth is boundless, while the human space is deepened by means of repeated supplementary distinctions (for example: cultivated space/inhabited space, village inhabited space/lineage inhabited space, lineage inhabited space/family inhabited space). Everything that does not belong to the place where a man was born, where he has procreated, where he has honored his ancestors, where he is destined to die, is unknown, dangerous space, bearer of the incite-

---

7. TN: This is a pun on two meanings of the word *sens,* which means both "sense, meaning" and "direction." In normal usage *le bon sens* means "good sense" or "common sense." By stressing the *bon,* in this context, the author shifts to a directional meaning, "the good direction, the right direction," while "common sense," with all its connotations, continues to hover in the background.

8. On the place of blacksmiths and *laobe* in Yatênga society, see my article: "La nature, les hommes, le roi," in *Systèmes de signes. Textes réunis en hommage à Germaine Dieterlen* (Paris, 1978), pp. 299–305.

ment to transgression. Here there appears an encoding of the individual destiny which, in reference to the earth, takes account of the opposition between the human center and the wild periphery, between immobility and wandering, between a relationship to the earth mediated by the human presence and an immediate relationship with the earth, the former beneficient, the latter malign. Not to copulate, not to die on the bare earth—whether the residual of the wild earth inside human space, or the wild space itself—amount to the same thing.

In this regard it may be enlightening to examine the fate reserved for certain dead bodies other than those of *yaralentîise*. The Moose give the name of "bad dead" *(samporoba)* to those who have died in conditions requiring ritual interventions distinct from those of ordinary funerals, whether these conditions involve the circumstances of death or peculiarities proper to the person when alive. Besides *yaralentîise*—the only *samporoba* who are not buried—the "bad dead" include: those who have died by accident (struck by lightning, drowned, burnt alive, etc.), suicides, men who died during the pregnancy of one of their wives, women who died in labor, albinos, hunchbacks, and also—here we find our subject once again—warriors killed in battle and hunters killed by wild animals (with the exception of *nakombse* in both cases).

The warrior and the hunter figure par excellence among those individual figures whose lives death transforms into destiny: the "good" warrior, the "good" hunter is the one who comes back home, the former returning victorious—or at least safe—from war, the latter bringing back game. These individual figures take shape as such on "wild" ground, distant or near; they are therefore in constant risk of death on the bare earth, they are in a state of potential transgression.

Let us consider this whole set of nonordinary figures: the Samo *zama*, the Mooga *yaralentîiga*, the warrior and the hunter:

1. the *zama* has sexual relations with the dead;
2. the *yaralentîiga* has sexual relations with animals;
3. the warrior kills "wild" men;
4. the hunter kills wild animals.

The activity—if we may call it that—of the *zama* and the *yaralentîiga* are inscribed in transgression; the activity of the warrior and of the hunter, through its subversion, is inscribed in the same place: the warrior killed by a wild man, the hunter killed by a wild animal. Everything suggests that the earth's positive or negative attitude towards human activity involves, among others, homologous oppositions of the type:

—licit sexual relations/illicit sexual relations;
—procreation/refusal of procreation;
—death given/death received.

The warrior and the hunter are in a state of potential transgression just as the *yaralentíiga* is in a state of assumed transgression. The warrior and the hunter choose their destiny individually and freely; the *yaralentíiga* passively undergoes a destiny chosen by others, without his knowledge. Here transgression is inseparable from social transversality and wandering. The eruption of individual choice—of lived freedom—into a hierarchized social universe, in which the individual is enmeshed in a network through which he is defined implicitly, means a subversion of the order of this universe; here freedom introduces the molecular, the transversal which the dominant ideological conformism sanctions—and so, in a sense, ratifies—when it is manifested as effective transgression in death. That there is a place for everyone and that everyone should stay in his place does not prevent the society from admitting that "displacements" can exist, as long as it is intended that these be only provisional, negative moments—solitary detours between socialized birth and socialized death—which could be said to have the function of reminding men of what each must conquer for himself and for all: the innocent dilution into the group which is the manifestation of peasant wisdom.

We have been speaking of "displacements." The warriors go far away, they route the enemy like hunters track game. Here we have blind, risky wanderings when, as far as peregrinations are concerned, the society knows only closed circularities. In wandering, there is a risk of "loss(es)": not all warriors and hunters come home again, and the ordinary form of social suicide is exile for life, the mark of refusal, and also of madness. In Mooga society warriors and hunters form groups outside the hierarchy, institutionalized as brotherhoods, or, for hunters, as a secret society: warriors and hunters, like boys undergoing circumcision, are initiates who also go into the bush, become *samporoba* if they succumb to their rough treatment, and, after emerging from the initiation camp, transversalize the social hierarchy with a network of solidarities based on membership in the same age-group. Compared with warriors, hunters, and young men undergoing circumcision, the *yaralentíise* form a strange brotherhood indeed, which can, at the limit, be seen as the inverse of a secret society, for instead of the *yaralentíise* knowing who they are while those around them are ignorant of it, it is the rest of society that knows and they themselves who are in the dark.

Warrior and hunter do not have the same place in the society's ideology. In this kingdom, in which an aristocracy of conquerors has imposed its power on a peasant population, the hunter is a figure from before the coming of the state, who brings enough negativity into the agriculturalists' world view for the latter to appear in many foundation legends as obsessively preoccupied with tying hunters down to the earth, reducing them to purveyors of meat for the abusive fathers-in-law who have seduced them with the pleasures of home life. The warrior is first of all the *nabíiga,* son of the chief, or more generally the *nakombga,* son of a *nabíiga* who did not become chief; a powerful man without power who lives in expectation of power and bides his time making war and looting. In the kingdom the name *nakombse* (pl. of *nakombga*) is kept for members of the vast royal lineage, from which the king comes, and a small number of whose members hold commands over villages. The *nakombse* transgress a number of prohibitions: alimentary, marital, and sexual. We have noted that they can have sexual relations with blacksmith women and still not become *yaralentíise;* similarly, a violent death does not make them *samporoba.* The *nakombse* are not exactly in the state of potential transgression; they are, rather, situated beyond norms and transgressions, since access to power, the passage from the status of *nakombga* to that of *naaba,* means a return to the norm. We could even say that they are outside the opposition between hierarchy and transversality, between immobility and wandering: these nobles become tramps from time to time; these kinsmen of well-established chiefs are men without women, without a village, without land.[9]

The morality of the people of the earth *(tengbíise)* establishes in a single movement its norm in social reality and the inverse of the norm in the social imaginary: the absolute transgression of the *yaralentíise,* impossible to surpass, provides the standard for all transgressions. Even if the referent of the absolute transgression is an imaginary one, society must nevertheless be able to point a silent finger at those who transgress, if only to root itself still deeper into the conformism of morality. The passage via the imaginary is necessary for the actual production, in the real, of an antisociety, for in order for the norm to be affirmed, confirmed, reinforced it is necessary both that the transgression be of the order of the unimaginable and that the transgressor take on the banal appearance of one's neighbor. Thus *tengbíise* and *yaralentíise* are indissociable in a rural society devoted to the cult of the earth and the ancestors, in which everyone is born, lives, and dies in his own village, in which the group defines its own measurement of time and is unable to think of space other than as a circle whose borders are, to say the least, hazardous to cross. Between the norm and absolute transgression comes the well-tempered transgression of someone who dares not to be afraid of the possible use of his freedom, who elaborates its notion in action. The hunter, the warrior, the madman are figures of rebellion who manifest that the reign of necessity is never indivisible, that there must be freedom in every society, even if it is there only to be denied. On the historical stage of every lineage, of every village, thus appears from time to time one of those characters about whom they say, "He was quite a guy, he didn't give a damn about anything...," one of those cranks his family hasn't seen in years, or decades, and about whom they soberly say, "He's rambling."

Together, then, *tengbíise* and *yaralentíise* form a society closed in on itself: a lineage-based society of sedentary agriculturalists, whose largest local unit is the village, which is constituted, on a homogeneous territory marked by the pres-

9. M. Izard, "La lance et les guenilles," *L'Homme* 13, no. 3 (1973): 139-49.

ence of an altar, by a certain arrangement of localized lineage segments, the "chiefs" of the lineage, segment, and family being the "elders." The "people of power" who impose their domination on the "people of the earth" introduce the concept of "power" *(naam)* as above and beyond the notion of "earth" *(tênga);* to the divinity Earth *(Tênga)* they oppose and add the divinity Wende, connected with the sky, and found a religious syncretism by associating Napaaga Tenga with Naaba Wende as a chief's wife *(napaaga)* to a chief *(naaba):* feminine earth, masculine sky. The conquerers' society opposes the figure of the "chief" *(naaba)* to that of the "elder" *(kasma)* of the society of the conquered, and introduces the subversive principle (subversive for the people of the earth) according to which "before the chiefs, age means nothing." The order of chiefs is superimposed onto the order of the old. The passage from a society without power to a society of power is thus marked by an inversion-transgression. The people of power initially form an equally closed society, within which there is a split between those who do not hold actual power and those who do, between the *nakombse* and the *nanamse* (plural of *naaba).* Within the society of the people of power the *nakombse* are wanderers who refuse to till the earth (and, more generally, refuse all work), who live off war and plunder, form a group of marginals living in expectation of or in nostalgia over its loss; the *nanamse* have a place (they rule villages), earth, women, and servants. The chiefs are at ease in their historical role. In relation to the *nanamse*, the *nakombse* are in a situation that cannot but remind us, in a highly attenuated form, of that of the *yaralentîise* in relation to the *tengbîise.* In the society of people of the earth, morality had to pose the existence of its opposite in order to exist itself. In the society of people of power, a single ethical system takes different, even opposed, forms depending on whether we are looking at those who hold power or those who do not, the ethicality of the chiefs presupposing the morality of the people. For the duality people-of-the-earth/people-of-power exists in history only to be superseded in politics: in order for the ideological discourse of power to be given as universal—which it must not fail to do—it is necessary and sufficient for it to take on the same moral language as that of its subjects, the better to delimit the sphere of its own political intervention. The *tengbîise* do not separate their resigned acceptance of the power of the chiefs from an attitude of avoidance towards the *nakombse,* who are feared and despised. As for the chiefs, they are able to exercise their power only by keeping their wild juniors at a distance, and making sure the latter manifest their predatory tendencies farther from, rather than nearer to, themselves and their subjects.

   This articulation of people of power to people of the earth defines a first form of the centralization of power, locally or regionally based, the network of local commands thus presupposing close segmentary relations between chiefs, and the figure of the sovereign emerging only through segmentarity: a king among his barons. The process of centralization at work from the first establishments of local commands leads to the sovereign's isolation in a transcendence of the duality between people of power and people of the earth. Characteristic in this respect is the passage from localities with a chief and an earth master to royal localities without chiefs—since the king resides or can reside there—and whose territoriality is outside the division of space into units of mastery over the earth. In the sovereign the subjects' morality and the ethicality of the chiefs, the reference to Tênga and to Wende, are totalized. But the radical differentiation of sovereignty is not separable from the constitution of a State apparatus, whose principal mark is the emergence of the group of royal servants and especially royal captives. These are wanderers from outside the kingdom, people who have been made prisoners, tossed about by history, and fixed in places of power around the solitary and immobile figure of the king. It is in the practical work of the people of the State apparatus that the concept of "force" *(panga)* is differentiated: the king is "master of force" *(pangsoba),* the people of the king's household are "people of force" *(pasdemba).* The concept of *panga* appears as a transcendence of *naam* and of "right," *buum,* which means both "justice" and "truth." The Moose say: "When *panga* follows the road, *buum* cuts across the bush"; *panga* is no longer *naam* in its immediate evidence, rallying consensus by an appeal to the legitimation of the earth—it is the violence of power. But on the level of the people of force the king and his servants do not occupy the same position; they are distinguished as the bestiary of fables distinguishes the lion from the hyenas who, say the Moose, "know the way to the henhouse." On one side, there is the solar effigy of the monarch as dispenser of boons; on the other, a sombre brood of men-at-arms, executioners, secret sacrificers, keepers of regalia, courtesans. Like the *nakombse,* the royal captives frighten people: beyond the death that they have escaped, they infest places of power and get their hands dirty; the *tengbîise* avoid *nakombse* and royal captives without discriminating between them: the former must capture wives, the latter marry among themselves and enjoy privileged marital relations with the king. The royal captives *(bingdemba)* who share the *nakombse's* lack of concern for the ordinary moral code, who can with all impunity steal, plunder, and kill, since they do it in the name of the king, have their own *cursus honorum* at court, at the top of which the chief of the royal captives ia a holder of *naam,* one of the four highest dignitaries of the royal government; of the members of the electoral college charged with selecting the king from among the candidates to the throne, it is before this chief that the designated candidate first prostrates himself.[10]

This is a society with three levels: people of the earth, people of power, people of force; an ideology is elaborated at each of these levels: that of right *(buum),* that of power *(naam),* and that of force *(panga).* Level 1 corresponds to a pre-state agricultural society, level 2 to a state society in formation, level 3 to a State with a governmental apparatus. Each of these levels has its own equilibri-

10. M. Izard, "Les captifs royaux dans l'ancien Yatênga," in C. Meillassoux, ed., *L' esclavage en Afrique précoloniale* (Paris, 1975), pp. 281-95; cf. also "L'odyssée du pouvoir," *Dialectiques* 21 (1977): 59-64.

um between two antagonistic but indissociable worlds: among the people of the earth between *tengbȋise* and *yaralentȋise,* among the people of power between *nanamse* and *nakombse,* among the people of force between the king, who bears the title of *Yatênga naaba* ("chief of Yatênga") and the *bingdemba.* Within each of these universes there is an opposition between a subuniverse of the norm and a subuniverse of transgression from the point of view of the social ethic involved. These three universes are solidary amongst themselves while having particular modes of articulation, since, while level 1 can exist autonomously, level 2 presupposes the existence of level 1, and level 3 presupposes the existence of levels 1 and 2. In relation to popular morality, the three-leveled structure of the universes of the earth, of power and of force, corresponds to a progressive weakening of the norm in favor of transgression, each of these universes being viewed as a totalization that includes its opposite moment. But we may also consider the substructure *tengbȋise-nanamse-Yatênga naaba* to represent an axis of the norm, and the substructure *yaralentȋise-nakombse-bingdemba* an axis of transgression; the maximal (ethical) gap between *tengbȋise* and *yaralentȋise* then leads, through the weakening of the difference between norm and transgression in their successive avatars, to a minimal (political) gap between the sovereign and the State apparatus.

The moral world view takes shape among the dominated—the people of the earth—and looks toward the dominators just as the political world view takes shape at the level of central power and looks toward the holders of local power and the mass of the subjects. On each of the social levels that have been considered we have a pole of the norm and a pole of transgression, so that at each of these levels and as a totality, the society is continually producing an inverted image of itself. On one side, all things considered, a world of transgression, transversality, wandering; on the other, a world of the norm, of hierarchy, of immobility. On one side the possible eruption of freedom; on the other the obviousness of necessity. On one side the dilution of temporality in spatiality; on the other the homogeneous and centered space of the transmutation of lived time into history, the place of emergence of a discourse of power with a claim to universal vocation. The unity divides into two, certainly, but only to close in upon itself all the more completely.

Dan Sperber

Appendix **Is Symbolic Thought Prerational?**

The Issue

Many philosophers, psychologists, and anthropologists have assumed that so-called symbolic thought processes are primary, primitive, or prerational. More recently it has been recognized (by Piaget and Lévi-Strauss for instance) that symbolic and rational thought processes are intermingled. This has sometimes been pushed to the point of rejecting the symbolic-rational distinction altogether and of extending the notion of symbolism so as to include all aspects of conceptual thinking. I have criticized this extension in Sperber (1974). Here I wish to argue both against the view that symbolism is prerational and against the view that symbolic and rational thought processes are indistinguishable. In attempting to outline the structure of interaction between the two types of thought processes, I also hope to shed light on some important aspects of symbolic interpretation.

In his survey of cognitive psychology, Ulric Neisser (1967) remarked:

> Historically, psychology has long recognized the existence of two different forms of mental organization. The distinction has been given many names: "rational" vs. "intuitive," "constrained" vs. "creative," "logical" vs. "prelogical," "realistic" vs. "autistic," "secondary process" vs. "primary process." To list them together casually may be misleading. . . . Nevertheless, a common thread runs through all the dichotomies. Some thinking and remembering is deliberate, efficient, and obviously goal-directed; it is usually expe-

This article is reprinted from *Symbol and Sense,* ed. M.L. Foster and S.H. Brandes (New York: Academic Press, Inc., 1980), and is used with the permission of the publisher.

rienced as self-directed as well. Other mental activity is rich, chaotic and inefficient; it tends to be experienced as involuntary, it just "happens." It often
seems to be motivated, but not in the same way as directed thought; it seems
not so much directed towards a goal as associated with an emotion (p. 297).

An equally vague and very similar distinction has been made in anthropology
under many different names: e.g., *logical* versus *prelogical, scientific* versus
magical, and today, usually, *rational* versus *symbolic.* Modern anthropologists
would not dispute the fact that rational thought is, on the whole, deliberate,
efficient, and goal-directed. But as for symbolic thought, they have tried to
show that it may be less chaotic and inefficient than would seem. Rather than
contrasting *rational* and *symbolic* as *consistent* versus *chaotic* and *efficient*
versus *inefficient,* they would prefer *directly consistent* versus *indirectly consistent* and *directly efficient* versus *indirectly efficient.* These interesting qualifications on the part of anthropoligists do not eliminate the similarity in psychologists' and their basic distinction between two different modes of thought. This
distinction should be clarified in two ways: *(a)* Since it is essentially a psychological distinction, even when made by anthropologists, the mental mechanisms
and processes involved should be more explicitly characterized: *(b)* The distinction has been and still is closely linked with the view that symbolic thought is in
some sense prerational; this view should be either developed and justified or
reconsidered and possibly abandoned.

The view that symbolic thought is prerational actually consists of three distinct assumptions:

1. A phylogenetic assumption according to which rational thought is a later
development in the history of the human species, following a first stage where
all thought was symbolic. Lucien Lévy-Bruhl (1910, 1922, etc.), with his notion
of a *pre-logical* stage, was the most cogent exponent of this view which, in spite
of numerous criticisms, notably those of Claude Lévi-Strauss in *The Savage Mind*
(1966), is still commonly held.

2. An ontogenetic assumption, according to which conceptual rationality is
a late acquisition in the history of the organism, the child having first to go (in
the terms of Piaget, 1968) through a stage characterized by *preconceptual* and
symbolic representations.

3. A cognitive assumption about the genesis of individual thoughts, according to which rational thought is a more directed, more attentive development
and exploitation of symbolic thought. In Neisser's terms:

Rational thought is "secondary" in the sense that it works with objects already
formed by a "primary process." If these objects receive no secondary elaboration, as in some dreams and disorganized mental states, we experience them
in the fleeting and imprecise way of iconic memory. However, the same multiple processes that produce these shadowy and impalpable experiences are
also essential preliminaries to directed thinking (Neisser 1967, p. 302).

Although these three assumptions are generally bundled together in one form or another, they are in fact mutually independent, and there is no logical reason to adopt them all simultaneously. On the other hand they could all three be refuted together if it were shown that the reverse of the third assumption were true: If one assumes that symbolic thought is necessarily built on some prior rational processing, symbolism could not have preceded rationality either in the history of humankind or in that of the individual. This is the rather paradoxical assumption I wish to defend. The argument will essentially bear on models in cognitive psychology. However, the choice of such a model may have important implications for both developmental psychology and anthropology.

Something seen, heard, smelt, felt—in other words a stimulus—can undergo several types of mental processing. To begin with, the stimulus can be identified, recognized as falling under a given conceptual category. For instance on hearing a specific sound one may build the corresponding elementary proposition: "This is the sound of a doorbell." Such processing is usually called *perceptual*.

Second, the identified stimulus may evoke other mental representations. For instance, an unexpected doorbell ring may evoke the idea of someone one wishes would come. Such processing has been described in terms of association of ideas, of connotation, of symbolic meaning. Here, I shall use the theoretically more neutral phrase *symbolic evocation*.

Third, the identification of a stimulus may be used as a premise in a logical argument. For instance, from the identification of a doorbell ring, one may infer that someone wants the door opened. Such processing is at the basis of *rational* thought.

Let us term *device* the set of mental operations that are part of the same type of processing. Let us term *perceptual device* a device that accepts as input the information provided by external stimuli, and that yields as output elementary identifying propositions. Let us term *symbolic device* a device that accepts as input propositions (from the perceptual device or from other sources) and that yields as output further propositions *evoked* by the input and retrieved from (or constructed on the basis of) long-term memory (LTM). Let us term *rational device* a device that accepts as input propositions and that yields as output further propositions *logically inferred* from the input (and other premises available in memory).

These notions will permit the characterization of three elementary hypotheses about symbolic and rational thought processes mutually incompatible but each compatible with the most general kind of evidence. Indeed, no obvious evidence precludes considering that the information yielded by the perceptual device is first symbolically and then rationally processed, or is simultaneously processed in both ways or is first rationally and then symbolically processed.

The first hypothesis (figure 1a) is the most commonly accepted: The output of the perceptual device is fed into the symbolic device; the output of the symbolic device can be fed into the rational device (both devices feed from and into memory). This hypothesis fits general intuitions: If no intellectual effort is made or if there is no cause for alertness, evocation tends to be the normal activity of the mind. A variety of loosely connected ideas follow either external stimuli or each other in a seemingly disorderly manner. On the other hand, it takes a certain effort to think rationally, for example, to construct or understand a logical argument. In that case, fewer closely connected ideas are processed in an orderly manner. There appears to be a positive correlation between the energy expended, the selectivity of recall, and the degree of organization of thought. It seems commonsensical to assume that a higher degree of organization, typical of rational

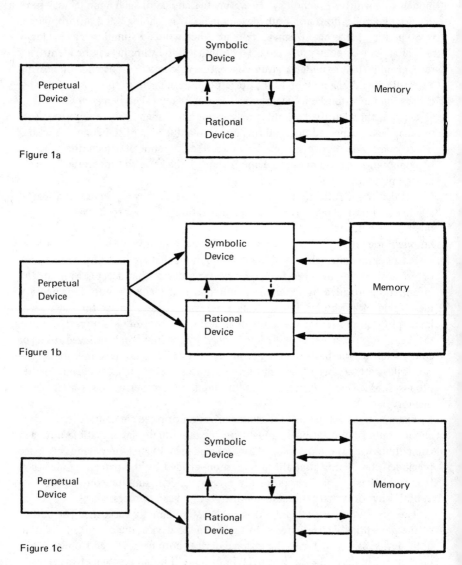

Figure 1a

Figure 1b

Figure 1c

processing, develops from a lower degree of organization typical of symbolic processing, rather than the other way around.

The second hypothesis (figure 1b) is the weakest and the least interesting one: The output of the perceptual device is fed both into the symbolic and into the rational devices. As part of this second hypothesis, it is assumed that according to the level of attention either the symbolic device or the rational device does the greatest part of the overall processing.

The third hypothesis (figure 1c) is the most paradoxical: The output of the perceptual device is fed into the rational device, and the output of the rational device can be fed into the symbolic device. It is assumed that if enough energy is spent on rational processing, symbolic processing need not take place at all. On the other hand, if rational processing is not carried out sufficiently, symbolic processing then takes over. When rational processing is minimal, the overall processing is mostly symbolic and may even give a false impression of being wholly symbolic.

These three hypotheses are compatible with simple introspective evidence. So are three slightly more complex hypotheses that can be constructed from the previous ones by allowing for feedback paths (dotted arrows on figures 1a, 1b, and 1c) and cyclical processing between the symbolic and the rational device. It seems likely that the processing of most information involves such interaction. But even when this element of complexity is incorporated into the model, the problem remains: In this interaction, which kind of processing initiates the cycle? Which device is directly fed the output of the perceptual device? The symbolic one? The rational one? Both simultaneously? The three possible models are still in competition.

There are neither commonsensical nor obvious phylogenetic or ontogenetic grounds to decide between these three models. The issue is rather to determine what kind of further evidence is needed to make a well-grounded selection. For example, relevant evidence would show that rational processing requires at least some prior symbolic processing or that symbolic processing requires at least some prior rational processing, or that neither of these requirements obtains, thereby favoring either the first, the third, or the second hypothesis, respectively. First I shall argue that some rational processing does not require any prior symbolic processing, and second that all symbolic processing does require some prior rational processing. If this argument is accepted, then the cyclical version of the third hypothesis (figure 1c) is to be preferred.

The Symbolic Contribution to Rational Processing

The rational device can be seen as deriving conclusions from premises. Some of these premises are the output of the perceptual device, others are taken from memory. To give just two simplified examples of rational processing:

There is the sound of a bell [premise from the perceptual device] .

When there is the sound of a bell, someone is ringing one [premise from memory].

Someone is ringing a bell [conclusion].

Peter is nodding [premise from the perceptual device].

Whoever nods is answering positively to whatever question he or she has been asked just before [premise from long-term memory].

Peter has just been asked whether he wanted some more coffee [premise from short-term memory].

Peter has answered positively the question as to whether he wanted more coffee [conclusion].

Symbolic processing could contribute (or even be necessary) to rational processing as a means of retrieving propositions from LTM that can then be used as logical premises. There is little reason to doubt that such contributions occur and even play a crucial role in creative thinking. For instance, it makes sense to describe one of the processes involved in scientific discovery as follows: Sometimes the scientist "lets his mind wander" around and about the problem at hand; in other words, the problem is being symbolically processed. It may happen that the considerations thus evoked, however farfetched they may seem at first, will provide crucial premises for a new—rational—treatment of the problem. More trivially, discovering a knot in one's handkerchief triggers a symbolic evocation which, if successful, will provide the additional premises to explain the knot rationally. In both cases a fairly free search of memory provides information which, when combined with propositions that are in the focus of attention, enhances rational understanding: Some symbolic processing is required for full rational processing.

These two typical examples are compatible not only with the "symbolism first" hypothesis, but also (and I would say even more so) with the cyclical versions of the second and third hypotheses. Intuitively, in the preceding cases, symbolic evocation occurs not before rational understanding but between two of its stages. Evocation serves as a kind of heuristic to retrieve from memory information too loosely specified for directed recall, or in Tulving and Pearlstone's terms (1966), information that is *available* but not quite *accessible*. The need for that information, the loose specification of it, the internally generated probe, one might say, is best understood as the outcome of a prior, initial stage of rational processing. For instance the knot example could be described (in a simplified way) as follows:

There is a knot in my handkerchief [premise from the perceptual device].

When there is a knot in my handkerchief it is because I made one in order to be reminded of something when I look at the knot [premise from LTM].

When I made this knot I wanted to be reminded of something [conclusion].

What did I want to be reminded of? [question raised by the conclu-
sion].   (3)

Having reached this stage, either the information in working memory will
provide the answer to the question or there is no logical algorithm, no manageable
sequential procedure that will make it rapidly accessible. The best way then is
to try and recreate the state of mind one had at the time one made the knot. In
order to do this, several cues, chronological, analogical, and otherwise, have to
be followed; varied connections have to be explored; vague suggestions tested.
In other words, symbolic evocation is the appropriate approach. If this description is a fair approximation, then, in this example at least, symbolic processing
must follow upon some prior rational processing and *may*, if successful, trigger
some further rational processing.

Consider, on the other hand, cases where all the information needed for the
rational processing of the input is already present in working memory. This is
typically the case when the input matches prior expectations so that all the
pertinent premises needed to derive relevant conclusions from the input are
already accessible and no symbolic evocation is needed. Example (2) is a case
in point: When one asks a yes–no question, one expects a behavior that stand-
ardly expresses a positive or negative answer. One knows in advance the relevant consequences of such a behavior, and no extra search in LTM is needed to
decide, for instance, to pour some coffee for someone who nodded when asked
whether he or she wanted some.

Similarly, when an experience is familiar (matches standard "schemata"—
see Bartlett 1932; Neisser 1967, 1976; and Norman and Rumelhardt 1975 for
various developments of this notion), no symbolic evocation is necessary. Identifying the stimulus already brings to working memory whatever background
information is needed for rational processing. Example (1) is a case in point:
Recognizing the sound of one's doorbell makes immediately accessible the
required premises that bells ring when triggered by someone, that whoever
rings a bell wants the door opened. A fairly elaborate deduction process may
ensue without ever requiring any loose, evocative, symbolic processing.

In short, there are cases where symbolic evocation provides crucial premises
to rational processing. However, this could be a feedback phenomenon rather
than a prerational one. There are also cases where the memorized information
needed for rational processing is directly accessible and where, therefore, no
symbolic evocation is a prerequisite to either the inception or the development
of rational processing. In other words, on the one hand no evidence points
unequivocally or even strongly towards the view that symbolic processing is a
precondition for rational processing. On the other hand there is evidence that
some rational processing requires *no* prior symbolic processing.

Evocation and Association

I want to argue that *any* symbolic processing requires *some* prior rational processing, and as a first step I shall try to show why accounts that do not make

and develop such an assumption fail to match some very general evidence. As a second step, I shall defend an account based on this assumption.

Any account of symbolism must answer two fundamental questions: *(a) Which stimuli get symbolic processing, under which conditions?* (henceforth the *Which stimuli?* question); and *(b) Which evocation gets triggered by which stimulus, under which conditions?* (henceforth the *Which evocation?* question).

Hypothetical answers to these two questions are constrained by various kinds of evidence from anthropology and psychology.

Anthropologists interested in symbolism have tended more or less explicitly to adopt a classical associationistic approach (see Lévi-Strauss 1963, p. 90; Turner 1967, p. 28). They assumed that ideas are associated by similarity or contiguity, that associated ideas tend to evoke each other, and that an idea with a great many associates is especially likely both to be evocative and to be evoked. Similar assumptions have been rejected or modified beyond recognition in experimental psychology (see Anderson and Bower 1973, for a review and a defense). Since this rejection has not been accompanied by any alternative theory to account for oneiric, poetic, or cultural associations, it is not surprising that psychoanalysts, rhetoricians, and anthropologists should persist in using associationistic principles. Hence it may be appropriate to show that the very data they intend to account for is the best evidence against these principles.

The psychological import of the anthropological evidence I shall adduce to counter associationistic principles is usually not considered. Most humans in most societies spend a share of their time, energy, and sometimes wealth in setting up simple or complex rites. In most cases, whatever effects these rites have derive from the triggering of a process of symbolic evocation in the minds of the beholders and of the participants. Even those anthropologists who think that indirect effects on social status, societal cohesion, economic exploitation, etc. are the crucial factors in explaining rites must base their sociological explanations on an implicit assumption of psychological efficaciousness. This in turn is based on two properties ascribed to cultural symbolism, its *selectivity* and its *directionality*. *Selectivity* means that out of the infinite range of available stimuli, a small, finite, but nevertheless quite varied set is selected to serve ritual purposes. Presumably the stimuli selected have a greater symbolic potential (i.e., a greater likelihood to trigger a rich evocation). *Directionality* means that different stimuli are carefully chosen for different rites. The expressed purposes of these rites (e.g., induce a rainfall) are usually not achievable by the chosen means. However one may assume that different rites achieve different symbolic evocations. If this is so, then at least the direction of the evocation (the part of LTM to be searched), if not its exact content, is somewhat determined by the properties of the stimulus.

Although these two points—selectivity and directionality—may be phrased otherwise or left implicit, all anthropologists dealing with ritual take them for granted. They are, if not sufficient, at least quite necessary to explain ritual action (and for that matter all forms of symbolic communication—i.e., communication through the triggering of an evocation in the receiver—ritual being just the most compelling case).

Given this, the answer to the "Which stimuli?" question cannot be expressed only in terms of the degree of intellectual alertness (a looser attention to ritual stimuli does not increase their symbolic import—if anything the opposite seems to be the case). Rather, it must specify a class of stimuli (or a class of paired stimuli–conditions) as being systematically symbolic. The answer to the "Which evocation?" question cannot limit itself to individual idiosyncratic factors (such as interest); rather, it must specify some systematic relationship between the stimulus and the content or at least the direction of the evocation.

These constraints rule out any account of symbolic evocation in terms of association based on contiguity or similarity because this would entail two predictions: *(a)* that a very frequent or a very trivial stimulus should, since it enters into many more relations of contiguity and similarity, be much more evocative than a rare or unusual stimulus; and *(b)* that the representations a stimulus is most likely to evoke are either those that co-occur most often with it or those that are most similar to it. Both these predictions are patently falsified by cultural symbolism. For example, according to the first prediction odd animals such as the pangolin (Douglas 1957) or the cassowary (Bulmer 1967) should be poor symbolic stimuli as compared to ordinary mammals and birds. On the contrary, they are highly symbolic (see Sperber 1975a for a discussion). A lion is both more often found with and more similar to a lioness than to a brave warrior; yet, contrary to the second prediction, the latter and not the former is evoked in most cultures in which the symbol is used. In other words, having a great many associates in terms of either contiguity or similarity is neither necessary nor sufficient to be a powerful symbolic stimulus. Close association to a stimulus is neither necessary nor sufficient for a representation to be evoked.

Whereas classical associationists may have underrated the selectivity and directionality of evocation, anthropologists are prone to overestimate them and to neglect some of the points suggested by experimental and introspective evidence: for instance, that any stimulus may trigger an evocation, given appropriate conditions, and that any representation can be evoked by any stimulus, given appropriate conditions. The first point is evidenced by free association: A sufficient condition for any stimulus to trigger an evocation is the simple decision to associate freely. The second point is evidenced by the success of mnemonic techniques based on deliberate association: A subject is instructed to associate two arbitrary stimuli in an image or in a story. Later, the use of one of the stimuli as a cue will facilitate the retrieval of the other (see, for example, Miller, Galanter, and Pribram 1960, chap. 10). Even without instruction, many subjects tend spontaneously to build associations as a mnemonic prop.

Between the idiosyncratic and occasional evocations of free association or cued recall and the more widely shared and more regular associations of ritual symbolism a continuum of intermediate states can be found (e.g., in poetry or the arts).

Besides this varying degree of idiosyncrasy, there is no empirical argument to suggest that cultural symbolism and individual evocation are based on different mental mechanisms; and anthropologists should reject models of symbolism not compatible with experimental evidence on associations. This puts important constraints on any view of symbolism otherwise based on anthropological evidence. In particular, it rules out from the start any so-called grammar of symbolism; that is, any explicit account of symbolism as a kind of language.

The idea of a grammar of symbolism is appealing because it immediately provides a frame to answer the "Which stimuli?" and "Which evocation?" questions.

By definition and in principle, it should be possible to formalize a grammar of symbolism so that it would generate, on the basis of a finite set of axioms and rules, a finite or infinite set of pairs, where the first element would be the representation of a stimulus and the second element the representation of an evocation. The general answer to the "Which stimuli?" question would thus be: A stimulus gets symbolic processing if and only if it corresponds to the first element in one of the grammatical pairs. The general answer to the "Which evocation?" question would be: The evocation triggered by a given stimulus is specified by the second element of the appropriate grammatical pair. When a stimulus is represented in several such pairs, several evocations would be possible. Then, answering more specifically the two fundamental questions and making detailed predictions would amount to writing the appropriate grammar.

However, since any stimulus can be evocative, all the possible psychological stimuli should be generated as first elements of the pairs; and since any representation can be evoked by any stimulus, there should be for each stimulus at least as many pairs as there are representations in the memory of the subject(s) considered. This is sheer absurdity. It would take more than elaboration and qualifications to redeem the notion of a grammar of symbolism and its purely metaphorical, not to say misleading, character.

Anthropologists have developed various versions of what could be called *cultural associationism* rather than a truly grammatical model (whose formal constraints have not always been grasped). Cultural associationists assert or imply three assumptions: first, that humans have the general ability to build associations on the basis of either contiguity or similarity, and to use them in retrieval, as described by classical associationists; second, that a finite subset of these associations is learned as part of the acquisition of the culture; third, that the subjects learn to give preference to these cultural associations whenever the proper stimulus is presented, that is, mainly on cultural occasions. In other words, a restricted and shared subpart of the overall individual associative network is used in prescribed cultural contexts. The answers to the "Which stimuli?" and the "Which evocation?" questions are provided by the cultural group itself and learned by the individuals who are socialized in the group.

This cultural associationism shares neither the pitfalls of the simple kind of associationism considered in the preceding (which fails to account for the selectivity and the directionality of evocation), nor the pitfalls of pseudogrammatical views (which could never handle the fact that any stimulus may be evocative and may evoke any representation). However, cultural associationism makes (and cannot but make) heavy and unwarranted assumptions about the learning of symbolism. For instance, Turner (1967, 1969) assumes, first, that the kind of exegesis that is sometimes taught in some societies provides the right associations to "make sense" of cultural symbols, and, second, that when exegesis is absent, the way the symbols are talked about or handled contributes to learning just as exegesis would. It is hard to see how a cultural associationist would dispense with these or similar assumptions. However, I have argued at length (Sperber 1974) that not only is exegesis rare and fragmentary but it also is as much in need of being "made sense of" as the symbols themselves. I have further argued that the only way in which rules for the use of symbols (and other peripheral data) can be considered as equivalent to exegesis is that they too need to be "made sense of." Exegesis and other types of data are stimuli for evocation rather than representations to be evoked. In short, only a small part of cultural symbolism is the object of teaching, and that teaching is itself quite symbolic. The only form of learning that then remains available in this associationistic framework is the building and strengthening of associations on the basis of contiguity and similarity. The cultural associationists will assume that specific associations are fostered in a cultural context by creating the right contiguities and pointing out the right similarities. However, once again, no amount of cultural contrivance will reverse the fact that a lion is both more generally contiguous and more similar to a lioness or to a lion cub than to a brave warrior. There is no way, in this account, of avoiding the prediction that the closest associates of a stimulus in terms of contiguity or similarity will be the most likely to be evoked. When that prediction can be checked against experimental or introspective evidence, it is often falsified. When it cannot be checked and is assumed to be valid, it usually fails to "make sense" of the cultural phenomena it was meant to explain in the first place.

To sum up this section, the answer to the "Which stimuli?" question must accommodate both the fact that any stimulus can sometimes trigger an evocation and the fact that some stimuli nearly always trigger one. The answer to the "Which evocation?" question must accommodate both the fact that any representation may be evoked by any stimulus and the fact that different stimuli differ as to the representation they are most likely to evoke.

It might have been thought at first that these requirements call precisely for the kind of probabilistic treatment that the notion of strength of association provides. But it turns out not to do so. Inasmuch as predictions can be made at all on the basis of number and strength of associations, they fail to be borne out by the evidence. Although the assumption of a cultural fostering of selected associations might draw attention to interesting facts, it does not radically improve the quality of predictions. To generalize the argument: Knowledge of prior associations is not sufficient to predict which stimulus is likely to get symbolic processing; and knowledge of both a stimulus and prior associations is not sufficient to predict which evocations are likely to be triggered.

Contextual Constraints on Evocation

What more than the stimulus and prior associations should one know to be able to predict which evocations (if any) are likely to be triggered? Even association-ists would agree that an evocation is a function not only of the stimulus and of prior associations, but also of the context. What is needed is knowledge of the context. However, references to it are generally a way of sweeping various pending questions under the rug, and the study of symbolism is no exception. How important are the questions thus disposed of?

If on the basis of prior associations a restricted class of possible evocations could be paired with a given stimulus and if the job of the context was just to permit a final selection, then indeed a vague reference to the context might do for the time being. But I have tried to show that in no way can prior associations restrict the class of possible evocations. If this is correct, the contextual selection is made out of the whole range of evocations available in memory, and association strength plays at best an ancillary role. In other words, what is being swept under the rug is the central problem, and what is being diligently studied is a side issue.

Why do students of symbolism hardly ever do more than mention in passing the relevance of the context, and never attempt to make explicit the psychological mechanisms involved in contextual selection? At least part of the answer is clear enough: By talking vaguely—and misleadingly—of "the role of the context," one minimizes the problem and postpones the challenge to basic assumptions that the study of contextual selection would involve. Indeed, properly speaking, not the context, but the intellectual *representation of* the context, can have a direct effect on symbolic processing. The intellectual representation of the context is not a matter of simple perception, but involves the integration into a logically consistent whole of various perceptual identifications with prior knowledge and expectations. In other words, the only way the context ever appears in conceptual processes such as the symbolic one is through the synthesis of diverse information by the rational device. But acknowledging the role of context and really trying to make it explicit would amount to admitting that rational processing is a prerequisite for symbolic evocation. This seems to be something that both classical associationists and cultural associationists do not want to do because their basic assumption is that symbolic evocation is prior to rational under-standing. All the shortcomings that I have tried to point out are linked to this basic assumption and to the concomitant refusal or inability to consider seriously the role of rational thought in the contextual selection of evocations. I believe that the repeated failure of generations of scholars to build a reasonably explicit theory of symbolism on the basis of that assumption is a sufficient reason to try and dispense with it.

Compare:

(a) Wine referred to as "wine"
(b) Blood referred to as "blood"
(c) Wine referred to as "blood"   (4)

(a) Lighting a cigar with a match
(b) Buying a cigar with a dollar bill
(c) Lighting a cigar with a dollar bill   (5)

(a) A cackling hen
(b) A crowing cock
(c) A crowing hen   (6)

(a) The issue number 1247 of a periodical
(b) A $1000 price tag on a second-hand car
(c) The issue number 1000 of a periodical   (7)

In the four examples, the *(c)* cases tend to be more symbolic (more likely to trigger a rich evocation) than the *(a)* and *(b)* cases. The stimulus or the symbol is present in the *(b)* cases but it becomes properly symbolic only when put in an *(a)*-type context. Innumerable examples such as these can be found, or coined at will. What do they have in common? There is something that could be described as incongruous, paradoxical, or striking in the relationship of one specific item with its given context. Notice that the relationship need not be especially unlikely: The issue number 1000 is not less likely than the issue number 1247. Nor need it be unexpected: Hearing wine called "blood" during the Mass is highly expected. Nor need it be mysterious: The newly rich are rather obvious when and if they light a cigar with a dollar bill. Nor need it be *meant* to strike you: The crowing hen is guileless. All one can say is that in each example an extra intellectual problem is raised by the *(c)* cases as opposed to the *(a)* and *(b)* cases. Even if you expect wine to be called "blood" at the Mass, you also have a much more general and practical assumption that words are used according to their meaning, and that assumption is challenged. The careful carelessness of the newly rich is hard to interpret as the unintended behavior it is intended to be seen as. A crowing hen challenges zoological common sense. Example 7, although very ordinary, is also subtler: The number of an issue is somewhat like a proper name with a semantic element in it expressing order of issue. It is not meant to express a quantity. To grasp the quantity expressed by a number such as "1247," an effort of artithmetical analysis would have to be made and usually is not when the number is used ordinally. When the number "1247" is seen on the cover of the periodical, the information grasped is precisely the relevant one and nothing more: It indicates the issue following number 1246 and preceding number 1248. However, when the number is "1000," it is hard *not* to grasp the quantity expressed. We have an unanalyzed (although, of course, analyzable) concept of "a thousand" but not of "a thousand two hundred and forty seven." When verbal (or numerical) information is given to us orally or in writing, our rational processing consists of establishing its relevance (see Sperber and Wilson, forthcoming). In this case, attaching relevance to the unwittingly grasped quantity is a challenge.

Thus in the four *(c)* cases the load on the rational device will tend to be much higher than in the *(a)* and *(b)* cases. I propose that this can be generalized to answer the "Which stimuli?" question: *Whenever the perceptual representation of an additional stimulus in a given context cannot be fully processed on the basis of the resources accessible to the rational device at that moment, symbolic processing will occur.*

Put differently, when the rational device cannot reach a satisfactory synthesis on the basis of information provided by the perceptual device on the one hand, and directly accessible memorized information on the other, then a nonsequential search is made in LTM for additional premises. It is this search that is intuitively grasped as an evocation: an awareness more of the activity of research than of the information actually parsed.

This proposition permits several general predictions. Indeed, if it is correct, then two factors will affect the likelihood of an evocation: The first involves the compatibility of the information to be processed with the frameworks or schemata of rational interpretation available to the individual; the second involves the intellectual resources actually mobilized or accessible at the time when the information is presented. Predictions are:

1. When some information challenges basic assumptions of a cognitive system, it will be symbolically processed, whatever the degree of intellectual alertness.

I would argue that this first prediction is borne out by most of cultural symbolism. Supernaturalism, mystical causality, and religious mysteries challenge basic cognitive assumptions and thus are sure to be processed symbolically. To consider things the other way round: If the assumption that overloading the rational device triggers a symbolic processing is right, then it is not surprising that this psychological liability should have been exploited sociologically in the surest possible way, by systematic irrationality. The selectivity of cultural symbolism should be explained along such lines.

2. When the degree of intellectual alertness is very low, most information processed tends to overload the rational device and thus to trigger a symbolic evocation.

This prediction might be borne out by "some dreams and other disorganized mental states" such as the hypnagogic states studied by Silberer (1909). Less dramatically, this prediction offers an alternative to the usual explanation of the introspective evidence that the lesser the intellectual alertness, the greater the symbolic character of the thought process. This evidence is usually considered crucial to justify the view that symbolic processing must be primary and prior to. rational processing. However, it corroborates as well if not better the opposite view defended here: If symbolic processing is triggered by an overload of the rational device, then the less the rational device can process at a given moment, the more the symbolic device will have to process.

3. Mastery of rational, culturally adapted schemata will proportionately limit the occasions on which symbolic interpretations must necessarily occur.

Again this prediction provides an alternative account of the assumed importance of symbolism both in technologically primitive societies and in children. The development of science and technology multiplies the possibilities of rational interpretation of, and rational dealings with, the environment and diminishes the chances that environmental facts will overload the rational device and be symbolically interpreted. However, this historical process is a very slow and marginal one. More dramatic is the case of children. They rapidly internalize a large number of adapted schemata, facilitating the rational processing of information and thereby diminishing the chances of overload and the probability of symbolic processing.

According to the traditional view, in the history of either humankind or of the individual, rationality was progressively acquired and tends to take the place of symbolic thought processes. According to the view advanced here, not rationality but only knowledge is acquired. It is organized in schemata for rational processing, and thereby enables the individual to process a greater load of information with the rational device he or she possessed from the start. The range of stimuli that are automatically processed symbolically is reduced accordingly. However, it need not decrease the overall use of symbolic thought since this depends also on other factors such as the level of attention or individual and cultural interests. The development of rational schemes makes this decrease possible, but not necessary.

There is no a priori reason to prefer the classical empiricist view or the rationalist one presented here; only empirical considerations such as the validity of predictions should decide. I have tried to show that concerning the "Which stimuli?" question, whatever valid predictions are implied by the empiricist view are also implied by the rationalist one, that further invalid predictions are implied by the empiricist view only, and that further valid predictions are implied by the rationalist view only, thus favoring the latter. I will now attempt to show that the same situation obtains regarding the "Which evocation?" question.

During the Mass when the wine is referred to as "blood," neither the close associates of wine nor those of blood, nor their common associates (such as other reddish liquids) are likely to be evoked. What is likely to be evoked (among other possibilities) is a transcendent order of reality where the evidence of the senses would cease to be reliable, where a superior power would be able and willing to transmute substances. In other words, a set of supplementary premises is evoked. Within the framework provided by these premises, it makes sense to refer to wine as "blood."

When someone lights a cigar with a dollar bill, what is likely to be evoked is such an extreme degree of wealth and such a complete indifference to the concerns of ordinary people, that the use of a dollar bill as a matchstick might deserve no more notice than the use of a matchstick as a toothpick. In other words, this striking use of a dollar bill evokes supplementary premises such that, within the framework they provide, the only striking thing that remains is that one should have been struck in the first place.

The crowing hen may not evoke much to the modern academic, but it was very evocative to traditional European peasants. Judging from the native commentaries compiled by Sébillot (1906, 3: 222-23), this anomaly was likely to evoke misfortunes or anomalies with which it was related either causally or analogically, or in both ways at the same time: The hen had copulated with a reptile, in its eggs were snakes, or the owner of the house was dominated by his wife, or husband and wife would quarrel, or someone would die (in the latter case the analogy should be: What the crowing cock is to life, the crowing hen is to death). Surely beside and beyond these traditional exegeses further representations could be arrived at; but the direction is fairly clear: What is evoked is a set of supplementary premises such that the isolated and unexpected crowing of the hen becomes part of a chain of expectations.

The thousandth issue of a periodical is likely to evoke the amount of time spent, paper printed, work done, as if part of the aim had been to achieve this precise quantity, as if an objective threshold were thereby passed. Thus, supplementary premises are evoked that would make the irrelevant but noticeable quantity incidentally expressed by an ordinal number become relevant. Notice that, conversely, to render a cardinal number symbolic, one way is to make it ordinally noticeable, for example, "*The Thousand* and One *Nights*," a title that evokes an important thousand-and-first night in a way neither "the thousand nights" nor "the thousand-two-hundred-and forty-seven nights" would do.

What the four cases have in common can be, I would argue, generalized to answer the "Which evocation?" question: *When the rational device is overloaded, the symbolic processing thus triggered consists of a searching on the basis of information available in long-term memory for supplementary premises that, had they been accessible in the first place, would have permitted a fully rational processing of the initial input.*

According to this view, at least three factors contribute to determine the content of the evocation: the input to the symbolic device, the state of the rational device, and the content and organization of LTM.

So far I have considered only one major type of input to the rational device, perceptually processed information about a stimulus-in-context. Two other types of input should also be considered: first, the grammar-based decoding of sound waves (or other types of linguistic signals), where the input to the rational device is a semantic representation (see Sperber 1975b; and Sperber and Wilson, forthcoming); second, the feedback of the symbolic device, i.e., the additional assumptions symbolically evoked that are fed into the rational device and that may in turn raise a new challenge and call for further evocation (I have suggested [Sperber 1974] that such cyclical evocation may be crucial in understanding both cultural and dream symbolism).

Whatever the inputs to the rational device, be they perceptual, linguistic, or endogenous, the outputs of the rational device capable of becoming inputs to the symbolic device are always of the same nature: The symbolic device is fed defective conceptual representations resulting from an incomplete rational processing of challenging inputs.

Beside the input to the rational device, the second factor determining evocation is the state of that device. Depending on the assumptions accessible to it at the time, the input will either get full rational processing or not, and if not, the search for additional premises will take specific directions. The direction of the evocation will depend on the nature of the intellectual challenge. When this is a challenge to the most basic cognitive assumptions, as in much cultural symbolism, the direction of evocation is fairly predictable. This is one more consideration when explaining the selectivity and directionality of cultural symbolism. When, on the other hand, the challenge is due to cognitive idiosyncrasies or to intellectual fatigue, the direction of evocation is much less predictable; this kind of susceptibility to symbolism is culturally exploited (as in some initiation rituals) or encouraged (as in many art forms) only by societies that favor a high degree of individuality.

Even when the directionality of symbolism is strong or, in other words, the focalization of evocation is narrow, the exact content of the evocation is still not predictable. Indeed, beside the initial input to the rational device and the state of that device, a third factor is crucial in determining the evocation; the content of long-term memory. Supplementary premises have to be retrieved or constructed from the information available in LTM, and this always comprises a high level of idiosyncrasy. In the present account, the most pointed kind of cultural symbolism cannot elicit a standard response. Evocation is an individually creative use of memory and can be manipulated to some extent only in its direction, not in its actual content.

The easy acceptance by humans of odd and sundry symbolic systems according to their milieu of birth has repeatedly been taken as an argument for the malleability of the human mind. However, if the present account is correct, these symbolic representations are internalized not as ordinary knowledge but, so to speak, "in quotation marks"; not as thoughts, but as starting points of evocations, as food for thought. Members of the same social group may take in the same so-called beliefs, but it does not follow that they think the same thoughts. Reports starting with "The so-and-so think that . . ." should be reconsidered. Cultural symbolism, often construed as an argument for a behavioristic, manipulative view of humankind, is better understood as based on the ability to search one's memory in a creative way, open only to limited and uncertain manipulations.

In addition to these three factors—symbolic input, state of the rational device, content of LTM—it is arguable that a fourth factor plays a role, namely, the associative network. It is possible that once a probe has been specified as a result of the shortcomings of the rational device, once a range of information in LTM has been focalized, then, within that range, associative paths are followed in priority. However, even if the present account is extended so as to include such associationistic considerations, it would still yield predictions fundamentally different from the classical associationistic ones.

Associationists predict that between a stimulus and its evocation there is an associative path. Even more than psychologists or anthropologists, rhetoricians have devoted themselves since the time of Aristotle to corroborating this view. However, this is trivially true: Not only between the representation of a stimulus and the representation evoked, but between any two representations whatsoever, there are always several relationships of contiguity or similarity or both. This might cease to be the case if strong constraints were put on the notions of contiguity and similarity (for instance, by considering these relations to be nontransitive). But to my knowledge, no constraints that would redeem the associationistic predictions from triviality without falsifying them have ever been proposed. Not an oversight but an impossibility, one imagines.

Still, it is hard to see how associationists could dispense with making at least one more prediction, implied by their whole approach, namely, that the stronger the contiguity or the similarity, the stronger the association and the greater the likelihood of mutual evocation. I have argued that this prediction is trivially false.

Whereas the associationist should predict that the stronger associates of a stimulus are its most likely evocations and that, among these, contextual factors may effect a final selection, I have proposed here a rationalist view that is the other way round. Contextually relevant representations are the most likely to be evoked; among these it may be that strength of association to the stimulus contributes to the final selection. But contextually relevant representations may include only very weak associates of the stimulus. Therefore the two types of predictions are quite different. The rationalist prediction is not subject to the objections raised against the associationistic ones. It is neither trivially true nor trivially false, and should therefore be preferred.

Conclusion

The fact that under appropriate conditions any stimulus can evoke any representation precludes any grammar or grammar-like method of symbolism. On the other hand, the selectivity and directionality of symbolism cannot be accounted for in simple associationistic terms. When an attempt is made, as in cultural associationism, to find a middle way between the too strong constraints of a grammatical model and the too weak ones of an associationistic model, it turns out that not just the strength of the constraints but also their nature has to be reassessed. Symbolic interpretation does not consist of recalling or reconstructing a strong or weak connection between a signal and a sense; it is rather a particularly creative form of problem solving. The main constraint on any problem solving lies in the problem itself; the main source of constraint is whatever specifies the problem to be solved. In the present instance, the problem is, generally speaking, one of retrieving or imagining supplementary premises that should make it possible to process fully some challenging input information. The specification of these problems has to be done by a device capable of synthesizing various input data, of evaluating these against accessible schemata, and, if this is not sufficient, of specifying what kind of supplementary assumptions are to be looked for. These abilities are characteristic of the rational device. There is no reason to assume that they are duplicated in the symbolic device, when it is much simpler to assume that some rational processing takes place before any symbolic processing. In other words, the constraints on symbolic evocation are typically those a rational device would put; the problems dealt with are those a rational device would raise. Therefore, in thought processes, the cycle of interaction between symbolic and rational processing should be considered as initiated by the latter. If so, then neither phylogenetically nor ontogenetically, nor in any other sense, can symbolic thought be prerational.

References

Anderson, J. R., and Gordon H. Bower. 1973. *Human Associative Memory*. Washington, D. C.: Halsted Press.

Bartlett, Frederic C. 1932. *Remembering*. London and New York: Cambridge University Press.

Bulmer, Ralph. 1967. "Why Is the Cassowary Not a Bird? A Problem of Zoological Taxonomy among the Karam of New Guinea Highlands." *Man* 2, no. 1: 5-25.

Douglas, Mary. 1957. "Animals in Lele Religious Thought." *Africa* 27, no. 1: 46-58.

Lévi-Strauss, Claude. 1963. *Totemism*. Boston: Beacon Press.

____. 1966. *The Savage Mind*. Chicago: University of Chicago Press.

Lévy-Bruhl, Lucien. 1910. *Les fonctions mentales dans les sociétés inférieures*. Paris: Alcan.

____. 1922. *La mentalité primitive*. Paris: Alcan.

Miller, George A., Eugene Galanter, and Karl H. Pribram. 1960. *Plans and the Structure of Behavior*. New York: Holt.

Neisser, Ulric. 1967. *Cognitive Psychology*. New York: Appleton.

____. 1976. *Cognition and Reality*. San Francisco: Freeman.

Norman, Donald A., David E. Rumelhart, and the LNR Research Group. 1975. *Explorations in Cognition*. San Francisco: Freeman.

Piaget, Jean. 1968. *La formation du symbole chez l'Enfant*. Neuchatel: Delachaux et Niestlé.

Sébillot, Paul. 1906. *La folklore de France*. Vol. 3. Paris: Maisonneuve et Larose.

Silberer, Herbert. 1909. "Bericht über eine methode, gewisse symbolische halluzinations–Erscheinungen hervorzurufen und zu beobachten." *Jahrbuch für psychoanalytische und psychopathologische Forschungen* 1: 513.

Sperber, Dan. 1974. *Le symbolisme en général*. Paris: Hermann. (English translation: *Rethinking Symbolism*. London and New York: Cambridge University Press, 1975.)

____. 1975a. "Pourquoi les animaux parfaits, les hybrides et les monstres sont-ils bon à penser symboliquement?" *L'Homme* 15, no. 2: 5-24.

____. 1975b. "Rudiments de rhétorique cognitive." *Poétique* 23: 389-415.

Sperber, Dan, and Deirdre Wilson. *Language and Relevance*. In press.

Tulving, Endel, and Z. Pearlstone. 1966. "Availability versus Accessibility of Information in Memory for Words." *Journal of Verbal Learning and Verbal Behaviour* 5: 381-91.

Turner, Victor. 1967. *The Forest of Symbols*. Ithaca: Cornell University Press.

____. 1969. *The Ritual Process*. London: Routledge and Kegan Paul.

Index